Rural Women in Urban China

Rural Women in Urban China

Gender, Migration, and Social Change

Tamara Jacka

An East Gate Book

M.E.Sharpe
Armonk, New York
London, England

An East Gate Book

Copyright © 2006 by M.E. Sharpe, Inc.

Library of Congress Cataloging-in-Publication Data

Jacka, Tamara, 1965-
  Rural women in urban China : gender, migration, and social change / authored by
Tamara Jacka.
    p. cm.
  Includes bibliographical references and index.
  ISBN 0-7656-0820-0 (cloth : alk. paper)
  1. Rural women—China—Social conditions. 2. Rural women—China—Economic
conditions. 3. Rural-urban migration—China. 4. Migrant labor—China. 5. Migration,
Internal—China. I. Title.

HQ1767.R327 2005
307.2'4'0820951—dc22   2005020340

Printed in the United States of America

The paper used in this publication meets the minimum requirements of
American National Standard for Information Sciences
Permanence of Paper for Printed Library Materials,
ANSI Z 39.48-1984.

BM (c)   10   9   8   7   6   5   4   3   2   1

For Misha

Contents

List of Figures and Maps

Figures

Maps

Acknowledgments

My heartfelt thanks go first to the many rural migrant women in Beijing and Hangzhou who have shared their stories with me over the years. I do not have the words with which to convey how much I have learned from these stories and how much they have impressed, moved, inspired, and sometimes disturbed me, but I hope that my deep respect for my interlocutors comes through in the writing that follows. My sincere thanks go also to Xie Lihua, Li Tao, Li Zhen, Ning Dong, Zhou Ling, and Wang Laoshi (the last three are pseudonyms used to protect identities) for their advice and for helping me so generously with my fieldwork.

Several other people gave advice and shared ideas and research findings with me: Sally Sargeson, Sarah Biddulph, Sarah Cooke, Josko Petkovic, Börge Bakken, Rachel Murphy, Luigi Tomba, Anita Chan, Pun Ngai, Yan Hairong, Arianne Gaetano, Alice Goldstein, Kenneth Roberts, Zheng Zhenzhen, Geremie Barmé, Jon Unger, and Andy Kipnis. I am grateful to them all. I particularly want to thank Rachel Murphy, Pun Ngai, and Andy Kipnis for their comments on my manuscript.

For inspiration and supportive friendship through some difficult years, I wish to thank my colleagues at Murdoch University: Carol Warren, Jim Warren, Sandra Wilson, Anne Marie Medcalf, Sally Sargeson, Tim Wright, and Carolyn Brewer. And for providing a truly wonderful environment for conducting research and writing, my warmest thanks go to Margaret Jolly, Jodi Parvey, Annegret Schemberg, Richard Eves, and the other members of the Gender Relations Centre at the Australian National University.

Many thanks to Jamie Greenbaum for his excellent research assistance and help with translations, to Arianne Gaetano for her help in implementing the questionnaire survey of the Migrant Women's Club in Beijing, and to Chen Jiazhong for help in drawing up tables. My sincere thanks go also to Annegret Schemberg and Ria Van de Zandt for their invaluable assistance with copyediting, and to Patricia Loo, Makiko Parsons, and Angela Piliouras at M.E. Sharpe for their wonderful efficiency in producing the book.

I would like to acknowledge the support of Murdoch University, The Australian National University, and the Australian Research Council in providing funding for fieldwork in China in 1995, 2001, and 2002, and Peking University in hosting me and my son for six months in 2001.

Finally, my deepest gratitude goes to my partner, Nick Chapman, for his love, support and editing; to my mother, Eleanor Jacka and my grandmother, Edith Dissky, who first taught me the importance of stories; and to my son, Misha Petkovic, for sharing life with me and making it all worthwhile.

Earlier versions of some parts of this book have been published elsewhere. I am grateful to Columbia University Press for permission to reprint extracts of the introduction to *On the Move: Women and Rural-to-Urban Migration in Contemporary China,* ed. Arianne Gaetano and Tamara Jacka (2004), which appear here in the introduction and chapter one. And I am grateful to *Critical Asian Studies* for permission to reprint a revised and extended version of "Finding a Place: Negotiations of Modernization and Globalization among Rural Women in Beijing" (*Critical Asian Studies,* vol. 37, no. 1, 2005, pp. 51–74), which appears here as chapter four.

Rural Women in Urban China

Introduction

From the "Margins" to the "Center"

Liang Chun and her family live in a migrant settlement in Haidian District, an hour and a half by bus northwest of downtown Beijing, with its vast, glittering malls and imposing office blocks. From the bus stop on the main road my son and I walk for twenty minutes along a dirt track. On the right there are vegetable fields and fruit trees and on the left an area recently bulldozed and then a jumble of stalls and repair workshops marking the edge of the settlement. Fifteen years ago when I was a student, my class took a trip to this area to see a model village. Nowadays, the whole of Haidian district is considered an inner suburb. The rural residents no longer farm, but instead make a handsome living renting out rooms to rural migrants who have come from all over the country.

The track narrows to a muddy lane, almost impassable after rain. On the left is a long row of low, makeshift brick pingfang (single-storied buildings), built specifically to rent out to migrants. Liang Chun and her family live in one of these rooms. They have been here for seven years, having migrated from a poor village in Anhui. Liang Chun takes in sewing at home and her husband is self-employed as a builder and interior decorator. Their two children attend a nearby primary school for migrant children. The room the family rents is about thirteen square meters with a dirt floor. Just inside the door is a long trestle table, with an old-fashioned sewing machine and piles of cloth stacked neatly to one side. Next to it is a small shelf and a gas cylinder with a single ring for cooking. In the center of the room a light bulb hangs over a small round folding table and two fold-up chairs brought out for our visit. At the back of the room is a double bunk bed. The whole family sleeps on the bottom and their belongings are stored on the top. When the weather is fine, Liang Chun

Figure I.1   **Approaching a Migrant Settlement, Haidian District, Beijing**

prepares their meals and does the washing outside, where there is a wa-
ter tap that they share with the neighbors. There is a public toilet just
down the lane. It is filthy, the stench is terrible, and there are piles of
rubbish outside. Residents pay a "hygiene fee," but the toilets are rarely
cleaned and the rubbish rarely collected. The hygiene is much worse than
in the village, Liang Chun tells me.

This is the first time that Liang Chun has met my son, and she greets
him enthusiastically. Beneath her cheerful welcome, though, I sense
anxiety. She explains that The International Student Games are due to
start elsewhere in Haidian later this month, so the local authorities
have been trying to make the migrant presence in the area less visible.
In the week since my last visit yet more buildings on the edge of the
settlement have been bulldozed and there are rumors that the entire
settlement is due for demolition ahead of the 2008 Olympic Games. In
addition, every night for the past week officials from the Public Security
Bureau—that is, the police—have been coming through the settlement
arresting migrants by the vanload and taking them away to the deten-
tion center in Changping, to the north of the city. No one knows how
long this will continue. (August, 2001)

This is a book about women who, at the end of the twentieth and the beginning of
the twenty-first centuries, left their homes in rural China to seek work in urban

centers, joining what has been characterized as the biggest peacetime wave of internal migration the world has ever seen. It is based primarily on ethnographic research with rural migrant women living in China's capital city, Beijing, and on an analysis of these women's stories of their experiences of migration and life in the city.

In the last two decades a massive increase in rural to urban migration has been one of the most significant corollaries of the Chinese state's efforts to develop a market economy and "join tracks with the world" (*yu shijie jiegui*). For both rural migrants and the urbanites into whose communities they move this has been conceived very much as a movement from the poorer, "backward," "margins" to the wealthier, more "civilized" and "modern" "center(s)."

Most of the people moving into urban centers are transient or "unofficial" migrants, belonging to what is termed the "floating population" (*liudong renkou*). Currently, this group includes somewhere between 80 and 120 million people and constitutes between one-fifth and one-third of the total population of most large cities.[1] The terms "unofficial migrant" and "floating population" refer to anyone who has moved, either temporarily or long-term, away from home without a corresponding transfer of their official household registration or *hukou*.[2] According to China's household registration system, which was introduced in the 1950s, all citizens are classified according to place of residence and as belonging to either agricultural or nonagricultural households. Household registration is usually inherited from the mother and for most people it is extremely difficult to transfer registration from agricultural to nonagricultural, from a village to an urban center, or even from a small town to a larger city.

Until the 1980s the combination of the household registration system with other aspects of Maoist political and economic management resulted in a perpetuation of rural/urban inequalities and put a brake on migration out of the countryside toward the more prosperous cities. In particular, when faced with the dilemma of how to develop and modernize a largely agrarian economy scarce in capital, the Maoist state resorted to the Soviet strategy of siphoning resources out of agriculture in order to finance the heavy industrial sector. At the same time, it guaranteed subsidized food and housing, lifetime employment and welfare benefits to urban residents, but not to those with rural registration (Zhang 1999, 821). Rural to urban migration was thus very effectively curtailed, for in the city it became impossible to buy grain or to find housing without local, nonagricultural household registration.

With the emergence of a market economy in the late 1970s and early 1980s, however, the effectiveness of household registration in limiting rural to urban migration greatly eroded. No longer reliant on the state for the provision of foodstuffs and other basic necessities, people registered officially as belonging to rural, agricultural households could nevertheless now live in towns and cities for months or even years at a time. Meanwhile, economic reforms led to a growth both of forces pushing rural inhabitants off the land and out of villages and of demand for rural labor in the industrial, commercial, and service sectors of towns and cities.

These economic reforms had been initiated in the late 1970s with the disman-
tling of the communal system and the return to household farming and with efforts
to stimulate diversification, specialization, and commercialization of agricultural
production. Initially, the new measures were successful in stimulating higher levels of productivity in agricultural production, which in turn provided the capital
and released the labor required for the expansion of rural industries and the development of private businesses. Income inequalities between different rural areas
increased, but were offset by an overall rapid improvement in rural incomes and
living standards, and a narrowing of the rural/urban income gap.

From the late 1980s onward, however, real incomes in rural areas stagnated,
while both intrarural and rural/urban income inequalities grew. Shortage of arable
land, lack of local employment opportunities, falling prices for agricultural products, and rising taxes, not to mention unscrupulous and corrupt local leaders, pushed
rural people out of their villages. A desire to see the world, now made more visible
through television and increased flows of people across areas, and a wish to improve their material life, in addition to, in some cases, the need to escape oppression or familial conflict, further propelled rural people toward towns and cities.

Meanwhile, an expansion of the urban economy resulting from deregulation
and from China's entry into the global market resulted in a huge need for unskilled
and cost-effective labor. The majority of the new jobs were temporary, offering no
security and very few welfare benefits, of low status, physically exhausting, and
carried out in poor working conditions. Not surprisingly, these jobs were largely
shunned by urbanites and, consequently, demand grew rapidly for rural migrant
workers who accepted the poor conditions and who were cheaper to hire.

In Beijing between 1977 and 1984 the average size of the floating population
was about 231,000. By 1994 the figure had jumped to 3.3 million (Poston and
Duan 1999, 27). In the mid-1990s, Beijing authorities began efforts to reduce the
size of the floating population, and in 1997 declared a target of 1.8 million people
(ibid., 11). By the time of the census of Beijing's floating population undertaken in
November 1997, the actual size of the floating population was calculated to be
about 2.3 million (Tan et al. 2002, 200). By 2001 it had increased again to 3.3
million, or about 23 percent of the municipality's total population (Beijingshi
Tongjiju 2002, 72 and 577).[3] The vast majority of these migrants had rural, agricultural *hukou*. Just over 37 percent were women, 72 percent of whom were between the ages of 15 and 35 (Beijingshi Tongjiju 2002, 579). Among female
migrants aged 6 years and above, about 4 percent were illiterate, 17 percent had
primary school education, 52 percent had completed junior secondary school, 17
percent had completed senior secondary school, and 10 percent had tertiary education. Most migrant women had been in the city for between six and twelve months
(26 percent), or for between one and three years (34 percent) (ibid., 579).

These "floaters" have been at the front line of the global capitalist economy,
many of the men working as building laborers, and the women working as poorly
paid waitresses, market vendors, maids, cleaners, and prostitutes, or toiling in

appalling conditions in multinational factories and sweatshops, producing clothing, toys, and electronics for the global market.[4] Similar to foreign immigrants in other countries, these migrants have only limited citizenship rights in the cities. In the larger metropolises in particular, local governments, employers, and others commonly discriminate against those who do not have local urban household registration, limiting migrant employment to a narrow range of poorly paid, menial jobs, providing migrant workers with none of the job security or welfare benefits extended to local urban workers, charging migrants exorbitant fees for the enrolment of their children in local schools, and conducting frequent campaigns to demolish migrant settlements and to detain migrants and deport them back to the countryside.

Given what we have learned about migration in other parts of the world, we can surmise that the experiences of rural to urban migrants in China will result in important changes in their worldview, sense of identity, and relationships with others. These in turn will translate into forms of broader social change that will constitute a central aspect of the particular meanings and consequences of capitalist development, modernization, and globalization in China in the coming years.

There are a number of ways in which an appreciation of the specific experiences of rural migrant women has particular significance for understanding the links between globalization, migration, and social change in China. First, although they comprise only a minority of the floating population in most cities,[5] migrant women workers dominate in some sectors of the economy, including domestic service, prostitution, sanitation, textiles, and the toy and electronic industries. Furthermore, across the country the proportion of rural women in the floating population is increasing.[6]

Second, gender relations and the experiences of women in the Chinese countryside are particular motivations for women's out-migration. They are also one area of social relations likely to be most affected by rural to urban migration. Some scholars have speculated, for example, that out-migration may provide an important avenue of escape for women suffering gender oppression or violence, and even that it may help to reduce suicide rates among rural women (Lee and Kleinman 2000, 224 and 234; Bossen 2002, 358). On the other hand, some studies in China and elsewhere suggest that rates of mental illness and suicide may be higher among rural migrant women who return to the village after a brief sojourn in the city (Murphy 2004, 265; Kearney and Miller 1987; Hickling 1991, 80–89). These findings are of particular importance because suicide rates in China are about three times the global average, and, unlike any other country in the world, most suicides are young rural women (Lee and Kleinman 2000, 224 and 234).

Rural Chinese women, like their counterparts in other developing countries, may well experience a liberating sense of autonomy from parental, spousal, and other forms of authority and a broadening of horizons when they migrate to urban areas. Certainly this appears to be an important motivation for migration. On the other hand, in the city, the exploitation and discrimination frequently suffered by rural migrants of both genders are often compounded in the case of women by sexual exploitation, discrimination, and abuse. In addition, there are major inequalities and differences in lifestyle and values, especially those relating to gender and sexuality, between rural and urban China, and these and the barriers placed in the way of rural migrants trying to integrate into urban society are likely to make the transition from country to city (and back) very difficult. For the majority, this is compounded by the fact that the move comes at a time when they are also trying to negotiate the shift from youth to adulthood. Finally, rural women's migration may pose particular difficulties, both for the individuals involved and their families and communities, because it conflicts with the expectation dominant in rural areas that a woman will marry in her early twenties, settle in her husband's village, and take responsibility for the domestic sphere, including child rearing, housework, and agriculture.

This book seeks to contribute to our understanding of rural women's experiences of migration and life in the city of Beijing.[7] The findings on which it is based come from two main sources. The first consists of interviews, participant observation, and other forms of research conducted with members of the Migrant Women's Club (Dagongmei zhi Jia). Set up in 1996, organizers claim that this was the first nongovernment organization established in China for rural migrants, and it remains one of very few such bodies.[8] It was established by the editorial office of the monthly journal *Rural Women* (*Nongjianü*), China's only national journal for rural women. Today the Club has a membership of over 400 people, most of whom are young rural women. The club's aim is to provide migrant women with a place to get together and share experiences, socialize, and participate in discussions and classes. Since 2002 the Club has also published its own journal, *Working Sister* (*Dagongmei*), and a migrant hot line and a Migrant Rights Group have been set up in affiliation with the Club.

In 1999 I collaborated with *Rural Women* and the Migrant Women's Club in running a national story-writing competition with the theme "My life as a migrant worker" (*Wo de dagong shengya*).[9] Some of the stories we received, along with others published in *Rural Women* and *Working Sister,* are analyzed in this book. Then in the year 2000 I ran a questionnaire survey of 100 members of the Club.[10] The questionnaire included sixty-nine questions on a range of topics, from reasons for migration and length of sojourn in Beijing, to occupation and housing in Beijing, to perceptions of identity and aspirations for the future. Findings from this survey are reported throughout this book.

Between 2001 and 2002 I spent seven months in Beijing, participating frequently in activities run by the Migrant Women's Club, interviewing Club members, and interacting with them informally. Altogether I conducted about fifty-five hours of formal, taped interviews with twenty-two female members of the Club, and another few hours with a couple of male members of the Club and with members of the *Rural Women* collective. The twenty-two women that I interviewed came from rural areas all over China and ranged in age from sixteen to thirty-eight. Most worked as maids, office cleaners, or factory workers. Three were married with a child, the rest were unmarried and childless. At the time, two of the married women were without work. One of the women had been in Beijing for just a few months, but the remainder had lived there for at least a year, most having migrated to the city in the mid- to late 1990s. Four had been in Beijing for eight years or more.

The members of the Migrant Women's Club and the migrant women writing stories for *Rural Women* are known as *wailaimei,* meaning "(younger) sisters from outside," or *dagongmei,* which means "working (younger) sisters" or "working girls." By definition, *dagongmei* work in waged employment, *dagong* referring to work done for someone else, as opposed to self-employment. Most, though not all, *dagongmei* are also young and single, *mei* being a somewhat patronizing appellation, meaning younger sister or girl.[11] The majority of rural migrant women across China are young, single, waged workers, and in urban discourse and in the media these *dagongmei* have become stereotypes eclipsing all other images of rural migrant women. All the same, there are thousands of rural women living in Beijing and other cities who are older than the typical *dagongmei,* are married and have children, and are either self-employed or care for their children while their husbands earn an income. Liang Chun and most of the other women in the migrant settlement in Haidian belong to this category. There is no separate term for these women—they are simply referred to as part of the floating population, or as "outsiders" (*wailai renkou; waidiren*).

My second source for this book is a series of conversations and interviews conducted with Liang Chun and her neighbors in 2001. Over the six months that I lived in Beijing in 2001, I visited the migrant settlement in Haidian once or twice each week. Aside from numerous informal conversations, I conducted two-hour-long interviews with fifteen women, and on one occasion had a lengthy discussion with a group of about twenty women. Most of the women with whom I talked were in their mid-thirties, and were married with one or, in most cases, two children. The majority were without employment or worked alongside their husbands selling vegetables. They came primarily from the provinces of Henan, Hubei, and Hebei, but again most had been in Beijing for a few years, since the mid- to late 1990s.

For comparative purposes, this book also draws on interviews conducted with ten women working as maids in Beijing in 1989 and another forty interviews undertaken in the city of Hangzhou in 1995 with *dagongmei* working in silk and textile factories, as restaurant waitresses and escorts, as salespeople, and as maids.[12] All the women interviewed for the book belong to the majority Han nationality.[13]

By comparing the stories told to me in interviews and conversations with migrant women in Beijing, with other migrant women's oral and written accounts and articles about migration published in the Chinese press, I have tried to understand the material and emotional consequences for women of the shift from the countryside to the city. I have also tried to appreciate the ways in which migrant women's identities, their status, their relationships with others, and their sense of belonging and place in society have altered as a result of migration. And I have examined the ways in which migration fits into women's life course and the impact it has on their sense of time, especially their aspirations for, and views of, the future. Finally, I have sought to understand the ways in which migrant women's experiences and stories have been shaped by dominant discourses and by individual women's varied ways of negotiating those discourses.

Experience

Numerous social scientists before me have focused on "experience," which is defined here as people's engagement with the world, including apprehension and interpretation, thoughts, feelings, and actions.[14] For example, a leading "anthropologist of experience," Edward Bruner, writes: "What comes first is experience. The anthropology of experience deals with how individuals actually experience their culture, that is, how events are received by consciousness. . . . The anthropology of experience sees people as active agents in the historical process who construct their own world" (Bruner 1986, 4 and 12). Anthropologists have traditionally always been concerned with personal experiences, using long-term participant observation as a means by which to get close to other people's inner perspectives. However, Bruner suggests, in interpreting and re-presenting their field data for publication, many have filtered out experience, instead emphasizing structure or culture, or else they have included the former only as snippets of personal narrative or excerpts from field notes as a way of enlivening the text. The anthropology of experience, in contrast, takes peoples' expressions of their own experience, whether these are in the form of personal narratives, dramas, or carnivals, for example, as the analytical focus. The advantage of this approach, says Bruner, is that "the basic units of analysis are established by the people we study rather than by the anthropologist as alien observer. By focusing on . . . expressions, we leave the definition of the unit of investigation up to the people, rather than imposing categories derived from our own ever-shifting theoretical frames" (Bruner 1986, 9).

A focus on experience has also been central to many feminist and other social historians concerned with the situation of marginalized groups.[15] As with anthropologists of experience, part of their motivation has been the desire to grasp reality as it is understood by subjects themselves, rather than by the external observer. There has also been a desire to "add to the record" the lives and stories of groups previously neglected, both because these stories are fascinating in and of themselves, and because they can be an important corrective to mainstream historical accounts. In writing this book, I too have sought to "add to the record" the lives and stories of a group of people who are particularly marginalized in China. In this sense, the book is not only about a movement of people from the rural "margins" to the urban "center," it is also an attempt to bring the experiences and voices of a group of rural migrant women from the margins of social and scholarly concern to a position of greater centrality. In addition, I have paid particular attention to the subjective aspects of these women's experiences—that is, the meanings and significances that they themselves have attached to what has happened to them and to how they have acted. An appreciation of this aspect of experience can be of crucial importance in an analysis. For example, the difference between a form of agency that is recognized by an outside observer as "resistance" but not recognized as such by a subject herself, and a type of agency explicitly characterized by the subject herself as resistance, can be highly significant for an understanding of power relations and social change.

At a more fundamental level, my research strives for a form of understanding and communication that overcomes strangeness and strangerliness but does not negate difference. This type of understanding and communication involves making connections with people on the basis of what we share—the fact that we all enjoy moments of happiness and triumph and periods of misery, confusion, and pain. And we all have a sense of self (however that might be defined), try to have that self recognized and appreciated by others, and strive for a sense of self-continuity (Moore, Henrietta 1994, 30). Understanding other people, on the other hand, also depends on learning about and respecting the uniqueness of the way in which not just each culture but each person understands and engages with the world; on understanding that while we each experience the world in the particular ways I have described above, none of the particulars are the same (Abu-Lughod 1991, 157–58). Appreciating the experiences of others is important because it enlarges the range of models available to all of us as to how to live together. To quote Clifford Geertz, "It is the asymmetries . . . between what we believe or feel and what others do, that makes it possible to locate where we now are in the world, how it feels to be there, and where we might or might not want to go. To obscure those gaps and those asymmetries . . . is to cut us off from such knowledge, and such possibility: the possibility of quite literally, and quite thoroughly, changing our minds" (Geertz 2000, 78). However, there are potentially serious limitations to the analytical force of the approach to experience that I have outlined thus far. As I will explain, these stem from a failure to fully account for the relationships between subjects, experience, discourse, and communication.

Experience, Subjects, and Discourse

In a recent critique of studies of experience the historian Joan Scott argues:

> When experience is taken as the origin of knowledge the vision of the individual subject (the person who had the experience or the historian who recounts it) becomes the bedrock of evidence upon which explanation is built. Questions about the constructed nature of experience, about how subjects are constituted as different in the first place, about how one's vision is structured— about language (or discourse) and history—are left aside. . . . Making visible

the experience of a different group exposes the existence of repressive mechanisms, but not their inner workings or logics; we know that difference exists, but we don't understand it as constituted relationally. For that we need to attend to the historical processes that, through discourse, position subjects and produce their experiences. It is not individuals who have experience, but subjects who are constituted through experience. Experience in this definition then becomes not the origin of our explanation . . . but that which we seek to explain. (Scott, Joan 1992, 25–26)

What might it mean to attend, as Scott urges, "to the historical processes that, through discourse, position subjects and produce their experiences"? And how might such an approach contribute to an understanding of the experiences of rural migrant women in China?

First, we must recognize that while each human experience is unique, it has nevertheless also been shaped by social practices. Through social practice, and specifically discourses, we learn to enact categories of identity, or what we might call "subject positions" such as those, for example, of "peasant" and "migrant woman." Following Michel Foucault, I understand discourses to comprise bodies of knowledge, and also the language, structures, and practices through which those bodies of knowledge are produced and conveyed (McHoul and Grace 1993, 31–56). Discourses embody relations of power in the sense that they set the conditions and the rules that enable and constrain what can be imagined, said, practiced, and even felt, how, and by whom. These rules vary historically, from one society to another, and from one discourse to another within the same society or culture.

Two sets of discourses that are central in shaping the experiences of the subjects of this book are those relating to gender difference and a rural/urban divide in China. These discourses involve particular relations of power, embodied and reproduced in language and knowledge about, for example, the qualities associated with "masculinity" and "femininity" and about "urbanites" and "the peasantry," each of these terms having particular histories in modern China. Relations of power are also embodied in, and enforced through, sociopolitical practices and structures. These include the practice of patrilocal, village-exogamous marriage in rural areas, and the institution of the household registration system. Understandings about what it means to be a "rural woman" and a "rural migrant woman," and the reproduction of marriage practices and the household registration system are mutually reinforcing, and both stem from and contribute to hierarchical distinctions between male and female, urban and rural.

A range of subject positions around these hierarchies can be imagined and enacted, with varying degrees of ease and desirability. A woman labeled as a peasant, can, for example, resist such a positioning, and seek instead the identity of the urbanite, but at the present time such an effort is fraught with difficulties that can have an enormous impact on both the material and emotional aspects of her life. It is also possible, at least to some extent and in some contexts, to refuse the categories both of "male" and "female" and of "urban" and "rural," but the consequences are generally such as to put a person beyond the realm of beings recognized socially as subjects. In China, for example, it is possible to become a "black householder" (*hei hukou*), that is, someone who has no household registration and is therefore not classified as either "rural" or "urban." To do so, however, is illegal, and it puts one beyond the bounds, not only of state regulation, but also of the provision of public goods such as legal housing, employment, education, and medical care. This is a position that Judith Butler, following Julia Kristeva, terms "abject": a position not socially recognized, the specter of which is nevertheless produced by, and indeed is of central importance to, the discursive production of the "rural" and the "urban" subject (Butler 1993, 3).

In later chapters, I explore in more detail the ways in which particular historical processes and discourses, especially those relating to gender and to rural/urban difference, have produced particular subject positions in modern China, and how they have prevented, excluded, or constrained others. I also try to indicate the directions in which these discourses and the range of subject positions they enable have been changing and how they might change in the future.

But what exactly is the relationship between discourses and the subject positions they produce, and persons; their identities, agency, and experience? Identities are not fixed attributes. Rather, they are a continual shifting between different overlapping and conflicting subject positions. For example, when I am in Beijing, my primary identity is sometimes that of an ethnographer with a certain status and power as a "foreign expert" and sometimes it is that of an Australian woman with only an imperfect grasp of the Chinese language and of what Chinese culture is all about. Sometimes I am a friend, and sometimes an outsider; and in some contexts I am an academic, while in others I am a mother.

The metaphor of location implied in the term "subject position" usefully suggests that, just as the view of landscape varies from one location to another, so too do understanding and knowledge vary from one subject position to another. The term implies, however, that there is a singular, unitary subject who shifts from position to position, taking on a new standpoint with each move, but nevertheless remaining essentially the same subject through the process. The understanding I want to convey here, in contrast, is that there is no singular subject outside of the taking up and performance of particular subject positions. A subject is not so much an entity, or even a collection of roles or positions. It is more like a series of performances, engagements, or ways of being. Put another way, a subject is a history of experiences. Each experience is different from those that came before. Critically, however, each new experience also includes, and is imprinted by, memories of prior experiences and by what, as I suggested earlier, seems to be a universal human desire for self-continuity; the desire to make some kind of link between past, present, and future.

Recently, several social theorists have contended that interconnected aspects of modernization and globalization—the development of technologies that increase

flows of goods, information, ideas, and people; and increases in commerce between regions and nations—result in a multiplication in the subject positions that
are available to, or forced upon, people. Craig Calhoun argues, for example, that

> the modern era brought an increase in the multiplicity of identity schemes so
> substantial that it amounted to a qualitative break, albeit one unevenly distrib-
> uted in time and space. In the modern era, identity is always constructed and
> situated in a field and amid a flow of contending cultural discourses. . . . The
> tension and even incommensurability among the various discourses—at the
> extreme where they claim autonomy—appears not just as an "external" diffi-
> culty for individuals but as a series of contradictions within the "subject-self."
> (Calhoun 1994, 12)[16]

Modernization and globalization have been occurring unevenly across the world
since the eighteenth century. However, their consequences have been felt more
intensely and by more people across the world since the late twentieth century,
with the advent of what has been variously described as "modernity at large"
(Appadurai 1996), "late modernity" (Giddens 1991), and "postmodernity" (Harvey
1990). Since then, the multiplication of identity schemes has increased and become more widespread as a result of new electronic media and large-scale movements of people (Appadurai 1996, 3–4; Bammer 1994, xi), and by late capitalist
industrial strategies of "flexible accumulation." These last aim to reduce turnover
time in both production and consumption, for example by dispersing production
to geographical areas of cheaper wages and easier labor control, by introducing
more flexible work regimes and short-term labor contracts, and by promoting rapidly changing consumer fashions and an aesthetic that celebrates difference and
ephemerality (Harvey 1990, 141–88).

In contemporary China, I suggest, rural to urban migration is emblematic of
twentieth- and twenty-first-century modernization and globalization. By this I mean
two things: first, at the macro level, it is a key outcome of the strategies of "flexible
accumulation" of both domestic and international capitalists, enabled by a state
that has tried to promote rapid economic growth and integration into the global
market by stimulating geographical and social mobility on an individual level while
at the same time maintaining key institutions of social differentiation and control
such as the household registration system. Second, for individual migrants, movement across the rural/urban divide in China results in experiences of dislocation
and the multiplication of different, often clashing, subject positions that are typical of the experience of modernization and globalization. In this volume I ask:
How do rural women respond to the proliferation of different subject positions
entailed in migration? Is it experienced as liberation and adventure, or, as Calhoun
suggests, does the multiplication of conflicting discourses and subject positions
present profound problems for the individual migrant? Alternatively, is it something that can either be "screened out" and ignored, or else seamlessly incorpo-
rated into consciousness and ways of being?

At a more basic level, what exactly determines the range of subject positions a person performs? Do migrant women have any choice about the subject positions they take up—are they agents who actively shape and alter subject positions or do they only choose subject positions from an already existing repertoire? Do they, in fact, have any choice in the matter or is the history of subject positions and experiences that constitute "the rural migrant woman" determined solely by discourses and the power relations they entail?

To discount human agency would be politically and ethically undesirable, because it would suggest that people are completely helpless victims and cultural dupes. It would also leave us unable to account for variations between people and the ways in which they engage with the world, for discrepancies between discourses and peoples' actual behavior and experiences, and for both social continuity—the reproduction of discourses—and for social change, involving resistances to or modifications of discourses. However, the notion that subjecthood and experience are formed through discourse need not mean that people have no agency. Rather, our understandings, not just of particular subjects or persons as, for example, "male" or "female," and particular forms of agency, but also of what "subjects," "people" and "agency" are at all, are constituted through discourse and through every instance of a specific subject position being performed and experienced.

Human agency is thoroughly social and discursive, but is made possible by the fact that societies consist of numerous different, competing discourses, and within any one discourse a variety of subject positions are available. Discourses confer the ability to make choices between these various subject positions, but the intimate relation between discourse, knowledge, and power is such that some people will be able to imagine a greater range of subject positions than others, and will be better placed to choose which of those to enact. Furthermore, there is always a hierarchy between different discourses and subject positions. In Louis Althusser's terminology, positions "interpolate" or "hail" their subjects. But some positions are more desirable, or hail with more force of persuasion, than others. Which subject positions are seen as more desirable is a matter of individual perception, but also, of course, relates to the values of others and to the very real material, social and economic benefits attached to certain subject positions and the disadvantages attached to others (Moore 1994, 65).

Thus, as I have indicated, it is possible in contemporary China to take on the position of a "black householder," eschewing both "rural" and "urban" identities. To do so, however, is undesirable because it means being cast as a criminal and consequently makes access to many of the necessities of life, including employment and housing, very difficult. If an urbanite were to take up such a position, she or he would most likely be labeled insane or exceedingly stupid. On the other hand, some rural migrant women do take on the status of a black householder because they feel they have no choice or because the alternatives open to them are even less desirable. In fact, as I will illustrate through this book, a great many rural migrant women in Beijing report themselves caught in a situation in which every subject position available for them to "choose" is undesirable in some important way. This is what it means to be marginalized and at the bottom of the sociopolitical order.

As Joan Scott explains, then, "subjects have agency. They are not unified, autonomous individuals exercising free will, but rather subjects whose agency is created through situations and statuses conferred on them. Being a subject means being 'subject to definite conditions of existence, conditions of endowment of agents and conditions of exercise'" (Scott, Joan 1992, 34). These conditions enable choices, but the choices are by no means unlimited.

This book is premised on a thorough acceptance of Joan Scott's critique of studies that use experience as evidence for a particular view of history. But I persist, nevertheless, in believing in the value of a focus on experience. My focus is not on "What experiences do rural migrant women have?" Rather, I ask, "What histories of experience constitute the rural migrant woman, and what discourses enable and constrain these histories?" While the book seeks in part to document the experiences of women traveling from the margins to the center and to bring these women's accounts of their experiences from the margins to the center of our attention, it also seeks to understand, question, and destabilize the meanings and understandings that are implicit in that very phrase, "from the margins to the center." In this sense, the title of this introduction has several question marks hidden in it: For starters, how is it that the rural is perceived as "marginal" and rural to urban migration is understood as a movement "to the center" by so many in Chinese society, and yet, not by all? Where, in any case, do these categories of rural and urban come from? And how is it that certain people moving from the countryside to the city, who in various other ways might be quite different, are understood as the same type of subject with largely the same experiences and the same social status? What are the discourses through which these various terms, subject positions, and experiences are created and reproduced?

Experience, Discourse, and Narrative

If it is problematic, as I have discussed above, to view the rural migrant woman as the author of her experiences and to use these experiences as evidence for historical explanation, it is yet more problematic to view migrant women's stories as mirrors directly reflecting experience. For storytelling, like any other form of communication, is itself a particular experience—a particular mode of engagement with the world. A story of an experience will thus always be different from the experience itself; in some senses less than and in some senses more than that experience.

I use the terms "story" or "narrative" here in the loosest sense to refer to a construct, conveyed through language, image, or gesture, that contains an actor or actors and a plot—a sequencing through which particular relationships are established between actors, events, time, and place. For the purpose of analysis, three other aspects of the story can be identified: The event or plot structure refers to the inclusion of some events and not others, and the order in which they are presented. The evaluative system is the set of values underpinning the narrator's interpretation of events and actors—which are good or bad, which are important, and which trivial. This can be conveyed in a variety of ways, including the use of emotive language or facial expressions, repetition, and the ordering of items within the story. The explanatory system refers to the set of assumptions that undergird the explanations the narrator gives (and those she does not give) for events in the story (Linde 1986, 186–90). The interrelations between these aspects of the story are important. In particular, the explanatory system may affect the set of events deemed worthy of inclusion in the story, the degree of importance accorded them, and the ways in which they are evaluated (Steinmetz 1992, 499).

Stories are a particular subset of discourse, drawing on and contributing to other discourses. They can be analyzed either as objects or texts, whether written or spoken; as acts of communication or performance; as a form—a particular structuring and arranging of knowledge; or, indeed, as a practice that characterizes the very way in which people engage with and experience the world. All of these approaches are important in this book.

Stories are one of the main forms through which categories and truths embodied in discourses are understood and communicated. In addition, through their own acts of making narratives, subjects interpret, negotiate, manipulate, incorporate, and resist those truths and the power relations that impact on their lives. This line of conceptualization confirms the notion that identities are not so much "constructed" through or by discourse, as narrated and performed. We perform our selves and our lives and attempt to make sense of them by reinterpreting, retelling and reenacting preexisting stories that circulate in our society, and the different subject positions that they offer (McLaren 1995, 90–98).

Like the metaphor of location suggested in the term "subject position," the notions of narration and performance here have limitations, for they suggest the existence of a unitary subject behind the various roles that are performed, or the "masks" that are put on. It needs to be stressed again that there is no subject outside of the history of its performances. The notions of narration and performance are useful, on the other hand, in suggesting both the agency and creativity of the subject, and the significance of discourses and the power relations they embody. A subject performs and creates herself and her life but, like a storyteller, she cannot do or be whatever she likes. She is constrained, if not by a script, then by certain broadly held understandings of what particular subject positions entail and of how, when, and by whom, they can be performed (Kenyon 1996, 27–28). And while, in its detail, each narration of a life is unique, some narrative structures and plots are more common in a given social setting than others. Which ones are dominant is something that is always contested and dependent on the distribution of power (Lee 1998, 30).

Carefully compared and analyzed, stories can illuminate a great deal about the dynamic interaction between social discourses and personal identities and experiences. Stories, however, take many different forms. In this book I draw on a range of different types of narrative, including articles written by scholars and journalists about rural migrant women, as well as stories told or written by migrant women themselves. All of these I view as "fictions"; none are privileged as any closer to "the truth" than others. Rather, each type of narrative tells a different set of "truths" and each is shaped by the identities and interests of their authors, the discourses in which they are placed, and judgments they make about their audience.

With this in mind, and in the interests of achieving as broad and thorough an understanding as possible of migrant women's lives and experiences, I juxtapose and compare different kinds of stories and voices. However, I focus particular attention on the stories told or written by migrant women themselves because they tend to say more about the subjective elements of migrant women's experiences. Among these, I am most interested in stories that encompass the whole trajectory of a woman's life, or at least a significant portion of it—in this case, the trajectory involved in rural to urban migration and life in the city. This is because the narration of a life story compels the author to move from accounts of discrete experiences to interpretations of how and why the life took the shape it did (Personal Narratives Group 1989, 4–5).

A critical examination and comparison of life stories, including their event structures and evaluative and explanatory systems, can reveal the ways in which—sometimes consciously, sometimes unconsciously—the identities, experiences, and understandings of numerous people are shaped by particular discourses. However, while certain dominant discourses, such as those relating to rural and urban identities and gender, are enormously powerful, they do not entirely determine people's lives and life stories. A comparison of life stories can also reveal the different paths steered by individuals in similar discursive environments, and the working out within specific life situations of different identities and courses of action that in turn have the potential to either undermine or perpetuate the discourses in which the life evolved (ibid., 6).

In addition, an analysis of life stories can illuminate people's responses to contradictions that emerge between different discourses or between expectations and experience (Skultans 1998, 27), or to instances when individuals' personal sense of identity are no longer recognized in a new social and discursive environment. They can cast light on the strategies that people employ in coming to terms with these contradictions and disjunctures, including the adoption of particular evaluative and explanatory systems, various forms of resistance to dominant discourses, and different attempts to recast personal identities. This is particularly important in this study, for, as mentioned, rural to urban migration commonly involves a shift between social values and expectations, especially as they relate to gender and sexuality.

It is important to bear in mind, though, that not everyone knows how to tell a life story. Not only does the existence and form of life stories vary from one society to another, but within any given society, the skills involved in the public narration of a life story are differentially acquired. Among my interlocutors in this study, not all were able or willing to reflect in detail on their major life choices and events. Most were though, and several talked at great length with very little prompting from myself, presenting articulate, detailed life stories, which included a great deal of critical reflection on their life thus far and the directions it might take in the future.

This is somewhat surprising in light of the ways in which power relations shape understandings of who can and cannot talk in public in China. "Knowing how to talk" (*neng jianghua*)—a term that refers to the ability to speak to strangers or in public with a high degree of articulateness and persuasiveness—is generally understood to be an attribute of formal education, worldliness, and maleness, and a key marker of superior social status. Rural inhabitants are commonly perceived as "dumb" in both senses of the word because they lack formal education and because their lives are confined to the farm and village and they have little contact with strangers. Furthermore, women, especially young women, are traditionally not supposed to "know how to talk" because they are supposed to be confined to the domestic sphere and to be subject to the control of the men and elders in their family. Though they turned out to be quite articulate, a number of my interlocutors in Haidian said at the beginning of our interactions that they "lacked education and did not know how to talk." And many members of the Migrant Women's Club told me that young migrant women have a sense of inferiority (*zibei gan*) and do not know how to talk because of sexism in the countryside, because they received relatively little education, and because as girls they were not allowed to speak up for themselves in the family and their interactions with people outside the family were restricted.

Several factors need to be taken into account in explaining my interlocutors' articulateness. First, older, married rural women tend to be more able and willing to speak in public than younger women (Lou et al. 2004, 213). This is a result of their greater experience and of a higher degree of social status and self-confidence obtained through employment and their roles as wives and mothers. This goes some way toward explaining the articulateness of my interlocutors in Haidian, all of whom were married mothers aged thirty and above. It also helps to explain the fact that, among members of the Migrant Women's Club, those who stood out as particularly vocal and articulate were older than the average, and most were married.

But many younger, single members of the Migrant Women's Club were also very articulate. This can be partially explained by the fact that on average they had higher levels of education than is the norm for women in rural areas. In addition, the impact of their involvement in the Migrant Women's Club must be taken into account, for, as I will discuss in chapter 2, it is one of the Club's central missions to help young migrant women overcome their sense of inferiority and improve their self-confidence and ability to speak out. In addition, the women who have been actively involved in the Club over many years have learned not only to talk about their own, individual experiences, but also to identify the experiences and interests of *dagongmei* as a collective. They are well practiced in talking to journalists, academics, and others about the issues facing *dagongmei,* and a number have also published articles in *Rural Women, Working Sister,* and elsewhere.

Apart from this, the high levels of articulateness and reflection found in my interlocutors' narratives undoubtedly reflect the impact of migration. Young migrant women themselves often claim that the experience of being a migrant—of going out into the world and learning to be independent—broadens their horizons, makes them more mature, and gives them a greater degree of confidence in themselves. That this also makes them more confident and able to talk in public is confirmed in studies conducted in rural China comparing returned migrant women with those who have not migrated. In a recent study conducted in Anhui and Sichuan, Lou Binbin and her associates noted that in focus-group discussions single returned migrant women were much more willing to talk than were single women who had never migrated (Lou et al. 2004, 213).[17]

Finally, it could be that, as the sociologists Mustafa Emirbayer and Ann Mische hypothesize, "actors who are positioned at the intersection of multiple temporal-relational contexts can develop greater capacities for creative and critical intervention" (Emirbayer and Mische 1998, 1007). In drawing up this hypothesis, Emirbayer and Mische refer to two sets of research, the first of which suggests that during periods of social upheaval or rapid change some actors may try to resist change and hold tightly to past routines, but others may be more likely than at other times to challenge existing norms and seek alternative futures (ibid., 1006). The second body of research referred to by Emirbayer and Mische suggests that "actors who are located in more complex relational settings must correspondingly learn to take a wider variety of factors into account, to reflect upon alternative paths of action, and to communicate, to negotiate, and to compromise with people of diverse positions and perspectives" (ibid., 1007). I have suggested above that women's experiences of rural to urban migration in contemporary China involve a multiplication of subject positions. Extrapolating from Emirbayer and Mische's hypothesis, one could further suggest that the high levels of critical reflection apparent in migrant women's narratives are a response to this multiplication of subject positions, and the challenges that these raise for women's sense of who they are and where they belong (cf. Lawson 2000, 174).

Narrative, Performance, and Re-presentation

So far I have blurred the distinction between narrative as a way of experiencing the world and narrative as an act or text that recalls and communicates past experience. But what is remembered and recounted from the past may differ from the previous experience, for memory is not so much a dredging up of the past, as a selective and imaginative creation of it. When recounting an experience we dwell on and embellish some aspects of it while leaving others out. And there are some experiences that we simply do not have the words for. Furthermore, the main purpose in telling one's life story is not so much to describe the past "as it really was" but to confer upon it a meaning that will help to make sense of the present (Bertaux-Wiame 1981, 257; Kenyon 1996, 29–30), so that one is better able to imagine a path into the future and to knit together past, present, and future in a meaningful whole.

In any case, none of us has just one, singular life story or even only a single story to tell about a particular experience. We all make up stories to suit the moment and perform them differently according to our audience. Stories do not exist prior to the particular collaboration between "narrator" and "audience" characterizing each telling or writing. Instead, each instance of story telling, whether it is an interview, a casual conversation, or a piece written for publication, is an interaction between at least two people, shaped by the audience's background, expectations, and desires as well as by those of the narrator (Shostak 1989, 231–32). In discussing stories published in *Rural Women* and *Working Sister* and those written and told by members of the Migrant Women's Club, I consider the politics and editorial stance of the journals and the numerous ways in which the Club's activities have shaped its members' outlooks. Chapter 2 provides an introduction to these issues. In analyzing the oral narratives of members of the Migrant Women's Club, and those of my interlocutors living in Haidian, I have also tried to be sensitive to the ways in which these narratives are likely to have been shaped by my relationships with my interlocutors and the context of our conversations.

In Haidian my interlocutors were first selected and approached on my behalf by Ning Dong, the principal of the local migrant children's school, all of the women being mothers of students in the school. In my first few visits in 2001 Ning accompanied me to each woman's home and spent several minutes introducing me and my project before leaving us to talk alone. Later, rather than accompanying me herself, she asked her students to show me the way to their home and introduce me to their mothers. This proved a much more satisfactory arrangement. Ning seemed to think that with an introduction from herself the women would be less wary of me as an outsider. In fact, though, the atmosphere was more relaxed when she was not there because both my interlocutors and I were intimidated by Ning's presence and her way of introducing me.

In my observation the relationship between Ning and these women was neither equal nor particularly close. Though they were all "outsiders" to Beijing, and though they lived and worked alongside each other, Ning behaved, and was perceived as, superior in status because she was an urbanite, an "intellectual," and a cadre, because she dressed in smart, expensive clothes, and because she walked and talked with an air of confidence and authority, all of which was off-putting to the other women. When she introduced me, she did so as a "fellow" intellectual and as a foreign "expert." In response, a number of women protested that they had no education and would be of no interest to me, and that they "did not know how to talk."

I too was more self-conscious in Ning's presence, feeling that my "expertise," in particular my language abilities and my skills as an interviewer, were under scrutiny. With Ning absent it was easier for me to relate to my interlocutors. I was still an outsider to be wary of, but I looked more like a student than an expert—my clothes were a good deal less smart than Ning's, and I did not speak with the same kind of authority. In addition, although in fact very similar in age to both Ning and the majority of my interlocutors, I was generally perceived as being younger. I also had in common with my interlocutors the fact that I was a mother with a young son. As is so often the case for parents "in the field," my son became an important point of connection between myself and my interlocutors.

On some occasions the schoolchildren who showed me to their homes would linger for a while, listening to my conversation with their mother, before going back to school. Sometimes other relatives and neighbors would also drop in. Usually, though, my interlocutor and I were left alone for the greater part of my visit. All of the interviews I conducted were in Mandarin, which, it should be noted, was a second language not just to myself but also to my interlocutors. In rural areas across China most people understand Mandarin but they do not use it in daily interactions, speaking instead in the local regional dialect. Upon migration to Beijing, they quickly learn to speak Mandarin. However, most migrants, especially the older ones, retain an accent and throughout their sojourn in the city this remains one of the key signifiers of their status as inferior outsiders in the eyes of urbanites. I had relatively little trouble conversing with my interlocutors and they were impressed by my fluency in Mandarin, but they nevertheless observed that I had even more difficulties with the language than they. This earned me some sympathy and helped to reduce the gap in status between us. It was also advantageous in that it seemed natural for me to ask "stupid" questions and for my interlocutors to give explanations about issues and terminology that were crucial to my understanding of migrant experiences but that are so taken for granted as basic features of Chinese culture and language that a native speaker would not have been able to raise them.

During my interviews I did not have a fixed set of questions, preferring, like Edward Bruner quoted above, that the focus and basic units of investigation be established, as far as possible, by the research subjects rather than by the outside researcher. I generally began proceedings by explaining that I wanted to hear the story of their lives, and in particular their experiences of migration and life in the city. As I have mentioned, some women responded by talking at length and with few hesitations and in these cases I intervened with very few questions. Others were less inclined to talk in any detail and I prompted them more frequently with questions.

After the first meeting a few of my interlocutors in Haidian were keen to develop a friendship with me, seeking me out when they heard I was visiting the area, and inviting me and my son to meals with their families. In most cases, though, I spent only one session with my interlocutors, and while we generally established good rapport, I was not able to engage with them on a deep enough level to get beyond a fairly superficial acquaintance.

With members of the Migrant Women's Club I was able to establish more longer lasting, deeper relationships. Although the bulk of my ethnographic research with the Club was not conducted until 2001, I had run projects and met with the Club's organizers and a few of its members on a number of occasions prior to that. Consequently, when I first participated in the Club's activities in July 2001 I was introduced as an "old friend." Though an exaggeration this, combined with my sustained involvement with the Club over the ensuing several months, helped to establish me as a partial "insider."

My regular participation in Club activities was of particular importance. I joined in all these activities, including self-introductions, singing and role-plays, with as much energy and enthusiasm as others, though with considerably less aptitude. My involvement in these activities not only taught me a great deal about relationships within the Club, it was also very useful in breaking down any wariness that might otherwise have arisen as a result of my status as a "foreign expert." This made it easier for me to develop relationships with Club members. I first got to know some of my interlocutors during Club activities and then asked for an interview. Others approached me after seeing me at the Club and learning that I wanted to talk to members about their experiences of migration. A few were introduced to me by Zhou Ling, whom I had met in 1999. A long-time member of the club, Zhou Ling had worked in the Club's office for a time and was much loved by other members. She became one of my key interlocutors.

As with the women in Haidian, during my first formal interviews with members of the Migrant Women's Club I usually explained that I did not have a fixed set of questions and that what I most wanted was to hear their life story, and in particular, their experiences of migration to Beijing and life in the city. As in Haidian, not all of these women were willing or able to narrate their lives without repeated prompting questions on my part, but the majority did. Some spoke at considerable length, and in such great detail, and with so few hesitations that it was all I could do to keep up. In several cases, our interviews were followed by ongoing casual interactions through which my interlocutors and I have become lasting friends.

Although my efforts to bridge the status gap between us were important for the development of relations with my interlocutors, my position of authority and status as a foreign expert was also important. In fact, the combination of an empathetic and approachable stance on my part with my status as a highly educated foreigner may well have been a particular incentive for Club members to speak with me. Rural migrants commonly feel that in the city they are surrounded by people who believe themselves to be superior and treat them with contempt, and there is no one who will listen to them. For members of the Migrant Women's Club these feelings are alleviated to some extent by their involvement in the Club. All the same, for many of these women the opportunity to talk with someone who, despite their high status, is empathetic and keen to hear their story is a welcome one.

For some of my interlocutors there was yet more to it than this. As mentioned, longer term members of the Club were well practiced in talking to journalists, academics, and others about the issues facing *dagongmei* and a number were also published writers. Their interactions with the staff of the *Rural Women* editorial office, combined with their activities in the Club and their interactions with the press, had taught these women that communicating their stories to the public was of potentially great importance for furthering the interests of *dagongmei*.

On the other hand, many members of the Migrant Women's Club had had unpleasant experiences with journalists and other outside "experts." Because the Migrant Women's Club is one of relatively few nongovernmental organizations in China, it has become something of a curiosity show for both local and foreign journalists, academics, and others. This is cause for widespread resentment among members of the Club, a number of them complaining that most visitors came only once, wrote up a story about them, and were never heard from again. There was a general feeling that these visitors treated them with condescension, used them for their own purposes, and gave back nothing in return. Other forms of exploitation were also reported. Zhou Ling, for example, complained that on a number of occasions her name and photograph had been published in the press without her permission. Another woman, Chunzi, had herself devoted enormous effort to producing a book of stories and interviews with other young rural migrant women, which was accepted for publication. However, the publishers had tried to make it more marketable by beefing up the melodrama and salaciousness of the stories, and to Chunzi's acute chagrin the end result bordered on the pornographic.

For all this, Zhou Ling, Chunzi, and many others were enormously generous and frank in telling me their stories. This may have been because they thought that as a foreign expert I could convey their story to a broad public and that, as someone genuinely sympathetic to their personal experiences and points of view, I might be able to get that story right. For me, this has been a formidable but seductive challenge. However, while I try to do justice by my interlocutors I do not pretend that this book is a straightforward, unmediated representation of the truth of their lives. If it achieves any semblance of veracity, it must be remembered that this too is only one person's story—the author's—and that just like any other story, it is partial and contrived.

Through the book I include numerous quotations from the narratives, both oral and written, of migrant women. In part, I do this out of a belief in the political and epistemological importance of heeding the experiences of others as they understand and represent them, and out of a desire to work against the grain of dominant, global discourses in which the subaltern are so often presented as passive objects, unable to speak for themselves. Of course, though, these quotations do not really give the reader direct, unmediated access to these subaltern women's voices, experiences, and understandings, for it was I who selected and translated them and placed them in the text in order to achieve particular effects.

In many cases, I chose these pieces because they seemed to me typical or representative in some way of migrant women's narratives. In some instances I have used excerpts of narratives because they summarize information about experiences that are common to many rural migrant women or because they convey, in a particularly succinct and evocative way, the "feel" of those experiences. In other instances I have quoted narratives in order to highlight terminology and narrative structures that are embedded in many migrant women's accounts, and that indicate values, understandings, and assumptions that are common both to migrant women and to dominant discourses.

It is a key aim of this book, however, to highlight the fact that, while inevitably bound in certain ways by dominant discourses and sharing certain commonalities with others, no single migrant woman's narrative can ever be entirely representative of the stories of migrant women in general. Within the category "rural migrant women" certain distinctions, based for example on age and occupation, and on membership or nonmembership in the Migrant Women's Club, can be seen to effect similar experiences and narratives. Other variables, including the circumstances in which narratives were told, have also resulted in identifiable patterns in migrant women's stories. In several places in this book, in order to facilitate an identification and discussion of patterns among migrant women's stories and the variables underlying those patterns, I have juxtaposed quotations from narratives that, individually, are representative of a particular narrative form or a particular subset of reported experiences, but that differ from each other.

Even within subgroups of migrant women, of course, no individual set of experiences, identities, and understandings will ever be exactly the same as another. Likewise, no narrative will ever be identical with another, regardless of similarities in the circumstances of their production and performance. In some places in this book I have quoted from narratives precisely because of the extent to which they differ from the "representative." I do so in order to both illustrate the power of dominant discourses—in other words, with the understanding that "the exception proves the rule"—and to demonstrate the importance of individual subjects' agency in shaping experiences, understandings and narratives.

Summary of Aims and Organization of the Book

Part I begins with a discussion of the discursive formation of rural migrant subject positions. Chapter 1 tracks the origins and history of key elements of these subject positions from the late nineteenth century to the present and examines the construction of rural migrant subject positions in contemporary urban discourse, especially the written media. Chapter 2 then discusses the *Rural Women* collective, the Migrant Women's Club, and the journals *Rural Women* and *Working Sister,* and the important ways in which these institutions have contributed to the formation of rural migrant women subject positions.

The remaining parts of the book focus on the experiences of migrant women themselves and what they have to say about them, each touching on several aspects of migration and life in the city, but from a different thematic angle each time. Part II looks at experiences and understandings of place, understood in both geographic and social terms. Thus, chapter 3 looks at the ways in which migrant women are both highly regulated and marginalized in the city—made to feel at once both "out of place" and "put in their place" as a result of the household registration system and accompanying regulations, and forms of discrimination, exploitation, and abuse that feed off those regulations. Chapter 4 then looks at the evaluations that migrant women make of different places, specifically their home villages and the city of Beijing.

Part III focuses on relationships and identities. Chapter 5 discusses migrant women's relationships with other people. This chapter seeks to comment on the literature on relationships within migrant families—the effect these family relationships have on migration motivations and decision making, and the effects of migration on family relationships. It also makes a contribution to the literature on the significance of networks and ties between migrants for the migration experience. Chapter 6 discusses migrant women's understandings of identities—who they identify as "us" and who as "them," the criteria upon which they make these categorizations, and the characteristics they attribute to the categories. This chapter is particularly concerned with the ways in which migrant women negotiate the dominant subject positions that are discussed in Part I, and with the extent to which analyses based on class, gender, rural/urban difference, and ethnicity can contribute to our understanding of migrant identities and experiences.

Finally, in Part IV the focus is on time and temporal change. Thus chapter 7 examines the relationship between narrative form, understandings of time as a central aspect of migrant experience, and migrant agency and resistance. Instead of focusing on discrete segments of migrant women's narratives, this chapter examines narratives as wholes, identifying particular narrative structures common to different groups of migrant women and analyzing them in relation to dominant discourses. Two types of narrative structure are identified and analyzed—one that positions migration and life in the city in relation to the narrator's life course, and another that is structured around complaints about migrants' circumstances in the city, their status, and the treatment they receive from others. This chapter introduces relatively little new material, instead drawing together the key strands in rural women's representations of migration and life in the city that are identified in previous chapters.

Appendix 1 contains a list of all interlocutors named in the book. All migrant interlocutors have been given pseudonyms, and the personal details of some have also been changed in order to protect identities. Appendix 2 has a map of the People's Republic of China and a map of the Beijing Municipality. A glossary of Chinese terms is also included at the end of the book.

To sum up, my first aim in writing this book has to been to understand and draw attention to the experiences of migrant women, while the second has been to unravel the processes through which these experiences are discursively and narratively constructed and performed.

I have called this introductory chapter "from the margins to the center" partly because I am focusing on the experiences of women who have moved from the countryside to Beijing, which is, both in dominant discourse and in the eyes of migrant women themselves, a movement from the poorer, "backward" margins to the center of civilization, wealth, modernity, and power. But I also want to destabilize the understandings entailed in the very set of distinctions between margin and center, rural and urban (and indeed between female and male) upon which my title rests.

Finally, I bring some of the most marginalized figures in Chinese society—that is, rural women and rural migrant women—into the center of my analysis. I do this, first, because the rural women who are now migrating to Chinese towns and cities to work are key agents in the global economy and in the social changes attending globalization. Second, as I will argue in chapter 1, the figure of the rural female migrant "other" plays an important part in elite and dominant discourses of modernity and of China's identity with respect to the rest of the world. Understanding how migrant women react to or work with the ways in which they are framed in those dominant discourses is essential for an appreciation of what migration and life in the city means to rural women and how it affects their sense of self. In addition, an examination of the particular ways in which migrant women's narratives reproduce, negotiate, and in some cases challenge dominant discourses will greatly enrich our understanding of globalization and social change in contemporary China.

Part I

The Subject

1

Between "Rural Idiocy" and "Urban Modernity"

As a way of beginning to understand the experiences of rural migrant women in China this first chapter looks at the genealogy of rural migrant subject positions. Two basic propositions underlie this chapter. The first is that migrants construct and perform their identities and understand their experiences both in reaction to and within the framework of dominant state and popular discourses[1] in which they have been cast as a group that is in essential ways different from, and outside of, the urban citizenry. In order to understand migrant women's lives, we need then to understand the construction of migrant subjects in dominant discourses. The second preliminary proposition is that the definition and representation of particular groups within a society as marginal, deviant, inferior, or outsider "others" can be central to the construction and maintenance of conventional or dominant notions about the identity of that society and about what constitutes a "normal" or "good" citizen. In the case of China, scholars have recently begun to examine the ways in which an "othering" of peasants, women, and members of ethnic minorities intersects with and contributes to elite or dominant discourses on modernity and national identity (Cohen 1993; Schein 1997; Feuerwerker 1998; Rofel 1999). In this chapter I demonstrate that the figure of the rural migrant is yet another signifier of "otherness" against and around which dominant national ideas about identity are constructed and reproduced. She is, to use Judith Butler's (1993) term, an "abject" that threatens the project of national modernity and in so doing gives it shape. She is also an object of pity, titillation, and fascination. And she is a subject that must be both put to work and worked upon, if the project of modernity is to succeed.

Where, then, does one begin a genealogy of this abject/object/subject? In previous studies a range of explanations for the high levels of discrimination and exploitation suffered by people of rural origin in the cities of contemporary China has been given. There are those who have attributed it to the notion that the beneficial workings of a free market have been stymied by the ongoing influence of authoritarian Maoist outlooks and institutions, most notably the household registration system (HRIC 2002b). Others have explained it in terms of the particular conjunction of Maoist institutions and market mechanisms characterizing post-Mao economy and society (Solinger 1999), and yet others have seen capitalism and the nature of the post-Mao regime's efforts to "join tracks" (*yu shijie jiegui*) with, and profit from, the global capitalist order as the root cause of the problem (Yan Hairong 2001, 2003a, 2003b).

I will state at the outset that I align myself most closely with those who analyze the status of rural migrants not in terms of the incomplete "liberation" of market forces in contemporary China, but as an outcome of the particular conjunction of Maoist institutions and market mechanisms that makes up the current sociopolitical and economic order in China. Thus I argue that the most pervasive and dominant understandings of the subject positions available to rural migrants and the social valuations attached to those positions in contemporary China result from the particular ways in which they are taken up by, and seen to function in, the post-Mao order. However, the various principles of categorization and evaluation according to which a person is identified as a rural migrant and which underlie understandings of what migrant subject positions entail did not arise "out of thin air" with the unleashing of market reforms in the late 1970s. Nor can they be explained as originating with the household registration system introduced under Mao in the 1950s. On the other hand, these principles of categorization and evaluation are also neither timeless nor "natural." Rather, what we see is the coming together of a number of ideas and concepts that emerged in an earlier period and new formulations, narrations, and performances of these concepts in new contexts, serving new functions. Specifically, I will argue in the first section of this chapter that the emergence of concepts that are key to rural migrant subject positions is intimately bound up with a form of "internal orientalism" on the part of Chinese intellectuals searching for a way to respond to Western projects of modernity and colonialism in the late nineteenth and early twentieth centuries.[2]

Among the various concepts that go into the identification of subjects as rural migrant women, the most fundamental relate to discourses of rural/urban difference, outsider/local status and gender, and to the ways in which these are intertwined with, and contribute to, notions of modernity. This is apparent both in other peoples' representations of migrant women, for example in the media, and in the narratives of migrant women themselves. This chapter, therefore, seeks to unravel the connections between the constitution of the female migrant subject and the genealogy of these discourses in the modern era. More specifically, the first section of the chapter briefly sketches out the emergence of the "peasant question" and the "peasant woman question" in the late nineteenth and early twentieth centuries and responses to those questions in the Maoist period. Section two of the chapter examines post-Mao reformulations of, and responses to, the peasant question. Section three then looks at the ways in which the constitution of rural migrant subject positions in the post-Mao period has brought into play and reworked these questions and answers, drawing also on notions of outsider and local status. This part of the chapter first discusses connotations embedded in the terms used to refer to rural migrants and then focuses on the ways in which rural/urban migration and migrants have been constructed in the Chinese media between the mid-1980s and the early 2000s.

Modernity and the Peasant Question Before and After 1949

In his book *The Country and the City*, Raymond Williams discusses the existence of a rural/urban divide and an assumption of urban superiority in the work of a large number of English writers from 1600 onward and traces the origins of that divide even further back, to classical Greek culture (Williams 1973). Frederick Mote claims, however, that no such rural/urban divide existed in imperial Chinese culture (Mote 1977, quoted in Cohen 1993, 156). There are plenty of grounds for contesting this view.[3] It is clear, nevertheless, that in traditional Chinese political and cultural discourse, the rural/urban divide was much less significant than a distinction between the scholar-official class (*shi*) and the ordinary people (*min*). This distinction had been given its classic formulation in the fourth century B.C., when Mencius stated that those who used their minds and hearts (*laoxin*) ruled and those who used their muscles (*laoli*) were ruled (Feuerwerker 1998, 11). It was thought that the power and authority of the ruling scholar-official class rested in their moral and intellectual superiority over the ordinary people. It was the former's duty to provide for the welfare of the people and to promote moral improvement and keep order among them by themselves being exemplars of self-cultivation and family regulation (ibid.; Bakken 2000, 42). If these duties were not properly upheld, the people would rise up in rebellion and the mandate to rule would be lost.

As various writers have documented, contact with the West and the decay of the imperial state system in the nineteenth and early twentieth centuries led to a crisis of identity among Chinese intellectuals and a subsequent struggle to shape for themselves new ways to exercise their traditional role of intellectual and moral leadership. Underlying the most significant discursive shifts that occurred in the course of this struggle was a drastically new concept of time and a new state teleology (Dikötter 1995, 9). Previously dominant ideas of the past as the golden age and of the fortunes of dynasties as cyclical, reflecting the gain and then loss of the Mandate of Heaven, were now replaced by various modernist discourses in which both individuals and societies were seen to evolve and "progress" in a linear line and through different stages toward maturity and modernity. It became intellectuals' urgent new task to guide and pull the rest of China along this path, so as to restore it to greatness.

Accompanying this new teleology two important new discourses relating to "the people" emerged. In the first, "the people" (*min*) became "a people" (*renzhong*), a "race" (*minzu*), and a "population" (*renkou*); an object of ethnographic and scientific investigation and definition and a resource to be improved for the good of the nation. As Dikötter has argued, by the late nineteenth century "political power was no longer considered to be the result of public virtue or individual morality:

demographic strength was the only criterion by which the expansion or destruction of the state could be measured" (ibid., 107–8).

Defining, measuring, and evaluating the "race" and the "population" were seen as essentially the equivalent of describing and evaluating the nation. It therefore became a central plank in intellectuals' attempts to answer the question, "What is wrong with China?" a question brought on by defeat at the hands of colonial powers that became, and has remained to this day, a key problematic for the educated elite (Fitzgerald 1996, 108). By the 1920s, it had become almost universally accepted by intellectuals that "what was wrong with China" were grave defects in the "national character" (*guomin xing*). Previously, as indicated above, the Confucian elite already drew a link between the maintenance of social order and harmony and human cultivation and improvement. Now, however, an improvement in the national character and in the quality of the population became a more pressing task with a definite goal: the modernization of the nation.

When Chinese nationalists, such as Liang Qichao and, later, Lu Xun, wrote about defects in the national character, they were reacting to, and in many cases mirroring, Western colonial treatises on the topic. One of the most influential Western critiques of the Chinese, a book called *Chinese Characteristics*, was written by an American missionary, Arthur Smith, and published in 1894. In this book, Smith detailed a long list of defects in the Chinese character including a "disregard of time and accuracy," an "absence of nerves," "intellectual turbidity," and an "absence of public spirit" (Smith 1894).[4]

Arthur Smith believed that these defects could be ameliorated only through conversion to Christianity. For many Chinese intellectuals the answer lay in the promotion of mass education and the popularization of culture. A key strand in the May Fourth Movement[5] was the promotion of mass literacy and of literature written in the vernacular. For others, concern about the defects in the Chinese national character led to an emphasis on the cultivation of "civilization" (*wenming*) and etiquette. In 1924 Sun Yatsen, in his last lectures on the Three Principles of the People, poured scorn on the manners of his audience and urged an improvement in public etiquette. Ten years later, Chiang Kaishek launched the New Life movement, central to which was the promulgation of ninety-six rules governing public conduct and hygiene, including "Be clean," "Do not spit in the streets," and "Button your suit properly" (Fitzgerald 1996, 104-5; Bianco 1971, 127–28).

For yet others, concern about the characteristics of the Chinese people led to support for a eugenicist program, targeted in particular at the lower classes. Numerous scholars from the nineteenth century on blamed racial degeneration on the overbreeding of the poor. Some advocated a selective, class-based program for limiting reproduction. Others warned against the dangers of disseminating contraceptive knowledge, for fear that it would be taken up disproportionately by the educated classes and the race would be swamped by hordes of inferior creatures born in the lower classes (Dikötter 1995, 120).

Alongside the emergence of the population and the national character as prominent concerns in intellectual debates, a second discourse emerged in the early twentieth century, in which the *shi/min* divide was reconstituted as one between the urban population or, more particularly, urban intellectuals and the "peasantry" (*nongmin*) (Feuerwerker 1998, 9).[6] During the late nineteenth century a differentiation between urban and rural society had begun to grow as a result of the establishment of foreign "treaty ports" and the example they set in the areas of commerce and administration. Administration, communication, capital, and mechanized industry became increasingly concentrated in a few coastal cities, especially Shanghai. As a consequence, the distinctiveness of the quality of life and culture of these cities relative to the rural hinterland also increased and city dwellers sought more and more to distinguish themselves from their rural cousins (Stockman 2000, 48–49). During this period several terms were adopted that had roots in classical Chinese, but which had then been (re)constructed by Meiji-era Japanese modernizers for use in translating works from the West. These included the neologism *nongmin* (peasant), which, as in English, had connotations of backwardness that had not been present in the previously usual term *nongfu* or farmer. It also included terms now used to describe "the peasantry," such as *fengjian* (feudal) and *mixin* (superstition) (Cohen 1993, 155).

During the May Fourth Movement, the "peasant" became a central theme in literature and sociopolitical discourse. According to Myron Cohen, only a minority of intellectuals during this period viewed peasants with any positivity:

The notion of the peasantry as a culturally distinct and alien "other," passive, helpless, unenlightened, in the grip of ugly and fundamentally useless customs, desperately in need of education and cultural reform, and for such improvements in their circumstances totally dependent on the leadership and efforts of rational and informed outsiders, became fixed in the outlook of China's modern intellectual and political elites. For the elites governing China, or seeking to assume power over it, this image of the peasant confirmed their own moral claim to an inherently superior, privileged position in national political life, and their conviction that populism or popular democracy were utterly unacceptable if China was to avoid chaos and achieve national strength. (Cohen 1993, 155)

My own sense is that intellectuals' feelings about the peasantry were rather more complicated than this suggests. Even among the most reformist, Lu Xun, for example, was scathing about the backwardness of village life and particularly adamant about the need for its destruction but, at the same time, evinced considerable nostalgia for it. The same kind of tension is evident in the essay "Youth and the Countryside" published in 1919 by Li Dazhao, a founding member of the Communist Party. In his essay Li claimed that "the darkness of the Chinese countryside has reached an extreme" and that peasants needed urgent liberation from their suffering, pain, ignorance, and sickness, but he also urged young people to travel to the countryside, saying that "darkness prevails in the city while brightness prevails in the countryside. Life in the city is almost ghostly while in the countryside activities are for humans. The air in the cities is filthy while the air in the countryside is fresh" (Li Dazhao 1984 [1919], 651). From the mid-1910s to the 1930s various intellectuals echoed Li's call to youth, exhorting them to "go among the people" and to "head inland" (Feuerwerker 1998, 29–30; Fitzgerald 1996, 136). The search was on for the "real" Chinese, untainted by contact with foreign influence or the corrosive, degenerative effects of life in the cities.

While this picture of the tensions and differences in intellectuals' images of the countryside complicates Cohen's argument that these images "confirmed their own moral claim to an inherently superior, privileged position in national political life," it by no means invalidates it. Common to the contempt and the fondness for the countryside on the part of May Fourth intellectuals and political leaders was what Johannes Fabian terms the "denial of coevalness" (Fabian 1983). In other words, in both cases, the countryside and the peasants were effectively "othered" by being denied temporal equivalence with the cities. Whether they symbolized the backwardness of an old society that had to be destroyed, or whether they were viewed with nostalgia as inhabiting an idyllic world untouched by modernization, peasants were set apart as "the past." This cleared the way, in effect, for the present and the future of modernity to be inhabited, taken charge of and shaped by those who were not peasants—the educated, urban elite.

As various scholars have noted, though, it is not just class or an urban/rural divide but also gender that "serves as one of the central modalities through which modernity is imagined and desired" (Rofel 1999, 19).[7] In the nineteenth and early twentieth centuries in China, as elsewhere in the colonized and semicolonized world, the poor treatment of women was, for Westerners and consequently for Chinese intellectuals also, a key sign of the inferior status of the nation (Fitzgerald 1996, 133–34). Consequently, from the May Fourth period onward, the "peasant question" and the "woman question" alike were high on the agenda of social and political reformers, and the female peasant "other" became a popular subject for literature (Feuerwerker 1998, 245).[8]

When the leaders of the newly formed Chinese Communist Party began formulating political theories in the 1920s, the peasant question and the liberation of the peasantry from the oppressive systems of political, clan, religious, and—in the case of peasant women—patriarchal authority were issues of particular concern. Karl Marx and Friedrich Engels, like other Western modernists, had been scathing about the peasantry, characterizing them as an anachronistic, backward-looking class "representing barbarism within civilization" (Marx 1895, cited in Swacker 1983, 125). They hailed the disenfranchisement of peasants from their land, the rise of modern, capitalist industry and of large-scale urbanization in Britain and other parts of Europe as "epoch-making" events that had "rescued a considerable part of the population from the idiocy of rural life" (Marx 1867;

and Marx, and Engels 1848, cited in ibid., 121–25). Mao Zedong, in contrast, became famous for his celebration of the revolutionary qualities of the peasantry. However, this reputation belies the considerable ambivalence that Mao and his followers felt about peasants.

As Daniel Kelliher notes, Communist efforts to formulate theories on the peasant question focused on two issues. The first was how to legitimize the Party's increasing reliance on the peasantry in the face of orthodox Marxist denigration of the "rural idiocy" of that class. The second was how to learn from history by determining why there had been so many peasant uprisings in the past in China that had, however, failed to change the social structure (Kelliher 1994, 389). Communist thinkers produced a broad spectrum of contending answers to these questions during the 1920s and 1930s. Gradually, however, these contending approaches coalesced into a theory of the "dual nature" (*liangchong xing*) of the peasantry. On the one hand, according to this theory, the exploitation and oppression long suffered by peasants in the traditional economy had instilled in them a natural instinct for rebellion. On the other hand, the fact that they were smallholders in a "semifeudal" society led to two forms of backwardness. First, it resulted in a tendency toward political conservatism and a susceptibility to feudal superstition. Second, it led to petit bourgeois aspirations that went no further than an obsession with gaining land and dividing it equally. Peasants, according to this view, were naturally inclined to rebel, but, left to themselves, would always seek to re-create a polity in which an emperor father figure would preside over an order of landlords and peasant patriarchs. Hence, in the past, "although some social progress was made after each great peasant revolutionary struggle, the feudal economic relations and political system remained basically unchanged" (Mao Zedong, quoted in ibid., 392).

The lesson Communist Party officials derived from the theory of the dual nature of the peasantry was that peasants could be usefully employed in the service of the revolution, but they could not lead the revolution themselves. They needed the leadership of the proletariat and its party, the Communist Party. Already the Bolsheviks had formulated the notion of a "worker-peasant alliance," but this was greatly elaborated by the Chinese Communists, who, anxious to repudiate both Stalin's and Trotsky's condemnation of the Party because of its lack of a base among urban workers, claimed that the Party was the most advanced element of the working class itself and that wherever the Party commanded peasants the worker-peasant alliance and the proletarian credentials of the revolution were intact (ibid., 393).

In the context of the 1920s through to the 1940s, the theory of the dual nature of the peasantry was a radical and innovative approach to the peasant question, which provided Chinese Communist Party leaders with both the practical insights and Marxist legitimacy needed for a revolution based in the countryside to succeed (ibid., 394). Kelliher suggests, however, that after 1949 the theory of the dual nature of the peasantry and the worker-peasant alliance took on new meanings and new ideological functions. Whereas before the revolution Mao had put most emphasis on the positive, revolutionary side of peasant nature, after Liberation, when the rebellious nature of the peasantry was no longer such an asset, concerns about the backwardness of peasant consciousness became more prominent in Party theorizing. Furthermore, by the mid-1950s, peasants had begun to complain that what the worker-peasant alliance really meant was the subordination of the interests of the peasantry to that of the urban working class and the Communist Party (ibid., 395).

Through the first three decades following Liberation, the Communist Party professed itself committed to women's liberation and to the elimination of the "three great differences" (san da chabie), that is, inequalities between city and countryside, mental and manual labor, and workers and peasants. In official media and in literature, peasants, including peasant women, were most commonly depicted as heroes leading the revolution or as the masses who had previously suffered from feudal backwardness, but had been lifted out of that backwardness and inspired to march forward by the Communist Party.[9] In short, they were depicted not as "barbarism within civilization" or as the backward past of modernity, but as a "forward moving" or "advanced" class central in the nation's drive toward communism (Kipnis 1995, 119–20).

In practice, peasants, especially poor peasants, gained a great deal during the Maoist period in terms of social and political status and also benefited from impressive efforts on the part of the state to improve basic health and literacy, to raise the status of women, and to promote free marriage. Many rural residents now look back on the Maoist period as a "golden age" of equality, dignity, and morality, when everyone's basic needs were met, there was little corruption or crime, and the population was united in a worthy cause, under a charismatic and powerful leader (Gao 1999; Dorfman 1996, 269). They do so with considerable justification, I would suggest, given Maoist achievements both with respect to prerevolutionary conditions in the countryside and with respect to the increases in inequalities, corruption, violence within the countryside, and an increasing social and economic divide between rural and urban that has characterized the decades since Mao's death.[10]

However, with regard to gender equality, achievements were decidedly less than state rhetoric might suggest. While innovative in so many other ways, when it came to women's liberation the Chinese state by and large adopted a simplistic, orthodox Marxist approach, according to which women would be freed from oppression once they had been drawn into social production. Furthermore, even this approach was put into practice only when it suited the demands of the economy, and not when unemployment pressures were high. Consequently, most analysts now argue that during the Maoist period the liberation of women, especially in the countryside, was "unfinished" or "postponed," with fundamental problems, including gender divisions of labor and unequal remuneration, the double burden, and lack of freedom and equality in marriage practices and family relations remaining (Johnson 1983; Andors 1983; Wolf, Margery 1985).

In addition to this, during the 1950s the Communist Party instituted two different forms of categorization and regulation that objectified a rural/urban divide and cemented it into place. The first of these was the assignation of class status, in the process of which citizens were split between those defined as either permanent urban residents or permanent rural residents of a specific village. The former were further categorized according to their occupation or their family's occupation before the revolution, while the latter were categorized according to land ownership. The second form of categorization instituted in the 1950s was the household registration system. As discussed in the introduction to this book, this system, combined with other aspects of Maoist political and economic management, made movement from rural to urban areas almost impossible and enabled the state to siphon resources out of the countryside for use in funding industrial development and the subsidization of urban living costs. The result was that rural living standards remained low and rural/urban inequalities were perpetuated.

During the Cultural Revolution decade (1966–76), the two extremes of the Party's perceptions of the peasantry, as enunciated in the dual-nature theory, became particularly apparent. On the one hand, the Party sent urbanites to the countryside both in order to redress the divide between urban and rural residents and so that the urbanites might learn from the revolutionary spirit of the peasants. In addition, during this period rural "Iron Girl" teams, modeled after a group of young rural women in the model Dazhai production brigade, became one of the most potent symbols, both of women's liberation and of revolutionary progress (Yan Hairong 2002, 10–11).[11] On the other hand, ultra-leftists in the Party became more suspicious than ever of the petit bourgeois tendencies of the peasantry, condemning rural families' efforts to supplement their incomes by raising a few pigs or chickens, or growing vegetables on private plots as "tails of capitalism."

By the end of the 1970s, as Kelliher notes, the theory of the dual nature of the peasantry had hardened into a set of essentialist clichés. The dominant image "presented peasants as enthusiastic, proud, physically powerful, easily led, defiant against oppressors, revolutionary, natural, and dignified under duress; yet the image also depicted peasants as cunning, stubborn, conservative, thieving, backward, selfish, superstitious, and acquisitive" (Kelliher 1994, 397).

The "Low Quality" of Peasants in Post-Mao China

Kelliher argues that under Deng Xiaoping in the 1980s, Party reformers tried to gather new information and to open themselves to a new understanding of peasants, but they were thwarted in this by the continuing influence of the dual nature theory, especially by the assumption that the peasantry was a backward, short-sighted class. In particular, when Party officials observed that decollectivization was accompanied by a resurgence in prerevolutionary village customs, they attributed this to a primordial, backward "peasant consciousness" (*nongmin yishi*), rather than, for example, to economic factors or to the Party's failure to address a sense of insecurity and uncertainty in the countryside (ibid., 401–2).

Kelliher claims that, unlike Party investigators who remained stuck within old and rigid perceptual frameworks about the essential backwardness of the peasantry, "artists and scholars of the 1980s brought unprecedented strains of objectivity, humanism and intellectual excitement to their depictions of the peasantry" (ibid., 401). It is certainly true that a great deal of careful research into the rural economy and society was published and that in cultural circles also, more complex characterizations of rural people and rural life were produced than under Mao. It is also the case, though, that essentialist views of the peasantry and in particular of peasant backwardness were influential right across the spectrum of academic, artistic, and official production. It appeared not only that older Party theories about the petit bourgeois tendencies among peasants had degenerated into immovable clichés about peasant backwardness, but that the Cultural Revolution policy of sending urbanites to learn from the revolutionary side of peasants' nature had been a singular failure. What most urbanites had learned, more than anything else, was how essentially different and backward the peasants were in comparison with themselves. This lesson, combined with a sense that on the world stage China as a nation was also backward, led to a reemergence of the question, "What is wrong with China?" and to the construction of a range of answers to that question by officials, intellectuals, artists, and journalists that drew their inspiration, on the one hand, from capitalism and, on the other, from intellectual discourses dominant in China in the early part of the twentieth century.

Hence, with the end of the Cultural Revolution decade peasants lost the moral and political status that they had gained under Maoism, and through the 1980s anxieties about weaknesses in the national character and the backwardness of the population, especially the peasantry and peasant women, once more featured prominently, not just in official pronouncements but also in academic and artistic productions and in the popular media. For example, in 1986 a State Council report on rural poverty laid the blame for China's backwardness on deficiencies in the rural population. This report, in turn, was used as background reference material for the controversial television series *Heshang* (River Elegy) in which one of the central messages was likewise, that China was being held back by its backward peasantry. Throughout the series, peasants were explicitly associated with stagnant tradition and condemned as weak-spirited, passive, and superstitious (Anagnost 1997, 121; Kipnis 1995, 122; Hao Jiaozhen 1990).[12]

The countryside and the peasantry were also of central interest in literature, especially that of the "roots seeking" school, and in the films of "Fifth Generation" directors, such as Zhang Yimou and Chen Kaige, produced in the late 1970s and 1980s. In these works, as during the May Fourth Movement, peasants were alternately portrayed as barbaric and abhorrent or as the longed-for essence of China's tradition and spirit, or quite often as both at once. And, as in May Fourth literature, the figure of the peasant woman often served as a metaphor of otherness in fictional portrayals of the educated urban elite male's relationship to the people.[13]

Through the 1980s and 1990s the state increasingly targeted rural people, especially women and those in the poorest areas, in a range of discourses that focused on *suzhi*, a neologism that translates into English roughly as (human) quality.[14] For example, improving the *suzhi* of the rural population, in particular by eliminating "superstitious" ritual practices, providing technical training, encouraging competition and commodification, and "liberating rural people from the fetters of traditional concepts of small production and egalitarianism" was a central aim both of the Party's campaign to improve "spiritual civilization" and of the All China Women's Federation's efforts to improve women's role in, and contribution toward, development (Jacka 1997, 95; "Kua Shiji. . ." 1999; Judd 2002, 19–32).[15]

Suzhi has become a central element in a variety of discourses on development and the achievement of modernity and national power. It can, and has been, used to refer to a host of attributes, including education, culture, morality, manners, psychology, physiology, and genetics. The key to understanding its significance is not to pin it down with a precise definition. Rather, it is important to recognize, first, the very utility and power of the term's flexibility. Another significant feature of the deployment of *suzhi* is that it focuses concern on the attributes of human beings and how to improve them, and diverts attention away from deficiencies and inequities resulting from structures, institutions, and practices either created, or endorsed by, the state.

Suzhi contributes to forms of social and economic differentiation and governmentality that are rather different from those of Maoist class categories. Superficially, "low *suzhi*" appears to be a less rigid category of inferior status than a bad class label had been under Maoism, for the idea that anyone and everyone can, and should, raise their *suzhi* has been promoted in a wide range of post-Mao discourses. In fact, one could suggest that *suzhi* itself is less central to post-Mao strivings for modernity than is the notion that a person's and a nation's *suzhi* are not fixed, and that they can either fall behind others' or be raised. This feeds and answers to new, very powerful desires and anxieties in the populace, for the possibilities of attaining higher levels of *suzhi* for oneself, of competing with others over who has the most *suzhi*, of feeling superior because of one's *suzhi* and looking down with either sympathy or contempt on those who have less, has proved enormously enticing.

The engendering of these new desires and anxieties, in turn, has become at least as crucial to the market economy and to state governance as are the desires for material wealth and consumption. Thus, at the macro level, raising the population's *suzhi* through, in particular, family planning, eugenics, crackdowns on crime and disorder, and the disciplining and training of the workforce has been seen, both by the state and in the general populace, as crucial to national "development," an all-important goal in China's competition with other nations for pride and power. And at the micro level, individuals' "self-development" (*ziwo fazhan*), based on efforts to improve their *suzhi*—through, for example, better diet and exercise, the provision of "quality" education for one's children, self-study in English and computing, and the broadening of horizons through travel to the city or abroad—have not only been promoted by the state as vital to national development, but have been internalized as powerful yearnings among ordinary people, including, as I will discuss in later chapters, rural migrant women. Desires and anxieties over China's *suzhi* as a nation thus fuse with competition over families' and individuals' personal *suzhi*, contributing to a powerful form of governmentality based on pressures toward self-regulation and self-development that are internalized among the people as much as they are imposed by the state from above.

In the post-Mao period, people in both rural and urban China have been inundated by state campaigns, popular media, and commercial advertising that promotes the possibility of raising *suzhi* and that pushes and pulls them into trying to achieve that possibility. Tragically for those concerned, however, those groups marked out as having the lowest *suzhi*, especially people of rural origin, have found that in practice this is a status that is even more difficult to change than the Maoist "bad class" label had been. *Suzhi* has been mapped onto a geography of social and economic differentiation between the poor "backward" rural hinterland and the urban cities and coastal provinces that, far from being ameliorated by market-oriented reforms, became ever more stark over the 1980s and 1990s. Thus, from the mid-1980s inequalities in income, education, health, welfare, and security increased, both within rural areas and between rural and urban areas. By 1995 the ratio of urban to rural incomes was 2.47:1 (Khan and Riskin 2005, 380), indicating a level of inequality higher than had pertained at the beginning of the post-Mao period in 1978 (Knight and Song 1999, 319). This rural/urban inequality was higher than any other form of inequality in China (Khan and Riskin 1998, 246) and also higher than the rural/urban inequality in any other country in the world except Zimbabwe and South Africa (Knight and Song 1999, 337). And it grew even higher in subsequent years—in 2002 the ratio of urban to rural incomes in China was 3.01:1 (Khan and Riskin 2005, 380).

The "Tide of Peasant Workers" in Post-Mao Discourse

> Regardless of whether it is the conversation of ordinary urbanites or the opinions of important government officials that one is listening to, regardless of whether one is watching a popular film or television program or reading the work of an authoritative expert, one will be given more or less the same description of rural people who enter urban areas: that is, that they are, in the main, stupid, dirty, lacking in breeding, and without any sense of shame. You will be told that the country people pouring into the cities are, if not active, then latent, robbers and plunderers, prostitutes and pimps, "out of plan guerrillas" [a reference to those who do not conform to family planning policies] and carriers and transmitters of contagious diseases. (Yu 1994, 38)

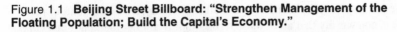
Figure 1.1 **Beijing Street Billboard: "Strengthen Management of the Floating Population; Build the Capital's Economy."**

Given general prejudices about the backwardness of peasants, encoded in the very term *nongmin*, reified and essentialized during the Maoist era in the theory of the dual nature of the peasantry and the household registration system, and once more highlighted in post-Mao anxieties and desires about *suzhi*, it is perhaps unsurprising that when large numbers of rural people began entering the cities in the mid-1980s they too should be viewed with contempt and distrust by urbanites. As the sociologist Yu Depeng notes in the quotation above, this attitude was readily apparent in ordinary conversations, in the popular media, and in official discourse.

In fact, among post-Mao urbanites the peasants in the "tide of peasant workers" or "floating population" have called forth considerably more anxiety and revulsion (but also, as I will discuss shortly, fascination) than do peasants in the countryside. This is partly because suddenly they are on urban streets in large numbers and much more visible and unavoidable than they had been in their villages. It is also because of their fluidity and liminality; because, having left their moorings in the countryside but yet not being true urbanites, they threaten the very distinction between "rural" and "urban" upon which the order maintaining both urban material privilege and notions of higher urban *suzhi* has been based.

These concerns about fluidity and liminality are clearly reflected in the terms most commonly used to refer to migrants, including *mingong chao* (tide of peasant workers), *mangliu* (blind drifters), as well as *liudong renkou* or floating population. It is noteworthy that all of these terms employ a water metaphor and contain characters with the water radical. Thus, in the first term, migrants are likened to a tide or a surge, and both the latter terms contain the character *liu*, which means to flow, float, or drift.[16] As several scholars have noted, Chinese culture has traditionally involved a particularly bunker-like attitude toward outsiders and a high degree of anxiety about people who are geographically mobile. Perhaps this is because it has been dominated to such an extent by a kinship-based sedentary agricultural society (Yang 1994, 193). Hence, rootedness in a spatially bound community has been an important element in mainstream ideals of what constitutes a desirable, moral life (Zhang, Li 2001, 33), and the character *liu* has very powerful, negative connotations.[17]

Other terms used to refer to migrants also encode a sense of threat by emphasizing their outsider status in their place of destination. Thus, the common terms *waidiren* (outsiders), *wailaigong* (outsider workers), and *wailaimei* (outsider sisters) most obviously indicate an outsider status because they point to the fact that the person comes from a different place. The terms *dagongmei* (working sister) and *dagongzai* (working son) are not as explicit about migrants' status as outsiders as are *waidiren*, *wailaimei*, and so on. However, the term *dagong*, which refers to temporary wage labor in contrast to a permanent occupation (*zhiye*) and has none of the status that was accorded to *laodong* (labor) under Maoism, also suggests that they are outsiders to the urban social order. For all the changes that have occurred with the introduction of a labor market and the growth in private enterprise, in the 1990s and early 2000s *zhiye* has still most commonly brought to mind a lifetime job in which a person is attached to a particular *danwei* (work unit). That *danwei* is the individual's anchor in society, providing not just employment but also housing, welfare, and a range of other public goods, and is responsible for monitoring and policing the person's behavior. *Dagongzai* and *dagongmei* are completely outside of the *danwei* system—they work on short-term jobs, quite often without any contract or other legal documentation, and because they are generally not provided with any welfare or other benefits (though factories do often house them in dormitories) they are also not beholden to their work units in the same way as other workers.

Finally, the words *zai* (son) and *mei* (younger sister; girl) in *dagongzai* and *dagongmei* also suggest that migrants are outsiders to, or at least not full members of, the social order because they indicate that the individuals being referred to are young and unmarried. For women in particular, marriage marks the entry into the social order. Thus, whatever position migrant women occupy in the city, it is seen as only temporary—their "real" adult status begins when they return to the countryside, "settle down," and become wives and mothers (Pun 1999, 2).

I now want to look at the ways in which assumptions, ideas, and attitudes embedded in the very terms used to refer to migrants are also played out in representations of migrants in the written media, this being one of the most visible aspects of urban culture, both reflecting and contributing to dominant discourses on rural to urban migration. In this section I examine a range of articles published in the national and Beijing media, including analytical pieces and survey reports by academics and officials; didactic pieces, including portrayals of models and heroes, and cautionary tales about the fallen; and human-interest stories and investigative journalism. The articles I discuss come from "official" newspapers and magazines, as distinct from "commercial" tabloids and other publications. It should be noted, however, that changes in funding and management of the media have complicated the distinction between official and commercial or unofficial media in such a way that both the "Party line" and the "bottom line" of commercial concerns are visible in both, and a range of discourses reflecting various interests, desires, and concerns can be discerned across the official/commercial divide.[18]

The single characteristic shared by the periodicals referred to in this chapter, as indeed by the vast majority of both official and commercial media in China, is an overwhelmingly urban perspective and an assumption that the main readership is the educated, urban population. For all their numerical dominance, the concerns and perspectives of rural inhabitants get little airing in the Chinese press, outside of a few specialist periodicals. In the next chapter, however, I will examine the journals *Rural Women* and *Working Sister*, which are directed specifically at rural women. Part of my aim in this next chapter will be to determine the extent to which the discourses that dominate the mainstream, urban media are also reflected in more specialized women's journals that purportedly write for a rural or rural migrant audience.

Most analytical articles on rural to urban migration published in China in the 1980s and 1990s portrayed it with ambivalence. One such article, written by officials in the Beijing Public Security Bureau (the equivalent of the police), began a discussion of the floating population in that city by claiming that

> since reform and opening up, and following the gradual establishment of a socialist market economy, the flow of people, finance and products has expanded day by day, and in large and medium sized cities across the nation the floating population, a dynamic and complex population group, has swollen to an extent and at a rate previously unseen. (Wang, Shi, and Zong 1993, 35)

The article outlined some statistics on the size and demographic characteristics of Beijing's floating population before discussing its impact on the city's economy and society. First, "positive" aspects were noted. These included the contribution that rural construction workers made in building the city and the fact that rural laborers had helped to "plug the gaps" in industries, such as construction, textiles, chemicals, sanitation, and coal that, because of their reputation for involving "dirty, tiring, and heavy" work, suffered from a shortage of labor. Also mentioned was the fact that rural people selling agricultural produce and other goods, repairing shoes and household implements, and providing cleaning and other services, had

made daily life in the capital a good deal easier. It was further pointed out that in their role as both retailers and consumers the floating population had greatly contributed to the growth of business in the capital (ibid., 36–37).
The article went on:

> However, every issue has two sides to it, and while the entry of millions of floaters has played an important role in developing the economy and constructing the capital, it has simultaneously also created a series of problems for the capital's economic order, urban management and social order. (ibid., 37)

It then discussed these problems, giving statistics to demonstrate that increased rural immigration has resulted in rising crime rates in Beijing, that rural migrants predominate in growing numbers of businesses operating without licenses and without paying taxes, and that the growth of the floating population is putting unsustainable pressures on public transport, the supply of water, electricity, and coal, and on public hygiene and family planning. There followed a brief forecast of growth trends in the floating population and then the article concluded with a substantial list of policy proposals. All of these were aimed at improving the management of the floating population. They included measures to "supplement, revise, and perfect the role of the legal system" in this area; the establishment of a "unified, authoritative structure for the management of the floating population," the continued promotion of the role of employers and other urban residents in the surveillance and regulation of migrant employment and accommodation in the city, and the implementation of a standardized "user pays" system of fees that would overcome the serious shortfall in the resources needed by the Public Security Bureau and other departments in the administration of migrant permits (ibid., 37–39).

Several aspects of the narrative structure, as well as content, of this article are standard features of analyses of the floating population published in the 1980s and 1990s. First, the analysis is premised upon a clear divide between "our" city, belonging to both the author and the reader of the text, and "the rest" and is written from a managerial perspective, underwritten, in particular, by an anxiety about urban stability and the maintenance of local urban living standards. Thus the overriding concern in the article is to establish the scale of the floating population phenomenon and to determine how best to control and manage it. No consideration is given to the welfare or needs of "floaters" themselves. Furthermore, as is the case with most such articles, this analysis mentions benefits to be drawn from the presence of the floating population in the city, but the discussion of the negative effects and of how to manage them takes pride of place, both in terms of sheer column inches and in its dominant position in the center, and at the end of, the narrative.[19]

Second, in this narrative an association is made between the market and migration, and the effects attributed to the floating population are very similar to those commonly attributed to the market. However, the narrative blurs the causal relationship between market reforms, migration, and social and economic change. The overall effect is that migrants become a metaphor for the market and anxiety about the floating population contributes to, and is itself reinforced by, general anxiety about the breakdown of central planning and the impact of market forces (cf. Solinger 1999, 100).

Accounts such as this thus reproduce associations between migration and disorder that are already encoded in the terms *liudong renkou* and *mangliu*. They express a nostalgia for a premarket reform system in which everyone was fixed in place, and, by giving the impression of constantly impending social breakdown, help to generate a desire for strong central control, thus legitimating the role of the state, especially the law-enforcing agencies. In addition, by highlighting the alleged dominance of rural migrants in urban crime, they construct an image of a dangerously antisocial, low *suzhi*, rural "other" against which contrasting notions of urban civilization and order can be built and maintained.

Between the mid-1980s and the mid-1990s, the image of the floating population as a flood threatening to overwhelm the city was by far the most dominant representation of rural migrants in the media. Thereafter, however, portrayals of rural migration and of migrants became increasingly diversified and included a growing number that focused on migrants as individual people, rather than viewing migration simply as a problematic phenomenon. They included, first, a growing number of articles that were positive about migration, and that even portrayed migrants as heroes of development. They also included reports that drew attention to the difficult lives of migrants and urged for a more sympathetic response to them, articles giving advice to migrants, for example, about local urban regulations, and others in which rural migrants, especially women, were objects of titillation and voyeurism. Like the threatening "peasant worker tide" image, each of these representations of rural migrants related in important ways to conceptualizations of "backwardness," low *suzhi* and liminality, and to a host of anxieties and desires attendant upon market-oriented "reform," "development," and "modernity," but they each did so in different ways.

Beginning in the mid-1990s, a small but growing number of scholars pushed for a sympathetic understanding of the situation of migrants and sought to repudiate urban prejudices against migrants by means of survey research.[20] More often, however, a focus on the lives of migrants in the city seemed motivated by a growing realization that, on their own, coercive restrictions and regulations on migrants would not prevent them from threatening social and political stability. Instead, some effort needed to be directed to incorporating them into the social life of the city and, above all, into instilling forms of *self*-regulation in the migrant population.[21] Hence, in the late 1990s some newspapers ran columns specifically for and about migrant workers. A large proportion of the articles published in these columns provided information directed at migrants themselves and pertaining to their legal rights and responsibilities. For example, in the regular weekly section on "migrant work in

Beijing," published by *Beijing Youth Daily* (*Beijing Qingnian Bao*) between January and April 1999, a large proportion of articles gave advice on permit requirements for people newly entering the capital, migrant workers' entitlements and duties in employment, and the procedures for reporting criminal behavior to the police. Other articles cautioned migrants not to become involved in drinking, gambling, or crime, or urged them to protect themselves against deception and theft.

While through the 1990s the focus in academic and official articles remained on the troubling impact of migration on law and order in the city, there were also a growing number that portrayed migration in positive terms because of its perceived benefit to rural development. The existence of these very different positions reflects the fact that even the official media do not represent a single, homogenous Party line. Rather, different press articles tend to reflect the interests of different arms of the state bureaucracy. The Public Security Bureau and the municipal governments of the metropolises most favored by rural immigrants are most vocal about the threats to urban security posed by the floating population. In contrast, the Ministry of Agriculture and the governments of provinces that have seen the largest flows of out-migration more often champion rural to urban migration as an avenue for rural development.

Beyond this, the growing presence in the media of the 1990s and 2000s of articles supporting rural to urban migration reflects a general shift in official approaches to rural development. The dominant view of the 1980s was that "surplus labor" from agriculture should be channeled into local, farm-based businesses, small local townships, and village and township enterprises but kept out of larger towns and cities. The slogan was "*li tu bu li xiang, jin chang bu jin cheng*"—"leave the land but not the village, enter factories but not towns and cities." Through the 1990s, this increasingly gave way to the view that industrialization and urbanization were essential for the modernization of the countryside and, therefore, the nation; but that they could not be achieved through the development of small towns and township enterprises alone.

At a convention on the administration of the floating population held in 1995, opinion among central-level leaders was still divided between those who argued that it was "necessary to absorb rural surplus laborers locally" and those who held that "firm and effective measures should be adopted to ensure a rational and orderly movement of rural surplus laborers" (Solinger 1999, 54). At the Sixteenth Party Congress in November 2002, however, President Jiang Zemin argued that "all the institutional and policy barriers to urbanization must be removed and the rational and orderly flow of rural labor guided" (Lague 2003, 25). By this time the realization that China's accession to the World Trade Organization would result in a loss of livelihood for yet more millions of farmers had led to a new slogan: "*li tu you li xiang, jin chang you jin cheng*"—"leave the land and the village, enter factories and towns and cities."

In the late 1990s and early 2000s, efforts have even been made to enable some rural migrants to gain permanent urban residency. However, this has so far largely been limited to towns with a population of less than 100,000 and to skilled and business migrants. The dominant official assumption through this period has continued to be that the majority of rural migrants in large cities will return, either to their home village or to a nearby township, after a sojourn of a few months or years.

Like the reports of migrant criminality, articles on the benefits of migration for rural development reinforce a view of the peasantry as backward, but they portray migration and work in the city as the means whereby that backwardness will be overcome. For example, one author writing for the sociology journal *Shehui* (Society), echoed the Communist Party's "dual nature" theory of the peasantry, claiming that

> research demonstrates that there is a close relationship between population quality and population migration. For a long period, a self-sufficient, narrow, xenophobic natural economy resulted in an extremely closed minded, isolated rural community and bred a small peasant consciousness according to which everyone took care of their own interests without regard for others and stayed on their own home turf with no interest in moving elsewhere. This meant that for a long period social production and consciousness remained within a narrow sphere, always cycling back upon itself, making it very difficult to raise the quality of the rural population. Since the 1990s, following the gradual breakdown of the rampart between city and country and the loosening of the household registration system, peasants have one after another left the countryside to become migrant workers, and migration between country and city has become livelier than ever before. . . .The departure of peasant workers out of the countryside and their entry into wage labor in the city has entailed a fundamental change in their survival-oriented mode of production and style of life, and the change in social and economic environment has been very effective in improving their quality. (Huang Chenxi 1995, 26)

Elaborating on this point, the author argued that their experiences in the city raised levels of culture and education (*wenhua shuiping*) among peasant workers and improved their technical expertise. By sending home remittances, these workers would also contribute to the funds necessary for the provision of education for other villagers. Wage labor in the city also transformed peasant workers' ideas and concepts (*sixiang guannian*). After working in the city, these laborers were less inclined to want numerous children and more likely to look further afield for a marriage partner, thus reducing the likelihood of marriage between relatives and, therefore, the risk of interbreeding and degeneration in the quality of the population. In addition, the author stressed, their experience in the city would strengthen peasant workers' understanding of the market and nurture an openness to new ideas, a willingness to take risks, an understanding of the importance of cooperation and competition, and an appreciation of the value of information and time.

Finally, while in the city, peasant workers would imbibe modern civilization, gradually adapt themselves to the urban rhythm of life and to the contractual nature of social relations in the city, and increase their first-hand knowledge of modernity (ibid., 26–27).

Other articles extol the particular values of domestic service as a formula whereby young rural women contribute to the economy by serving urban families, and in exchange—and in the process—are themselves civilized and modernized. This is viewed not simply as a process whereby rural women gain new skills, but one in which their very bodies and minds are altered. An example is an article published in the Communist Party's *Half Monthly Forum* (*Ban Yue Tan*) reporting on the transformation of young women from Wuwei county in Anhui from being peasants to domestic workers to entrepreneurs. The author notes:

> Tempered by work in the city, these smart and hardworking girls quickly become a new generation combining the cultures of the city and the countryside. When they walk out of the fields they carry with them a rustic air [*tuqi*] and physical strength [*liqi*]; when they return they carry with them not just capital, information, technology, and market experience, but also new ideas, new concepts and the ability to explore the market economy, none of which people at home have. (Wang and Li 1996, 24)

Implicit in this piece, and in the *Society* article just cited, is a condemnation of Maoism for failing to lift the countryside out of a traditional, largely subsistence-based agricultural economy, and for failing to change the "backward," "narrow-minded" peasant mentality. Only since the 1990s, it is claimed, is the *suzhi* (quality) of the peasantry being improved, and that by getting them out of the countryside and into the modern, urban market economy. In these, as in many other accounts, a juxtaposition is drawn up between several terms, as follows:

Negative	Positive
country	city
peasant	urbanite
old	new
tradition	modernity
Maoist	post-Mao
self-sufficiency	market
survival	development
isolation	openness
conservatism	progressive thought
backwardness	civilization
physicality	mental abilities
poor quality	high quality

Migrants are the nexus between these two sets of concepts. As noted in the quotation from Yu Dapeng, they are figures of contempt because of lingering associations of peasantness, being regarded as stupid, dirty, lacking in breeding, and without any sense of shame. In addition, migrants are regarded with suspicion and anxiety because they cannot be pinned down, either literally or metaphorically, in either rural or urban categories, and because of what Yu Dapeng refers to as the "riding the train effect"—because those already on the train (in the city) resent the crowding caused by others (rural migrants) trying to get on (Yu 1994, 37).

However, individual migrants are sometimes praised for their achievements in escaping backward peasantness, as models pioneering the modernization of the countryside and providing inspiration to other peasants to do the same. In the *Half Monthly Forum* article mentioned above, for example, three model women from Wuwei were mentioned. The first studied Chinese medicine part-time while working as a maid in Beijing. After a few years, she returned to Wuwei and established a highly successful factory, producing medical products for both domestic and overseas markets. The second woman worked for several years in domestic service and other occupations in Beijing and was then recognized for her talents by officials in her home village and recruited to become the local representative of the Women's Federation. And the third woman, who had left home before she finished junior secondary school, found work as a maid with an intellectual family in Beijing. She later won first-class grades when she sat for senior secondary school-level examinations in Beijing and a story she wrote was published in the press. According to the authors of this article, these *dagongmei*

> have taken the lead and bravely left the closed up world of farm and field. Through life in a strange city they have been baptised in civilization [*shoudao wenming de xili*] and increased their abilities. They have awakened their thousands of brothers and sisters in the countryside and led them toward the great classroom of the city to be tempered and trained by the market economy. They have brought important benefits to their home county by dealing a blow to their fellow villagers' traditional concepts and ways of thought, and at the same time they have trained a production army that dares to weather the ups and downs of the market; their actions have opened up their home counties to the fact that the outside world is broad and expansive, and once you have left the narrow fields you can change everything. To transform your poverty-stricken, backward home you must rely on yourself, blaze a path for yourself, and fight. (Wang and Li 1996, 24)

In celebrating the achievements of these women, this article obscures the fact that for thousands of young rural women domestic service is experienced as profoundly humiliating labor that leads nowhere in terms of career advancement or training. Furthermore, while ignoring the pitifully low wages paid to those in domestic service, the article fetishizes the supposed gains that these women have made in self-development, in improving their own and their fellow villagers' *suzhi*, and in leading other villagers to the "great classroom of the city." In the process it erases the problem of the class exploitation of migrant wage laborers (Yan Hairong 2002, 7).

In another example, in 1997 the official magazine of the Communist Youth League *Zhongguo Qingnian* (Chinese Youth) ran a report about migrants who had been awarded the title of "outstanding migrant worker youth" (*jiechu wailai wugong qingnian*) by the Youth League. These included a young man who toiled in a shoe factory, enduring the abuse of the manager and suffering serious work injuries over a period of six years, after which time he returned home to set up his own shoe factory. Also praised was a young woman who, as a street cleaner, endured eleven years of contempt and sexual abuse, before being recognized by the Youth League for her service to the urban community. And a final case raised for emulation was that of a young woman who worked for three years in urban restaurants and as a maid, before she could take the humiliation and exploitation no more. She returned to her poverty-stricken village and, using money borrowed from relatives, she built a school for local children (Liu Xinping 1997).

Aside from celebrating the industrialization and commercialization of the rural economy and the proletarianization of rural labor, accounts of model migrants such as this perform two important functions for the state. First, by extolling the successes to be achieved by those who leave agriculture to seek work on the urban job market, learn new skills, and venture into business (preferably back in their home county), they lend legitimacy to state policies promoting a market economy. Indirectly, they also lend legitimacy to the post-Mao state's explicit prioritization of economic growth ahead of, and at the expense of, concerns over social inequalities.[22] For although the exploitation and hardships suffered by these migrants are recognized in these articles, it is not as a problem, but rather as a kind of "trial by fire" that is necessary to each individual's self-development and improvement of *suzhi.*

Second, these articles promote an internalization of values and attitudes seen as necessary for national development. These include adaptiveness, endurance, self-sacrifice, and a willingness to take risks, be flexible, and improve oneself. Central to the *Chinese Youth* and *Half Monthly Forum* articles cited above is the fact that the migrants raised their *suzhi.* The message is that self-development and the improvement of one's *suzhi* is the beneficial outcome of, and reward for, joining the modern market economy. At the same time though, recognition of low *suzhi* and of the need for self-improvement of *suzhi* on the part of each and every individual is the essential prerequisite for national development. As Yan Hairong explains, the post-Mao regime's efforts at "joining tracks with the world" is a social engineering project crucially conditioned upon the formation of a subjectivity through which people come to see themselves as underdeveloped and lacking in quality and the engendering of a desire within each person for self-development and *suzhi* (Yan Hairong 2002, 4–5).

Articles that extol the benefits of labor out-migration and celebrate the successes of individual rural migrants suggest that the road to development and self-development lies in rural people breaking out of the narrow confines of the traditional peasant economy (in most cases later returning to transform it). One aspect of peasantness, however, is seen as a virtue to be retained: the ability to "eat bitterness" (*chi ku*), or endure hardship. In fact, it is precisely the ability to tolerate years of low-paid backbreaking toil, abuse, and exploitation without welfare or security of employment, that makes them heroes. Here, then, we see the rural migrant constructed, not as the "abject" other, but as the subject of post-Mao development. This time it is the urbanite, specifically the urban worker, laid off from employment in the moribund state sector, whose association with Maoist central planning and "dependency" on the "iron rice bowl" of life-long employment and welfare has become the cause of her abjection (Yan Hairong 2002, 8–9).

While articles portraying migrants as heroes play important discursive functions, they still have been relatively rare in the media of the 1990s and early 2000s. Accounts portraying migrants as victims have been far more common. In particular, stories of *dagongmei* victims have abounded, especially in tabloids and other forms of commercial media, but also in the official press. There has been, for example, a substantial and growing body of investigative journalism into the exploitation of migrants, especially *dagongmei*, working in the foreign-invested factories of Shenzhen and other Special Economic Zones. These articles often provide graphic and harrowing details about the long hours *dagongmei* endure for appallingly low wages, the abuse they suffer at the hands of employers, the inhuman conditions in which they live and work, and the high rate of work-related injuries and medical problems that they suffer.

As Anita Chan suggests, these articles are often motivated by an urban liberal concern at social injustice and are used by journalists seeking to apply moral pressure on the state to improve workers' rights (Chan, Anita 2001, 4–5).[23] However, the discursive effects and functions of such articles may go beyond concern for the migrants themselves. Significantly, most such articles expose exploitation in foreign-invested factories. Relatively few discuss the exploitative practices of domestic private or collective enterprises, and even fewer expose the exploitation of migrant workers that occurs in the Chinese state sector. This, I argue, is not just because the degree and scale of exploitation in the foreign-invested sector is greater than in the domestic sector. It is also because of the relative risk involved in criticizing domestic managerial practices and the political mileage to be gained from a critique of foreign capital. To give one example, in the second half of 2001 a prominent story in the media in Beijing, as elsewhere in China, was that of a group of fifty-six *dagongmei* who filed a lawsuit against their employers at a South Korean-owned wig factory in Shenzhen, alleging that they had been subjected to rough body searches. Though they had undoubtedly been humiliated, none of the workers had been injured. Nevertheless, this story was reported at length in the media, often accompanied by large pictures of women workers traumatized and weeping.[24] The interest in this case stems, I argue, not so much from concern with the plight of the individual victims, but rather from the use of the body of the *dagongmei* as a metaphor for the nation, threatened by foreign capital.

Articles such as this are unlike those about migrant criminality in that the figure of the migrant functions not as a stand-in for the market, but as a trope of its disturbing consequences. However, in other ways these different genres are similar. Both reinforce suspicion about the market. Perhaps more significantly, both lend legitimacy to the role of the state in maintaining social order. The former draws attention to the ways in which "our" cities are being threatened from "within" by rural migrant criminality and lends legitimacy to the state by highlighting the need for law enforcement in the face of such threats. The latter highlights threats to "our" citizens from "outside" the nation, drawing on nationalist anxieties and foregrounding the role of the law in protecting citizens' rights and dignity. Finally, this article is an illustration of how closely discourses on nationalism and those on gender can be interwoven. In this respect, in China as elsewhere, external threats to, or humiliation of, women serve as a particularly potent focus of nationalist anxiety and outrage because gender discourses are such that the figure of woman is more easily rendered than man as a trope of a precious object (the nation) that belongs to, and must be protected by, the state and the citizenry.

Another genre of female victim story that has burgeoned in the Chinese media of the 1990s and 2000s is that of reports of sexual violence perpetrated against women who work as maids and of accounts of young rural women who have been deceived and either forced into prostitution or sold in marriage. In these stories we see, once more, significant overlaps between discourses on the market, governance and social order, migration and gender. For example, as Sun Wanning has discussed, in 1998 several newspapers, including both commercial papers and those published under the auspices of the All China Women's Federation, published stories about a twenty-year-old rural migrant woman, Hong Zhaodi, from Anhui whose prospective boss attempted to force her into prostitution. When she refused to cooperate, the man kicked her repeatedly, stripped her, and photographed her. When she was later taken to the hospital, the staff ignored her pleas for help in contacting police. Out of despair, Hong attempted suicide by throwing herself out of a second-floor window and ended up with first-degree spinal damage (Sun 2004).

Sun Wanning notes that the press drew two kinds of didactic message from this story. First, *Anhui Fuyun* (Anhui Women's Movement), an official monthly magazine of the Anhui Women's Federation, used the story as a cautionary tale, advising rural women against urban migration and warning those who did intend to migrate to be wary of possible deceptions and criminal activities (Sun 2004).

Second, in both the commercial and the official press, Hong Zhaodi was praised as a *lienü*, a Confucian concept of a woman who exemplifies female heroism, because she would rather die than have her sexual virtue compromised. As Sun Wanning discusses, the celebration of Hong Zhaodi as a *lienü* in the press of the Women's Federation is an illustration of the contemporary Communist Party's support for a thoroughly traditional and patriarchal discourse on gender and sexuality, and of the complicity of the Women's Federation, whose task is supposedly to further the interests of women, in that support. Numerous other stories reported in both the commercial and the official press tell of migrant women who have been deceived by "human peddlers" (*ren fanzi*) and sold into either prostitution or marriage.[25] Here, once more, the *dagongmei* functions as a metaphor for the corrosive effects of the market and the market itself is represented in the figure of the human peddler who takes commodification to an extreme. In addition, these stories reinforce a view of the countryside as barbaric (because the trafficking of women is seen as a rural phenomenon, even if the actual kidnapping occurs quite often in urban areas). And the fact that the victim is almost always portrayed as naive and ignorant further reinforces an urban/rural divide. The implicit message is that while the kidnapping and sale of women is linked with market forces, it only happens to ignorant rural *dagongmei*—more sophisticated urban women would not let themselves fall into this kind of trap (Evans 1997, 172).[26]

Finally, like the articles documenting the criminality of the floating population, these stories serve to underwrite the importance and legitimacy of the state's control over society. This they do both by documenting the alarming scale on which kidnapping and sale occurs, thereby invoking concerns about social stability and demonstrating the need for strong state intervention, and by citing impressive statistics relating to the number of kidnappers arrested, thereby indicating that the state is dealing with the problem (cf. Anagnost 1997, 135).

Similar to the account of Hong Zhaodi, none of these accounts of *dagongmei* victimization criticize the patriarchal structures and discourses in which such terrible violations of women's basic rights are grounded. Instead, it is precisely these discourses that make young rural *women*, rather than men, such appealing objects of consumption for an urban media audience. As Rey Chow has argued,

> the representation of subalterns shares a major characteristic with pornographic writing in the sense that it depends on a certain objectification and specularization of the "other." . . . If the excitement of pornography can be described as something like "the dirtier, the better," then the excitement of subaltern representation may be described as something like "the more socially deprived, the better." Both types of excitement depend on the object's lack—that is, her great wantingness (or shall we say wantonness) and thus her invitation to the reader to actively fill that lack. (Chow 1994, 243)

Hence, the gender oppression of *dagongmei*, when added to the oppression that results from the rural/urban divide, serves to increase the distance between them and the urban audience. This both heightens urbanites' sense of superiority and adds to the appeal of *dagongmei* victims as objects of sympathy, titillation, and voyeurism, thus making them favorite fodder for the increasingly profit-driven Chinese media.[27]

Conclusion

In this chapter I have shown that the genealogy of contemporary understandings of rural migrant subjects is intimately tied up with the history of notions of modernity, development, and nationhood in China. Thus it can be seen that the careers of rural and rural migrant subject positions, on the one hand, and concepts of modernity, progress, and nationhood on the other, are underwritten by elite modernist teleologies that first emerged in the late nineteenth century. Ever since then, intellectual and political leaders have seen it their role to either develop or revolutionize the nation out of a backward, traditional past, toward a better, modern future. And within these elite, linear teleologies the peasantry and, later, the tide of peasant workers have been constructed above all as a question for the progress of the nation.

The exact framing of this question and the solutions espoused have varied significantly from one discourse and from one period to another, with important consequences. For example, the post-Mao question of how to use rural to urban migration to improve the quality of the peasantry so that it might better serve a market economy, while at the same time minimizing the threat that peasant migrants pose to urban order, has led to very different attitudes and policies than the Maoist question of how to harness the rebellious qualities of the peasantry for the purposes of socialist revolution.

Nevertheless, and regardless of how and where exactly the peasantry or the tide of peasant workers have been positioned along the line of progress—as an advanced and forward-looking class or as a backward, less-developed class—the very framing of the peasantry as a question or problem within a linear teleology of advance toward modernity has resulted in important continuities. First, the construction of the category of peasant involved processes of differentiation based on place of residence (rural versus urban) and occupation (agricultural versus nonagricultural). Furthermore, from the very beginning, those processes of differentiation were also processes of constructing inequalities. Subsequently, and despite efforts in the Maoist period to put a more positive spin on the peasant question, through the twentieth and twenty-first centuries the range of essential differences attributed to the rural and the urban has been elaborated and the fit between perceptions of essential difference and patterns of material inequality has become tighter and tighter. The origins of this process are not specific to either Maoist socialism or post-Mao capitalism, but in different ways it has been exploited and furthered by both. Since the 1980s rural to urban migration, combined with an enormous growth in rural industry and in towns and suburbs, has in some ways blurred the distinction between rural and urban. In other ways, however, the distinction has become even sharper, with rural/urban inequalities increasing and with urbanites becoming ever more energetic in their efforts to distinguish themselves from the peasants.

Second, in the construction of the peasantry, the tide of peasant workers, and so on, as a problem, the people themselves—the men and women labeled peasants, outsiders, working sisters, and the like—have been rendered silent and passive. By this I mean not just that the problem of the peasantry and the solutions posed have been constructed, by and large, by national elites and very little by rural people themselves. In addition, it has been extremely difficult to hear the opinions and sentiments of rural residents or rural migrants. Under Maoism, poor peasants did learn to "speak bitterness" in public forums; that is, they were taught to voice and share an understanding of preliberation suffering in terms of class exploitation. This was a particular type of subject formation through narrative that, as I will discuss in chapter 7, contributed to a new, powerful, and long-lasting sense of agency, or at least a sense of a right to agency, among peasants. This agency, cultivated under Mao, was, however, carefully shaped and highly restricted by the state. Since Mao's death it has been similarly restricted, and much less deliberately cultivated, by the state. Today, peasants and peasant workers are construed at different times as the objects of concern, fascination, and contempt, and sometimes, even, of admiration. However, by and large, they are constructed as voiceless objects, rather than as speaking subjects.

Third, the identification of the peasantry as a problem has made it possible to dissociate explanations for failures or inadequacies in programs aimed at rural development from other social groups and from state-promoted structures or practices, and has enabled elites, both before 1949 and since, to assign the cause of these failures to qualities supposedly inherent in the peasantry itself (cf. Escobar 1991, 667).

Finally, the demarcation and evaluation of groups of people according to their "peasantness," when combined with other forms of categorization—most notably those based on gender and insider/outsider status—has enabled a proliferation of forms of "othering." These, in turn, have contributed to a variety of discourses, furthering a range of interests. In this chapter I have shown how, in the post-Mao period, an "othering" of rural residents and rural migrants has fed into a range of desires and anxieties surrounding market-oriented reform. Thus, in some press articles links made between market reform and the rise of a threatening tide of backward, low quality, criminal rural migrants reinforce popular anxieties about the disruptive effects of the market and thereby lend legitimacy to the state and, especially, to law-enforcement agencies.

In other articles, however, the figure of the rural migrant is used, not to draw attention to the dangers of a market economy, but to support its growth. Here, she is portrayed, not as a criminal endangering state and (urban) society, nor as the backward inferior of urbanites, but as a hero of development and self-development that urbanites are urged to emulate. She is a model of labor for both domestic and global capitalists—cheap, flexible, hardworking, and uncomplaining.

In yet other articles, the migrant is neither a criminal nor a hero, but a helpless, pitiful victim of exploitation, violence, and sexual abuse. Like other representations, this image harks back to representations of peasants, and especially peasant women, that emerged at the beginning of the twentieth century and can be seen to derive from practices of "orientalism" on the part of Western colonialists and "internal orientalism" on the part of Chinese modernist elites. Some of these portrayals of migrants, especially *dagongmei* victims, reflect and reinforce anxieties about a market economy. However, very often they are also a form of fetishization, used by the media to extract profits from a largely educated, urban audience eager for the pleasures entailed in fetishizing or pitying a group of people less privileged and less powerful than themselves, and in the process thereby confirming their own superior status.

In short, inferior, low-quality peasants, the tide of peasant workers, and working sisters are representations whose origins and development have been closely tied up with Chinese struggles for national identity and modernity in the twentieth and twenty-first centuries. Today these figures play an important role in a range of dominant discourses relating to urban and national identity, order, development, and modernity.

2

Assembling Working Sisters

In the previous chapter I demonstrated that in dominant discourse the rural migrant is most commonly objectified as either a backward, low-quality outsider to be blamed and shunned or a naive, helpless victim to be pitied and fetishized. In the few instances in which she is portrayed as a model agent, rather than a victim, it is because, through self-sacrifice and "self-development," she has turned herself into an object of exploitation, putting her body on the line for the market economy.

It will become increasingly clear through this volume that these subject positions carry enormous weight, for they are supported by capital and by interests in the state and the urban, educated elite and they both contribute to, and are themselves reinforced by, profound structural and material inequalities. However, in the previous chapter we have already seen that there has been some change over time in official and mainstream media constructions of migrants. In this chapter, I turn my attention to the ways in which Beijing's Migrant Women's Club and its parent body, the *Rural Women* collective, have also contributed to changing migrant subject positions. To what extent and in what ways, I ask, have the collective and the Club challenged prejudiced assumptions and objectifications of migrants? Through their efforts at supporting rural migrant women have they contributed to alternative migrant subject positions that are more empowered and empowering than those that have dominated urban- and national-level discourse?

I draw here on the theorizations of Nancy Fraser and other critical and feminist theorists, according to whom key to the advancement of democracy and social equality in any stratified society is the development of a public sphere made up of numerous and various "publics," especially "subaltern counterpublics," where members of subordinated social groups can withdraw to an extent from the forms of domination and subordination to which they are normally subjected by dominant discourse, regroup, and "invent and circulate counterdiscourses to formulate oppositional interpretations of their identities, interests, and needs" (Fraser 1999 [1992], 123–24).

Rural Women (formerly *Rural Women Knowing All,* Nongjianü Baishitong) was founded in 1993 by Xie Lihua, a well-known social activist and deputy editor of the All China Women's Federation's daily newspaper, *China Women's News.*[1] *Rural Women* is the only national periodical devoted to rural women, with an impressive circulation of more than 230,000 (CDCRW 2001).[2] The journal provides some technical information, for example on innovative farming techniques, and publishes reports on successful rural women. It is unusual in running numerous letters and stories sent in by rural women and migrants themselves, and in discussing controversial issues, including suicide, which other periodicals avoid.

In addition to the *Rural Women* journal and the Migrant Women's Club, the *Rural Women* collective runs a Rural Women's Technical School on the outskirts of Beijing and has funded various development projects aimed at providing practical assistance to rural women, including literacy training and microloans for business ventures (CDCRW 2001). In the paragraphs that follow I demonstrate that the *Rural Women* collective is an important contributor to a burgeoning public sphere in contemporary China, and that in the process of assembling migrant women into a formal organization, the Migrant Women's Club also contributes to the assemblage of collective understandings of migrant women's interests and the subject positions they can and should take up. Whether they constitute a "subaltern counterpublic"—a space where migrant women assemble and perform oppositional interpretations of their identities and interests—or whether they have merely reproduced the hierarchies of dominant discourses is the key question with which this chapter is concerned.[3]

The chapter is divided into three sections. The first provides a broad introduction to the organization, aims, and activities of *Rural Women* and the Migrant Women's Club and their relationship to the Chinese state and, specifically, the All China Women's Federation.

The second section examines the migrant subject positions that were constructed and promoted through the *Rural Women* journal and the journal of the Migrant Women's Club, *Working Sister*, in the decade 1993–2002.

These periodicals are the official, public faces of the Migrant Women's Club and the *Rural Women* collective. They include numerous stories by members of the Club and other migrant women, which have nevertheless been strategically selected, assembled, and editorialized in order to convey messages determined, not by ordinary members of the Club, but by professional editors under the direction of Xie Lihua, chief editor of *Rural Women*; Li Tao, a journalist with *Rural Women* and the person in charge of the Migrant Women's Club; and Li Zhen, chief editor of *Working Sister*. These individuals are outstanding in their dedication to women in the floating population, but both their socioeconomic status and their attitudes set them apart from "floaters" themselves. One member of the Club voiced a common perception of Xie Lihua when she said:

[She] is a good person, but she doesn't have much feeling for *dagongmei*. And she doesn't have a lot of respect for us. You can feel it. I'm saying it the way it is—I'm not saying anything behind her back. She grew up in the city and she has an urban identity, so it's not possible for her to understand our situation the same way we do. . . . She's made this her cause, but it's not the same as it is for us. We want to change the discrimination against ourselves and people like us and that desire is very strong. But she's up above, looking for a cause. It's not that she really speaks from the heart on behalf of this group. (August 2001)

As for Li Zhen and Li Tao, neither are Beijingers, but are originally from rural Shandong, having come to Beijing to attend university. Most people, however, do not count university students and graduates as part of the floating population, but as belonging to the educated elite, and while my interlocutors generally felt there was less distance between themselves and Li Zhen and Li Tao than was the case with Xie Lihua, they nevertheless still did not feel they were "one of us." Like the previous chapter, then, this section discusses migrant women subject positions that have been created across fundamental sociopolitical hierarchies, and assembled by members of the educated elite, rather than by migrant women themselves.[4]

The third and final section of the chapter is based on participant observation of activities held at the Migrant Women's Club in the second half of 2001 and in December 2002. It discusses the construction and performance of migrant subject positions through Club activities. Again, it is important to note that these activities were shaped primarily, though not solely, by nonmigrant Club organizers and staff and by urban "experts," including lawyers and others, who were invited to present talks. This section of the chapter focuses on the internal micropolitics of the Migrant Women's Club, revealing some tensions and disagreements between the Club's organizers and its members and a degree of uncertainty and instability in the Club's construction of migrant subject positions that is not apparent in its publications. I will show that some Club members readily embraced the migrant subject positions created through Club activities. Others accepted some aspects of those positions and ignored, rejected, complained about, or tried to change others.

This theme, of migrant women's varying negotiations of migrant subject positions assembled by the Migrant Women's Club, as well as through other institutions and discourses, is continued through the remainder of this book. Then, in the final chapter, I revisit the Club, this time exploring signs that, despite the unequal terrain on which it has been created, the Club has served, not just as a space in which migrant women receive and negotiate subject positions essentially created by others, but as a base from which they have begun to wrest for themselves new, collective identities as agents of social change and resistance.

Structures and Orientations

Staff at *Rural Women* established the Migrant Women's Club in 1996, in response to numerous letters they had received from rural migrant women complaining of the hardships, exploitation, and discrimination they faced in the city, and the loneliness and alienation they felt. The Migrant Women's Club, whose Chinese title translates literally as "The Home for Working Sisters" (Dagongmei zhi Jia), was set up in response to these expressions of alienation. A letter aimed at recruiting members to the club said:

> From today, you people who have come from far and wide at last have your own home in Beijing. . . . The Migrant Women's Club is a place of warmth, where there is no discrimination, no cold indifference, no inequality. Everyone will be able to say what is on their minds without feeling inhibited, will encourage each other and will make many new friends. ("Zhi Dagongmeimen de Yi Feng Gongkai Xin" 1996)

When first established, the Migrant Women's Club was housed with *Rural Women, China Women's News,* and other offshoots of the Women's Federation in a shabby building in an alley off Beijing's most expensive and cosmopolitan downtown shopping street, Wangfujing. It came under the direct authority of *Rural Women,* which was in turn formally answerable to *China Women's News* and the All China Women's Federation. Li Tao was put in charge of the club, and its day-to-day business was run by two office staff. Through the late 1990s and early 2000s, the office moved and its staff changed several times. For most of this period, however, the staff included one—usually older, better educated—urban woman, and a young *dagongmei.*

In 2001 the *Rural Women* collective underwent major restructuring. The *Rural Women* journal remained under the auspices of *China Women's News,* but the collective's projects, including the Migrant Women's Club, were grouped under a new, independent umbrella organization, the Cultural Development Center for Rural Women, administered by Li Tao.

Through the late 1990s and early 2000s the Migrant Women's Club engaged in three different kinds of activities. First, it held a meeting every second Sunday, to which it often invited guest speakers. It also organized social gatherings and outings, especially around National Day and Spring Festival, and on one occasion it put on a joint wedding celebration for a number of migrant couples. The Club also ran classes, for example in literacy, basic computing skills, and English.

Second, the Club provided some help to migrants looking for work and gave support to migrant women in difficulty. For instance, in 2001 members of the Club helped two women who had been violently abused in their jobs as maids. Chen Ailing, a seventeen-year-old from Shanxi, had been beaten daily over a period of ten months, and had no wages paid. Members of the Club visited her in the hospital, made donations, helped find a lawyer who took her case to court and defended her for free, and went along to the court hearings. Liu Yu, also seventeen, from Sichuan, was locked in a room by her employer and raped repeatedly. She jumped out of a window on the third storey and ended up in the hospital, seriously injured. When members of the Migrant Women's Club learned what had happened in the press, they visited Liu Yu in the hospital and from then on did their best to offer her support and to help her take her case to court. They failed in this latter aim, however, because the Public Security Bureau refused to file the case, citing insufficient evidence.[5] In part in response to Club members' experiences trying to support Chen Ailing and Liu Yu, in 2002 the Cultural Development Center for Rural Women established a hotline for migrants seeking help and advice regarding labor disputes, violations of their rights, and violence. It also set up a Migrant Rights Group, which provided counseling, emergency relief, and legal aid to migrant women who had suffered abuse, and published a newsletter that was designed as a platform for the exchange of ideas and information among legal experts, volunteers, and migrants (CDCRW 2002, 1).

The third area in which the Club has been involved is in the media and in lobbying the state. Thus, through the 1990s Li Tao and Li Zhen between them probably wrote more articles exposing the problems faced by migrant women in Beijing than anyone else, publishing in *Rural Women* and other local and national papers. Members of the Migrant Women's Club have also been frequent contributors to *Rural Women*. In addition, in late 2001 the Cultural Development Center for Rural Women began publication of a new journal, *Working Sister*. It appointed a team of five journalists and editors, headed by Li Zhen, and members of the Migrant Women's Club contributed stories.

In addition to this, Xie Lihua and other staff of *Rural Women* and the Cultural Development Center for Rural Women have lobbied, with some success, for a simplification and reduction in cost of the procedures that rural people must go through to become legal residents in Beijing and for the Women's Federation to pay more attention to the rights of rural migrant women. Finally, *Rural Women* has organized two national forums on the rights of migrant women workers. These involved the participation of more than one hundred grassroots Women's Federation representatives, local government officials, journalists, academics, and activists from across China and other parts of the world, and several members of the Migrant Women's Club. One of the central issues debated in these forums was the need to reform or abolish the household registration system.[6]

The *Rural Women* collective and its constituent bodies are a good example of the difficulties involved in trying to understand contemporary social activism in China in terms of Western concepts of "civil society" and "nongovernmental organizations," for while it receives the bulk of its funding from overseas donor agencies, especially the Ford Foundation, the collective retains close links with the Women's Federation. In addition, while Xie Lihua and her team have taken on causes neglected by the Women's Federation, such as rural migrant women and suicide, the orientation and approaches of the Women's Federation, the *Rural Women* collective, and indeed most other Chinese women's organizations working with rural women are quite similar, having developed in tandem, and often through mutual reinforcement, in response to the reforms of the post-Mao era.[7] The overriding aim of all these groups has been to improve women's competitiveness in the market economy. It is generally believed that market-oriented development offers new opportunities, and that it is important to position women to maximize these opportunities and not be left behind in the race for development and modernity (Judd 2002, 19–32). Women's groups have by and large not challenged the premises of the state's program for market-oriented development and modernization, nor the most basic institutional gender underpinnings of the contemporary sociopolitical order.

The activities of *Rural Women* and the Women's Federation aim to do the following: (1) cultivate women's "four selfs" (*sizi*)—self-respect (*zizun*), self-confidence (*zixin*), self-reliance (*zili*), and self-strength (*ziqiang*); (2) boost training in literacy and technical skills; (3) provide microloans and other forms of assistance to women in small-scale business; (4) stimulate competition and enthusiasm for entrepreneurship among women; (5) combat problems, such as arranged marriages and trafficking in women, that are attributable to "feudal remnants" and the "lingering effects" of "traditional" sexism and that threaten social stability and economic development; (6) teach women to use the law to protect their basic rights and interests (Jacka 1997, 90–100; Judd 2002).

Through the 1980s and 1990s both the Women's Federation and the *Rural Women* collective commonly couched these aims in terms of raising women's *suzhi*.[8] Thus, at the First National Forum on the Protection of the Rights of Migrant Women Workers, organized by the *Rural Women* collective in 1999, Li Tao presented a paper on the Migrant Women's Club, in which he argued that the cause of the social problems faced by rural women in the city—the frequent violations of their basic rights, their difficulties in finding a marriage partner, their sense of inferiority and their feelings of hopelessness about the future—all boiled down to one thing: in essence, their low *suzhi* meant that they were unable to manage the obstacles thrown up by a society in transition. Consequently, raising migrant women's *suzhi* was the most important means by which to address their problems (Li Tao 1999a, 75–76).

For Li Tao, there were three aspects of club members' low *suzhi* that needed to be addressed: first, their "psychological quality" (*xinli suzhi*) needed improving. Through group discussions, excursions, and holiday celebrations, he hoped that Club members would feel like one big family and would be able to speak freely and give each other encouragement, and thereby overcome their feelings of inferiority and loneliness. And through talks on issues relating to marriage and to adapting to city life Club members would overcome their bewilderment in the city and learn a greater degree of endurance and adaptability. Second, the quality of their thinking (*sixiang suzhi*) needed to be improved. He felt that by listening to the stories of rural women model achievers, migrant women's fighting spirit and creativity would be kindled and they would be inspired to adopt a sense of historic responsibility for building the urban economy and lifting their home counties out of poverty. Finally, Li Tao felt that Club members' educational or cultural quality (*wenhua suzhi*) needed raising, in other words, they needed to improve their basic education and to develop technical skills (Li Tao 1999a, 75–76).

In the third section of this chapter I explore in some detail how Li Tao's rhetoric on *suzhi* has translated into concrete practice in the activities of the Migrant Women's Club, and how these activities have been received by migrant women.

Before moving to this level of detail, however, I want to discuss for a moment some of the more general advantages and disadvantages of a *suzhi*-centered approach to gender relations and the position of women in Chinese society. Using this approach, the Women's Federation, *Rural Women,* and other women's organizations have made some important contributions to gender equality in rural China, in particular by providing literacy programs, microloans and training for rural women. On the other hand, the stance taken by the women's movement has at times resembled a "blame-the-victim" approach in reinforcing assumptions about women's "weaknesses" and putting the onus on individual women to overcome those weaknesses, while investing considerably less effort into combating fundamental institutional and structural barriers to gender equality. In its tendency to assume that rural women have particularly low *suzhi*, and that they can and should be helped by others of higher *suzhi*, that is, educated, mostly urban activists, women's organizations have also often reproduced urban elitism and rural lack of status and authority.

The Chinese women's movement has not neglected institutional and structural problems entirely. As mentioned above, it has addressed some problems that can be explained in terms of the "lingering effects" of "feudal remnants" and traditional sexism, and that can be said to impede social stability and economic development. These include arranged marriages, discrimination against girls in education, domestic violence, the kidnapping and sale of women, and pressure on women to withdraw from paid employment after marriage and childbirth. Criticism of these phenomena has been seriously weakened, however, by a reluctance to acknowledge that these are not just remnants of a past order. On the contrary, they have been greatly exacerbated by the contemporary state's naturalization of gender inequality as resulting from biological difference; its reprivatization of issues relating to sexuality and intrahousehold decision making and divisions of labor; its collusion with the commodification of women's bodies that has become so central to the promotion of capitalist consumerism; and its withdrawal generally from direct efforts to overcome social inequality (Evans 1997; Jacka 1997).

At an even more fundamental level, there has been a general blindness to the deep, institutionalized imbrication between gender and power in contemporary society. Thus, violence against women is rarely attributed to the unequal power relations between men and women. More commonly, women's organizations conform to dominant state and popular understandings of such violence as resulting from the female victim's passivity, ignorance, and failure to protect herself, or alternatively her provocative or immoral sexuality; from corruption and the abuse of power among male officials and businesspeople; from feudal remnants and from rural backwardness, lack of education, economic stress, and poverty (Evans 1997, 167–88). To give another, very important example, contemporary women's groups have not tried to change the rural practice of patrilocal marriage, despite the fact that it underpins discrimination against girls in education and contributes to rural women's marginalization in employment and political participation. And finally, neither the Women's Federation nor other groups, like *Rural Women,* have mounted any serious challenge to gender segmentation in the workforce, whereby women are concentrated in the most poorly remunerated, low-status trades and occupations.

The focus on overcoming individual weaknesses rather than underlying structural inequalities that is characteristic of *suzhi* discourse has led many Western feminists and development activists to criticize the Chinese women's movement's use of such discourse. As a result, in the early 2000s there has been an observable decline in usage of the language of *suzhi* in the women's movement.[9] Simultaneously, women's activists have referred increasingly to the global language of development. For example, in the promotional leaflet for the Cultural Development Center for Rural Women, published in 2001, the center's goal is described as being to

> support Chinese women, especially poor women, [in their efforts] to improve their position with regards to production, living conditions, health and education, and through the provision of health, cultural, technical, legal and information services, promote *gender awareness* [*shehui xingbie yishi*], raise capabilities for *community development* [*shequ fazhan*] and realize *self-empowerment* [*ziwo fuquan*] and *sustainable development* [*kechixu fazhan*] for rural women. (CDCRW 2001, 2; italics added)

Whether usage of the terms italicized in the quotation above, which are central to global development discourse but new in China, heralds a substantive change in direction or whether it is simply a focus on "raising women's *suzhi*" couched in slightly different language is not yet clear.[10] When I talked to Li Zhen about this, she said that "raising *suzhi*" is part of "self-empowerment" and confirmed that the emphasis on "self-empowerment" rather than on *suzhi* was simply a change in terminology rather than an indication of a change in direction (December 2002). Yet, as I will discuss shortly, under Li Zhen's editorship, *Working Sister* seemed to reflect a greater concern with, and criticism of, at least some of the structural and systemic inequalities faced by rural migrant women than had been apparent in *Rural Women.*

Li Tao, talking with me about *Working Sister* in 2002, remarked:

> After so many years working with migrant women I have a strong feeling that we've done a lot of work, but our work is limited in its real effect to 500–1,000 people—[not much more than] the members of the club. But China has more than 90 million migrant women. We're not

the government, so we can't help or represent them all. But the journal can serve, and give a voice to, a much larger number of people. Another important issue is that through the work of the Migrant Rights Group and work with migrant women we've discovered that there are a lot of difficulties that are not created by the migrant women themselves, but by inappropriate government policy. So, when we say you must have self-confidence and strength, and you must learn how to protect yourself and so on—that serves no purpose. It's very difficult to change the larger context. There are some problems they just can't solve themselves. So how are you going to influence government and society? That's the purpose of the *Working Sister* journal. It's no use going directly to government to discuss problems. Influencing government is one aspect of the journal's purpose. But more important is to influence more ordinary people—make them recognize the importance of migrant workers. Another function is to enlighten this group [that is, migrants] as to their rights—raise their rights consciousness. So we work from below and above to enact reform. We put pressure on the government from above and below. Otherwise, if we always write reports, give opinions, telephone them, its very hard to influence them. . . . A lot of department heads understand the reasoning—they understand we shouldn't do things this way—so why do they still do it like that? It's because there's no pressure on them to change. If this group—the migrants—were awakened to their rights, they could put pressure on the government. Then the government would feel that if they did not change things their status would be affected. (December 2002)

Here, Li Tao is critical of his own, earlier emphasis, apparent in his 1999 discussion of the Migrant Women's Club, on raising migrant women's *suzhi* and the neglect of broader policy issues. It is noteworthy, though, that he assigns different functions to the Club and the *Working Sister* journal, and that he does not seem to see the Migrant Women's Club as a space in which, by coming together, migrant women might empower themselves and come to realize their own collective interests and from there play a role in awakening other migrants to their rights, or in pressuring the government. Rather than advocating the provision of conditions for migrants' self-empowerment, Li Tao reproduces here an assumption that people like himself—the educated elite—can and must help the subaltern, for they cannot help themselves. This is a form of intellectual elitism that he has inherited from Xie Lihua's generation, and that runs, in fact, all the way from Confucianism, through the May Fourth movement, to the current discourse on *suzhi*.

Let us now look at the ways in which the general orientations adopted by Xie Lihua, Li Zhen, and Li Tao are reflected in the journals *Rural Women* and, more recently, *Working Sister*, and in the activities of the Migrant Women's Club.

The *Rural Women* Journal

Through the 1990s *Rural Women* ran numerous letters, autobiographical accounts, and articles devoted to the experiences of rural women working in urban areas.[11] These included a wealth of detail about the lives of individual migrants and focused on many of the issues of most concern to migrant women. In doing so, they provided an important counterbalance to the mainstream media's dehumanization of migrants as a problematic phenomenon, and a source of support to migrant readers, who could now feel that at least they were not alone in the difficulties they experienced.

On the other hand, the representation of migrant women in these stories and in the editorials that accompanied them often closely mirrored the portrayals of migrant women in the human-interest and didactic genres of the mainstream press. For one thing, the stories were almost all about *dagongmei*, that is, young, mostly single women in wage labor. Furthermore, the primary focus was on the adventures, challenges, and dangers faced by *dagongmei* as young, vulnerable girls and daughters away from home for the first time, rather than, for example, as workers.[12] Older married women with children, like my interlocutors in Haidian who were either without employment or who worked alongside their husbands in family businesses, were essentially invisible in *Rural Women*, as they were in the mainstream media. This focus on the vulnerable, young, unmarried daughter subject position left migrants' inferior position in dominant discourses undisturbed and unthreatened. It also reinforced the dominant position of the state in the 1990s, which was that urban migration could be but a temporary, transitional phase in the life of an individual; that young, rural women would mature as a result of a brief sojourn in the city, but fully adult rural woman belonged in the village.

This position was further reinforced in the messages conveyed in didactic pieces, including both positive stories about model migrant women and cautionary tales about young migrant women who had run into difficulties. Thus, in the earliest issues of *Rural Women*, in particular, numerous articles warned of the difficulties and dangers involved in moving to the city. These were frequently very condescending, portraying migrant women in the same way as countless articles in the mainstream press—as ignorant, naive, pitiful victims and potential victims.

To give one example, the April 1993 issue began a discussion of the experiences of rural women working as maids with an article by one of the reporters attached to the journal, which described in graphic detail the fate of a young maid named Yu Xiaoqing, whose male employer beat her so badly that she ended up in hospital with broken ribs, a broken nose, damaged kidneys, and cuts and bruises all over her body (Wang Lingshu 1993). The editorial that preceded the story explained that

> [T]he aim of the collection of reports about Yu Xiaoqing being beaten up is just to let young rural women going to the city know that the city is definitely

not everywhere dripping gold—the asphalt roads are nice to walk on, but you can still go astray, and urbanites receive education in how to be civilized, but there are still some uncivilized people. All the same, the city is certainly not just one big trap. So, before you go knocking on the city gates, you must first examine whether you are fully prepared. It's not enough to have brought sufficient clothes, nor is it enough to have sewn some aspirations and courage into the seams. You must also have some basic understanding of the city that you're stepping into. Just as a person arriving in a strange place needs a map, you need to know how to protect yourself in your new environment—how to quickly find a suitable place to live and work, and in case of unforeseen circumstances, how to quickly find someone who can help you. ("Bianzhe de Hua" 1993)

In addition, the story itself was followed by another, contrasting account, in which a second young woman goes to work with the same man as Yu Xiaoqing but avoids her fate by demanding to leave at the first sign of the man's abusiveness. When he refuses to let her go, she threatens to kill the couple's child and they have no choice but to release her (Wang Lingshu 1993). The implication is that Yu Xiaoqing would not have met such an awful fate if she too had known how to stand up for herself. This message was reinforced by a letter commenting on the two stories, in which another woman working as a maid in Beijing sympathized with Yu Xiaoqing but was critical of the fact that she was so unable to look after herself. If Yu Xiaoqing had had some knowledge of the law, the correspondent suggested, she would have been able to use it to protect herself, and the employer would not have dared to abuse her in the way that he did (Han Chun 1993).

In emphasizing the dangers met by women entering the city, this set of articles accorded with official concerns about the influx of rural migrants into urban areas. In addition, in blaming Yu Xiaoqing's unhappy fate upon her inability to stand up for herself, they matched the All China Women's Federation's focus on the need for women to understand the law and to strengthen their "four selfs" and their disinclination to challenge the cultural and structural underpinnings of women's difficulties. None of the contributions to the discussion of Yu Xiaoqing's plight pointed out that the male employer's abusive behavior toward the maid was grounded in patriarchal discourses that accorded him, as an older, urban male, a great deal more power and authority than her, as a young rural woman. Nor did they note that, isolated as they are within their employers' homes, women who work as maids are very vulnerable to abuse. And none of the contributions attended to the fact that, far from being determined by individual failings, Yu Xiaoqing's exploitation and abuse was directly related to a segmentation of the urban labor market according to both household registration and gender, whereby most rural migrant women are to be found in low-status jobs in the service sector.[13] Finally, the voyeuristic objectifications of young rural women in this set of articles are disturbingly similar to those of human interest stories published elsewhere in the official media, and most commonly in more popular, entertainment-oriented media that aim to generate sales through titillation and sensationalism.

In later issues of *Rural Women* there were fewer articles and editorials warning *dagongmei* of the dangers of the city and more positive stories praising individual model *dagongmei*. These were very similar to articles promoting the value of urban migration for development that were to be found in the mainstream press. They emphasized the same goals of self-development through education, training, and economic achievement, and extolled the virtues of hard work, persistence, and a willingness to endure hardship on the road to success. However, in most stories, the model migrant woman's ultimate success was located in the future and back in the countryside, rather than having already been achieved, again reinforcing the notion that migrant labor in the city is a temporary, developmental phase. For example, Zhang Yangqin, a young rural woman interviewed by a scholar affiliated with the journal, spoke of her efforts to further her education in Beijing while working concurrently as a shop assistant. After one year she graduated from senior technical college, with plans to continue on to tertiary technical college and university. "Afterward," she said, "I want to go back. I won't stay in Beijing. I think about my home county—my home county is very backward and I want to go back to build it" (Ma 1998, 28). The interviewer concluded this article with the words:

> This is without doubt a clever, wise, and strong girl—a *dagongmei* with a clear goal, who has come to Beijing in search of an opportunity to study and with a plan for development. And the city has provided girls like her the possibility to get diplomas and certificates through part time work and part time study and training. It is evident that five years from now, ten years from now, Yangqin will no longer be the sixteen year old Yangqin who first arrived in Beijing, and nor will she be the Yangqin of today. Hence, we can say that coming into the city and, in particular, striding once more through the school gates, has changed the life trajectory of this rural girl—it has changed her fate. And this change, this opportunity and possibility, provided and created by mobility, has been grasped firmly by Zhang Yangqin herself. (Ibid., 28)

In addition to didactic pieces, through the 1990s *Rural Women* ran numerous autobiographical stories, portraying *dagongmei* life in the city as being a mixture of excitement, enlightenment, and fulfillment—and hardship, alienation, and confusion. Like the report on Yu Xiaoqing, and like other articles in the mainstream press, migrant women's own stories commonly recounted lives full of struggle, including encounters with extremely cruel people, and instances of gross exploitation. Unlike the former, however, they almost never portrayed the women as helpless victims. On the other hand, nor did they provide any real critique of the discourses and structures that undergirded their exploitation. Instead, as elsewhere in the press, the contribution of hard work and struggle to both national and self-development was emphasized. In addition, an ability to use the law to stand up for oneself was often held as the key to success. The story "The law is by my side," contributed to the "My life as a migrant worker" competition, is typical. In it a rural woman from Guizhou tells of her experiences working in a joint-venture factory in the Shenzhen Special Economic Zone. The migrant women in this factory were forced to work long hours of overtime with very low pay in hot, humid workshops overcrowded with machines. If they complained they were fired. The narrator confronted the boss one day, showing him a copy of the Labor Law to demonstrate that his treatment of the women workers was illegal. When she pointed out that he would get in serious trouble if the workers complained to the Labor Bureau, he agreed to improve their conditions and wages, and promoted the narrator to the position of assistant to the deputy manager (Huang, Zhihua 2004). This story provides what could potentially be an indictment of capitalist labor relations, but that indictment is negated with the highly unrealistic message that individual workers can bargain successfully with their bosses for better conditions. Like numerous other accounts in the media, this story contributes to a discourse that promotes capitalism by depicting survival and success as a result solely of individual talent, effort, and entrepreneurship, by promoting individual forms of negotiation, rather than collective attempts at resistance, and by trivializing the class and gender hierarchies and inequalities that capitalism in China, as elsewhere, has perpetuated and thrived upon (Jacka 2004, 283).

Working Sister

When *Working Sister* began publication in 2001, its stated aim of "serving migrant workers and furthering urbanization" (*fuwu dagongzhe, tuijin chengshihua*) reflected a shift in official discourse toward more positive appraisals of rural to urban migration (see Figure 2.1). As indicated by its title, the new journal once more focused on *dagongmei*, but its contents and tone were quite different to that of the columns on *dagongmei* in *Rural Women*. In general terms, it ran both more success stories and more stories and articles discussing the problems faced by *dagongmei*, including a large proportion of critical, investigative journalism of a kind not found in *Rural Women*. It also contained a lot more facts and figures than the older journal.

Each of the six issues of the journal published in 2001–2 included a mix of autobiographical stories, articles about *dagongmei* success stories, investigative reports, letters seeking advice with responses from the editors, brief news reports— for example about changes in policy toward migrants in different cities—and book reviews. Most issues also included a page of pithy quotations aimed at exposing injustices and overturning common prejudices about rural migrants.[14] In each issue, at least two *dagongmei* success stories were written up in full one- or two-page articles. These articles were similar to those in *Rural Women* in describing young women who had gone to the city to work and/or study and who after several years of hard work and perseverance made impressive gains in their education, skills, and economic status. As in the older journal, the virtues promoted were

Figure 2.1   **Front Cover, *Dagongmei* (Working Sister)**

those of hard work, persistence, and a desire for self-development and, perhaps simply because more time had lapsed, the editors of *Working Sister* were able to find more migrant women who not only embodied these virtues, but who had achieved the ultimate goal of setting up their own business. Unlike in the older journal, though, most of these women remained in the city and expressed no desire to return to the countryside.

These articles conveyed the optimistic message that through hard work and persistence young migrant women could change their fates for the better. Other articles, however, painted a much less favorable picture, focusing on serious problems facing migrants in the city. These differed from the cautionary tales of *Rural Women* in two significant respects. First, rather than warning of the dangers that they would encounter in the city and urging young women to think carefully and prepare themselves thoroughly before migrating, these articles were underpinned by the assumption that rural women were already in the city. Second, instead of emphasizing the personal qualities of individual migrant women as the key to their fate, these articles focused on the external circumstances they encountered in the city and the ways in which they were treated by urban employers and others.

A comparison of the set of articles on Yu Xiaoqing mentioned above with an article on Chen Ailing published in the first issue of *Working Sister* in 2001 is instructive in this regard. The former focused on the personal failure of Yu Xiaoqing to stand up for herself and was put forward explicitly as a cautionary tale to other young rural women. In contrast, the latter sought to understand what had happened from the maid's perspective and to uncover the injustice of the employer's behavior. It also explained Chen Ailing's inability to prevent or escape the violence, in part in terms of the fact that she was very young and inexperienced, but primarily as a consequence of her employer's intimidatory tactics, her lack of money, and the failure of neighbors to respond to her cries for help (Li Tao 2001a).

Aside from individual case studies, *Working Sister* also included several investigative reports on the circumstances of *dagongmei* as a collective. Two, by Li Zhen, examined the fate of *dagongmei* who married and returned to the countryside (Li Zhen 2002a, 2002b). They were far from glowing in their findings. Other reports detailed forms of injustice and exploitation facing migrants working in the city. These included pieces on several issues to be discussed in chapter 3 of this volume: the obstacles that the household registration system presented to migrant women who married in the city (Li Tao 2001b), the injustices of the detention and repatriation system and the large number of illegal and arbitrary fees and fines charged migrants (Cheng 2002a; Li Zhen 2002c), employers' failure to pay wages on time (Cheng 2002c), the exploitation and dangerous, unhealthy working conditions endured by *dagongmei* factory workers (Li Zhen 2002d), and the lack of insurance and workers' compensation for migrant workers (Li Zhen 2002d; Cheng 2002b). These were complemented with columns providing statistics and details of relevant laws and regulations—something again not found in *Rural Women,* for all its emphasis on the need for women to acquaint themselves with the law.

In these investigative reports the journalists and editors of *Working Sister* moved the focus of readers' attention and concern decisively away from the *suzhi* of migrant women themselves, to a broad range of issues relating to state policies and institutions and the practices of government officials, employers, and others, and subjected the latter to a critical, analytical gaze.

In the process, they also engineered subtle but highly significant shifts in subject positions, both for those whose lives they reported and for their readers. First, in the range of concerns addressed they conveyed an understanding of *dagongmei* identities that was different from that conveyed in *Rural Women*. In particular, the several articles concerned with the exploitation of both male and female migrants in factory employment suggested that *dagongmei* were to be identified first and foremost as migrant workers, rather than as women. Other articles, including those on migrant women who married and settled in the city and those who married and returned to the countryside, gave the impression of *dagongmei* as being older and more experienced than the naive, vulnerable "low *suzhi*" young girls entering the city for the first time who dominated *Rural Women*.

Because workers' concerns have a higher status and political import than "women's issues" and because adults (especially men) are taken more seriously than youths (especially girls), the combined effect of these articles was to accord a new respect and importance both to *dagongmei* as agents and to the difficulties that they faced. On the other hand, like the articles in *Rural Women*, the reports in *Working Sister*, critical as they were of the institutional underpinnings of class and rural/urban inequalities, paid very little attention to the significance of gender as an institutionalized basis for discrimination and exploitation in Chinese society. They were underwritten by an assumption that, because of their gender, *dagongmei* were even more at risk of discrimination, abuse, and exploitation than male migrants. However, rather than understanding this in terms of the ways in which social hierarchies and power relations in general are thoroughly gendered, the marginalization of *dagongmei* as women continued to be understood as a weakness or vulnerability within *dagongmei* themselves. In Li Tao's terms, this was a "vulnerable group" (*ruoshi qunti*) particularly in need of support and representation.[15]

The editors and journalists of *Working Sister* further contributed to the assembly of new subject positions by means of the journal's new orientation and tone. Simply put, the pointed quotations, statistics, legal information, book reviews, and critical analyses hailed a community of readers who were more savvy and socially aware than the naive young *dagongmei* constructed by *Rural Women*. The earlier journal assumed a readership of rural women and *dagongmei* who needed to be advised and encouraged to stand up for themselves. The later journal assumed a readership of *dagongmei* and others who, provided with information and critical analysis, could and would use it not just to stand up for themselves but also to change the society around them. In fact, not all readers were assumed to be *dagongmei*—as indicated in Li Tao's quotation above, the journal was targeted at government officials and other urbanites as well as rural migrants and was aimed at enlightening both groups as to the importance of migrants and the injustices they faced. The effect of combining the two groups in a single project in this way was to reduce the gap between them—to hail them as a single community of subjects equally capable of absorbing information and acting upon it and equally concerned with and able to address social injustices and inequalities.

At the beginning of the twenty-first century, reports of the kind published in *Working Sister* that uncovered serious social problems and were critical of government policies were by no means unique in the Chinese media. *Working Sister* was, nevertheless, at the forefront of critical journalism, pushing the envelope of political acceptability, the risks of which were compounded by the fact that the journal was not registered with an ISSN number different from that of *Rural Women* in the way that it should have been to be strictly legal. In acknowledging the dangers they faced, Li Tao explained to me that one protective measure the editors took was to publish an introductory piece by a high-ranking official at the beginning of each issue of the journal—"When they see such big names writing for us, they'll feel it hard to clamp down on us." They were also careful, he said, to write only those things that could be verified, and they held to the principle of not being critical of shortcomings that stemmed from the country's (low) level of development and that the government did not have the capacity to address (December 2002).

Despite this, the journal's publication of critical investigative journalism was short-lived. In 2003 Li Zhen and Li Tao left the journal and the Cultural Development Center for Rural Women. *Working Sister* continued under new editors and gained its own independent registration and ISSN number. A detailed analysis of the new journal is beyond the scope of this volume. Suffice it to say that it continued to publish a mix of success stories and reports on difficulties facing *dagongmei*, but the latter were less numerous and less critically incisive and informative than the investigative reports published under the previous editors. In addition, while the journal continued to publish autobiographical stories and letters from migrants, there were no more pithy quotations and no more columns setting out details of specific laws. In terms of the overall content, layout, and accompanying imagery, the new journal looked more like an entertainment-oriented women's magazine than its more serious predecessor.

A "Home for Working Sisters"

When organizers chose the name "Home for Working Sisters" (Dagongmei zhi Jia) for the Migrant Women's Club, they no doubt had in mind an image of the "home" or "family" (*jia*) as a haven from alienation, hardship, and struggle; a place of reassurance, community, and harmony. Yet families and homes, as we all know, are generally characterized by shifting internal hierarchies of power, tensions, and conflicts, and the "Home for Working Sisters" is no exception.

In 2000 the day-to-day business of the Club was managed by Zhou Ling, a woman in her thirties who had originally migrated to Beijing from a poor village in Jiangsu in 1982. Zhou Ling had built a strong rapport with Club members.

Figure 2.2   **A Meeting of the Migrant Women's Club**

During the week people often dropped into the office to chat with her, and on Sundays the Club activities were attended by upward of a hundred people. There were, however, serious tensions between Zhou and Xie Lihua, and to a lesser extent Li Tao. According to Zhou herself, these arose largely from the fact that Xie Lihua and Li Tao expected her to put an enormous amount of work into organizing Club activities and recruiting as many members as possible, but gave her no authority and very few resources. Consequently, Zhou Ling left the office in early 2001, though she continued to participate occasionally in Club activities. After her departure, she was replaced by a series of people who were less popular, and the number of members visiting the Club and participating in its activities declined markedly.

In the second half of 2001 the office was staffed by Wang Laoshi,[16] an elderly Beijing woman who had taken on her position with the Club voluntarily after retiring from the editorial office of *Rural Women*, and a migrant woman in her twenties who acted as her assistant. Wang Laoshi was a kind, motherly figure, but she was not "one of us" with whom Club members felt they could chat frankly, and so few people came into the office during the week and usually no more than thirty people attended the Sunday sessions that she organized. These were mainly young, single women who were working in waged labor or looking for work. There were also a few young men who came, in part in search of a marriage partner.

The sessions that Wang organized lasted for three hours. We usually began with introductions and singing, and the rest of the session was devoted to discussion of a specific topic. Some of these discussions were organized and chaired by one of the participants, while at other sessions invited specialists gave talks. During the second half of 2001 Wang Laoshi invited a counselor to talk about psychological issues. Two lawyers came to talk about the Labor Law and the protection of migrant workers' rights, one session was about environmental protection, and on another occasion Wang invited someone to speak about HIV/AIDS.

The most prominent theme running through these Sunday sessions, as through the columns devoted to the situation of migrant women in *Rural Women*, was that migrant women should overcome their sense of inferiority and that they can and should "stand on their own two feet." Frequently, however, the presentation of talks worked against this message, for Club members were expected to treat the "expert" guests with great formality and respect, the speakers lectured their audience at length, and there was little encouragement of, or opportunity for, debate or interaction between the speakers and Club members.

Furthermore, in urging them to stand on their own two feet these expert speakers were often highly condescending and attributed *dagongmei* problems to their own lack of *suzhi*, without acknowledging the widespread discrimination, exploitation, and abuse that they faced. The psychological counselor, for example, criticized *dagongmei* for a lack of agency and independence, saying:

Some people decide that their environment doesn't suit them. In fact, that is the wrong way of looking at things. You must look for a way to adapt to your environment, not the other way around.

Afterward I wrote in my journal:

I was sitting there, opposite Liu Yu, whose legs are still so smashed up she can't even sit properly, let alone walk any distance, and behind her was Chen Ailing's sister. The distance between their realities and her little speech, all carefully prepared and written down and said with such "expert," "scientific" authority, quite appalled me and I kept thinking "I bet they've been through more than she would ever be able to come to terms with psychologically." (September 2001)

Club members themselves were largely silent in response to this talk, as they were to the talk given by the two lawyers about the Labor Law. The lawyers urged *dagongmei* to acquaint themselves with the Law, saying that as long as they signed written contracts with their employers they could use the Labor Law to protect their rights or to seek redress should those rights be violated. Later, two of the Club members confirmed for me what everyone in the room at the time must have known—that the Labor Law was of little use to migrant workers because few employers provided contracts to their migrant employees, and without a contract it was very difficult to use the law to seek justice (see chapter 3).

In other sessions, Wang Laoshi showed the same inclination to lecture Club members as did guest speakers, but she did not have the authority that would enable her perspective to go unchallenged. Consequently, these sessions were characterized by more debate and dissension, and were therefore probably more useful than the guest speeches for developing women's self-confidence and independence.

As an example, in one of the first meetings I attended, the theme Wang Laoshi chose for discussion was "What is time?" Before the session started, Wang wrote on a whiteboard, "Time is life, time is money, time is a resource." She then proceeded to argue essentially that it is important to manage one's time and not waste it, and to be on time, for example, for meetings and when starting work. These themes were then taken up by the young woman who had been assigned the task of guiding the group discussion for the day. She gave each participant a strip of paper with a literary quotation reiterating one or other of the themes that Wang Laoshi had outlined. She then asked us each in turn to discuss the significance of the quotation we had been given and to provide examples drawn from our own lives. Some did so, including one woman who complained about a friend's failure to meet her at an agreed time, and a few others who engaged in self-criticism about their inability to get to meetings or work on time. However, several of us could not read our quotation or did not understand its import and had to ask our neighbors to explain it. Others expressed disagreement with the quotations they had been given or with the propositions that Wang Laoshi had made at the start of the session. Zhou Ling said that having to wait for a friend for an hour or two was nothing; she felt that much of her life had been wasted because, as a young girl in a very poor village, her wish to go to university had been thwarted and then, as a migrant worker, she had been continually exploited in dead-end jobs in which she could not develop her abilities. Wang Laoshi responded that one should not think like that—that everyone, no matter what their situation, had the ability and the responsibility to make the most of their time. Zhou countered by saying that we cannot always blame ourselves for things that happen to us and another woman joined her saying, "We don't have any choice [about wasting our lives]—there's a whole generation of people for whom there's been no choice [mei banfa]" (August 2001).

Aside from the formal talks and discussions that I have described here, perhaps the most significant aspect of the Sunday sessions was the informal get-togethers that occurred at the beginning and end of the sessions. Most of the young women and men who came regularly to the Sunday meetings did so, in fact, to meet up with other migrants more than to hear the formal talks. Some came early and chatted before the formal meeting got going, others came late, paid little attention during the meeting or chatted with their neighbors while the formal talk was going on, and then hung around afterward chatting, and often a group of us would go out to lunch together. These informal get-togethers were vitally important to participants, many of whom traveled up to two hours on the bus just to get to the Club. As the recruitment letter suggested it would be, the Club had indeed become like a second home, where they could make new friends and meet up with old ones and exchange gossip and news.

In 2002 declining participation in the Migrant Women's Club led Li Tao and his colleagues to ask Wang Laoshi to leave. In an effort to stimulate greater participation, they advertised for new staff and nine people responded. They then held a public meeting, at which Club members chose Zhang Hong, a *dagongmei* and veteran Club member, and Xu Min, a young local Beijing woman who had recently graduated from a tertiary law degree.

Zhang Hong was responsible for organizing the Club's activities. She and Xu Min also worked with other staff of the Cultural Development Center for Rural Women on a new venture aimed at broadening participation in the Club. Observing that many *dagongmei*'s long work hours did not permit them to come to Club activities on Sundays, they themselves visited three worksites with a large concentration of *dagongmei* each week, running activities there similar to those held at the Club. In addition to helping Zhang Hong with Club activities, Xu Min worked with Li Zhen in the newly established Migrant Rights Group and was responsible for answering the Center's hotline telephone. Staff at the Cultural Development Center advocated "self-management" for the Club, which according to Li Tao, meant that "we rarely participate in the club's activities, so it's more natural, and they organize them themselves. The problem is, though, that they have very little experience organizing and managing" (December 2002). My own observation was that, while they rarely participated in the Club's activities, Li Zhen and other staff of the Cultural Development Center supervised Zhang Hong and Xu Min quite closely.

Under Zhang Hong and Xu Min, the Club's activities continued to involve about thirty people at a time, but they were held every Saturday and Sunday. Saturday sessions were relatively unstructured and were run by the club's "cultural entertainment troupe." During December they were devoted primarily to preparing songs and performances for a New Year's soiree to be held at the end of the month. These sessions were lively, relaxed, and full of camaraderie and banter—a marked contrast to the subdued and restrained atmosphere that had prevailed the previous year. This seemed to be connected to the fact that, under its new management, the club had attracted a different set of participants, with a larger proportion (a third or more) of men involved than previously and more, better educated migrants who had been in the city for several years and attained relatively high-status white-collar jobs. Fewer younger, recently arrived migrant women came to the Club than previously, and those that did were generally very quiet. The Club, it appeared, had transformed itself from a matriarchal "home" into something more like a young people's association that was lively and democratic, but at the same time exclusionary for those who lacked the self-assuredness to participate in the performances and banter.

Some of the Sunday sessions held that month were devoted to English lessons. Others were conducted by a small group of student volunteers from the social work department of the Beijing Women's College, with whom Xie Lihua had close connections. In one of these sessions the students divided us into small groups. After self-introductions, each group was asked to draw up a list of basic rules for the conduct of Club sessions, after which we reported back to the larger group and one of the students wrote up suggestions on a whiteboard. Lively disagreements ensued, with some people arguing for very strict rules and a few for none at all. One woman in my group complained that they had rules for everything at work, but they wanted to come to the group to relax, not to be bound by more rules. The final list of rules drawn up included "turn off your mobile phone," "do not leave in the middle of an activity unless it's an emergency," "respect others while they are speaking," and "raise your hand when you want to say something." These were immediately disobeyed, both by the student organizers and the migrant participants.

Next, the students asked each small group to discuss strategies for stimulating members' enthusiasm for Club activities. At the end of the session the students wound up by asking everyone to submit a strip of paper with their opinions of the day's activities.

These exercises appeared to be aimed at inculcating in Club members some understandings of social citizenship and participatory democracy, but they were not well received. In a casual conversation a couple of days later, one of the women who had participated in the session asked me what I thought of it and I confessed I thought it was boring. Our companion, who had not been present, commented "that's what they all said." The first woman said, "You're right, it wasn't very interesting and it wasn't much use." On her strip of paper at the end of the session she had written that the activities were fun, but that there was one person in her group who had not said anything the whole afternoon. "They didn't do anything to arouse her enthusiasm!" she said. In a second conversation, Chen Ailing's sister similarly said that the session was very boring and that on her strip of paper she had asked that they not hold any more like it. When we explained the activities to Liu Yu, who had not been present, she commented, "It sounds like those were things for them [the student organizers] to work out; they didn't have to involve everyone" (December 2002).

On the whole, in 2001 and 2002 my interlocutors were commonly dissatisfied with the activities that the Club ran. They also felt that the Club and its associated activities—the hotline and the Migrant Rights Group—lacked the resources to be of much use. Liu Yu, Chen Ailing, and her sister commented, for example, that the Rights Group could offer advice, but they had neither the power nor the money to do anything more substantial. They really needed a full-time lawyer working for *dagongmei*, Liu Yu noted, but they lacked the resources for that (December 2002).

As a way of extending beyond the limited capabilities of the Migrant Women's Club, Li Tao and other staff of the Cultural Development Center for Rural Women emphasized the importance of using the media to draw the public's attention to social injustices and change public opinion about migrants, and thereby to put pressure on the government to change its policies. Aside from publishing in *Rural Women* and *Working Sisters*, this strategy entailed inviting journalists to visit the Club and write up stories about it, and publicizing individual case studies of human rights abuse, such as those of Chen Ailing and Liu Yu. These latter two strategies were not appreciated by the members of the Migrant Women's Club, however. As I mentioned earlier, many resented the presence of journalists at Club activities. Others did not acknowledge the value of focusing on just a few cases of abuse, emphasizing instead the Center's inability to help the majority of *dagongmei* and complaining that Center staff focused on "models" like Chen Ailing and Liu Yu simply as a way of publicizing themselves and their work.[17]

Club participants did, however, appreciate the opportunity to make friends with other migrants and so overcome the loneliness they felt in the city. While noting that the Club did not have the resources to provide much in the way of concrete support to its members, Chen Ailing's sister, for example, nevertheless said that it was just good to have somewhere where they could meet their "brothers and sisters" to chat and also to look for a partner (December 2002).

Many members also felt that their involvement in the Club had been important in giving them a feeling of self-confidence and teaching them that the discrimination they faced was neither legitimate nor inevitable. Despite her differences with Xie Lihua, Zhou Ling was among the most appreciative of this. She said that when she first left home she was very self-effacing:

When I first came out I thought rural people had to stay in the countryside and then slowly, by meeting people at the Migrant Women's Club and taking part in meetings, I came to feel that I should fight for my rights. How could I not feel that after so many meetings and talking with people like you? So there needs to be someone to do these things, to talk. (August 2001)

This was also something noted by outside observers. Wu Qing, an adviser to the Club, observed, for example, that the most obvious change that occurred in migrant women who became members of the Club was that they acquired a greater sense of self-confidence (Milwertz 2002, 109).

Conclusion

In the 1990s and early 2000s nongovernmental organizations were a new phenomenon in China and there were few people who had any experience in either managing or participating in them. It is not surprising, therefore, that *Rural Women, Working*

Sister and the Migrant Women's Club struggled to find an identity and a direction for themselves and the collective of migrant women that they sought to serve and represent.

The *Rural Women* collective and, within it the Migrant Women's Club, made a pioneering contribution to furthering the interests of rural and rural migrant women. However, their efforts were limited by the fact that, by and large, they did not challenge the fundamental underpinnings of gender and rural/urban hierarchies and inequalities. Thus, until about 2001 the primary subject position assembled, both in the columns of *Rural Women* relating to migrants and in the activities of the Migrant Women's Club, was that of a vulnerable young *dagongmei* who could benefit from a sojourn in the city, but who needed to be cautioned and taught to stand up for herself and whose *suzhi* needed to be improved; a subject position that reproduced many of the hierarchical and discriminatory understandings of dominant discourse and did not challenge the power relations underpinning either gender or rural/urban inequalities.

Migrant women themselves contributed to the assembly of this subject position, sending in stories to *Rural Women* and participating in activities of the Migrant Women's Club. However, the assembly was very much orchestrated from above, in the sense that those in charge of the journal and the Club belonged to the educated elite and were bound by an assumption that the subaltern or "vulnerable groups" in society needed their help and leadership.

By the early 2000s, however, the construction of the "low *suzhi*" subaltern *dagongmei* subject position and its "other," the concerned social activist, was coming under pressure from a number of angles: Feminists abroad criticized the *suzhi* discourse, global funding agencies pressed for more participatory approaches to development, and migrant women "voted with their feet" and stayed away from the Migrant Women's Club. The response of the *Rural Women* collective was decisive. It underwent major restructuring, setting up a new, independent organization to take charge of the Migrant Women's Club and other projects, began publication of a new journal, *Working Sister*, established a new Migrant Rights Group and hotline, and changed the management of the Migrant Women's Club.

In 2001–2 *Working Sister* moved away from the focus on *dagongmei* as vulnerable young women whose problems stemmed from their low *suzhi* and inability to stand up for themselves, concentrating instead on the institutions and policies that discriminated against migrants, exploited them, and stymied their citizenship. The shift, through which we can see the development of a "counterdiscourse," was highly significant. This was not just because it promoted a more useful understanding of the sources of social disadvantage but because it contributed to the imagining of rural migrants, not as a fundamentally inferior "other," but as equals to educated urbanites, as entitled to, and as capable of, citizenship as they were.

In the same period, staff at the Cultural Development Center for Rural Women tried to put new life into the Migrant Women's Club by increasing migrant involvement in its management and by expanding its activities. To some extent they succeeded, and there was more lively participation in Club activities than previously. Members continued to complain, however, that activities were boring and that the Club did not do enough for migrants. On the other hand, there was wide appreciation for the Club as not so much a "home" as a meeting place for friends and as a site where migrant women could overcome their feelings of inferiority and gain the confidence to stand up—and speak up—for themselves.

This was one of the most important achievements of the Migrant Women's Club, for although the Club was not a "subaltern counterpublic" in that it was not managed and shaped primarily by subalterns themselves, it did act as a space for migrant women to "withdraw and regroup" and from there to begin to "invent and circulate counterdiscourses to formulate oppositional interpretations of their identities, interests, and needs," as Nancy Fraser (1999 [1992]) put it. Ironically, migrants' dissatisfaction with the "failures" of the Club was closely bound up with this, its greatest success, for learning to articulate what they did not like about the Club was very much a part of learning to stand up for themselves and to formulate new understandings of identities, interests, and needs.

In 2001–2 this contributed to a growing call among members of the Club for migrant women to "unite" and "fight for their rights" and even to some discussion of strategies that they could adopt as a collective in order to further their own interests without relying on urbanites like Xie Lihua. In other words, members of the Club were beginning to think of themselves not just as subjects and agents but as agents of resistance.

This topic will be examined further in chapter 7. Before that, however, we need to look in more detail at how migrant women's lives have been shaped by the discourses outlined in this part of the book, and how they have responded to and negotiated the subject positions created and assembled through those discourses. We turn first to the ways in which state policies and institutions, and the discourses and practices they uphold, have both put migrant women "in their place" and made them feel "out of place" in the city.

Part II

Place

—— 3 ——

In and Out of Place

In this second part of the book I focus on aspects of experience and identity that relate to place and emplacement, examining migrant women's experiences both of geographical location and physical environment and of social "place," that is, of status and position with respect to other people.

Practices of social control often entail placing people in particular spatial relationships to other people and to their physical environments. In modern institutions such as factories and prisons, for example, the power and authority of superiors is often exercised and expressed through forms of emplacement and limitations on movement of those over whom control is sought (see, for example, Foucault 1977 [1975]; Dutton 1992; Rofel 1999, 257–76). Clearly, the Chinese household registration system, which for decades has shaped citizens' status and life chances by fixing them to particular places, is another type of social control through emplacement. In this chapter I demonstrate that even for rural people who have migrated to the city the household registration system and regulations supplementing it continue to act as a form of control through emplacement, making them feel both marginalized and "out of place," as well as highly restricted, subordinated, and "put in their place" in the city. Just how consequential this can be is illustrated in the following account given by Chunzi, a long-time member of the Migrant Women's Club.

What do I get from the household registration system?

Being what's known as a working sister [*dagongmei*] and enjoying freedom in love and marriage, marrying into Beijing would seem to be a lucky thing indeed, but in the past two years I've had a thorough taste of the misfortune it can bring!

Because I don't have a Beijing *hukou* [household registration] my husband lost his right to assigned housing. Since 1997, when we married, we've always rented on the market and it seems as though we have to move to a new place every year. For a while this year it was difficult to find a suitable place and we were almost living on the streets. . . .

However, there is something that makes me even more dispirited than all of this: my daughter is already two years old, but all along she has been a "black householder" [*hei hukou*, i.e., without household registration].

Is this because I am unwilling to have my daughter registered at home [in the countryside]? Not at all! I had thought that although my daughter could not inherit registration from her father, she could take mine. If it came to it I thought she could be a working sister like me, but it hadn't occurred to me that it wouldn't be so easy for her to inherit my *hukou*!

When she was nearly four months old, I was forced to take her to my distant home to be raised, in the hope that in a settled environment she could find her own place and a foundation for her growth. But my daughter never really got used to the place, and nearly lost her life. So, after a month my mother brought her back to Beijing. When I took her home I had taken her birth permit, birth certificate, and other relevant documents in order to process her *hukou*. But I couldn't complete the process, as I had forgotten to take my husband's ID card.

After returning to Beijing I got all the documents (including the one-child certificate that I had obtained in the village), photocopied them and mailed them back to the village. For my daughter's household registration, my elderly father unquestioningly followed up futile leads. In the end he told me on the 'phone: "It was easy to get the village authorities to issue your daughter with a certificate, but they registered her as a boy and now it all has to be done again. Also, you have to quickly mail back your husband's ID card; the photocopy was unacceptable!"

How could photocopies be unacceptable? Here in Beijing an ID card could be necessary at any moment. So I thought about it and then rang back home and told them not to process the *hukou* for the moment—that I'd sort it out when I returned to the village. . . .

For the sake of my daughter's *hukou* and some other matters, I had no choice but to borrow some money to return home again. But what I hadn't reckoned with was the new land policy in the village: girls who had married out had become spilt water [that is, the village considered that it had lost these women's labor power]. Those who had married out like me, yet had no way to change their *hukou*, were just considered to be "empty registers" [*kong gua*]. "Empty registers" are those who, although their *hukou* lies in their natal village, have no rights to the land (in the last few years the state has collected more and more of the land belonging to my mother's family, so I won't be getting any money from the sale of that land in the future). In reality I no longer belong to my mother's family, but I still have to follow the old pattern with respect to state taxes and obligatory work.

In the face of this new land policy, what should have been a strong position now looked so feeble. I am fully aware that this type of land policy is not protected by law, and I also know that I can fight to have my legal rights enacted, but such a "fight" is far from easy. How much time and energy would I have to spend? And money? I have to admit that I can't afford it. . . .

Without any bad intentions on anyone's part, my child has become a "black householder." Actually, though a citizen of the PRC, I am even lower than a "black householder." I don't count as a member of the family that raised me, and I don't count as a city person—so, when it comes to it, what kind of a person am I? Needless to say, I have to process all types of certificates and be "managed" by officials both in my natal village and in the city, but contrary to what you'd expect, when I should have been managed, no one did so! Take family planning for example. Both my husband and I married when we were over thirty and when we wanted a child I was already thirty-three (and my husband thirty-four). That's late for both marriage and pregnancy, but before I got pregnant no family planning official came to tell us the necessary information [about regulations relating to marriage and childbirth]. . . .

When I was about two months pregnant, I accidentally mentioned this in a telephone call to my sister-in-law in Hefei. . . . Later she rang me back saying that I had to return home for an examination, and only then could things be settled! So at four months pregnant I had to make the special trip back home (it came to nearly 1,000 yuan for the return trip for me and my husband). The local Family Planning Bureau wasn't interested in our exceptional circumstances. They fined us 400 yuan on the spot, and asked me to pay another 100 yuan deposit (for the insertion of an IUD after childbirth). Unfortunately, because of my caesarean section and puerperal fever, an IUD could not be fitted successfully (when they tried fitting it I lost a lot of blood and they had to remove it). I asked the doctor to provide a certificate for this, but the doctor said that this type of certificate could only be issued once the hospital officials had made a diagnosis. I knew that doctors these days understand only money! Therefore I had no choice but to spend time and money to get this certificate. . . .

In June of 2000 the Family Planning Bureau at home sent another notice to my family, demanding that I complete a migrant worker family planning contract within a certain period, otherwise there would be such and such a fine. My old father couldn't explain it all clearly to me on the telephone, but he asked me to send home a recent photograph immediately. My parents paid for me yet again—this time a 200 yuan deposit and several tens of yuan in procedural fees. After this I received, posted from my family, the "contract for family planning for a woman of child bearing age who has left her native place" and a year's supply (four copies) of a migrant worker's family planning circumstances receipt form—quite standard—with my photograph attached, and the seal of the local Family Planning Bureau stamped on top, asking me to return one form every three months, and asking me to have my (Beijing) hospital and Family Planning Bureau put their seals on it. So, once again I had to visit hospitals and family planning bureaus. And as a result of the fact that, in the process of implementing family planning procedures, the Family Planning Bureau at home had already stamped "insert IUD" in one column, the Family Planning Bureau in Beijing refused to affix their seal and wanted me to again bring proof or go to a designated hospital and have an IUD inserted. Once again I had to turn myself inside out! (Chunzi 2001)

The subordination of rural migrants in contemporary Chinese cities results from a unique combination of ongoing state regulation centered on the household registration system and the unleashing of market forces. On the one hand, with deregulation and increased competition across the economy, employers have been both motivated and enabled to hire migrant labor in large numbers on wages and under conditions greatly inferior to those enjoyed by urbanites. The household registration system did not create these practices but it was integral to it, for it institutionalized sociocultural divisions and inequalities, providing employers with a ready-made category of subjects whose inferior treatment was already socially sanctioned. Migrants' vulnerability to such treatment has been compounded by failures in state power, in particular by the state's inability to put in place a legal structure that would curb the worst excesses of capitalist exploitation. This is similar to the situation faced by people at the bottom of the social hierarchy in many other developing capitalist economies, but in China the state's failure to curb rampant lawlessness and abuse has been exacerbated by the massive rapidity of the shift from a state-planned to a market economy (Solinger 1999, 197).

On the other hand, the subordination and disadvantage suffered by migrants has also been exacerbated by "the lingering clout of the state," as Dorothy Solinger puts it, although I would argue that the state's clout has not so much "lingered" in the wake of a growing market economy as modified and developed in tandem with it. In the 1990s, recognizing that the household registration system no longer functioned to regulate rural to urban migration, the state augmented it with a bewildering array of other policies and regulations, in effect constructing new regulatory regimes that governed all aspects of migrants' lives. There were considerable variations in the regimes instituted by different provinces and cities, but all were characterized by discriminatory restrictions on migrants' movement, employment, fertility, education, and housing. All entailed complicated certification procedures; quotas limiting, for example, the number of migrants who could be employed in a city or to whom housing could be leased within a district; punishments for violations; and, in the large cities, periodic "clean-up" campaigns involving the detention and repatriation of migrants to the countryside (HRIC 2002b, 35). Like the regulatory regimes imposed by other countries upon overseas migrant "guest workers," all were aimed at minimizing the cost to the state of the influx of migrants by ensuring that they did not acquire the rights of urban citizenship.[1] The remainder of this chapter first outlines the regime of regulation and surveillance to which migrant women are subjected in the city. It then discusses the multifarious ways in which this regulatory regime contributes to migrant women feeling both "out of place" and "put in place," underwriting marginalization, subordination, exploitation, discrimination, disadvantage, and restrictions in all aspects of their lives.

Regulation and Surveillance

In the large metropolises of Beijing, Shanghai, and Guangzhou, regulations relating to migrants are particularly numerous, complex, and onerous. Rather than attempt a comprehensive account, I provide here just a brief summary of the minimum requirements that a woman with rural *hukou* needed to meet in order to qualify for legal residence and employment in Beijing in the late 1990s and at the beginning of the 2000s.[2] Some changes to national and Beijing regulations were introduced in the early 2000s. These changes and their likely impact on the lives of rural migrants are discussed briefly in the conclusion to this chapter.

According to national regulations, rural residents seeking to leave home to work in another province or directly administered city, including all those seeking to enter Beijing from outside the municipality, were required to first register with the local office responsible for labor recruitment and employment services and to obtain from it a "registration card for personnel leaving the area for work" (*waichu renyuan liudong jiuye dengji ka*). Once in the city, migrants seeking work in most occupations were also required to obtain a "work permit for personnel coming from outside" (*wailai renyuan jiuye zheng*) from the local labor department (HRIC 2002b, 54; Liu Ling 2001, 103-4). According to Beijing regulations this permit was to be given only to those migrants over the age of sixteen, with a minimum of junior secondary education (Liu Ling 2001, 104). The work permit was not required for women seeking work in Beijing as maids. They, however, were required to first register for work with a domestic service introduction agency and to apply for a domestic service permit (*jiating fuwuyuan zheng*).

Before leaving home, married migrants of childbearing age were also required to obtain documentation indicating their marriage and fertility status from officials in their place of household registration. On arrival at their destination they then had to report to the local family planning department to have this documentation examined, and to receive an acknowledgment of it. If their documentation was incomplete, they could be ordered to return to their place of origin to have valid papers issued (HRIC 2002b, 57–58).

Once in the city, anyone over the age of sixteen away from their place of household registration for more than a month was required to apply to the local Public Security Bureau (that is, the police) for a temporary residence permit (*zanzhu zheng*).

When applying for a temporary residence permit, applicants were required to present their identity card (*shenfen zheng*) and, if renting in the city, a copy of their lease. If the applicant lived within a work unit or workplace, the employer was permitted to apply for the permit in her stead (HRIC 2002b, 53). Women of childbearing age seeking a temporary residence permit were required to present documentation from their home county relating to their marriage and reproduction status (State Family Planning Commission 1998; Beijingshi Gong'an Ju 1995). Temporary residence permits were issued for a maximum period of one year, after which they could be renewed. Migrants were required to show their permit to the police upon request (HRIC 2002b, 53–54).

In Beijing, once issued a temporary residence permit, a woman of childbearing age was further required to obtain a "marriage and reproduction permit" (*hunyu zheng*) from the local family planning office in the area where she was living. This had to be done within ten days of her arrival in the area (HRIC 2002b, 63). Beijing regulations further stipulated that married migrant women in the city were to undergo checks of their contraceptive use and fertility every six months (ibid., 63; Liu Ling 2001, 106). Without a marriage and reproduction permit, a woman was not permitted to give birth. If she did, she could be fined and all permits allowing her and her partner to live and work legally in Beijing could be confiscated (HRIC 2002b, 63–64). Without a temporary residence permit (and a marriage and reproduction permit in the case of women of childbearing age), a migrant could not obtain a work permit or business license, and work units and employers were prohibited from employing any such person (ibid., 53 and 57).

This sketch leaves out many details and does not take into account variations in legal requirements and procedures that existed between occupations and between districts within Beijing. Nor does it take into account changes that were made to regulations in the period covered; discrepancies between national and local-level regulations; and widespread corruption on the part of officials, employers, landlords, and others. I have also not yet said anything about the fees migrants were charged for legal documentation. These could be substantial, but they varied enormously, due both to regional variations and to corruption. As one migrant in Beijing commented:

> I really can't figure out how much they are supposed to cost. Two yuan per year, 180 yuan, 240 yuan, 360 yuan, it's as if migrant people's money just comes down from heaven. If you've got the papers in Dongcheng District, Xicheng District won't recognize them, so you have to do them again, or perhaps they need to fill up a [police] van, so they don't even look at your [temporary residence] permit. "It's expired, get in the van!" they say, tearing it up. (an anonymous posting on www.NewsHoo.com, 10 March 2000, cited in HRIC 2002b, 85)

Finally, a crucial aspect of the way in which regulatory institutions and policies were experienced by migrants was the sheer lack of information available, the

widespread rudeness and uncooperativeness, not to say violence, that characterized officials' interactions with migrants, and the reinforcement at each step along
the way of an understanding that the system was a tool devised solely for the
purposes of surveillance, discrimination, and punishment.

Chunzi's story above illustrates how time-consuming, frustrating, unpleasant, and expensive it could be for a migrant to obtain legal documentation. In
many cases the struggle to conform to the law was complicated by bureaucratic
hurdles in the migrant's home county as well as Beijing, and it went on for
years. Furthermore, the very act of conforming to authorities' demands often
resulted in yet more burdensome, not to say humiliating, demands. Migrant
women such as Chunzi, who married and had a child in Beijing, were especially
likely to enter into, and then find themselves trapped in, a vicious circle of struggle
to conform to regulations, increased demands, surveillance, and humiliation from
the authorities, and ongoing marginalization of themselves and their families.
Such women were particularly motivated to comply with the law and to improve
their own and their children's legal standing because of a very valid concern that
if they did not their children would suffer both material deprivation and social
ostracism as they grew up. The state's concerns over family planning, seen almost always as a "women's issue," meant, however, that the legal demands placed
on migrant women seeking to marry and to give birth were particularly numerous and onerous, and subsequent surveillance could be particularly frequent
and invasive.

The difficulties faced by migrants were compounded for migrant women by the
fact that some of the most basic regulations and practices governing social and
economic relations in both rural and urban China are underwritten by a profound
gender bias. Thus, aside from the assumption that family planning is a "women's
issue," migrant women have had to come to terms with the fact that, as mentioned,
their children's *hukou* status follows their own and not their husbands'. As will be
discussed later in this chapter, children without local Beijing *hukou* face severe
discrimination in education, not to mention in other aspects of their lives in later
years. In order to improve their children's life chances, rural women who marry a
Beijing man and have a child have sometimes tried to obtain local Beijing *hukou*
for themselves. In this they have had to face a particularly hard battle. Zhou Ling
spent ten years struggling to change her *hukou* status and that of her daughter's.
Finally, she and her daughter were granted local Beijing status, but only because
her husband's work unit obtained it for them. Were it not for her husband's relatively privileged status as an editor in a central state publishing house, this would
not have been possible. Certainly, such a thing was beyond Chunzi's dreams. In
August 1998 the State Council approved a change in policy, allowing children to
inherit *hukou* from either of their parents. This is potentially of enormous significance to people like Chunzi. However, local governments, especially in larger
cities, have been slow to implement this reform. By 2003 it had still not been
systematically implemented in Beijing.

As Chunzi's story illustrates, rural land practices that discriminate against women can also make life for migrant women particularly hard. Following decollectivization in rural China in the late 1970s and early 1980s, use-rights to land were distributed to households according to their size. In theory, village land allocations were to be adjusted every few years for changes in household size resulting from births and deaths and from women's marriages—the most common pattern of marriage involving the bride leaving her natal home to join her husband's household, often in another village. There were several problems with this system. Administratively it was complicated and it resulted in insecurity over land tenure. In many places, therefore, villages readjusted landholdings relatively rarely. On the other hand, the system was open to corruption and abuse, and some local authorities made land readjustments to suit their own interests and those of their cronies. There were also numerous reports of villages with scarce land refusing to increase the land allocation of households in which a wife had recently arrived, while taking away land from households from which a woman had married out.[3]

In 1998, in a bid to improve farmers' sense of security, the central state passed the Land Management Law, according to which farmers were to be given thirty-year written contracts for the ownership of land use-rights over a piece of land. In practice, this law has been widely abused. Of particular concern here is the ongoing abuse of women's rights to land. Legally, women share equal rights with men to land and other property, and women who marry out of a village are entitled to retain their rights to land use and to a share of collective assets until they are allocated household registration, and land use-rights in the case of women marrying into another village, in their husbands' place of residence. Commonly, though, a woman is not allocated new land use-rights upon marriage into another village, and if she marries a man with urban *hukou*, she usually cannot obtain urban *hukou* for herself. On the other hand, villages often withdraw all or part of a woman's rights to land use and collective assets when she marries out, leaving her and her children with "empty" household registration or turning them into "black householders" with no registration, as in Chunzi's case.[4] These rights are not returned to the woman if her husband dies or if she divorces, in which case she loses whatever use-rights to land and other property she might have gained through her husband.[5]

The All China Women's Federation reports that in the first half of 1999, 40 percent of letters of complaint that it received from rural women related to the loss of land use-rights (Yang and Xi 2004, 2). In 2002 a study conducted by members of the Ministry of Agriculture found that in a sample of 400 rural households in the provinces of Hunan and Shanxi, 11 percent of married women aged between eighteen and sixty had no rights to land in the village in which they were living. They comprised 96 percent of all married people in this age bracket who were without land rights (ibid., 8,10).

Some scholars predict that gender inequalities in land use-rights and their consequences for gender inequalities more broadly will become yet more serious with the implementation of the Rural Land Contracting Law passed in March 2003.

This new law reiterates and reinforces the thirty-year no-change rule. It also empowers landholders to rent out or transfer ownership to land and to enter into shareholding arrangements (Lyengar 2003). According to Chinese economists, this means that rural out-migrants will be able to capitalize on their land use-rights, thereby improving their incomes and enabling them to start up a business. The existing gross gender inequalities in the distribution of rural land use-rights mean, though, that this commodification of land will further disadvantage rural women and rural women migrants (informal communication, Sally Sargeson, July 2003).

There is a general understanding among migrants that one gets very little in return for going to the considerable trouble and expense of registering for the permits that are required in order for one's sojourn in the city to be recognized as legal. Almost no institutional services or assistance are provided specifically for migrants in the city and migrants are not entitled to forms of government assistance, such as housing subsidies for the poor and retraining for the laid-off, that are offered to underprivileged locals. Furthermore, migrants are fully aware that, with or without legal documentation, they are marked as "outsiders." Not only does legal documentation not entitle them to equal treatment or opportunities relative to urbanites, it does not even protect them against police harassment. For this reason, some migrants refuse on principle to register for a temporary residence permit. One person said to me, "Why should I [register]—I won't get anything in return. If you register for a temporary residence permit, it just makes it easier for them to track you down." Other migrants go to considerable lengths to try to obtain legal documentation, but give up after being confronted with a long series of bureaucratic hurdles.

Lax enforcement and illegal behavior among officials, employers, landlords and others also contributes to low compliance rates (HRIC 2002b, 87). A woman interviewed for *Working Sister* said:

> Tell me, what crime have we migrant workers committed? Frankly, nowadays many of us don't even have a temporary residence permit. It isn't just the cost. The police station requires documentation from your landlord, but most landlords don't go through the legal formalities because it costs them,[6] which means there's no way you can get a temporary residence permit. But that's okay. If you're detained you have to pay; to get a permit you have to pay. It's all much of a muchness. If I'm detained once in two years I'm in the lead. If I get caught twice in one year it's just bad luck. These last few years I've only ever had an ID card [*shenfen zheng*], and I've always been lucky. (Cheng 2002a, 12)

Discrepancies between statistics on the number of temporary residence permits issued and estimates of the total number of migrants living in Beijing suggest that something like 1.5 million people, or about half of all migrants who have been in the city for a month or more, do not have temporary residence permits (HRIC

2002b, 24; Beijingshi Tongjiju 2002, 579). Among my interlocutors, by no means all had obtained temporary residence permits and only a few had documents proving their marriage and reproduction status.

One can conclude, in short, that the legal status of rural migrants residing in Beijing is highly tenuous and uncertain. And despite the defiant attitude of some, this means that even those migrants who do their best to comply with regulations are easy targets for extortion, discrimination, intimidation, and violence on the part of officials and others.

In large cities, and especially in Beijing because it is the capital, "clean up campaigns" aimed at reducing the numbers and visibility of migrants in the city were common in the 1990s and early 2000s. During these campaigns, large numbers of migrants were rounded up by police, "fined," taken to detention centers, and repatriated to the countryside. It has been estimated that in Beijing in the late 1990s at least 10 percent of migrants were subjected to detention and repatriation each year (HRIC 2002b, 24). Efforts to round up and detain migrants were particularly vigorous in the months and weeks leading up to major "showcase" events such as the Fiftieth Anniversary of the Founding of the PRC on 1 October 1999, and the hosting of the International Student Games in Beijing in 2001, but they also occurred at other times throughout the year. In fact, each local police station in Beijing had its own monthly target for the number of people to be taken into detention. In 2001, the Chaoyang District Public Security Office detained a total of 120,000 migrants, or about 18 percent of the district's total migrant population (Chaoyang District Public Security Office, cited in Cheng 2002a, 13; Beijingshi Tongjiju 2002, 577).

A "clean-up" campaign occurred in the migrant settlement in Haidian while I was conducting my research there in 2001. In the month leading up to Beijing's hosting of the International Student Games in August–September the demolition of migrant housing, which had already begun on the edges of the settlement, was stepped up and, in addition, Public Security Bureau officers began to come through, checking migrants' papers and detaining large numbers. My interlocutors said that they came with a few vans each time. First they took men without temporary residence permits, but if that did not fill the vans they started taking women and children and people whose paperwork was in order. They demanded a "fine" of 300 yuan from each person they detained. Those who could pay were let off. The rest were taken to the detention center in Changping county, north of Beijing. Some were kept there indefinitely, but most were kept only briefly before being put on a train back to the countryside. These detentions continued on a daily basis through September and then less frequently for the remaining three months that I was in Beijing.

Detention centers are officially deemed "welfare" facilities, set up to provide relief to vagrants, beggars, and the homeless, but a person detained has no choice in the matter, and there is no judicial process for determining whether she falls into a category of people legally subject to detention or for determining the duration of detention. Both national and Beijing regulations stipulate that people should not normally be detained for more than a month, but they also allow for several conditions under which a person may be detained indefinitely (HRIC 1999, 10, 12).

Centers are underresourced and conditions are notoriously bad. A writer, detained in the detention center in Changping for a month in 1995, described it as "hell on earth. It is much worse than normal prisons. The people detained there were mostly migrants from outside Beijing and they are not treated as human beings. Considering all living conditions, including food, I say that that is not a place for a human being" (HRIC 1999, 44).[7]

According to officials the primary targets of detention and repatriation are the *sanwu renyuan* (three-without personnel), that is, people without legal documentation, stable employment, and residence. In practice, through the 1990s and early 2000s most detainees were rural migrants, but by no means all were so destitute as to be without papers, employment, and residence. Most detentions occurred in sweeps of migrant settlements, such as at Haidian, and media reports suggest that less than 50 percent of those detained and repatriated were *sanwu renyuan*. In 1999, ahead of celebrations of the Fiftieth Anniversary of the Founding of the Republic, the Beijing government announced that it would demolish 2.6 million meters of migrant housing and deport 1 million migrants. The total *sanwu renyuan* population that year has been estimated to be 400,000 (HRIC 2002b, 24, 26)—a large number in absolute terms, to be sure, but only 40 percent of the total targeted for repatriation.

Among my interlocutors, some lived in migrant settlements in the suburbs of Chaoyang and Haidian that were threatened with demolition and subject to frequent police sweeps. Numerous others had been waylaid by the police while on the street and only narrowly missed being sent to a detention center. In December 2002, when members of the Migrant Women's Club met to determine at what hour of the day they should hold their New Year soiree, one of the deciding considerations was that most migrants would not venture onto the street after dark for fear of being stopped by the police.

Aside from resulting in coercive and unpredictable forms of surveillance and regulation, the household registration system and accompanying regulations form a highly effective structural basis for, and visible marker of, difference and inequalities—inequalities that are exploited and perpetuated by local governments, employers, landlords, and others. Most obviously, the regulatory regimes governing migrants in the city undergird inequalities between "locals" and migrant "outsiders," but they also feed into class and gender inequalities. As I will discuss in the remainder of this chapter, rural migrant women, positioned at the intersection between these different inequalities, are vulnerable to discrimination, exploitation, and abuse in every aspect of their lives.

Employment

Through the 1990s and 2000s, the urban job market was highly segmented both between those with local *hukou* and those without, and according to gender.

However, the nature of work available to migrants, and specifically to female migrants, varied from one city to another. In Beijing, for example, a large proportion of migrant women were employed in domestic service, whereas in Hangzhou more migrant women worked in catering and other services or in cotton or silk factories. In Shenzhen most migrant women worked in export-oriented light industries. This section focuses on migrant employment in Beijing.

In 2001, 78 percent of all migrants in Beijing were self-employed or worked as waged laborers and another 13 percent were categorized as dependants of migrant workers in their family (Beijingshi Tongjiju 2002, 580).[8] Among male migrants in employment, 29 percent worked in construction, 18 percent in catering and other services, 15 percent in industry, and another 15 percent in commerce. In comparison, among female migrants in employment, 25 percent worked in commerce, 22 percent in catering, and 25 percent in other services; 14 percent worked in industry (ibid.).

Among my thirty-five female interlocutors living in the migrant settlement in Haidian, the great majority were married with children and were without paid employment, although some worked alongside their husbands selling vegetables. Only two had jobs that earned them an independent cash income: Liang Chun took in sewing, and another woman put together gas lighters at home. Some of the other women told me that they had tried to find waged work but had failed because they lacked education or because employers considered them too old. One woman said that she could find work as a live-in maid, but had rejected this option, as it meant being away from her children.

Most of the women whom I got to know in the Migrant Women's Club, on the other hand, were in waged employment working as maids, cleaners, factory workers, in hairdressing salons, or in clerical positions.[9] Almost all had worked as a maid in the past, though only a few were in such work at the time that I got to know them. In the 1990s domestic service was almost the sole province of rural migrant women. It was the entry point into the urban labor market for the majority of young, single women, mainly because such work was relatively plentiful, the requirements for skills and education were generally minimal, and a job as a live-in maid guaranteed housing. However, even relative to other jobs undertaken by migrants, domestic service is poorly paid and of low status. Once they find their feet in the city, therefore, most migrant women try to move out of domestic service into other forms of employment. In the early to mid-1990s, it was generally only older rural women without education who remained in domestic service for long periods. However, from the mid-1990s the employment opportunities for migrants in Beijing constricted, as a result of both increases in the migrant population and because of the Beijing government's efforts to limit the employment of migrants in favor of the growing numbers of local unemployed. Consequently, it became harder and harder for migrant women to find jobs other than as maids. Even those jobs became harder to obtain, as more and more urban women, who previously disdained such work, now turned to it after being laid off from the state sector.

According to national regulations in the 1990s and early 2000s, businesses wishing to hire migrant labor from outside the province or, in the case of Beijing outside the municipality, could only do so under highly restrictive conditions and with the permission of a local labor recruitment agency and the local labor department (HRIC 2002b, 54–55). Furthermore, in the mid-1990s the Beijing government began to impose annual restrictions on the type and number of trades and occupations in which migrants could be employed (ibid., 99).[10] In 1997 it promulgated a list of just 12 trades and 200 occupations in which migrants could legally be employed. Without exception, these were all likely to be shunned by locals as tiring, heavy, dirty, and/or dangerous jobs (Liu Ling 2001, 104). In 1999 Beijing fixed a target limit of 950,000 on the number of migrants employed across the city and removed 70,000 migrants from their jobs, replacing them with Beijing people who had been laid off (*xiagang*) or were unemployed.[11] In December that year, the Beijing Municipal Labor Bureau also promulgated regulations stipulating 103 types of occupation barred to migrants (Li Tao 1999b, 129).

What impact these regulations have had on the *actual* employment and occupational distribution of migrants is hard to say. Anecdotal evidence suggests that the regulations have been widely ignored. Even in those trades in which their employment has been banned, a great many businesses have preferred to hire migrants because they are cheaper than locals, and they have done so without going through labor departments or labor recruitment agencies, using advertisements and personal contacts instead. Overall, government restrictions and crackdowns have probably had only a minor effect on the broad occupational distribution of migrants. All the same, they have limited the employment opportunities of thousands of individuals. Furthermore, as testified by the numerous bitter complaints I heard from members of the Migrant Women's Club, they have created a general perception among migrants that they face a highly discriminatory job market.

Work Hours and Conditions

"Get out of my way, I have to punch my card!"—the first thing a migrant woman factory worker who had fainted from exhaustion said after being revived. (cited in "Dagong Yulu" 2002, 2)

Under China's Labor Law, in effect since 1994, employers and employees must sign a legally binding written contract, setting out each party's responsibilities and entitlements. Workers are to work no more than eight hours a day and forty hours a week on average, and are entitled to at least one day off in a week.[12] Overtime is not to exceed three hours per day or thirty-six hours in a month, and is to be paid at no less than 150 percent of the normal wage rate. Wages are to be paid monthly and in full, at a rate not lower than the minimum wage set by the local provincial or municipal government. Occupational health and safety must conform to standards set by the state, and workers are entitled to social insurance benefits upon retirement, illness or injury, unemployment or childbirth. Female workers are entitled to a minimum of ninety days of maternity leave (*Labour Law of the People's Republic of China* 2002).

Most of my wage-earning interlocutors were familiar with these provisions but felt them to be quite irrelevant because, when it came to migrant workers, the law was honored more in the breach than in the observance. And, indeed, among the fifty or so *dagongmei* working in factories, in restaurants, and as cleaners that I interviewed in Beijing and Hangzhou between 1995 and 2002, not one worked in conditions that accorded fully with the Labor Law. In particular, very few had contracts and none had any form of social insurance. They knew that if they were to fall seriously ill, be injured on the job, or become pregnant, they were more likely to lose their job than to receive any form of compensation or leave of more than a few days. Some of my interlocutors had been refused contracts by their employers and felt this was a serious problem because they knew that without a contract it would be extremely difficult to seek justice should their rights be violated. Others did not want a contract because they feared that it if they signed one, it would prevent them from leaving a job that turned out to be exploitative or otherwise undesirable in some way. In the minority of instances in which migrants did have contracts, they were not legal and did not protect the workers from exploitative and illegal practices. For example, contracts that one cleaning company required its employees to sign stipulated that a "pledge fee" (*baozheng fei*) was to be deducted from workers' wages each month, to be returned only upon completion of the one-year contract. This company also required its employees to sign statements to the effect that costs incurred as a result of injuries or illness on the job were to be borne entirely by the workers themselves.

As will be discussed, a large proportion of migrants earn less than the minimum monthly wage set by local authorities. Delays of several months in the payment of wages are also very common.[13] In addition, it is very common for employers to deduct "deposits" of at least one month's wages upon employment of migrant workers as a way of deterring them from leaving the enterprise before the end of the month. Sometimes employers also take workers' temporary residence permits and identity papers for "safekeeping," leaving migrants vulnerable to police detention if they go out, and unable to leave the enterprise in search of another job (Chan, Anita 2001, 9; Zhang, Li 2001, 130). Such practices are illegal but very common. They are an example of how, as Anita Chan observes,

> the household registration system provides the perfect conditions for forced and bonded labor. . . . Western criticism of China's forced labor system usually focuses on prison labor, but China's household registration system to all intents and purposes leads to a situation of forced bonded labor for millions of "free" workers. (Chan, Anita 2001, 9)

The discrepancy between the minimum monthly wage and the wage earned by migrants is compounded by the fact that a large proportion of migrants work a great deal more than forty or forty-four hours a week, and they are usually not paid overtime rates. A Sino-German questionnaire survey conducted among 200 migrants in Beijing in 1999 found that 77.9 percent of those surveyed worked seven days a week, and only 9.5 percent worked five days or less. Only 12 percent worked eight hours a day or less, while 55 percent worked more than ten hours every day.[14] In my own survey of members of the Migrant Women's Club conducted in 2000, I found that only 10.2 percent had worked forty hours per week in the previous month; 33 percent reported having worked an average of ten hours or less per week. Some of these people are likely to have had full employment for only part of the month, others may have worked part time, for example doing domestic work on an hourly basis. On the other hand, 32.8 percent of respondents worked between forty and sixty hours a week and 11.2 percent worked sixty hours a week or more (N = 88).

Migrant stories document shockingly poor conditions and coercive and exploitative practices in enterprises employing migrant labor. For example, in the story "The law is by my side," mentioned in chapter 2, the author writes that in the joint-venture factory in Shenzhen in which she was employed, migrant women toiled in overcrowded workshops where the extreme heat made it "like being inside a steamer basket." Workers were driven to utter exhaustion, but even then were compelled to work overtime on a daily basis, those who resisted being threatened with expulsion (Huang, Zhihua, 2004). Investigative reports and scholarly analyses suggest that work conditions like these are by no means unusual. For example, Anita Chan claims that in a survey she conducted of 1,530 migrant workers in fifty-four footwear factories of all types of ownership, nearly one-third reported that their factories used physical punishment against workers (Chan, Anita 2001, 10). An investigative report translated by Chan claims that in the mid-1990s in the city of Putian in Fujian province, some 70,000 young *dagongmei* worked in foreign-invested shoe factories where the concentration of poisonous chemical fumes was several times higher than allowed under national standards and extremely dangerous (ibid., 83–97). Another report documents how, in 1993, a fire engulfed Zhili Toy Factory in Shenzhen, leaving eight-seven *dagongmei* dead and forty-five with severe burns and permanent injuries. Investigators blamed the high toll primarily on the fact that managers had seriously violated safety standards, for example by cramming merchandise into corridors in order to maximize productive space, and blocking exits and putting bars on windows in a bid to control workers' movements (ibid., 106–36).

Zhang Li writes also that in the migrant settlement of Zhejiangcun in Beijing some 40,000 young migrants, most of them teenage women, toil in household-based garment sweatshops, often spending more than fifteen hours a day in front of the sewing machines. They live and work in the same cramped quarters, shared with their employers, and are subject to strict discipline at all times, being told when to get up and go to bed, and rarely permitted to take breaks from work. They lead very isolated lives, rarely being allowed to leave the house and, in some cases, never venturing outside of the settlement (Zhang, Li 2001, 128).[15]

Most studies of the conditions under which migrants work have focused on factories and sweatshops. They indicate that conditions and management practices that violate the Labor Law are evident in all parts of China and across all ownership sectors. However, conditions in the state sector are somewhat better than in the private, collective, and foreign-invested sectors. The worst forms of exploitation, intimidation, and coercion appear to be concentrated in factories under Korean, Taiwanese, and Hong Kong ownership (Chan, Anita 2001, 10–11). In the 1990s these and other foreign-invested factories were concentrated in the Special Economic Zones of southern China, but increasing numbers are now moving inland.

To date, relatively little has been written about the circumstances of the millions of migrants working in other forms of wage labor, including the men who work in construction and the women who work as waitresses, kitchen hands, and maids.[16] Yet migrants in these circumstances are also subject to coercive management and discipline, harassment by employers and managers, and long work hours in poor conditions. Both waitresses and maids, for example, routinely complain of being on their feet for twelve or more hours a day, six or seven days a week, and of being continually subjected to humiliating treatment from their bosses.[17]

A large proportion of young migrant women—those who work as live-in maids and as sweatshop employees—live and work in the same space, within the home of their employer. The particular issues that arise from their location in this "private" sphere are discussed below.

Housing

In Beijing, as in other large cities, most migrants live in the suburbs. As indicated in Map 2, Appendix 2, the urban districts and counties of Beijing are grouped for administrative purposes into four broad geographical areas: the central urban area, the inner suburban area, the outer suburban area, and outlying districts and counties. According to official figures,[18] in 2001, 1.98 million migrants, or 60 percent of Beijing's total migrant population, lived in the inner suburban area. Of these, the majority were concentrated in Haidian district (750,000 people), Chaoyang district (650,000), and Fengtai district (420,000). Another 763,000 people (20 percent of the migrant population) lived in the outer suburban area.[19]

Through the 1990s and 2000s pressure on migrants to move further away from the city center has increased. This is because, in its efforts to "cleanse," "urbanize," and "green" the city's suburbs, the government has been "upgrading" the status of more and more local peasants in these areas to that of urban resident (*chengshi jumin*), moving them to high-rise apartments, meanwhile demolishing the settlements of old *pingfang* (single-storied buildings) that they had rented to migrants and that had been migrants' chief source of housing, and putting in office blocks, apartments, and parklands in their place. According to one newspaper article, between 1990 and 2002 the agricultural population of Chaoyang District declined from 1 million to 200,000. And under government plans to turn Chaoyang into a showcase of national and international modernity, by 2010 there will be no more peasants and the whole district will be classified as urban (Dong 2002).

The distance of one's residential location from the center of Beijing is not a good indicator of class, for while the poorest—that is, rural migrants—are concentrated on the outskirts, many of the luxurious housing estates of the extremely wealthy are also located in these areas (Hu and Kaplan 2001, 69–74). However, for migrants who lack the resources of the rich, such as cars, being located far from the city center compounds a sense of marginalization and isolation. Young women, in particular, complain that they "might as well not be in the city at all," because they live so far out that they are very rarely able to travel in to enjoy the pleasures of modernity in downtown Beijing. And migrant entrepreneurs complain that the further out they are, the harder it is to conduct business. Furthermore, the demolition of housing and the forced relocation of migrants, conducted without compensation and often without warning, is highly disruptive and alienating and compounds the sense migrants have that they are not wanted and "out of place" in the city.

With regard to type, quality, and cost of housing, the household registration system underpins one crucial difference between migrants and locals: Among those with local, urban *hukou*, the majority live in apartments that have either been leased to them at extremely low rates or sold to them, again at highly subsidized rates, by their work unit or that of another family member. In addition, since the 1990s a small but growing number of locals have bought better-quality housing on the commercial market.[20] In contrast, as Chunzi indicates in her account above, without local *hukou* migrants, and even local residents married to migrants, are not entitled to accommodation from their work unit. Furthermore, programs aimed at helping the urban poor by providing housing subsidies do not include temporary residents in their target population. Only a tiny percentage of migrants can afford to buy commercial housing.[21]

In 2001 approximately 49 percent of migrants in Beijing lived in rented housing, 23 percent lived in a collective dormitory provided by their work unit, 15 percent lived on a construction or other worksite, 4 percent lived with relatives, and about 3 percent lived with their employer (Beijingshi Tongjiju 2002, 581). All of my interlocutors in the migrant settlement at Haidian lived in housing rented from local peasants. Among members of the Migrant Women's Club that I surveyed, however, a larger proportion lived in either a collective dorm (47 percent) or their employers' home (24 percent), rather than rented housing (17 percent).

Much of the housing available to migrants is a very visible reminder, both to themselves and to urbanites, of migrants' low and marginal status in the city. On construction sites across the city, for example, rural migrant workers live in flimsy, makeshift shacks without amenities in full view of everyone. And in the suburbs, the areas where migrants are concentrated are characterized by crudely built shacks and *pingfang*, sweatshops and stalls, narrow dirt lanes, and piles of rubbish. To the migrants who live in these areas, the poor conditions and lack of amenities provided are a constant reminder of the contempt with which they are treated by urbanites. To urbanites they are an eyesore, and evidence of migrants' "low quality."

Other forms of migrant housing are much less visible to outsiders, but this very invisibility contributes to migrants' sense of marginality and is a powerful metaphor of the status of the floating population. This is particularly so in the case of migrant women: hundreds of thousands work as maids isolated in their employers' apartments and others who work as waitresses sleep on restaurant floors or tables at night. Yet more working on the factory assembly line live on site in collective dormitories, while others, working as cleaners in the large office blocks downtown, live in damp, dark bunker-like dormitories in the basements of the office blocks. And finally, while the external features of migrant settlements are highly visible and aggravating to the urban public, within their walls there are sometimes thousands of young women who toil night and day in clothing sweatshops, almost never going outside the bounds of the settlement.[22] All of these women are essentially invisible to the urban public eye. They feel their contribution to the economy to be unacknowledged, yet, as they point out, life in Beijing would grind to a halt without them.

My interlocutors were often acutely aware of the sociopolitical significance of control over housing and the types of spaces migrants occupy in the city. Zhou Ling told me about a conference on the floating population that she once attended:

High-level officials were discussing whether they should build a compound for outsiders out at Hongmen [in Fengtai district]. Someone said, "We shouldn't do that—if we do, the outsiders will be concentrated in one place, and they'll be able to make trouble." So they decided not to build them. They thought it was better to have the outsiders scattered, living among Beijing people, so it wouldn't be so easy for them to get together and cause trouble. But then others pointed out that if they lived with Beijing people, these outsiders were too dirty and they'd spoil the living environment of Beijingers; so it was better to build some housing for them out in the suburbs. They only considered things in terms of urbanites' interests—in terms of stability and how to maximize Beijing people's comfort and pleasant environment. They didn't think in terms of the contribution that outsiders make to Beijing and how to provide them with some services and opportunities for them to develop. They never raise those issues. They're just concerned with managing them, with making sure they don't cause trouble, with educating them so they do their work well without running all over the place and spoiling the Beijing environment, and so they won't be so dirty. (August 2001)

In practical terms, the different forms of housing available to migrants each have their own advantages and disadvantages. In general, however, their housing not only reflects migrants' marginality but also reinforces their vulnerability and insecurity in very concrete ways. This is particularly the case for migrant women, whose housing very often leaves them highly vulnerable to physical and sexual violence and other forms of abuse; abuse to which, as migrant women in a study conducted in Beijing, Guangzhou, and the Pearl River Delta in 1994 pointed out, they are already more vulnerable than urban women because, as outsiders with a low social status, they are "easier to bully" (Tang, Can 1998, 69; see also Lou et al. 2004, 227).

Whether leased or provided by employers, friends, or relatives, the housing of migrants is also invariably smaller in area and inferior in quality to that enjoyed by those with urban *hukou*, and often also inferior to the housing in their home village. In Beijing in 2001, the average living floor space per person among those with local *hukou* was about 14 square meters (Beijingshi Tongjiju 2002, 503), but in the numerous migrant households that I visited in Haidian, and the few in Chaoyang, families consisting of three or four people lived in rooms between nine and thirteen square meters in area. In contrast, in 2001 the average living floor space per person in rural China was just under twenty-six square meters (*Zhonghua Renmin Gongheguo Nianjian 2002* 2002, 1194).

For many of my interlocutors, rented accommodation was the preferred form of housing because it afforded a greater degree of autonomy, privacy, "hominess," and potentially better living conditions than the alternatives. In any case, many employers did not provide housing for migrant workers. But decent rental housing was hard to find and very expensive. According to official statistics, in 2001 permanent Beijing residents spent on average 87 yuan on rent, which amounted to less than 1 percent of their discretionary income for the year (Beijing Tongjiju 2002, 495 and 500). In contrast, most of my interlocutors who were renting paid between 200 and 300 yuan each month for a space accommodating three or four people. Both married women who lived with their husband and children and single women who split the rent with housemates paid between 20 and 50 percent of their total household income.

Most migrants who rent housing are congregated in settlements like that in which Liang Chun lives, in the inner or outer suburban areas. Here, work is easier to find and rooms, rented out by former farmers, are cheaper and more readily available than closer to the center of the city. Conditions in these settlements are poor, police harassment is common, and the rates of crime—especially burglary, but also violent crime, including sexual violence—are high. As noted in chapter 1, urbanites often view the floating population as naturally more inclined to criminality than locals, and the zones in which they congregate, in particular, as hotbeds of crime. But as Zhang Li notes in her study of Zhejiangcun, crime in such zones is generally perpetrated by a small minority, and the prime victims are other migrants. As Zhang explains, "criminals have learned that as long as they raid migrants only,

Figure 3.1 **Residential Yard in a Migrant Settlement, Haidian District, Beijing**

they are less likely to be arrested by the police, who are primarily interested in protecting the locals" (Zhang, Li 2001, 145). Furthermore, houses in these zones are often flimsily built and easily broken into, and there is no policing of the lanes and streets. In contrast, in areas closer to the center of the city there are more police on the streets and most urbanites live in apartment blocks in walled compounds, often with a security guard at the gate.

As noted above, among members of the Migrant Women's Club, dormitory living was common. Conditions in dormitories are usually very basic. Each room houses anywhere between eight and twenty women, in metal bunk beds. There is very little in the way of furniture, and toilets and washing facilities are shared between the residents of several rooms (see Figure 3.2). Workers usually eat in communal canteens. They are subject to strict surveillance and discipline by management, outside of work hours as well as during them.

The dormitories that I visited around Beijing were in solid buildings in gated compounds or in concrete basements, and my guess is that women living there were less vulnerable to attack than in rented housing in migrant settlements or in accommodation in individual employers' homes. However, reports suggest that that is not always the case; that some factories, especially smaller private enterprises and those run by villages and townships, are able to provide their female workers only with dormitory accommodation in flimsy or dilapidated buildings that are frequently broken into by local youths (see, for example, Chan, Anita 2001, 32–35). Furthermore, female migrant factory workers commonly report that

Figure 3.2 **Migrant Women Workers' Dormitory**

Photo courtesy of Arianne Gaetano.

they are often harassed and bullied by local youths, as well as the police, when they go out (ibid., 32; Tang, Can 1998, 66). Sexual harassment on the factory floor is also common (Tang, Can 1998, 65).

By working in a factory and living in dormitory housing, most women can save or remit at least some of their earnings. However, most view this as only a temporary phase in their life. There are many migrant women who are single, have worked and lived in a factory for several years, and are in their late twenties or older, but they are considered very unfortunate. They are "destitute" (*yi wu suo you*), both because they are unmarried and without children and because they do not have a physical home of their own.

Young women just arriving in the city often do not have the resources (contacts, skills, and/or money) necessary to find factory work or rental accommodation, and so many first take up jobs either as live-in maids or in home-based clothing sweatshops. Aside from the convenience of this, there is a common perception among young rural women and their families that such work, because it is located in the private sphere, is "safer" (*anquan*), less "chaotic" (*luan*), and more respectable for young women than other work. There is an understanding that these work situations offer women a family-like atmosphere, in which their employers will protect them in much the same way that parents would protect their child. And it is believed that in such sheltered environments there is less likelihood that young women's reputations will be compromised than if they worked in mixed-sex venues, including large factories, and in particular, in restaurants, karaoke bars, and beauty parlors, where sex is marketed and consumed along with other services (Gaetano 2004, 53).

Precisely because of their location in the private sphere, however, women in these jobs are highly vulnerable to exploitation and abuse, including sexual abuse.[23] Zhang Li says that in the garment sweatshops in Zhejiangcun, Wenzhou migrant bosses justify harsh discipline over their young, female migrant employees by saying that because they are junior members of the household their activities should be directed and scrutinized by the household head. At the same time, a perceived gap in class status between wealthy entrepreneurs and their employees exacerbates the former's poor treatment of the latter. In addition, the social isolation of these young women makes them vulnerable to physical and sexual violence from their employers (Zhang, Li 2001, 128–29).

Similarly, paid domestic service is widely considered in the same way as unpaid "housework," rather than as an occupation, and maids are viewed as members of the employer's household rather than as independent workers. For this reason, domestic service is not covered by the Labor Law, coming only under the Civil Code, which is less comprehensive. In Beijing domestic service is regulated by guidelines from the Municipal Labor Bureau, which are meant to be enforced by domestic service introduction companies, many of which are run by the Women's Federation (Gaetano 2004, 57). However, there is a general perception among migrant women, first, that while introduction companies require both employers and maids to sign contracts, they have no way of keeping check on whether conditions set out in these contracts are observed. Second, it is common for employers to limit maids' use of the telephone and their movements outside the household, which makes contacting an introduction company or the Women's Federation very difficult. Finally, even if they were to contact them, workers are largely skeptical that companies could enforce regulations, and there is a general feeling among migrant women that the Women's Federation does not care about them and that it would not support them in a dispute with an urban employer (ibid., 57–58).

Many live-in maids are treated well and some claim to feel "just like one of the family." As in the case of sweatshop employees, however, a family ideology combined with isolation in their employer's home makes maids vulnerable to heavy discipline and micromanagement of their behavior and person, and to intimidation and violence, including sexual violence. Even more so than in the case of sweatshop employees, this vulnerability is exacerbated by the very low status of their occupation. Not only are urban women reluctant to take on jobs as domestic workers, but migrant women who work as maids often try to hide this fact from their friends and family in the countryside. This social stigma arises, in part, from the association with low-status housework but also because of associations with extreme poverty and slavery. This latter stems from the prerevolutionary practice in which poor rural families sold total control over their daughters to wealthier families who put them to work as domestic servants. As I have mentioned, many rural families see domestic service as relatively "safe" because of its location in the private sphere. However, the social stigma of such work is compounded by the fact that, like all forms of employment for women that entail them moving away from their own family's sphere of influence, it also has associations, for both urban and rural people, with sexual transgression and immorality.[24]

Income and Expenditure

On average, migrant incomes are considerably higher than nonmigrant rural incomes, but expenditure in the city is also higher than in the countryside. Nationally, the average annual per capita net income among rural families in 2001 was 2,366 yuan. Annual expenditure per capita came to 1,741 yuan (*Zhonghua Renmin Gongheguo Nianjian 2002* 2002, 1194). According to a survey conducted by the Ministry of Agriculture, the average national per capita annual income of migrant workers was 5,502.6 yuan in 2001 ("Rural-to-Town Labour Force on the Rise" 2003). In Beijing in 2001 most of my interlocutors earned an average annual per capita income of between 2,400 and 7,200 yuan.[25] However, their living expenditure amounted to at least 3,600 yuan each year.

Largely because of the segmentation of occupations along the lines of *hukou* and gender, migrants generally earn less than urbanites, and female migrants earn even less than male migrants. A Ministry of Agriculture survey of rural migrants from

Anhui and Sichuan conducted in 1995 found, for example, that the average income of female migrants was only 55.3 percent that of male migrants (Fan 2004, 184).

In Beijing, a comparison of data from recent surveys—one by the Municipal Statistical Bureau, the 1999 Sino-German survey, and my own survey of the Migrant Women's Club in 2000—indicates that about two-thirds of all migrants (male and female) earn less than the average urban income. About 17 percent earn less than the minimum monthly wage set by the Beijing authorities and less than the poorest 20 percent of the urban population, which includes the families of laid-off workers. Among *dagongmei*, more than 90 percent earn less than the average urbanite, and more than 30 percent earn less than the official minimum monthly wage and less than the average income of the poorest 20 percent of the urban population.[26]

Though they indicate a range of incomes, figures such as these nevertheless still mask enormous discrepancies between the incomes and lifestyles of different types of migrants—the floating population is commonly regarded as a homogenous mass of paupers, but it is far from being so (Zhang, Li 2001, 30–31). It is, rather, characterized by class and gender inequalities similar to those found in the rest of the population. Thus, a minority of migrant entrepreneurs, almost all of them men, are able to earn incomes of tens of thousands of yuan a month, several times higher than the average urban income. They and their families are still affected by the household registration system in some ways, especially in relation to their children's education and future life chances (ibid., 44–46). However, through conspicuous consumption, they are able to craft new identities and a relatively high status for themselves. As one Wenzhou migrant woman commented to Zhang Li:

> Look at those arrogant Beijing *xiaojie* [ladies]—they work in state-owned units but make little money. They cannot even afford to go to expensive restaurants or to shop at Saite and Guomao [the International Trade Center Mall] as we do. How can they be so proud? Just for the piece of *hukou* paper? . . . Don't they realize that today's society belongs to those of us who have money? As long as we have money, Beijing is the place for us. (ibid., 44)

At the other end of the scale, in Beijing in the mid- to late 1990s, the lowest-paid work engaged in by men—garbage picking and reselling—earned between 400 and 600 yuan per month, usually with accomodation provided (Feng 1997, 59–60). In a similar period, most *dagongmei* who had been in Beijing for a while, including the majority of my interlocutors in the Migrant Women's Club, earned a monthly income of between 200 and 600 yuan.[27] This included women working as domestic workers, whose wages were generally the lowest, but covered room and board;[28] and cleaners and factory workers, who generally earned a little more and were also provided with free accommodation, but who paid something like 150 yuan each month for food. In one large company, several cleaners that I got to know in 2002 earned a monthly wage of about 400 yuan, including bonuses. Other *dagongmei* that I knew earned higher wages than this but had to pay for both food and rental accommodation, the latter usually costing them at least 50 yuan each month.[29] Most of my interlocutors in the Migrant Women's Club had little or nothing in the way of personal savings. Practice with regard to remittances varied enormously—some women remitted one or two hundred yuan each month, while some remitted this much every two or three months. Others remitted nothing at all.

In this period, some *dagongmei*, particularly those newly arrived or just starting in a job, earned less than 200 yuan a month and had great difficulty making ends meet in Beijing, let alone saving or remitting any money.[30] Indeed, in my 2000 survey of the Migrant Women's Club about 29 percent of respondents indicated that in their first month in Beijing their income was 200 yuan or less. Another 53 percent indicated that their income was 201–400 yuan.

In the migrant settlement that I visited in Haidian in 2001, most families earned a total of about 1,000 yuan a month, although the nature of the business they were involved in was such that the amount they could earn was unpredictable and varied from one month to another. In the mid- to late 1990s, many of these families had earned more than 1,000 yuan a month, but more recently had fallen on hard times. During the earlier period they had been able to remit a significant amount of money home (to the husband's family) and with this money, supplemented with money borrowed from relatives or friends, most had built houses in the husband's village, at a cost of 20,000–40,000 yuan. In the early 2000s some of the families in Haidian who had previously earned a living selling vegetables had their market stalls demolished or were forced to give them up because their income was not enough to cover the cost of the fees levied on the stalls. Other men, who were self-employed—for example renovating apartments—similarly found that business opportunities constricted. With a lower income, these families remitted less money, if any at all, were unable to repay debts they had incurred in building a house or in setting up business in Beijing, and were anxious about their ability to make ends meet in the city. In 2001 rent in this area was between 200 and 300 yuan a month. On top of this, families spent between 400 and 600 yuan each month on food and other essentials and, in most cases, at least another 60 yuan in school fees per child per month.[31]

Health

In several families that I visited in Haidian, one or more adults suffered from stomach problems and/or what they termed neurasthenia (*shenjing shuairuo*). I am not able to pinpoint the precise causes of these problems, but my interlocutors themselves made a clear link between their medical problems and the poverty and stress that had characterized their lives in both the countryside and in Beijing. As one woman explained, "It's probably to do with the pressures of life [*shenghuo yali*]: our bodies are weak, we get tired easily, the pressure of thinking is great and in the evening you can't sleep, and it goes on like that till you get neurasthenia."[32]

The prevalence of this and other forms of ill health is compounded by the fact that migrants, who usually earn low incomes and do not receive medical or other insurance, often cannot afford the treatment they need for medical problems. Chunzi, who suffered complications during childbirth resulting in partial paralysis and debilitating weakness, had to rely on borrowed money to pay for vital medical treatment. Two years later her condition was still serious, but she no longer had the money for hospital stays or for anything more than intermittent treatment.

For migrant women, lack of maternal health and family planning education and services, and the poor quality-medical facilities that they often resort to, pose yet another threat to health. Women with urban Beijing *hukou* either work in enterprises that provide them with medical insurance, family planning education and services, including the provision of contraception, or come under the jurisdiction of a residential committee that provides services and education in family planning. In contrast, although the state is enormously concerned with the reproductive activities of migrants, and its regulation and surveillance of migrant women in this regard is particularly harsh, the vast majority of employers and of residential committees does not consider it their duty to provide either family planning education or services to migrant women. According to one study, only 22.5 percent of the 604 migrant women surveyed in Beijing received maternal health and family planning education, compared to 100 percent of urban residents (Wang Y., et al. 1999, cited in Zheng et al. 2001, 119).

Unplanned pregnancy is common among migrant women, especially those who are unmarried. Premarital sexual activity has increased among both rural and urban youth since the 1990s.[33] The use of contraception among unmarried migrant couples, however, is strikingly low. A survey of urban spouses-to-be found that among those who admitted to premarital sex, 85 percent said they used contraception (Zhang J., et al. 1996, cited in ibid., 123). However, according to another study[34] most premarital sex among migrants is unprotected—a finding that has potentially alarming consequences for the spread of sexually transmitted diseases. The researchers explained this finding in terms of a combination of ignorance and other factors: some women were ignorant about contraception, while others did not use it because their boyfriends did not want them to. Some interviewees said they did not try to obtain contraception from family planning service stations because such stations catered only to married, urban women. They did not buy it elsewhere, either because they did not know that the pill and condoms are widely available in shops or because they did not want to spend their hard-earned wages on such things, or because they were too embarrassed to do so. Most interviewees in the study said that premarital pregnancy would cause a couple and their parents to lose face if others in the village found out. So a woman's only choice in such circumstances was to get married before the baby was due or have an abortion (ibid., 2001).

Among migrant women who have abortions and those who give birth, many do so with the help of unlicensed, illegal medical practitioners and facilities. According to concerned deputies to the Guangzhou Municipal People's Congress, it was for this reason that, in 2000, 76.9 percent of maternal mortalities in Guangzhou occurred among migrant women. The deputies attributed migrant women's use of unlicensed medical facilities to the fact that they were poor and "had a weaker sense of self-protection." Unfortunately, they failed to appreciate that, aside from the expense involved, these women may not have gone to licensed medical practitioners because they had not conformed with family planning rules and were, therefore, likely to be barred from using licensed facilities, and/or would be reported to the authorities and subsequently fined and deported from the city (HRIC 2002b, 106–7).

Marriage and Children

Only a minority of migrant women are married and living in the city with their husbands and children. One of the reasons for this is that it is difficult for already married migrant women with children to find work in the city that can be juggled with child care and that can contribute enough to the family finances such that they can all afford to live in the city. Among married rural couples with children, therefore, it is more common for the children to be left at home with one parent (usually, but not always, the mother) or other relatives, while the parent(s) migrate to the city in search of work. In addition, it is relatively rare for single migrant women to marry while in the city and to remain living there. Some migrant women do marry migrant men, but then they usually return to their husbands' village, at least for a time. It is much rarer for migrant women to marry urban men. This is not necessarily because they do not want to—as Chunzi indicates, marriage to an urbanite is considered by many to be a very lucky thing indeed. However, it is a dream that few can realize. Most urban men are reluctant to marry rural migrant women because their social status is much lower and because, as mentioned, children's life chances are diminished if their mother does not have local, urban *hukou*.

There are, nevertheless, hundreds of thousands of married migrants with young children in cities such as Beijing. Indeed, in Beijing in 2001 there were 246,000 migrant children aged under fourteen (Beijingshi Tongjiju, 2002). Education for this large group of children is a serious problem. In 1986 China enacted the Compulsory Education Law, according to which all citizens have equal rights to nine years of compulsory education, starting at the age of six or seven (HRIC 2002a, 18). Under this law, all school-age children must enroll in a school near to where they live and local officials must assume the responsibility of educating them (ibid., 19). Despite this, up until 1996, most migrant children were refused permission to enroll in urban state schools, responsibility for their education being seen to lie with the governments of their home counties rather than with those in their areas of destination (ibid., 7).

After 1996 the state tried to improve the opportunities for migrant children to receive compulsory education (see ibid., 19–23), but in Beijing in the early 2000s it remained the case that very few migrant children were enrolled in urban state schools. This was largely because local urban governments wanted to deter migrant families from settling in the area and because state schools did not wish to enroll nonlocal students, because they were not funded for such students. For these reasons, most state schools either continued not to permit entry to children who did not have local *hukou* or charged them exorbitant "temporary schooling fees" (*jiedu fei*) and "donation fees" (*zanzhu fei*), on top of the numerous unofficial fees that had become the norm for all school children (ibid., 7).[35] Despite all children's legal entitlement to nine years of free education, in Fengtai District in 2000, both local and migrant primary school children were charged 300 yuan per semester in tuition fees, and migrant children also had to pay a "temporary schooling fee" of 1,200 yuan per year, reduced to 600 yuan in 2001. Fees at state secondary schools were even higher—one source claims that Beijing secondary schools charged nonlocal students anywhere from 10,000 to 30,000 yuan for annual "donation fees" (ibid., 26–27). These fees were well beyond the means of most migrant families.

Large numbers of migrant children have been enrolled in private schools run solely for them, mostly by migrants. By the end of 2000 there were between 200 and 300 such schools in Beijing, most of them primary schools, catering for somewhere between 30,000 and 40,000 migrant children (ibid., 16). However, the great majority of these schools were unregistered with the state. This meant that they did not receive state funding and the qualifications they offered were not officially recognized. Conditions in these schools were poor and the teaching they offered was often substandard because they did not have the resources to attract good-quality teachers. In the migrant settlement in Haidian, the conditions of the migrant primary school to which most of my interlocutors sent their children were, according to my migrant friends, on a par with those back home in the countryside. In 2001 the school enrolled approximately 300 children, at a cost to each child of 300 yuan per semester, a rate similar to most other migrant schools (Han Jialing 2002, 271). It was housed in a set of rough brick buildings around a square dirt yard. There were no toilets and no play equipment. Inside the classrooms, the paint on the walls was peeling and all the desks were old and broken. This was light-years away from the bright, clean rooms and modern facilities of the kindergarten catering for the children of Peking University employees that my son attended.[36]

Through the 1990s and early 2000s, instead of increasing migrant children's access to state schools or improving the facilities of the private schools they attended, the Beijing government periodically closed down the latter type of school. In 2001, for example, the Fengtai District government closed down fifty migrant schools without providing alternative schooling to the children affected, the stated aim being to "clear out low quality people" (HRIC 2002a, 4).

Conclusion

In this chapter I have outlined the regulatory regime based on the household registration system that governs migrants in Beijing and have discussed the specific ways in which this regulatory regime underpins practices through which migrants are made to feel both "put in their place" and "out of place" in all aspects of life in the city.

In the case of migrant women, the marginality and discrimination they suffer as rural outsiders is compounded by their inferior gender status. Thus, migrant women are concentrated in occupations in which they earn not just less than urbanites but also less than migrant men, and they are subject to invasive regulation and surveillance of their reproductive activities, and sexual harassment and violence, as well as to the other forms of regulation and violence suffered by migrant men. For these subjects, both geographical and social place contribute to, and are the result of, the complementarities and mutual reinforcements that occur between the household registration system and power differentials between rural and urban, outsider and local, high- and low-status occupations, employer and employee, male and female, and, in some cases, youth and adult.

This is perhaps most readily apparent in the case of maids. To summarize: domestic service has a very low status, in great measure because of its location in the "private" sphere. For this reason few urban women take jobs as maids, and there is, thus, a high demand for rural female migrants to take on such work. Young, single migrant women, newly arriving in the city, are particularly motivated to take such jobs because of the difficulties they have in finding alternative employment and housing—difficulties that arise from the fact that the household registration system underwrites a regime in which migrants have access to only a limited range of occupations and to housing that is limited in availability, poor in quality, and mostly very expensive. There is also a perception that such work is appropriate to young women because of its location in the private sphere. Ironically, however, this very location in the private sphere leaves maids vulnerable to exploitation, harassment, and violence, including sexual violence, from their employers. The potential for such violence and harassment is relatively high because of the inequality in status between young, female maids, whose occupation has associations with domestic slavery and their older, male (and female) employers. It is also compounded by rural/urban inequalities, meaning that the gap in status between a rural maid and her urban employer is even higher than it is in the case of an urban woman working as a maid.

In this chapter I have outlined the regulatory institutions and practices that governed the lives of migrants in Beijing from the late 1990s to the early 2000s. Since the year 2000 the central state has attempted to introduce some reforms to the treatment of migrants in urban areas. This is largely as a result of a shift in top-level official attitudes, discussed in chapter 1, toward a recognition of the importance of opening the urban labor market in order to absorb labor made "surplus" to agriculture, an issue of major concern in the late 1990s, which became yet more pressing as a result of China's accession to the World Trade Organization (WTO) in 2001. Additional motivation for the reforms has come from rural riots, escalating conflicts between migrant factory workers and their employers, and growing pressure from scholars and social activists both within China and overseas, to improve the human rights situation of rural migrants.

In 2001 the State Council announced that all towns and small cities with a population of less than 100,000 should grant local urban registration to those with stable employment and residence in the city (Jacka and Gaetano 2004, 19). Since that time, a number of large cities also have announced reforms to household registration rules. In the majority of large cities, including Beijing, however, local governments have not really loosened the household registration system overall. Instead, they have moved closer to a dual regime similar to that imposed by many national governments on overseas immigrants, whereby skilled or business migrants are encouraged to enter and settle in the city, but control, restriction, and surveillance of the majority of unskilled rural migrants is maintained, if not increased. In Beijing, for example, eligibility for urban registration has been limited to educated professionals, commercial home buyers, and entrepreneurs who have made a substantial investment in the city. At the same time, in June 2001, the Beijing government introduced a new categorization of temporary residence permits into grades A, B, and C. I was told by staff at a local police station that to obtain an A permit, a migrant had to have lived in Beijing for five years or more, and be married to a Beijing person, be a skilled worker, own a house in Beijing that cost 300,000 yuan or more, or have made an investment in Beijing of at least that much. In order to obtain a B permit you needed a certificate from a landlord or residence committee to show that you had lived in Beijing for more than one year, and C permits were for those who had lived in Beijing for one year or less. When I asked why migrants were now being divided into three categories they said: "If you've got an A permit it means you've been in Beijing a while without causing trouble, so the police don't have to worry about you. To a lesser extent that's also the case with B. But if you have a C category you're an unknown quantity, so we keep a stricter watch on people in that category."[37]

In 2001 and 2002, some provincial governments went so far as to announce the abolition of the legal distinction between agricultural and nonagricultural *hukou*. Nevertheless, they continued to register people as either local or temporary residents, with the same limitations on acquisition of permanent, local residency status applying. Furthermore, in mid-2002 the central government ordered a stop to the removal of the rural/urban distinction (Wang, Fei-ling 2004, 121).

In 2002 the State Council issued statements urging that migrants be encouraged to move to urban areas and that they be treated reasonably and without bias. In January 2003 a new State Council decree brought together and augmented these previous calls for reform, presenting the strongest case for the abolition of discrimination against migrant workers the central state had made to date. Like earlier statements, this document emphasizes the importance of rural to urban migration for the absorption of rural surplus labor and for economic and social development. It also repeats the slogan of "fair treatment, reasonable guidance, improvement of management, and better service" that the State Council had raised in its statements in 2002. The decree lists several specific measures aimed at overcoming the problems faced by migrants. These include, first, the abolition of restrictions on the type of jobs in which they may be employed, the charging of extra fees, and repatriation by administrative means. Second, the document says that proper legal procedures are to be followed in the employment of rural workers, including contracts and on-time payment of wages. Third, there is to be an improvement in occupational health and safety, in the provision of insurance for migrant workers, and in the hygiene of migrant places of residence. Fourth, rural migrants are to be provided with technical and legal training on a voluntary basis and at reasonable cost. And fifth, compulsory education is to be guaranteed for all migrant children and the cost and quality of education available to them is to be improved (Guowuyuan Bangongting 2003). In June 2003 the State Council instituted a further change in state policy toward migrants, announcing that police would no longer have the power to detain and repatriate rural migrants and calling for the restructuring of existing detention centers to improve humanitarian relief to vagrants, beggars, and the homeless. These measures were taken in response to public outcry and petitioning by legal scholars occasioned by the beating and subsequent death in custody of a university graduate, who had been detained by police in Guangzhou for failing to produce a temporary residence permit (Kwan 2003).

Whether local governments will implement the central state's new policies, or how long they will take to do so, remains to be seen—they have previously been very tardy in introducing reforms in this area. As of late 2004, there had been no substantial improvement in the situation of migrants.[38] Furthermore, while the State Council's 2002 and 2003 statements signal a fundamental shift in attitude, we have yet to see a concomitant change in the institutions most basic to the maintenance of rural migrants' second-class citizenship: The household registration system, with its distinction between rural and urban citizens, and permanent and temporary residents, remains, as does the requirement for city-bound migrants to obtain temporary residence permits and a raft of other documents. In addition, urban state schools are not funded for migrant children, and government programs providing subsidies for the urban poor and welfare support and retraining programs for the laid-off and unemployed do not include migrants.

In discussing their experiences in Beijing with me, migrant women almost always emphasized marginalization, discrimination, and disadvantage, which they attributed primarily to the household registration system.[39] In this chapter my main concern has been to explain the causes of those experiences. However, my interlocutors did also speak of positive aspects of their present situation in the city and, when discussing the future, most said they would rather stay in the city than return to the countryside. This will be discussed in the next chapter.

4

The Place of Desire

Wang Lan: I came to Beijing in 1995. My home is in Shaanxi. I'm twenty-two this year . . . When I first came to Beijing, my single aim was [pause], that is to say, at home I really wanted to go to school, but my family was very poor. So I thought if I could come out, I'd have an opportunity to study—it was just for that aim that I came. . . .

Tamara Jacka: You've been here such a long time. Do you feel you now count as a city person?

Wang Lan: No, I'm still not a city person. I face a lot of suffering. My future—at the moment I have nothing. This city has given me an opportunity only to solve my problems of food and clothing, my survival. But I feel my future is very hazy. So I don't feel like I belong in this city. And in this city I receive a lot of discrimination, a lot of unfair treatment. In the eyes of these people, outsiders are contemptible. . . .

Tamara Jacka: Do you want to stay here long term or do you think you'll go home?

Wang Lan: I really like this city, so I'd very much like to stay here long term. There are a lot of opportunities here. At home—my mum, that generation—they get married, have kids, die. That's their whole life—they're very poor, they just work in the fields and they have absolutely no status—they're just housewives. So now my ideal, my goal, is to use my opportunities here to develop and give full play to my own worth—I want to continually study and perfect myself, so that I can become part of the city as fast as possible. Now China has already entered the world,[1] so it's in contact with the whole world. Here I can see the culture and history of the whole world. I really want to develop myself and I can do that here. Even though Beijing has given me a lot of pain and lots of bad impressions, on the whole people mature through struggle. (November 2001)

One of the first things that struck me about migrant women's narratives was the variety of evaluations of place presented, not just by different women, but also by the same individuals. We could understand this as resulting from a failure on the part of these women to fully comprehend reality, or from a confusion about who they "really" are and what their interests are. However, I suggest that it is more productive to think in terms of conflicts and contradictions within narratives as indicating that, in fact, subjects are not singular identities for whom we can determine objective sets of interests. Rather, subjects are series of different positionings with respect to the various discourses circulating in society, these different positionings involving different experiences and desires. In this chapter, my aim is first to identify the evaluations and desires about place most frequently articulated in migrant women's narratives, and then to explain these different evaluations and desires in terms of the discourses and discursive positions from which they arise.

In this chapter I concentrate on elucidating static images of the countryside and the city contained in migrant women's narratives and do not delve into their understandings of the *temporal* aspects of finding a place in the world—that is, of the ways in which the countryside, the city, and the movement between the two fit into the life course. This latter issue will be discussed in chapter 7 in relation to experiences and perceptions of time. However, time also plays a role in this chapter, for one of the key factors in shaping different representations of place is the temporal context in which it is discussed. For example, the same person might characterize her home life in the village as being one of boredom, in response to a question from me about her motivations for leaving, while also describing it with a great deal of nostalgia when reflecting upon the past, but with dread when discussing the future.

The chapter is divided into three sections. The first examines images of country and city in migrant women's reflections on their pasts in the countryside, the second discusses the reasons they give for migrating to the city, and the final section analyzes migrant women's perceptions of city and country as places in which to live in the future and the long term.

The Place Left Behind

Tamara Jacka: Tell me about the house you lived in when you were young.

Zhou Ling: [Suddenly animated] Oh, it was such a decrepit broken-down house! When I was small I cared very much about face. The house was on a main road. I don't know when it was built—it was very old. . . . When there was a strong wind—and the typhoons reached us there in Jiangsu—I'd be really scared that the wind would knock the house down, and when there was a lot of rain the water would leak in and we'd have to get out all our pots and pans to catch the rain. . . . Our house was on the way to school, and students would go back and forth every day past our door. I felt very embarrassed about going into our decrepit old house. I was afraid my classmates would laugh at me for living in such a decrepit house. This house always weighed on me. . . . Because of poverty, people around you, including your relatives, would discriminate against you. When I was little I wasn't that lively, because there was always a kind of pressure on me, because my family was always worried. So, even though I was small I was probably rather sensitive. I wasn't a very lively or open child. And it was probably because I didn't talk much that people could say I was simple-minded. I didn't endear myself to others. Even when I was at school I felt that the teachers didn't like me because I didn't have any nice clothes to wear, my family was poor, and I didn't like to talk much. Probably I wasn't very cheerful. After I left home, I had no nostalgia [*liulian*] for my family whatsoever. There was nothing in my childhood to be nostalgic about. . . . So, my leaving home was connected to some of the things that happened to me when I was small. The relationship is very strong. What's more, after I left home I suffered so many hardships, but I never once thought of going home. The poverty and the discrimination I received really affected my character and had a strong effect on the road I chose to take. (August 2001)

Zhou Ling's narrative conveys certain experiences of the countryside that are very common among migrant women. At the same time, however, this narrative is unusual in its detailed description of place and in the degree of bitterness with which its telling was invested—a bitterness that is informed both by her own personal circumstances and by a high degree of sensitivity to, and articulateness about, the dilemmas faced by rural migrants as a collective. In the paragraphs that follow, I first discuss the commonalities among discussions of life in the countryside prior to migration in the narratives of Zhou Ling and other migrant women. I then look at the more unusual aspects of Zhou Ling's narrative, using a comparison between it and the accounts of other migrant women to indicate the range of experiences and understandings that different women have of the place they have left behind and to try to understand the ways in which these women's different representations relate to, and engage with, dominant discourses on rural/urban difference.

Among both the members of the Migrant Women's Club and the migrant women in Haidian, the great majority made reference to economic difficulties in their families in the countryside prior to migration and the limitations that poverty placed upon their lives. There were, however, some differences between reflections of life in the countryside as it was in the 1960s and 1970s and those of life in the countryside in the reform era of the 1980s and 1990s. Women in their thirties, who included all my interlocutors in Haidian as well as Zhou Ling and a few others in the

Migrant Women's Club, commonly spoke of extreme poverty in their childhoods in the countryside in the 1960s and 1970s, by which I mean they said that they and their families did not have enough to eat. In reflections upon life in the countryside in the 1980s and 1990s, few said that they did not have enough to eat. The majority, nevertheless, spoke of "bitterness" and hardship (*ku, xinku*), and a number spoke of the humiliation of being poor. Han Haiying, who was born in 1966 in Hubei and came with her husband to live in Haidian in 1995, characterized her childhood as being full of suffering. When she was small, she said, "we had nothing. It's not nice to hear this, but we didn't eat properly." All the children in the village worked, she said, and in primary school there were no books. She left school after primary school. By the 1990s things had improved a little, but still, she said, "there's no cash expenditure at home, but you don't earn anything either. If you do things right you have enough to eat, otherwise you don't." Han Haiying explained that her husband came from an especially poor area and their family was even worse off than most. They had no money to pay their child's [primary] school fees, and so they migrated to Beijing in search of work. When they left they had to borrow, just to cover the cost of the bus fare, and their neighbors laughed at them. Other families were better off than they,

> but now they've all come out. At home, how do I put it, conditions in the countryside are lacking [*hen cha*] and on top of that you can't earn money. Our home county doesn't have any big enterprises and you can't earn anything trading. You depend on a bit of land and that basically isn't enough to support life. (August 2001)

In all instances, references to economic difficulties, the constraints they imposed, and attendant humiliations went hand in hand with unhappy reflections upon experiences of schooling or of the discontinuation of schooling. Education is a very important component of social status in China and, undoubtedly, my interlocutors' concern to explain the impact of poverty on their schooling stemmed in part from a sensitivity about their lack of education relative to urbanites in general and to myself in particular. In part, though, economic difficulties and schooling were linked with such frequency simply because attendance at school was one of the dominant experiences of life outside of the family for girls and therefore the sphere in which the social consequences of poverty were most obviously felt during childhood.

In addition, in China today, as has been the case for centuries, education is prized by rural families as a central, indeed often the only, route out of rural poverty (Kipnis 2001, 6). At the same time, though, limited finances mean that the education of many rural children is broken off earlier than they and their parents would ideally wish. Even in many areas where rural incomes have increased since the introduction of economic reforms in the 1980s, this has remained a problem because, with deplorably little in the way of either central state or local government funding, schools have charged individual families increasingly high fees. In poorer areas the problem is worse, because county governments have been less able, or less willing, to provide funds to maintain schools. Girls have been hardest hit, being most commonly withdrawn from schooling before boys because of patrilocal, exogamous marriage patterns, which mean that educating daughters is considered a poor investment because they are *feishui wailiu*—"fertilized water (that will) run into someone else's garden."[2]

In a few of the accounts given by older women who had grown up during the Cultural Revolution it was clear that the family's "bad class" background had exacerbated poverty, humiliation, and restrictions on schooling.[3] For many other women, including both those who grew up during the Cultural Revolution and those who grew up in the post-Mao period, a combination of sexism and large family size made life particularly tough.[4] Chunzi said that when she was growing up in the 1970s it was the norm in her home county for girls to discontinue their schooling after just a few years. Chunzi had two older brothers and one younger brother and her family was very poor. Her mother, though, made enormous sacrifices, selling her blood to keep all her children in school. Consequently, during her childhood Chunzi was the only girl in her village who went to secondary school. By the time she graduated from junior secondary school her oldest brother was at university. The financial burden of having all four children in school was so great that at home they did not have enough to eat—such poverty, Chunzi said, that she could not bear to recall it. So she decided not to continue her schooling, going to work in the fields instead. In contrast, all three of Chunzi's brothers continued school, eventually graduating from university.

Chunzi's family was unusual in terms of the lengths to which her mother went to keep her children in school and in terms of her brothers' educational achievements, but in other respects Chunzi's experiences in this area were typical of the members of the Migrant Women's Club with whom I talked. Most had left school after graduating from primary or junior secondary school, mostly voluntarily, but in the face of enormous pressure due to constraints on family finances and because of the understanding that it was not important for a daughter to receive an education. In hindsight, the majority of the women felt sad about this. This was the case as much with the younger women who grew up during the post-Mao period as it was for those, like Chunzi, who were children during the Cultural Revolution. Qiao Xue, for example, was born in 1981 and grew up in a village in Shaanxi. She has four older sisters, one younger sister, and a younger brother. Her parents, she said, were feudal and superstitious and cared more about males than females (*zhong nan qing nü*), and so kept trying for a son. Other villagers made comments about her family because "they thought we had too many children. They had particularly low regard for girls." She left for Beijing at the age of sixteen, before finishing junior secondary school, because the family could not afford to continue her education.[5]

The above accounts give a sense of some of the hardships that were common to my interlocutors' experiences of home in the village. They will probably come as no surprise, for they accord closely with, and provide backing for, what is the dominant understanding of life in the Chinese countryside, especially in the past, in both the Western and the urban Chinese imagination—that is, of poverty, a cruel struggle for survival and dignity, and discrimination against girls. They confirm discourses, discussed in chapter 1, in which the countryside is cast as the primitive, backward "other" of the modern city.

It is important to contextualize this, however. In Haidian, most of my interlocutors emphasized the negative in their discussions of their past in the countryside, but they were negative about their present circumstances in the city too. Life for these women was one of poverty and struggle, both in the past and the present, the country and the city. Some women, however, did express nostalgia for the past. For example, when I asked Jin Rong, a thirty-eight-year-old from Hebei, to compare the present with the past she said:

In the past living conditions weren't quite as good, but there was freedom. Now, with two children, I'm forever worrying about how to manage. There's really no freedom. Now if you want to study something or do something [pause] but the children aren't grown up yet. You have to think how to manage that.

In response to my request to tell me about her childhood, Jin Rong also said:

I was born in 1963, so what I remember is the Cultural Revolution. . . . During the Cultural Revolution it was a lot of fun. At school we sang and danced all day. There were a lot of performances. . . . At that time we'd go to the county town to sing and dance. We sang all the way from primary school to senior high. (August 2001)

Members of the Migrant Women's Club frequently mentioned hardship and suffering, but these were usually not *dominant* elements in discussions of the past in the countryside. Indeed, the detail and emotion invested in Zhou Ling's account of her family's low status and poverty are unparalleled in the narratives of other members of the Migrant Women's Club. Even when Chunzi talked about her childhood, her focus was not on the hardships that her family endured. Rather, she focused on her love for her mother, who, she felt, had made heroic self-sacrifices on her children's behalf, and she emphasized her own efforts to improve her fate despite her family's poverty (see chapter 7 for further discussion).

The majority of the members of the Migrant Women's Club with whom I talked, including those who mentioned hardships, reflected positively on life at home in the countryside in the context of their past. Typically, they remarked that as children their lives had been happier and more carefree than they were at present. For example, Qiao Xue, quoted above, who complained about poverty and gender discrimination in the village where she grew up, nevertheless said:

> I was happier then [as a child]. Even though I didn't have anything much good to eat or good clothes to wear because there were so many children, I still feel that I was happier then than now. I didn't have to think about anything. (August 2001)

Expressions of homesickness and nostalgia were common, especially among younger women who had been in the city for a relatively short time, and among those who had left a spouse and children behind in the countryside. For example, Ma Hua, a twenty-eight-year-old woman from Guizhou, left her husband and one-year-old child to come to Beijing three years previously. At first, she said, she found living in Beijing extremely difficult because her separation from her family caused her much pain, she found her work as a cleaner very tiring, she did not understand things in Beijing and found Beijing people unpleasant (October 2001).

Gao Xinran, a twenty-one-year-old from Hebei, had been in Beijing only three months when I met her. Already engaged to a man in her home county, she had postponed her wedding and come to Beijing against the wishes of both her own parents and those of her fiancé, in what she herself characterized as a desperate last-ditch effort to experience a little freedom before marriage closed in upon her. She was, however, highly aware of the contempt with which she and her fellow "outsiders" were viewed by Beijingers and of the ways in which the company at which she worked as a cleaner exploited its migrant workforce. She was very lonely and missed home terribly. Life in the countryside was more comfortable and relaxed than in the city, she said. When I said "but farming is hard and full of suffering [*xinku*] isn't it?" she countered that during the busy season it was, but that otherwise one was free to arrange one's own time. She also said that the city was very *luan,* meaning chaotic and unsafe, the air in Beijing was bad, and living conditions were cramped. Furthermore, she said, country people were warm, whereas city people were cold and they looked down on others (December 2002).

In light of the anxieties, loneliness, insecurity, and hardships that they suffered in the city, *dagongmei* such as these looked back on their childhoods in the countryside as being of carefree happiness and freedom, located in a set of intimate and harmonious family relationships, in a place of space, safety, and tranquility, where life proceeded at a relaxed pace and villagers treated each other warmly and with respect. This image of rural life contrasts sharply with that conveyed in Zhou Ling's narrative. It also contrasts with numerous journalist, academic, and official reports of life in the countryside that document gross inequalities, severe poverty, and underdevelopment in some areas, high levels of suicide, especially among young women, and alarming and rising levels of violent conflict, directed both at local officials accused of corruption and injustice, and against other villagers (Unger 2002, 171–222; Jiang 2004). In nostalgic *dagongmei* narratives these difficulties are subsumed by a focus on the hardships and alienation suffered in the city, and a subsequent idealization of the past and of the countryside.

Such expressions of nostalgia for home, for the countryside, and for the past are, of course, not unique. On the contrary, nostalgia is everywhere a common response to dislocation. Nostalgia for the past and for a home village in the countryside (*guxiang*) has been a powerful thread in modern Chinese literature, exemplified in the 1930s "native soil" fiction of Lu Xun and Shen Congwen and in the contemporary "search for roots" fiction of writers such as Han Shaogong, Gu Hua, and Mo Yan.[6] In addition, several scholars have noted a rise of other kinds of nostalgia in Chinese popular culture since the late 1980s.[7] As Wang Ban notes,

> nostalgia has seeped into many departments of cultural production and threatens to become a general structure of feeling. . . . The consequences of modernity as a process of rationally restructuring society in one decade brutalize consciousness and daily life with violence and anxiety. . . . All of a sudden the pre-Revolutionary times and even Mao's years are glowing in their simplicity and solidarity, in their inexhaustible hopes and common destiny, their poverty and cruelty conveniently forgotten. (Wang, Ban 2002, 670)

Migrant women's nostalgic narratives both draw on, and contribute to, this general structure of feeling.

Apart from maintaining an image of the past and childhood as carefree and secure in contrast to the troubles of the present, and of the countryside as peaceful and safe in contrast to the dangers of the city, the association or conflation in nostalgic *dagongmei* narratives between the countryside, childhood, and the past in itself has important discursive effects. First, while these narratives express a yearning for the countryside of one's past, they also suggest an understanding of the countryside *as* the past; as a place and a period in one's life that one has lost or left behind. This is at the individual, personal level. At the social level, this conflation of the countryside with the past tends to reinforce the "denial of coevalness" discussed in chapter 1—the understanding that the countryside and its inhabitants belong to the past that modernity has left behind. Second, the association between childhood and the countryside that is apparent in so many of these narratives reinforces the notion, often conveyed in dominant discourse, that the countryside is a place of innocence and country people are like children—simple and naive. The city, in contrast, is a place of trouble, but also of more "adult" sophistication. Just as children must grow up into adults—and indeed as part of this maturing process—the countryside must be left behind for the city.

These particular understandings of time and place are often quite explicitly articulated in nostalgic *dagongmei* narratives, and in other cases they can be readily interpreted. It is noteworthy, for example, that among the many women I talked to who were nostalgic about the countryside, very few expressed a desire to return there. Furthermore, I have encountered very few expressions of pride in the home village among migrant women, nor have I heard of any sustained effort on the part of the members of the Migrant Women's Club to preserve or share memories, or to maintain aspects of village life or native-place culture in the city. Thus, while many of the Club's members were interested in photography, and often shared with me and with one another photographs that they had taken at tourist sites around Beijing, they very rarely showed photographs of themselves or others in their family or village and did not display such photographs in their living space. This suggests an orientation very different from that of overseas immigrants for whom the preservation and observance of home traditions is often central to the maintenance of community and individual identities (see, for example, Ralston 1992; Werbner 1996). It is also somewhat surprising, given the common assumption that Chinese migrants strongly identify with native place. As I will discuss in the next chapter, networks among people from the same region in China are important to migrants looking for employment and housing. However, such networks are not maintained through shared cultural activities.

Rather than conveying pride or enthusiasm for their home village, when members of the Migrant Women's Club expressed nostalgia or a longing for home it was most commonly in order to highlight the hardships and dislocation they suffered in the city. Furthermore, the homesickness itself was represented as a weakness. For example, Ma Hua, whom I cited above as being extremely homesick, nevertheless said that she had learned to put up with the suffering. If you come out to work, she said, you have to expect to suffer, so from now on she would not complain about missing home or about working hard or getting tired (October 2001). Numerous other women said that most of the fellow villagers with whom they had originally migrated had missed home so much that they had been unable to bear it and had returned to the village shortly afterward. These women presented themselves as superior to their "sisters" by saying that while they too missed home, they felt that they would lose face by returning empty-handed after such a short while, and so they had stayed on.

Through the 1990s, *Rural Women* published numerous migrant stories that were nostalgic about the countryside (see, for example, Chen Aizhen 1994; Cai Peng 1994; Zhang Shenhong 1996; Mian 2004; Zhou, Rencong 2004). Some of these combined a rose-tinted view of childhood in the countryside with a representation of migration to the city as a process of maturation. These convey, even more powerfully and directly than do oral narratives, the sense that the countryside is the place of childhood and of children, and that it must be left behind.

An autobiographical account of migration to Beijing, written by Mian Xiaohong, a long-time member of the Migrant Women's Club, is a good example. At the

THE PLACE OF DESIRE   127

beginning of her story, Mian identifies herself and her fellow villagers before migration as "newborn calves," carefree and ignorant of the outside world. Later in her account, nostalgia for home in the village in response to the hardships of work in the city is expressed in a passage that also very firmly puts the rural home in the past, and that makes a clear identification of the narrator's past, rural self as being that of a child. "At home in the village," she says, "I was never aware of this thing called time. I was naive and innocent then, living without a care. Time went by like a light breeze. But now the wings of happiness had been clipped, and time was like a net that trapped me." Yet further into the story, the passage most nostalgic about home in the countryside is closely followed by one that links it once more with childhood, and places it firmly in the past. Thus, upon return to the village after a difficult short period in Beijing, Mian says, "From the hills of our hometown I looked down at the smoke curling up against the sunset. The red sun was like a balloon sitting on the mountains opposite, and it was so peaceful and quiet." However, a few sentences later she says, "Having been to Beijing, my closed world had been opened, and I could not be confined again. What's more, having been to Beijing, I could never return to my original carefree, naive and innocent state." In the remainder of the story, her experiences working in Beijing are portrayed as a form of maturation—a "painful process of awakening" through which she learns to find her way around and is taught some technical skills, "lifts the veil on the mysteries of society," "sees the true face of people from all walks of life," and comes to a new understanding of herself. In the final paragraph, this personal experience of maturation is then transformed into a social movement of development and liberation; a movement that is simultaneously one away from the countryside toward the city, and also out of the past and into the future: "Peasants who've been locked away for thousands of years, at long last have the opportunity to go to the outside world. Through struggle and hard work they are changing their lives. Reality has proven that we were right in having stepped forth" (Mian 2004).

Not all nostalgic *dagongmei* narratives express as clearly as does Mian Xiaohong's the notion that the countryside belongs to childhood and to the past and that leaving it behind is a necessary component of both personal and social progress. In fact, while almost all the oral narratives from members of the Migrant Women's Club that expressed nostalgia for the countryside nevertheless also expressed the desire to leave it behind and remain in the city in the future, only about half of the numerous nostalgic narratives published in *Rural Women* during the 1990s expressed this desire. In the other half, accounts of nostalgia and homesickness are used to convey quite different messages. For example, Chen Aizhen begins her narrative by writing: "I returned to my home village [*guxiang*] once more and breathed in the smell of the earth, and I finally realized: I always have and always will belong to this patch of yellow earth." Later, she writes:

Although my city life was rich and colorful, whenever I had spare time a picture of my mother and father, my stooped grandmother, and my brother and sister hard at work would slowly unfurl in my mind. . . . Last year the factory office gave me time off to go and see my family, and I went back to the home village I had been separated from for two years. When I walked on my native soil I cried, I cried deeply. The outside world and the bustling city are so distant and strange to me—it is only my native land, my native soil, that is real and close to me. I have always truly belonged in my home village after all. Home village, even though I have had to leave you again, I will return for certain. After my contract is up I will definitely return and make you into a place where "the land is oh so fertile and the water is oh so beautiful." (Chen Aizhen 1994)

One cannot say that this narrative expresses or reflects an understanding on the part of the author of the countryside as the past and the city as the future. On the contrary, I would argue that the reason this account, and others like it, was published in *Rural Women* was the perception on the part of the journal editors that nostalgia was being put to work in support of the dominant state position at the time that, while their sojourn in the city was valuable to themselves and to society and the economy, migrant women's futures ultimately lay back in the countryside.

All the same and despite the explicit, surface claim as to the desirability of making the countryside the place of the future, Chen's narrative is like Mian Xiaohong's in actually reinforcing associations between the countryside and the past. Thus, like Mian's, Chen's descriptions of her village home link it with the past, with childhood and family, and with hard work. This contrasts with the description of the city to which she has moved as a place of bustle and color. The pull on Chen to return home comes primarily from the notion that that is where she belongs; a claim that appears more as a reaction to a sense of failure at overcoming her feeling of alienation in the city than to anything else. This is combined in the last line with the suggestion that if she returns home she might be able to make that "home" a better place. The appeal to return to the village then comes from the claim that that is where a rural woman belongs, combined with an appeal to individual self-sacrifice to a greater, patriotic cause; an appeal that is reinforced by Chen's usage of the terms "yellow earth" (*huang tudi*) and home village (*guxiang*). These are powerful clichés in Chinese culture, connoting Chinese tradition, the essence of Chinese national identity, and a sense of belonging to the fatherland.[8] The appeal to return to the countryside does not come from any claim that it is a better or more desirable place to be, or that a rural woman will have a better life in the countryside than in the city. Ironically, in fact, Mian Xiaohong's narrative conveys a far more positive image of the countryside as a place to live than does Chen's brief description of her home village as a "patch of yellow earth" and, by implication in the last line, as a place that is (at present) neither fertile nor beautiful.

This combination of a claim that rural women belong in the countryside and a call to self-sacrifice, with a failure to represent the countryside as a desirable place in which to live, is characteristic of appeals to migrants to return to the countryside after a brief sojourn in the city, whether those appeals are expressed in migrants' own stories or made more directly in official pronouncements. It is a combination that reflects, first, a tragic failure on the part of the state to take concrete steps to make the countryside a more desirable place to live by successfully addressing severe social and economic inequalities, poverty, rampant official corruption, and high levels of discontent among villagers. Second, it could be argued that this combination reflects a high degree of coercion, hypocrisy and discrimination in the call made by urban elites for migrants to return to the land. This latter point was brought home to me most dramatically by Zhou Ling, whose explicit anti-nostalgia was clearly informed by a recognition of the ways in which nostalgia has been employed by others to argue that rural women belong in the countryside. Zhou Ling was bitterly critical of the argument made by Xie Lihua and other urbanites that rural migrant women should return to the countryside after a brief sojourn in the city:

Why should we [rural migrants] go back to the countryside? If the countryside needs developing, why don't they go there themselves? Why don't they send their children to the countryside instead of to America? . . . During the Cultural Revolution urbanites felt that being sent to the countryside was a kind of exile; but what about rural people, having to endure the same kind of exile for their whole life, generation after generation? (August 2001)

Finding a Life

Tamara Jacka: Why did you come to Beijing?

Han Haiying: [With a short laugh] Life is too bitter in the countryside. (Haidian, August 2001)

My clash with my mother came from the so-called "important event in my life" [that is, marriage]. The custom of "Marry a chicken, follow a chicken; marry a dog, follow a dog" was to me like a huge black net in which all my dreams and aspirations would be swallowed up. There had been enough tragedy amongst the women around me, including the suicide of Auntie Yinxing, who cared for me when I was young. I had always considered myself no ordinary person. I was a girl with some ideas and some know-how, already rewarded for years of struggle with the fortune of publishing a collection of short stories called *Bamboo Walls*. . . . But I was still just a twenty-four-year-old woman with rural household registration in a remote mountain village. In the countryside, I should long ago have become someone's wife or mother. But I didn't want that. When my mother lost patience and gave me an ultimatum, I couldn't go along with it, but I could also no longer say no. All I could do was run away. (Zhou, Rencong 2004, 298)

In light of their negative reflections upon the poverty that characterized their past in the countryside, it is easy to understand why the women in Haidian, and also Zhou Ling (from earlier in this chapter), might have wanted to migrate to the city—they did so to escape poverty. In fact, things are not as straightforward as this, even among these women. And what about the *dagongmei* who were so nostalgic about their childhoods in the countryside? Why did they all leave for the city when they were in their teens or early twenties? Were they pushed out by hardship or unhappiness, the memories of which they later downplayed, or were there other reasons for their departure? In the previous section I suggested the former—that homesickness brought on by their alienation in the city caused these women to paint a somewhat rosier picture of life in the countryside than they might have presented before their departure to the city. In this section I point to other factors at work.

To date, most analyses of motivations for migration in China, at both the micro- and macrolevels, have emphasized economic factors. For example, a 1988 survey of temporary migrants to the city of Wuhan, in Hubei province, found that 84.3 percent of men and 70.3 percent of women migrated to the city for "job related" reasons or "to improve conditions" (Goldstein and Goldstein 1996, 198).[9] Likewise, most of the older, married women I talked to in Haidian said that they and their husbands had come to Beijing together to earn money or because life in the countryside was too "bitter" (*ku*)—in other words, it involved too much hardship and suffering. The majority presented the move as a necessary, even desperate, attempt to meet basic needs. Han Haiying, for example, said that she and her husband "had no choice" but to leave home in search of work.

It is clear, however, that the basic needs these couples sought to fulfill were not just related to subsistence. Also of particular importance were the wish to educate their children and the desire to accumulate money to build a new house, most of these couples having lived with the husband's family in a relatively old, poor-quality building prior to migration.[10] The expression of desires such as these suggest once more that, for all the emphasis on poverty and bitterness in the narratives of women like Han Haiying, there has been significant economic improvement in the villages from which these women have migrated since the years when, as children, they "did not have enough to eat." It also lends strength to the finding of several surveys that it is not the poorest rural people who leave home for work in the city, since these lack the start-up money and other resources to migrate (Lou et al. 2004, 211).

All the same, as Rachel Murphy has suggested, we should not view desires such as those relating to house building or children's education as any less urgent or basic to the individuals involved than the drive for sheer economic survival. Both are fundamentally linked with the basic human need for self-respect and positive evaluation from one's community (Murphy 2002, 89). As I have indicated, education has traditionally been seen in rural China as crucial to social standing. So, too, has the quality of a family's dwelling. When I asked Zhou Ling to describe the house she lived in as a child, I hit a nerve, for—as her narrative quoted earlier indicates—the quality of one's house not only determines material comfort, it is also a marker of a family's social status, or lack thereof. It is the family's public face, demonstrating to others the extent to which the family has control over economic and social resources (ibid., 103). For this reason, the house has long been a key resource used by families in marriage negotiations, marriage of their children being one of the most important life goals for rural families. It is no coincidence that when Chinese people talk of the importance to the success of a marriage of matching the social status of the bride and the groom's families, they use the phrase *men dang hu dui,* "the doorways are well matched" (ibid., 105).

Since Zhou Ling was a child, social and economic change, including migration, have upped the stakes in the achievement of the goals of house building, material comfort, marriage, and social standing in much of rural China. Most obviously, economic diversification, including work outside the village, has provided the resources for at least some rural families to build more comfortable and more prestigious houses. This, however, has changed norms of "comfort" and "prestige" to the extent that poor people are forced into both out-migration and high levels of debt in order to achieve them. As one returning migrant explained to Rachel Murphy:

> Working outside is like a drug, the more you go out the more you spend, and then you have to go out again. It is just like opium. I still haven't cleared the debt from house building and people never clear their debts with me. A triangular debt is prevalent in the countryside. Everyone is spending money that they don't have. Everyone is trying to run ahead of others for a face that is not really theirs. You build a house so I build a house. You give a 20-yuan wedding present, so I give a 30-yuan wedding present. (Murphy 2002, 111)

Rachel Murphy notes that in Wanzai county in Jiangxi province, villagers aspire to spacious, double-storied homes with cement floors, termed *xiaokang lou.* Murphy points out that the word *xiaokang,* meaning comfortable living, has important political significance. Deng Xiaoping prescribed three stages of national development—subsistence, comfortable living (*xiaokang*), and prosperity—and in the late 1990s the state promoted *xiaokang* as the nation's goal, to be achieved in the immediate future (ibid., 104). As Murphy explains it, therefore, "in describing their ideal house as a *xiaokang lou,* petty commodity producers adapt the state's discourse of development and modernization targets to make sense of their own goals for securing the material and social advancement of both their families and native place in the reform era" (ibid., 104).

Sally Sargeson writes that in the wealthy province of Zhejiang, aspirations are even higher than in Jiangxi. In five case-study villages in Zhejiang in the period 1990–2000, more than half of all households built a new house and some built, demolished, and rebuilt two or three times during this period (Sargeson 2004, 155). About one-quarter of the villagers surveyed by Sargeson claimed that the need for funds for house building and marriage necessitated rural to urban migration (ibid., 159). Standards for new houses in Zhejiang are high—the preference is for multistoried mansions built of concrete and bricks, fitted out with air conditioning and other appliances, and incorporating decorative flourishes, such as baroque architraves, sweeping semicircular entrance stairs, and courtyard fountains. Much of this, Sargeson argues, is being driven by the agency of young women. There is a perception among villagers that "no woman would marry a man without a new house" and, increasingly, young women are determining whom they will marry and are basing their choice on the size and quality of housing that the families of prospective grooms can offer (ibid., 154–61).

Among my interlocutors in Haidian it was taken for granted that the construction of a new house in the village was a necessity, both as a place for them to retire to when they were too old to work in the city and in order to attract wives for their sons. Almost all achieved this goal in the late 1990s, a few years after they (or at least their husbands) had first migrated to Beijing. Though my interlocutors did not themselves say this, it seemed that the building of a new house was often an even higher priority than children's education. Certainly, these families did not wait to see their children through school before pouring huge sums of money into building a new house.[11] Furthermore, while many families had borrowed to finish their house, none spoke of borrowing money for their children's education. Han Haiying and her husband, for example, built a house in 1998 at a cost of 30,000 yuan. At that time, they borrowed 5,000 yuan from his younger sister's family, which they repaid in early 2001. However, by mid-2001 they were making only just enough money to cover their rent, their two children's school fees, the fee for their vegetable stall, and other basic needs. For the previous two years, lack of money had prevented them from visiting home or remitting any money. When I asked what her hopes for her children were, Han Haiying said:

> We have hopes for our children, but we aren't able to fulfill them, so there's nothing we can do. I'd still like the oldest to go to senior high after graduating from junior high. But at the moment we're not earning money and her dad's health is not good and he's getting on. Looking at our family's circumstances, if she can finish junior high, we'll be doing well. (August 2001)

A few married women migrate to Beijing not so much to improve their family's circumstances, as to fulfill more individualist needs. Two women in Haidian, for example, did not go to Beijing until some time after their husbands had been there. They followed them, they said, mainly because they found it too hard managing on their own in the village, and because they wanted the family to be together. There were also some indications that one of these women wanted to "keep an eye on" her husband to ensure that he did not engage in extramarital affairs (for further details, see chapter 5).

Domestic violence is another reason some married women leave home to work in the city. In one of very few stories about the experiences of married women published in *Rural Women*, Pang Hui writes:

> My husband was a gambler and a drunkard and boozed till he was completely legless every day. When he lost money he'd come home and beat up his wife and children. One of those awful beatings three years ago made me deter-mined to leave him, and that's how I started my life as a migrant worker. (Pang 2004, 294)

Ma Hua, one of the few members of the Migrant Women's Club who was al-ready married at the time of her migration to Beijing, pointed to yet another factor motivating married (and unmarried) women to leave home. Like Pang Hui, she had migrated alone, leaving her husband and one-year-old child at home in the village. When I asked her why she had come out to work she said "because I had nothing to do at home [*mei shi gan*]." This is a common response among both married and single young women that conceals rather more than it explains. Broadly speaking, it points to the marginalization of young women in the rural economy. Shortages of land and divisions of labor based on age and gender are such that these women often find that there are no opportunities for them to earn an income: Farm work is already being done by their parents, parents-in-law, brothers or other male relatives, and the little off-farm employment that is available is also domi-nated by men. In some cases domestic chores may also be taken care of by an older woman or may only take up a couple of hours of a woman's day, leaving her, literally, with "nothing to do." In Ma Hua's case it is hard to imagine that this could be so, given that she had a baby to look after, although her mother-in-law probably helped her. But childcare and domestic chores, because they do not bring in an income, are so devalued in rural China that they are not considered "work"; they are "nothing" (Jacka 1997, 101–19). Thus the phrase "nothing to do" connotes not just inactivity and the boredom that goes with it but also a sense of worthlessness.

In areas where out-migration is common it is likely that the departure of a large proportion of the village's young people further contributes to the sense of bore-dom, worthlessness, and also loneliness, of those left behind. In fact, it is debat-able which came first—out-migration or the widespread notion that there is nothing to do in the village. Certainly, the opportunity to "see the world," combined with the promotion in dominant discourse of the superiority of the city, has greatly compounded the understanding among young women, both married and unmarried, that there is nothing to do in the countryside.

Let us now examine in more detail the factors motivating the migration of young, unmarried women. In 1989 a manager at the March 8th Domestic Service Company, one of Beijing's largest recruiters of young rural women for domestic service in the capital, said that young women generally migrated to the city for one of three reasons: to see "the big lights" of the city, to help out their family financially, or to save money for a dowry (interview with Li Ruijin, August 1989). My own conversations with *dagongmei* in Beijing that year, and in Hangzhou in 1995, confirmed Li's observations that some women had come to the city to earn a bit of money for their family (but they did not generally talk about saving for a dowry). Others said that they came to see the city, broaden their horizons, and taste a little freedom, or else that there was nothing to do at home and they wanted to "come out and have a good time" (*chulai wanr*) (Jacka 1998, 67).[12] Among members of the Migrant Women's Club in the early 2000s, economic motivations seemed less important. Thus, Figure 4.1 shows that, when asked their main reasons for leaving home, 23.9 percent of respondents to my 2000 survey of the Migrant Women's Club cited the backwardness of their hometown or the poverty of their family (*jiaxiang luohou, jiali qiong*) as an important reason for out-migration, and another 22.8 percent said there was nothing to do at home. However, the most frequently cited reasons for out-migration were "to develop myself" (*xiang fazhan ziji*) (48.9 percent), "to broaden my horizons" (*xiang kaikuo yanjie*) (38.0 percent), "to exercise independence" (*duanlian yixia ziji de duli shenghuo nengli*) (32.6 percent) and "for my education" (*weile ziji de jiaoyu*) (30.4 percent).[13]

These findings suggest that young *dagongmei* are most commonly not pushed out of the village by economic necessity or by past experiences of deprivation or suffering. Perhaps, after all, the yearning for home expressed in the nostalgic *dagongmei* narratives that I discussed earlier is not such a retrospective whitewash of the place of the past as it was experienced by these women when they were children. The expressed desire to develop themselves, to broaden their horizons and to test their sense of independence suggests, rather, that these women are concerned that their futures will be constrained in the village, and that they have a desire for new experiences and for personal development beyond what their village has to offer.

Other studies confirm that young, single migrants are more interested in exploring the world, trying new experiences, testing new identities, and developing themselves, and are less concerned with providing a secure future for themselves and their families than are older, married migrants (Lou et al. 2004, 219; Woon 2000, 151). Being younger, members of the Migrant Women's Club are also likely to be more influenced than the older women in Haidian by new social norms and discourses. They will have been particularly influenced by the recent spread of television culture across the countryside and by the allure of urban and global

Figure 4.1 **Reasons for Leaving Home** (as percentage; N = 92)

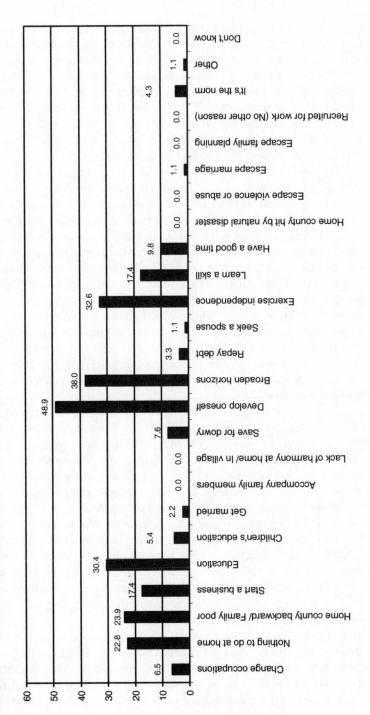

consumption-based capitalism and modernity that television advertisements and popular programs promote.[14] They will also have been more influenced by the state's official rhetoric of modernization, the improvement of *suzhi* (human quality) and "self-development" than the women in Haidian who were teens in the early years of post-Mao economic reform, before aspirations for these goals became such a dominant feature of both state and popular discourse. And, through their involvement in the activities of the Migrant Women's Club, the respondents to my questionnaire have been influenced, to a particularly high degree, by the state's promotion of "self-development" and *suzhi*.

Gender and marriage patterns also play an important part in unmarried women's reasons for wanting to migrate. First, as I discussed above, young women are very often considered marginal to the rural economy. For single women this is compounded by the assumption that the main thing that lies ahead for them is marriage and departure from the natal family and in most cases the village. For a single man, in contrast, the assumption is that in the near future he will bring in a wife and take over the running of the family economy. This does not prevent young men from migrating—in fact, nationally, more single men than women leave their villages in search of work. It may mean, though, that young single men and their female counterparts have a different orientation toward migration. A number of studies claim, for example, that single sons who migrate remit more than daughters because of the pressure on them and their families to construct a new house to attract a bride (Murphy 2002, 107; Cai Qian 2003; Sargeson 2004, 159).[15] More generally, men may be more inclined to view migration as a way of fulfilling their obligations as a family breadwinner, whereas young women may feel those obligations less strongly and may therefore be relatively "free" to pursue more individually oriented goals. I would not wish to be too absolutist about this though, for most young women, as well as men, do remit at least *some* of their earnings, suggesting that they too feel obligations toward their natal families. And, as I will discuss in the next chapter, some *dagongmei* express deep love for their natal families and a strong desire to repay their mothers for the suffering they endured in bringing up their children.

While impending marriage might, to some extent, free women from economic obligations, it is also very often viewed as a looming threat. In my survey of the Migrant Women's Club, only one respondent said that her out-migration was motivated by a wish to escape marriage. However, in conversation, my interlocutors time and again confirmed what Zhou Rencong says in a previous quotation about the significance of escaping, or at least delaying, marriage in the countryside.[16]

In two instances my interlocutors talked of migration as a chance to escape or to delay a marriage that had already been organized. Zhu Jin, a thirty-year-old from Jiangsu, said that four years previously she had tried to break off her engagement to a local man, but he still wished to go ahead with the marriage and refused to break off the engagement or take back the gifts that his family had given her. Her parents also put pressure on her to continue with the marriage. In the end, she said, she had no choice but to run away to Beijing (December 2002).

As mentioned above, Gao Xinran had come to Beijing to postpone the wedding that had been planned for her. She disliked being in Beijing and missed home, but at the same time was upset at the enormous pressure on her to return to the countryside to get married. With real desperation in her voice, she said: "There is no way I'll be able to go out after I'm married. When I'm married, that will be the end of all my hopes" (December 2002). Part of the problem for Gao seemed to be that although she had been introduced to her fiancé, she knew him only very superficially.[17] She was also concerned that he had not worked outside of the village and that this would mean he was less worldly and more conservative than she would wish. Gao said that she would try to get to know the young man better, and if she did not like him she would break off the engagement, even if that meant, as it would, that her family lost face. However, she was very dubious about her chances of finding a husband and in-laws who would allow her to migrate after marriage. It just was not done, she said: "Your mother-in-law wouldn't let you go because she'd lose face, because other people would think the daughter-in-law had been forced to go out to earn money for the family doing something shameful"(December 2002). When I said to Gao that in Australia a lot of people did not get married, she clapped her hands in delight and said, "What freedom, I really envy you, I wish I didn't have to get married" (December 2002).

While Zhu Jin and Gao Xinran were the only women to speak of migration as an escape from a *specific* marriage, many others expressed a desire to avoid or to postpone *any* marriage in the countryside. As she indicates in the quotation at the beginning of this chapter, Wang Lan, for example, rejected the village life that her mother's generation had led as offering only marriage and the drudgery and low status of farm work and childrearing that went with being a married woman in the countryside. Similarly, Chunzi said that when she was in her early twenties she rejected all the boyfriends that were introduced to her because,

I didn't want to get married, have kids, that type of life. I felt that what I needed wasn't that. It was strange, I just didn't want to get married and I didn't want to be like other people. I simply could not look up to other people who had that kind of life. (October 2001)

Some of my interlocutors seem not to have been consciously motivated to escape or delay marriage in the countryside at the time they left home, but later realized the benefits of out-migration in this regard (see Beynon 2004, 135 for similar comment). This was suggested in my conversation with Qiao Xue, whom I introduced above, as follows:

Tamara Jacka: Why did you come to Beijing?

Qiao Xue: Actually, at the time I didn't really think about why I came. There wasn't any particular reason. At that time, my younger sister had to start junior high and my younger brother was also going to school. Me, I didn't finish junior high, because things were hard at home financially. Where we lived, if you had three or four children who had to go to junior high school, like us, it was rather difficult. We really couldn't afford it, because both mum and dad were just farmers. So at the time I was sure it would be a bit better coming out than staying at home. . . .

Tamara Jacka: What were your hopes in coming here? [Long pause] Was it just to earn a bit of money?

Qiao Xue: When I first came I just wanted to earn some money so I could go home and go to school. But at that time, my mum also had chronic stomach problems—her health was no good. The money I earned I sent straight back. I very quickly gave up that idea [of saving up to go to school]. . . .

Tamara Jacka: Do you think you'll stay here long term?

Qiao Xue: I have no plans to go home. I seem to have got used to life in Beijing. If I went home I wouldn't be used to it. . . .

Tamara Jacka: Do you think coming out to work is a way to find a new life?

Qiao Xue: That's right, you could say that. If I was still at home, I'd probably be married by now. (August 2001)

If Wang Lan, Chunzi, or Qiao Xue had responded to my survey, it is unlikely that any would have marked "to escape marriage" as their reason for migration to Beijing. They are much more likely to have given "to develop myself," "to broaden my horizons," "to exercise independence," or "education" as their motivations. However, their narratives, and those of other *dagongmei,* suggest that the desire to escape marriage in the countryside and the desire to pursue self-development in the city are closely related. A future in the countryside means, to these women, being married to a rural man, having children, and working in the fields. The image that this conjures up is very different from the rural idyll that is painted by migrant women reflecting nostalgically upon their childhoods. It entails low status, predictability, monotony and drudgery, and an end to autonomy and to the pursuit of personal hopes and aspirations. This is the backdrop to the desire to leave the village in search of self-development.

Beyond dreading the confining ties of marriage *per se, dagongmei* often express a particular aversion to marriage into rural, agricultural households in which traditional patriarchal attitudes are strong and women are "doomed," as they see it, to lives of servitude. As alluded to in the narratives of Zhou Rencong and Wang Lan, their dread is informed by observations of their mothers and of other older, married women in the village. Such feelings of dread have long characterized young rural Chinese women's outlooks on marriage, but for recent generations they may well have increased, ironically because of new ideas and new possibilities opened up through migration and a growing level of communication between villages, cities, and other parts of the world. These mean that Zhou Rencong and other young women hope and to some extent expect that migration will provide a route out of the married life in the village that their mothers have led. Yet, to date, because the obstacles to settlement in the city have been so high, most women have continued to return to the countryside to marry after relatively short sojourns in the city. As Rachel Murphy and others have documented, migration increases the resources, including personal power and autonomy, of some of these returning migrant women. However, the majority go back to a life of marriage, domestic work, and agriculture not so very different from that of their mothers' generation. Having tasted the freedom and excitement of single life in the city, many of these women find it difficult to adjust to married life in the village and express high levels of discontent (Murphy 2004, 264–65; Lou et al. 2004, 236–39). The example these women provide can only reinforce among younger village women a desire to taste the freedom of the outside world and a dread of return and marriage in the village.

Among the members of the Migrant Women's Club and other migrants, including both men and women, married and unmarried, the question of whether or not leaving home and working as a migrant is "a way to find a (new) life" is a common one.[18] To married migrant women, such as my interlocutors in Haidian, this is primarily a question of whether or not work in the city can earn them enough to fulfill the life goals of feeding the family, educating children, and building a house back in the countryside. To young, single *dagongmei,* the question is whether or not work as a migrant in the city provides the opportunity to achieve a positive alternative to married life in the countryside. The next section, which looks at the impact of migrant women's experiences in the city on their views of, and aspirations for, the future, casts further light on these questions.

The Place of the Future

I can look back on the road that we've taken—the migrant worker road. Is it really a way to find a life? No, it's not. *Dagongmei* come out thinking it's a beautiful dream, but they're mistaken. People hardly ever tell them "don't come out, there aren't any advantages. This isn't a way to find a life." But what life can you find in the countryside? Nowadays the countryside is becoming more and more desolate and abandoned, so everyone's children are leaving. When they all go, how do they manage [in the countryside]? Everyone has left. More and more people are staying long term in the city. No one wants to go back. Take the people in the suburbs who sell vegetables or are builders—if they can survive there they stay, but they don't think about the quality of life, they just try to stay and make do. You know, all those houses in the suburbs are very crude, yet they cost 200–300 yuan a month. And there are *dagongmei* who say they don't mind if it's bitter and tiring, they still don't want to go back. Some are married and more than thirty and they can't afford to have a child. They'd really like to have a child, but they can't—How would they look after a child? They can hardly look after themselves. (Zhou Ling, August 2001)

To date, scholars and officials have assumed that rural migration in China is mostly seasonal and/or circulatory, that rural migrants still see "home" as being in the countryside, and that their sojourns away from that home, though they may be repeated, are brief; hence the terms "temporary" or "transient" migrants and "floating population." This perception has been supported by large-scale surveys. For example, according to the Ministry of Agriculture survey of 20,000 rural households in 319 villages conducted in 2002, the average migrant worker spent 8.9 months away from home. This survey also found, though, that 58 percent of all migrant workers spent more than ten months away from home ("Rural-to-Town Labour Force on the Rise" 2003). There is some evidence that migrants' sojourns are increasing in length, and in support of Zhou Ling's claim that increasing numbers of migrants view their residence in the city as long term. In Beijing, for example, the 1997 census of the floating population reported that 64 percent of migrants had been away from home for more than six months (Poston and Duan 1999, 17). By 2002, that figure had increased to 74 percent ("Beijing qunian wailairenkou . . ." 2003). Some studies also indicate that women migrants tend to stay away from the village for longer periods than men. A large-scale survey conducted in 1995 by the Ministry of Agriculture found, for example, that among rural migrants from Sichuan and Anhui, the average length of sojourn away from home was 9.3 months for men, but 10.7 months for women (Fan 2004, 184). Wang Feng and Zuo Xuejin suggest that women migrants' longer sojourns may be due to the fact that more male migrants are already married and have ties to families in the countryside, whereas the majority of migrant women are unmarried and may have fewer obligations and less motivation to return to the village (Wang and Zuo 1997, cited in Jacka and Gaetano 2004, 36 note 77). Other studies indicate that among migrants residing in large cities, women express greater satisfaction with their situation than men, and a greater desire to stay there permanently (Goldstein, Zai, and Goldstein 2000, 227; Song 1999, 85).

My own study is not representative of the floating population as a whole, or even of the population of female migrants, for most of the migrant women I talked with had been in Beijing for some years and expressed a desire to remain in the city in the long term. In this section, however, I will try to extrapolate from what I learned of the desires and aspirations of my interlocutors to suggest why significant, and possibly growing, numbers of migrant women wish to stay away from their "home" in the countryside for as long as possible, despite the discrimination and hardships they face in the city.

None of my interlocutors in Haidian expressed a positive desire to return to the countryside—all said they would prefer to stay in Beijing in the long term. Few, though, believed that would be possible. It was often difficult for me to fathom why these women would want to stay in Beijing, given what I saw of their objective circumstances. During the period that I met with them in the second half of 2001, business was poor and many families were in debt and only just scraping by. And as Zhou Ling says in the quotation above, these people lived in crude dwellings, even by their own village standards, and it was hard to see what they could enjoy in the way of quality of life. What is more, buildings in the area were being demolished and police sweeps were frequent. There were palpably high levels of tension, anger, and unhappiness in the air. All the same, many of my interlocutors conveyed a sense that there were slightly more possibilities in the city than there were back in the village. Zhang Xiaohua, a thirty-six-year-old from Henan, had no work when I met her, and the small demolition company that her husband ran with a few others from the same village was doing very poorly. She told me that life was very tough and she complained that the costs of living and of sending her son to primary school were much higher in Beijing than at home. The village where she and her husband came from was not particularly poor, she said. All the same, she continued,

At home, once you've planted your one *mu* [1 *mu* = 0.0667 hectares] of land there's nothing to do and you have no money to spend. Here, you might not earn any money for four or five days, but if you earn a bit it's enough to use for ten or fifteen days. So there's no point farming. If you can earn a bit of loose change it's enough. (August 2001)

Jin Rong, whom I introduced earlier, lived in a single-room house with her husband and two school-aged children. They dubbed the room "the cave" because there were no windows and the room was dark and cramped, with rough, cracked, dirty walls. Jin apologized for the place, saying that her house in the village was much better. Since they had arrived in Beijing four years previously she and her husband had tried a number of enterprises, selling first handicrafts, then running a bookstall, and then making and selling pancakes. When I met them, neither had any work and they still had to pay back 20,000 yuan from the funds they had borrowed to set up their handicraft stall. When I first asked Jin why they had left home, she said their home village was on the plains and was reasonably well off. They came, she said, "just so we'd have a bit more money, less worries." She did not want to return there, though. She explained that if they went home, it would be very difficult for them to repay their debt, whereas if they could find some opportunity in Beijing to earn some money, they could pay back their debt and would feel a little more stable. "I don't have any hope anymore," Jin said. "If you want to go back home you can't, you don't have any money. If you go back you have to set up house again, and how are you going to do that without money? So you just have to stay here and make do" (August 2001).

Though none were positive about returning to the countryside, it was clear that the migrant couples in Haidian retained close links with their homes in the village. Some had left young children there in the care of older relatives. And, as I indicated earlier, most had built new houses in the husband's village. A few of these houses had been rented out or were being occupied by the husband's parents. The general assumption was, though, that at some stage these migrants would "retire" from work in Beijing and return to the house they had built in the village.[19] The preferred ideal was for this to happen only once they were too old to continue laboring in the city, and their children were old enough to take their place. Most assumed this would be when the couple were in their mid-forties, five to ten years off. However, a number of my interlocutors voiced the concern that their bodies would not be up to that many more years of hard labor. Both Han Haiying and her husband, for example, suffered from lack of sleep, serious stomach problems, and neurasthenia. Her husband, who was thirty-eight, said that because of his poor health he would not be able to work beyond age forty. The couple planned to retire to the village then and to send their daughter to Guangdong or Shenzhen to work as a *dagongmei*.

Even among the younger, healthier migrants the majority felt that they would be driven out soon, either by lack of business or by the government's campaigns to "clean up" the area ahead of the 2008 Olympics. In the same courtyard as Han Haiying lived Yong Binbin (thirty-four, junior secondary school education), her husband, and their two teenaged sons. They had been in Beijing since 1994, having also come from Hubei. On the morning that I went to visit them the Public Security officials came through. I had just sat down on a stool in their single-room house, when Yong's older son came rushing in, yelling "lock the door, they're coming!" Yong assured me that she had a temporary residence permit, but she was still very nervous about being arrested. Yong's husband was out at the time, looking for work. He later returned without having found anything. The couple used to earn a living selling vegetables. Within the last few months, though, the stall that they were renting had twice been demolished. Without a stall now they could not sell vegetables, and they had been unable to find other work, so they were thinking of going back to his village.

While I was there, Yong Binbin's older sister and her husband, who lived in another courtyard nearby, also came to visit. Their business was doing relatively well—they rented a vegetable stall in town for a monthly fee of 700–800 yuan, from which they earned a net income of about 1,000 yuan a month. When I asked Yong's sister if she wanted to stay in Beijing long term, she gave a short laugh and said, "yes, but we can't. They'll send us back." She and her husband were bitterly certain that sooner or later they would be detained by the police and sent back to the countryside. "It makes no difference if you have a temporary residence permit," he said. "They rip it up . . . Jiang Zemin [then president of the Republic] isn't a Beijing person either—why don't they arrest him and send him back?" (August 2001)

In my survey of the Migrant Women's Club, 37 percent of respondents answered "do not know" in response to the question "If it is possible, do you think you will live long term in Beijing?" (*ruguo keneng ni xiang zai Beijing changqi shenghuo xiaqu ma?*). Another 30.4 percent indicated that they would not stay long term in the city, and 32.6 percent said they would (N = 92). The high percentage of respondents who answered "do not know" is a reflection of the sense of uncertainty and ambivalence that *dagongmei*, like other migrant women, feel about their future in the city. The 32.6 percent figure for those saying they would stay in the city is higher than has been reported in other studies. All the same, my research suggests that this figure underestimates the extent to which *dagongmei* commonly wish to stay in the city.[20]

Most *dagongmei* say that life in the city is hard. Asked about the greatest difficulties they faced in their first month in Beijing, a large proportion of respondents to the survey of the Migrant Women's Club said that they missed home, found their work very hard, were not used to life in the city, felt that urbanites looked down upon them, and/or had economic difficulties. Only 5.6 percent said they had no difficulties (see Figure 4.2).[21] In the month prior to the survey a greater proportion of respondents said they had no difficulties, but it was also the case that more respondents reported economic difficulties, and that significant numbers said their work was too hard, they faced too many regulations and restrictions, they had trouble finding work, they missed home, and they were lonely (Figure 4.3).

As Wang Lan puts it in the quotation at the beginning of this chapter, the city offers *dagongmei* the opportunity for little more than basic survival. They find that they can earn just enough to get by in the city and, if they are doing well, to send a bit of money home each month, but they can do little else. They live in poor-quality housing and struggle to find work that is relatively stable, where the wage is not too low and their employers not too abusive. The jobs they find generally involve tiring, menial work and provide few opportunities for advancement or the acquisition of transferable skills. They also feel lonely and constantly looked down upon by urbanites. When they have work, these women have little leisure time, their movements and contacts with others are often restricted by their employers, especially in the case of live-in maids and workers in small sweatshops, and, in any case, they usually lack the money and the energy to go out in their time off work. For all this, and despite bitter complaints about their marginalization, many *dagongmei* believe that they are better off in the city than they would be at home in the countryside. As can be seen in Figure 4.4, most respondents to my questionnaire survey of the Migrant Women's Club indicated that their living conditions (*shenghuo tiaojian*) in Beijing were better than those in their home village, though

144

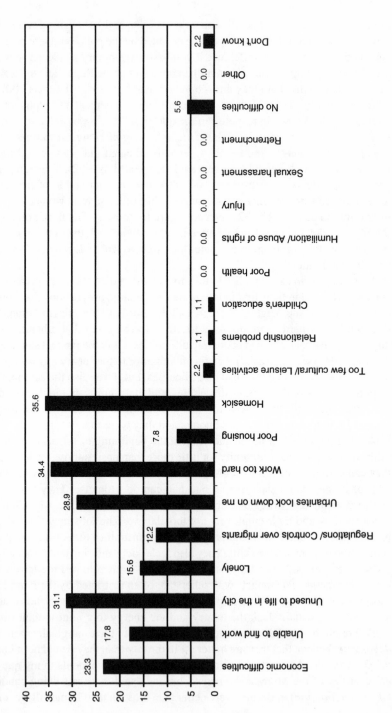

Figure 4.2 Difficulties During First Month in Beijing (as percentage; N = 90)

Difficulty	Percentage
Economic difficulties	23.3
Unable to find work	17.8
Unused to life in the city	31.1
Lonely	15.6
Regulations/ Controls over migrants	12.2
Urbanites look down on me	28.9
Work too hard	34.4
Poor housing	7.8
Homesick	35.6
Too few cultural/ Leisure activities	2.2
Relationship problems	1.1
Children's education	1.1
Poor health	0.0
Humiliation/ Abuse of rights	0.0
Injury	0.0
Sexual harassment	0.0
Retrenchment	0.0
No difficulties	5.6
Other	0.0
Don't know	2.2

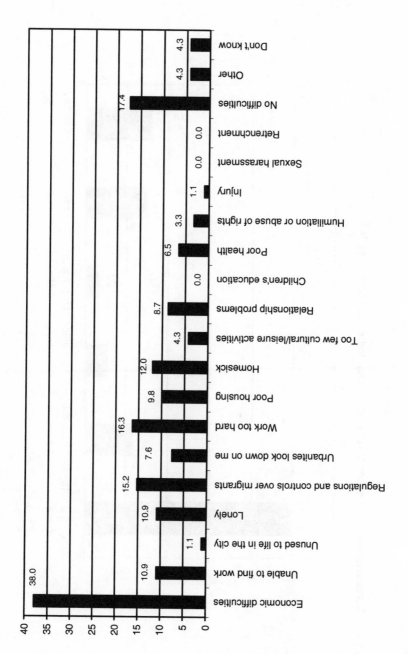

Figure 4.3 **Difficulties During Past Month in Beijing** (as percentage; N = 92)

Economic difficulties — 38.0
Unable to find work — 10.9
Unused to life in the city — 1.1
Lonely — 10.9
Regulations and controls over migrants — 15.2
Urbanites look down on me — 7.6
Work too hard — 16.3
Poor housing — 9.8
Homesick — 12.0
Too few cultural/leisure activities — 4.3
Relationship problems — 8.7
Children's education — 0.0
Poor health — 6.5
Humiliation or abuse of rights — 3.3
Injury — 1.1
Sexual harassment — 0.0
Retrenchment — 0.0
No difficulties — 17.4
Other — 4.3
Don't know — 4.3

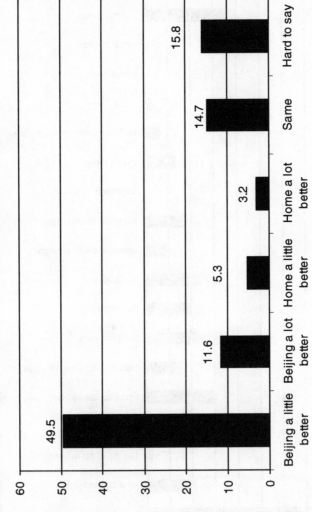

Figure 4.4 **Comparison of Living Conditions in Beijing/Home** (as percentage; N = 95)

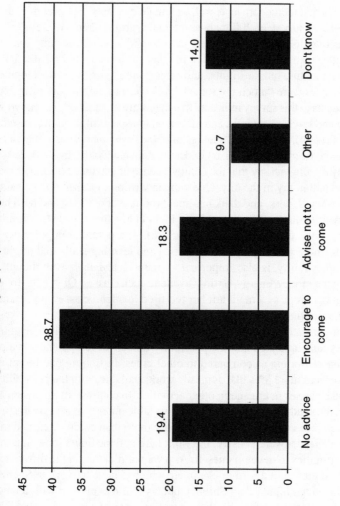

Figure 4.5 Advice to Others About Migration to Beijing (as percentage; N = 93)

only 11.6 percent said they were a lot better. When respondents were asked what advice they would give to relatives or fellow villagers thinking of migrating to Beijing, 38.7 percent said they would advise them to come, and only 18.3 percent said they would advise against it (Figure 4.5).

These findings hardly point to thorough satisfaction about life in the city among *dagongmei*. All the same, they suggest somewhat higher levels of satisfaction than do surveys that include male as well as female migrants. For example, in the 1999 Sino-German survey of 200 male and female rural migrants in Beijing,[22] respondents reported on average that their income and level of consumption in the city were better than previously, but that in other respects, including standards of living, social status, human rights, and opportunities for (self) development, their circumstances were "much the same" (*chabuduo*) as before (Liu Ling 2001, 118). Respondents to this survey indicated that they were dissatisfied (*bu manyi*) with their housing and levels of savings, and that all other aspects of their circumstances were "so-so" (*yi ban*), rather than "satisfactory" (*hai suan manyi*) or "very satisfactory" (*hen manyi*) (ibid., 121; see also Goldstein, Zai, and Goldstein 2000, 227).

Many *dagongmei* say that they enjoy a sense of expanded horizons and of freedom and autonomy in the city. One woman writing to *Rural Women* said that she lived in a small, dark, and dank basement room, worked long and hard hours, and had very little money, but "in my heart I feel I have some space that is mine" (Sun Hongzhi 1996, cited in Beynon 2004, 138). The potential opportunity for self-development, especially by taking classes and learning skills that might improve their employability, is also important to many *dagongmei*, even though most do not have the money, energy, or time to attend such classes. Qiao Xue, for example, said that her work as a maid left her too tired to attend classes at present, but her aspiration for the future was to study hairdressing.

Ruan Shilin, a twenty-three-year-old from Shandong who had been in Beijing for five years, indicated that the possibility for self-development was a particular attraction of Beijing as compared to other cities. In Beijing one might earn less, but there were more jobs like domestic work available, with the possibility of time off to take classes or engage in other activities. In contrast, in Shenzhen and other cities in the south, there was little work available other than jobs on the production line. Such jobs generally paid substantially more than could be earned in Beijing, but the managers were abusive, the work hard and the hours long, and there were no opportunities to develop oneself. As a way of illustrating the differences, Ruan Shilin told me about a former classmate who had gone to work in Shenzhen. Her wage was much higher than Shilin's, but, as Shilin explained with a laugh, when asked if she often surfed the Web, her classmate had no idea what Shilin was talking about (November 2001).

Finally, the sense of being at the heart of global modernity, and the aura of excitement associated with this, is also an important attraction of Beijing. This was indicated in Wang Lan's narrative quoted at the beginning of this chapter. Similarly, asked if she wanted to stay long term in Beijing, Ruan Shilin replied:

I definitely won't go back in the short term. In Beijing I have things I want to do. If you go home there's nothing much to do. Of course, there are things you can do—you can farm—but [pause] I feel I definitely couldn't go back in the short term, because now Beijing has entered the world and it's won the bid for the Olympic Games. The pressures here are very great. You might feel if you go home there's no pressure—you can feed and clothe yourself without feeling pressured—but it's boring. Even though working outside is full of suffering—you go to work at seven in the morning and don't finish till nine in the evening, and in the evenings it's cold and you feel very tired—but, still, it's interesting. After all, we're young. Maybe when I'm fifty I'll feel "aiya, it's so cold in winter, having to get up to go to work." [pause] But now when I phone home, nothing much is happening. (November 2001)

Once more, for the majority of *dagongmei,* the excitement of the modern city is more a matter of hope and imagined possibilities than of present reality. One woman named Shanshan, who worked as a kitchen hand, wrote:

Even though I live in the bustling city, I have a loneliness that I've never felt before. I'll never be on the same level as city people, never be on an equal footing. Once a customer asked me: "Little sister, you're so young, why are you here suffering and being exhausted and not at home studying?" I was speechless. To earn money?—My salary is so low it's pitiable. To blaze a path into the world? It's difficult for me to even step outside this shop a few times a day, what world would I blaze a path into? To extend my experience? All of the customers here are other migrant workers or lowly paid city dwellers, and once they come in all they do is order some food, eat, pay the bill, then leave. I don't even exchange a sentence with them—how would I extend my experience? (Shanshan 1998, 53)

But despite the reality of low pay for hard work under bad conditions, limited opportunities, discrimination, and loneliness, the belief that the city holds the possibility for making money, extending experiences and developing oneself, and being a part of a more exciting, modern world continues to be a powerful incentive for young migrant women trying to remain in the city for as long as possible.

Conversely, *dagongmei* often express an even stronger desire not to return to the countryside because it is too poor, rural people's thinking is too "backward" and "feudal" and farming is too draining, and because the women feel they would not be able to readjust to that life after living in the city. The longer they remain in the city, the more this feeling grows, despite a realization that their future in the city will also be limited. Zhang Ning had been in Beijing for eight years when I first met her in 2001. She had recently married another migrant and the couple lived in a small, rented room in a migrant settlement in Chaoyang under conditions similar to those in the settlement in Haidian. At that time, Zhang Ning had been unemployed for eighteen months. She remarked:

> In Beijing it's very hard to develop oneself. Originally I wanted to set up a school because I like being with children—when there's a whole lot of them together it's very lively. But you need a lot of capital. Even if the two of us [that is, she and her husband] pooled our money it wouldn't be enough, and I don't dare try, I don't dare do it. (August 2001)

However, when I asked her about prospects back in her husband's home county in Hebei, Zhang Ning said that there were no industries there and she did not know how to farm. "I feel that if you made me go back to live in the countryside now, I wouldn't be used to it. I feel that I've been here eight years and studied a few things and if you told me to go back I wouldn't be willing." Like many *dagongmei* who had been away from the countryside for some years, Zhang Ning said that her thinking had changed a great deal in the time she had been in Beijing. After she had worked in Beijing for a while, and participated in the Migrant Women's Club, she said,

> My worldview broadened a lot, and I wasn't just trying to earn a bit of pocket money the way I had been when I first came out, or thinking I'd just come out to have a look. I wanted to find a way of living for myself. I didn't want to go back because going back there'd be no way to find a life, only farming. It'd be as if I'd never come out. If you want to do something like run a factory, if you don't have capital you won't be able to. It's too backward. A lot of young people have left. Mostly it's just old people and children at home, and those who can't leave because they're sick. (August 2001)

Despite the hardships they faced as "outsiders" without local registration in Beijing, Zhang Ning and her husband had no thoughts of returning, either to her home county in Anhui or to his in Hebei. His family, she said, had not built a new house, "so if I went back there I wouldn't have anywhere to live, so I'm not going back. His parents just live in a mud house in the mountains" (August 2001).

In 1995 in Hangzhou, a great many of the *dagongmei* with whom I talked about their hopes for the future said that they wanted to "be a little boss" (*dang ge xiao laoban*), running their own business in Hangzhou or in a township or county seat in their home county.[23] Their chances of achieving such a goal appeared to me to be slight because they had no experience or training in running a business, few if any technical skills, and very little money saved up. It was an important dream nevertheless—being their own boss, these women felt, would free them from the exploitation they suffered as wage laborers in the city, and give them a much-sought-after chance of autonomy and control over their own lives. As discussed in chapters 1 and 2, entrepreneurship among migrants has been much encouraged by the state and by the Migrant Women's Club, and most of the models raised for emulation in the press, including in *Rural Women* and *Working Sister*, are migrants who have made it as entrepreneurs, either in the city to which they migrated, or, more commonly, in their home county. In some places, local governments have also provided concrete incentives to encourage returning migrants to set up business in a rural town or county seat.[24]

In contrast to the *dagongmei* in Hangzhou I spoke with in 1995, very few of the women in the Migrant Women's Club that I met in 2001 expressed any aspiration to be a boss. I can only speculate as to the reasons for this difference. It may be that it is harder for a migrant to run a business in Beijing than in other cities. My discussions with migrant traders in Haidian also suggest that it became much harder in the late 1990s and 2000s to run a successful business in the city than it had been previously. Two of my interlocutors at the Migrant Women's Club had tried their hand at business in the city but had failed and lost large sums of money in the process. Neither had plans to try again. Others either did not have the skills or the capital to think about starting up a business in the city, or were disillusioned by their own struggles or by stories of the difficulties and failures experienced by others. Shanshan, quoted above, wrote that she had originally been inspired to migrate to the city in search of work by a story she read in the newspaper about a *dagongmei* who had become a successful entrepreneur. However, she said that "a month of working in the city made it very clear to me that not every migrant can work a miracle. Success not only requires diligence and good sense, it also requires an opportunity. For the average migrant worker it's very rare that these things all appear at the same time" (Shanshan 1998, 53).

Zhou Ling told me that, for the first edition of *Working Sister,* members of the Migrant Women's Club thought they should write an article about *dagongmei* "success stories" (*chenggong zhe*). To this end, she and a few others combed the city in search of *dagongmei* who had become successful entrepreneurs. They wrote up the stories of four women, but Zhou Ling considered none of them to be genuine *dagongmei* success stories. One woman, who ran a book shop, hardly counted as a *dagongmei* in Zhou's eyes, because she was a technical school graduate and, in any case her shop was struggling. The other three had been in Beijing for several years before setting up their own businesses, but despite working extremely hard, they earned very little and their businesses were very small. Some migrant men, she said, became successful entrepreneurs in Beijing, but they were the ones who had been businesspeople in their home county, came to the city with capital, and depended on supply networks with their home county. Young *dagongmei* simply did not have the resources to compete with them (August 2001).

One might expect that the chances of establishing a business in a township in one's home county would be better than in Beijing, and certainly a number of returnee migrant entrepreneurs have been promoted in the press. However, in the countryside, as elsewhere, business and the resources required to run a business, including loans, political backing, and contacts, are heavily dominated by men (Jacka 1997, 154–57). In her study of returnee migrants in Jiangxi, Rachel Murphy found that just 15 percent of returnee entrepreneurs were women, and while some men ran large-scale manufacturing enterprises, the women's businesses were all small in scale, made low profits, and were concentrated in the service sector (Murphy 2002, 169–75).

Among my interlocutors at the Migrant Women's Club, only Chen Ailing said her dream was to open a tailoring shop in her home county, and she acknowledged that for the foreseeable future it was an unobtainable dream. Others, like Zhang Ning, said that their home county was underdeveloped with few enterprises, and with neither skills nor capital they had little chance of either obtaining a stable factory job in a local township enterprise or of starting their own business. The great majority of my interlocutors equated a future in the countryside with marriage, childrearing and the drudgery of housework and agricultural labor, and with the closing down, rather than the opening up, of possibilities for self-development, for earning an independent income, and for exercising autonomy.

Caught between disillusion about their possibilities in the city and the disheartening prospect of a return to the countryside, *dagongmei* dilemmas over the place of their future are often expressed through their anxieties about, and deliberations over, marriage. The pressure on young women to marry is enormous, and this, combined with their struggles and sense of alienation in the city, leads the majority of single *dagongmei* to return to the countryside to get married when they are in their early to mid-twenties. There are signs, though, that their experiences of migration are leading increasing numbers of rural women to delay marriage (Davin 1997, 311). Away from home, and earning their own income, young migrant women often gain a greater self-confidence and independence and feel they have some power to postpone their marriage to a later age than would normally be possible in the village. In this, they are helped by the example of fellow villagers and kin who migrated before them. For example, Qiao Xue, who was twenty when I met her, said that all her former classmates back at home were already married. She herself did not yet want to get married, and explained:

I feel I'm too young still. I shouldn't have to think about such things now. When it's time, I'll think about it. My older sister [also living in Beijing] is twenty-six and she hasn't married yet. If I leave consideration of marriage to when I'm her age, that still won't be too late. (August 2001)

Dagongmei exposure to modern, urban values also means that they often expect to have more say in whom they marry, and that they look for a man who will be less conservative than the average farmer, whom they disparagingly refer to as "dirt head, dirt brain" (*tutou tunao de*) (Beynon 2004, 142; Murphy 2002, 113). Some *dagongmei* look for an urban husband who, they hope, will be more modern and will enable them to stay in the city. Zhu Jin, who, as I mentioned, had left home to escape a marriage, was one example. Her main ambition, she said, was to marry a Beijing man, so that she could stay in the city and not be so lonely. She wanted someone steady and dependable who loved her as much as she loved him— it was no good, she said, being involved with someone you loved more than they loved you. Her main requirement, though, was that the man have his own apartment (December 2002).

Two of my interlocutors, Zhou Ling and Chunzi, succeeded in the ambition of marrying a Beijinger. However, the majority of *dagongmei* recognize that the dream of a stable, happy marriage to an urban man is a near impossibility. Some are wary of becoming involved with a Beijing man, fearing that the gap in status will result in disharmony and mistreatment of themselves from the husband's family (Beynon 2004, 143). To some extent, Zhou Ling suffered from this, for even after ten years her husband's parents still treated her with contempt. Other *dagongmei* shy away from relationships with urban men, fearing that the only Beijing men who would want a migrant wife are those who, because of disadvantage or disability, cannot find an urban woman to marry (ibid.).

A great many *dagongmei* seek marriage with a fellow migrant. This need not be someone from the same county or even the same province as themselves, but someone who has at least had some exposure to the world as a result of migration, and who might, therefore, be more open-minded and less conservative than a man in the village who has never been away from home. Some such women go with the man to his home village, settle, and have children there, but those who are allowed to by their in-laws often make return trips to the city to work, both before and after their children are born. Others, like Zhang Ning, remain in the city, at least for a time.[25]

The dilemmas that young single *dagongmei* face in finding a future place for themselves are such that they are often vague and indecisive when asked about their aspirations and talk simply of "living one day at a time" (*zou yitian, suan yitian*) (Jacka 1998, 69–70; Beynon 2004, 144). At the same time, though, many feel that time is running out on them because they are approaching an age when they will be considered "old maids," too old for anyone to want to marry. This anxiety is compounded by the understanding that most urban employers in the manufacturing and service sectors prefer to hire migrant women in their teens and twenties and commonly fire women past the age of thirty (Beynon 2004, 144–45). One waitress I spoke with said that restaurant customers expect waitresses to be young and pretty and complain if they are not good-looking or are too old. Generally, she said, restaurants employ women between the ages of eighteen and twenty-five and some state explicitly that they do not employ women outside that age range. As a twenty-nine-year-old, she herself was starting to feel uncomfortable and concerned that she would not be able to retain her job for much longer (December 2001).

In the 1990s and early 2000s most *dagongmei* were like Gao Xinran, in that they conformed to the dominant rural expectation that they return to the countryside to marry in their early twenties. Nevertheless, there were enough who did not conform to this pattern that Xie Lihua expressed the view—as early as 1995—that the number of unmarried rural women in their late twenties and thirties who had been *dagongmei* in Beijing for up to thirteen years and had little prospect of marrying had reached "crisis" proportions (personal communication, September 1995). In the eyes of Xie Lihua and many others, including migrant women themselves, this is a serious and growing social problem. For example, two studies argue that a failure to marry and have children by the age of twenty-five is reinforcing a sense of rootlessness and an inability to adapt back to rural life among increasing numbers of migrant women (Feng Xiaoshuang 1997; Tan Shen 1996, cited in Beynon 2004, 144). Others worry that women who stay in the city and do not marry will find themselves without an income and without financial support when they are older. Zhou Ling lamented that one of her younger sisters, who worked in a beauty parlor in Shenzhen, was already thirty but was destitute (*yi wu suo you*):

I've already realized that in the future I'll have to take care of my younger sister. She won't have anything. What will she do? She hasn't married and she doesn't have children. She's more than thirty and she doesn't have her own family. When she gets to forty, she won't be able to find work, so how will she live in the city? I'll have to look after her. She has an older sister, but what about all the others? So, how come I can stay in the city? It's just because I have a husband. If I didn't have a husband here I don't know how I'd manage either. (August 2001)

Of the twenty-two female members of the Migrant Women's Club with whom I had in-depth discussions, only five expressed a clear wish or plan to return to the countryside. I sketch out two of their positions here because, although they were unusual in their desires for the future, their cases illustrate a number of issues and dilemmas that are common to *dagongmei* trying to find their place in the world.[26]

Liu Yu left her home village in Sichuan at the age of seventeen in order to earn some money so that her younger brother and sister could go to school. When I first met her in 2001, Liu Yu was unhappy in the city and wanted only to return home. However, her future in the village had been greatly compromised by the fact that she had been raped by her employer in her first job in Beijing as a maid. Apart from an older male cousin whom she had contacted for help when she was in the hospital, no one in her family or village knew that Liu Yu had been raped. Word did get out, though, that she had been in the hospital, and this, combined with a general anxiety about the loose morals of women who left home to work, was enough for villagers to suspect that Liu Yu was a "fallen woman." Rumors caused Liu Yu's fiancé, to whom she had been engaged before her migration, to call off their wedding. Even before this happened, Liu Yu felt that, despite being in love with her fiancé, the stigma of rape meant that she had to end their engagement and that she would never marry. Even if she could find a man willing to marry a fallen woman she would always feel bad about herself and it would always be something in the way between them.

Several months after the rape, Liu Yu recovered enough to work and found a job in a factory in a Beijing suburb. She had conflicting thoughts about her future. On the one hand, she wanted to return home in order to look after her parents, who suffered from ill health, and because she disliked living in the city. On the other hand, she did not know what work she would do back in the village. Unlike most *dagongmei,* she was not averse to working in the fields, but she doubted she had either the skills or the strength to be a farmer and felt that, in any case, such work would not bring in enough money. She was hopeful that she might find work in one of the factories that had been set up in her home county in the last few years, but with only three years of schooling she did not rate her chances highly. Then there was the problem of marriage and what people would say about her in the village, and she was afraid of running into her former fiancé. For the time being, Liu Yu said, it was all too hard to think about. She would just take each day one at a time and try to have a bit of happiness for herself.

In early 2003 Liu Yu returned to her natal village. Shortly afterward she wrote that she was back at home but it wasn't really her home. She explained:

In China the only home a girl can have is that of her husband once she has married. Where I live now is my younger brother's home, not mine. I don't want to marry. My parents are angry at me for that and I feel my future is uncertain. I am tired of living. I'm another year older already. Sometimes I wish that time would stop and go no further. That way I would no longer cause my family such trouble. (June 2003)

Several months later she was back in Beijing, once more working as a maid. Her letter explained:

I really didn't want to come back to Beijing, but I had no choice. The gossip in the village was so frightening and I couldn't take villagers' old ways of thinking. To be a farmer and have my own farm—that's just a dream now. Coming back to Beijing I feel so lost. Today is the first day of the new year. . . . For three years I've worked hard to be a normal, happy girl, but today I still have tears pouring down my face. During the day I can steel myself to smile, but in the evening I face my shadow and I know I'm alone. Sounds so poetic, doesn't it? My whole life is a tale of sorrow and misery . . . But I'm just one of millions of *dagongmei*. (January 2004)

Deng Yiyan is my second example of a *dagongmei* who expressed a desire to return to the countryside. Originally from a village in Shandong, Yiyan migrated to Beijing in 1989 at the age of seventeen because her relations with her family were tense; she felt that she had had no status or autonomy at home and her contribution to the household economy was unrecognized. She worked in Beijing for many years, but her ambition was to return to the land, and during her spare time she studied accounting and read up on fruit farming techniques. After saving up for a while she gave up her job in Beijing and went home. She explained:

I thought I'd go home and go into business with members of my family. I thought I could plant fruit trees or else seedlings, because you can also earn a lot of money planting seedlings. I've had a look at the market. Everyone cursed at me. Then they sent me away. They wouldn't agree. They felt that the status of rural people is very low and it's full of hardship. They felt that if you work in the city it's clean, while in the countryside you spend the whole day covered in mud and it's very dirty. Moreover, other people will look down on you, and the conditions are poor. They said that, as a girl, I might be able to marry into the city and change my fate—that city people have better lives than rural people. That's why people sometimes buy urban household registration [in a nearby township or in the county seat]. It's really stupid. It amounts to giving away your land to someone else. You lose your land and you have to pay out money as well. That's an expression of real ignorance, isn't it? So I thought I'd sign a contract [with the local government] to run an orchard. But I'm not the head of a household, so I couldn't do that independently. That is to say, even if you have money, you can't necessarily be the one to make the decisions. Girls can't do anything in the countryside. You can only become independent of your family once you've married, but then you must do as your husband says. If my family had been willing for me to stay at home, they could have let me take my portion of land. But they wouldn't let me, they believed I was just a dependant. (August 2001)

Deng Yiyan disagreed with her family that the countryside was too dirty and too poor. "I don't think earth is dirty . . . and farming isn't necessarily hard work—

it depends how you do it." She had read several books on agriculture and had various ideas on how to farm more efficiently, how to process agricultural products and how to sell them in the city to make a larger profit. But her family just laughed at her.

I thought I'd earn some money and do things on my own. What I didn't expect was that as a girl I wouldn't have the power to do that. Even if I just grew vegetables, if I took them to sell in the city I'd make more profit than just farming. What's more, I could get them interested and make them believe me, so that they would no longer envy city people and would like the countryside. I really hate them. I hate the people in my home village. I feel I've done so much study and it's all been for nothing. Later, when I came back [to Beijing] I didn't feel like doing anything. I was really pissed off. (August 2001)

When I met Deng Yiyan in 2001 she was twenty-nine and had been in Beijing for almost thirteen years, although during that time she occasionally had returned home for short periods. At the time, she was employed in a real estate firm, having previously worked in a long string of jobs, including as a maid, a hospital orderly, a cook, a canteen manager, an accountant, in an advertising company, and as the owner of a clothing stall. She still hoped to marry and have a family because she was lonely, and because "that way it's more convenient, because Chinese people's opinions on this are still very strong" (August 2001). Her other ambition was to earn a huge sum of money so that she could buy some land in the countryside somewhere to set up a farm and start an elderly people's home without having to get her family's permission.

Deng Yiyan's aspirations to return to the land and her forthright repudiation of the assumption that city people have better lives than country people run counter to dominant official and popular urban discourses on development, modernity, and the superiority of the city. They are also very different from the views of most rural migrants and villagers, such as Deng Yiyan's family, among whom the superiority of urban life is generally taken to be simple common sense. Some *dagongmei* are drawn home to the countryside by homesickness or by a sense of obligation to their rural families and to their home village. Many others return to the village because of pressure from their family, because they feel that an urban future is beyond them, or because of harsh experiences in the city. The great majority, nonetheless, equate the city with desirable modernity and self-development, while the countryside is associated, at best, with security and stasis. Deng Yiyan is extremely rare among *dagongmei* in perceiving the countryside as a potential site for both self and collective development.

By being the exception to the rule, Deng Yiyan's narrative illustrates the potency of discourses relating to rural/urban difference and modernity, and their hold on the mind-sets of urbanites, ruralites and rural migrants alike. Like Liu Yu's, Deng Yiyan's narrative also demonstrates the power of discourses on gender, sexuality and marriage in shaping women's sense of place. Thus, Deng Yiyan is unusually vocal about the restrictions that gender places on rural women and bitter about the fact that gender discourse has both pushed her out of the village and thwarted her return to it. And yet, for all her rebellion, Deng Yiyan longs to be able to conform to gender and marriage norms, because to be outside of them is both less "convenient" and lonely. In the narratives of both Deng Yiyan and Liu Yu, as in fact in those of many others, one gets the sense that gender is at least as important as discourses on rural/urban difference in shaping women's desires regarding place and the possibility of them achieving those desires.

Conclusion

In chapter 1 I argued that a "denial of coevalness" between city and country could be observed in Chinese intellectual discourses on modernity and nationhood in the early twentieth century. In these discourses the rural was cast as China's "traditional," "backward" past, while the urban was seen as both the site and the engine of the nation's modern future. In some ways, the Communist Party under Mao Zedong overturned this modernist teleology, promoting the revolutionary, future-oriented role of the countryside and the peasantry. However, at the same time, and with more lasting consequences, the Maoist approach to development, entailing a siphoning of resources out of agriculture into industry and the imposition of the household registration system, thoroughly entrenched a denial of coevalness, such that the countryside was maintained, in material as well as symbolic ways, as the backward other of the city.

If the Maoist approach to development included at least some attempts to ameliorate the denial of the countryside's coevalness with the city, in the post-Mao period that denial returned with a vengeance, with state officials, intellectuals, and capitalists all seeing it in their interests to promote the city as the site of modernity and the future and the countryside as the place of backwardness. This shift did not occur in full and immediately with the introduction of post-Mao reforms—in the early 1980s, for example, rural-urban inequalities were actually reduced, and it was not until the late 1990s that all-out urbanization became such a dominant feature of China's pursuit of modernity.

Since the late 1990s, however, the countryside has very much been relegated to second place in national strategies for development and in the country's culture of modernity. This is not to say that it has no place or function—on the contrary, as an object or site for nostalgia it has played an important part in contemporary culture. It also plays a vital role in national development strategies, both as an object to be developed and as a source of resources, including cheap labor. However, towns and cities are, once more, both the site and the engine of modernity.

In this chapter I have shown that dominant discourses on modernity and the denial of coevalness that they entail have had powerful material effects on the ways in which the countryside and the city are experienced by rural migrants. They have also become so thoroughly absorbed in the outlooks and subjectivities of individuals, and are generally so central to the evaluative and explanatory systems of their life stories, that to hear a rural migrant deny the superiority of the city and to advocate the countryside as the site of self and collective development is truly startling.

Both at the level of dominant national discourse and at the level of individual experiences, subjectivities, and narratives, however, modernity, urbanity, and the denial of coevalness between the city and the countryside are thoroughly entangled with gender relations and with discourses relating to age, marriage, and the life course. Under Mao the countryside could be a site for young people, both male and female, to become political activists and model laborers and thereby to join the national march of revolution and progress, albeit as lesser participants than industrial workers. For men, these social identities and roles often solidified once they married and started their own families, fading later with their retirement from collective labor. For women, in contrast, marriage usually entailed moving to their husband's household in a different village and, both because they were "outsiders" in their husband's community and because of their new responsibility for childrearing and housework, women rarely continued to be as active in politics and collective labor after marriage as before.

Since the 1990s the countryside has ceased to provide an identity for young people in the way that it did in the past—to be a part of the nation's project of development and modernity, a young rural person must now migrate to the city. However, the positioning of young rural men and women with respect to such migration is different. Once more, the implications of patrilocal, exogamous marriage practices are crucial. These practices mean that young women are regarded as marginal to their rural families and when they migrate they tend to feel less obliged to remit their earnings than do their brothers who, in many cases, are saving up money to build new houses to attract brides.

Impending marriage also lends a different coloring to migrant women's and migrant men's reflections on the countryside. For men, marriage marks the achievement of identity as a full member of his community and the assumption of responsibility for the maintenance and reproduction of his family. When a rural migrant man in the city thinks back on his home in the countryside, he is most likely to think of it as the primary locus of his identity and in terms of a continuing tie and commitment. For women, in contrast, marriage marks a radical disjuncture: a departure from her natal home, a loss of autonomy, a loss of support from kin and friends, and the assumption of heavy new responsibilities and tasks, under the authority of scarcely known in-laws. The rupture and loss of identity that looms with marriage may well mean that rural migrant women look back upon their childhoods in their natal families in the countryside with greater nostalgia than do male migrants. It also means, though, that compared with men migrant women tend to see a future in the city as holding greater potential for development than life in the countryside, and they commonly view return to the countryside with greater anxiety and dread than men.

This picture is complicated by gender inequalities and by discrimination and sexual violence against women. Relative to men, young women migrants have fewer chances of advancement in terms of income generation, skills acquisition, and the achievement of status in the public sphere in both rural and urban areas, and are more vulnerable to sexual exploitation and violence. They are also more subject to censure with regard to their sexual morality and behavior.

We have here a complex weaving together of dominant discourses and personal subjectivities, and of tradition and modernity: Modern urban development involves capitalist factory managers making full use of traditional gender inequalities and rural marriage practices to exploit young rural migrant women as a cheap, expendable labor force. It also involves traditional sexual discrimination and sexual violence, directed disproportionately against young rural migrant women. And yet, young rural migrant women are often the most enthusiastic proponents and subjects of urban-oriented modernity and development, in large part because of their positioning in, and negativity toward, traditional rural gender relations and marriage practices. However, as we have seen in this chapter, how all of this pans out in the experiences, stories, and behaviors of rural migrant women varies, in surprising and sometimes tragic ways, from one individual to another.

Among older, married migrants the picture is somewhat different. In modern China, as elsewhere in the modern world, young adults have always been seen as the prime subjects of social change and progress. Older people, like children, are marginal in this discourse. In the post-Mao era, rural migrants past the age of about thirty are less favored as employees in urban enterprises and they are less the targets for the state's and the market's promotion of consumption, self-development, and development. In any case, with marriage, childbirth, and the assumption of family responsibilities, both men and women tend to be less oriented to the achievement of self-development and more to the survival of their families and the enhancement of their children's life chances. This is particularly the case for rural women because of the dominant gender division of labor, whereby the private sphere of childrearing is seen as women's work. This gender division of labor means that, on average, rural women migrate less frequently after marriage than men. When they do migrate, some are motivated by personal needs, including escape from boredom, overwork, and domestic violence, but for most the chief aim is to improve the situation of their family.

Older married migrants, both men and women, also tend to differ from younger migrants in their perspectives on the place of the urban and the rural. Thus, while younger migrants' search for self-development and the expansion of horizons draws them to the city, older migrants' concerns about the reproduction of their family and about their own increasing age tend to lead them to view their futures in terms of retirement to the countryside, even if that retirement is many years off and, as is often the case, holds little appeal.

Taken as a whole, the narratives of both groups reflect and reinforce dominant discourses on modernity, urbanity, and the denial of coevalness between the city and the countryside. Thus, in the narratives of most migrants, as in the rest of the population, the countryside is the place of the past, of stasis and confinement, childhood, old age, and retreat. The city, for all its hardships, is the place of the future, modernity, youth and desire, and development.[27]

Part III

People

5

Relationships

In Part II I focused on place, arguing that conflicting experiences and evaluations of place are a central component of migrant women's understandings of their lives and identities. In Part III my focus is on interpersonal relations and identities with respect to other people.

In this chapter I look at what rural migrant women in Beijing say about their relationships with the people closest to them. The chapter is divided into two sections. The first focuses on migrant women's relationships with close family members, particularly parents and husbands. The second discusses their relationships with other migrants and with urbanites. Throughout this chapter my aim is to learn how migrant women's relationships with others shape their patterns and experiences of migration and life in the city and to further our understanding of the impact of migration on rural women's relationships, especially with members of their families.

Family Relationships

Filial and Rebellious Daughters: Dagongmei Relations with Their Parents

Since the 1980s it has been common for scholars to analyze labor migration in terms of "household strategies," this being something of an intermediate point between the two approaches that had hitherto dominated the literature, one taking the individual migrant as the unit of analysis and the other focusing on macrolevel structural forces (Trager 1988, 6–8; Wolf, Diane 1992, 12–20). In some studies a household strategies approach has simply entailed replacing the individual with the household or family as the primary actor in migration decision making. Labor migration patterns, in these studies, are understood as determined by rational strategies adopted by households or by heads of households, in the interest of maximizing economic returns. Feminists have argued that these studies underestimate the degree to which decision making within families and households is shaped by conflicts between the desires, expectations, and understandings of different household members, gendered differentials in power and control over resources in the household, and intrahousehold divisions of labor, all of which are shaped by society-level discourses relating to gender (Chant and Radcliffe 1992, 23; Wolf 1992, 20–23).[1]

In taking these concerns on board, recent studies of the labor migration of young, unmarried women have developed two contrasting models. Following Yuen-fong Woon, I call these the "filial daughter" and "rebellious daughter" models. The filial daughter model posits that young women leave home to work primarily as a result of decisions made by their parents, taken in order to maximize economic benefits to the household. Being at the bottom of hierarchies of both age and gender, and subject to powerful patriarchal discourses, young women have no choice but to accept these decisions (Woon 2000, 160). Lydia Kung is a key proponent of this filial daughter model. In her study of young rural women's entry into the industrial labor force in Taiwan in the 1970s, Kung argued that neither separation from home nor the earning of an independent income resulted in any significant reconfiguration of the relations between these women and their families. Parents continued to wield a high degree of control over their daughters' lives and expected a large proportion of the women's earnings to be remitted to them. Having internalized the belief that they were "useless daughters" who would soon be married out, these women acceded to their parents' expectations, regarding migrant work primarily as a chance to repay their parents for the burden of raising and educating them. Factory work, Kung concluded, "is a new activity that permits the achievement of traditional goals, and filial piety continues to be a motivating force" (Kung 1983 [1978], 203).[2]

In contrast to the filial daughter model articulated so well by Lydia Kung, proponents of the rebellious daughter approach portray young women's decisions to migrate as their own, taken independently of the patriarchal family and in rebellion to it. Their migration, in this model, is seen as motivated not by family needs but by young women's individual desires for personal autonomy, self-actualization, and improved life chances. According to some writers, this type of rebelliousness is particularly prevalent among relatively highly educated young rural women and stems from a clash between their subordination and lack of opportunities in the patriarchal family, and new ideas and aspirations to which they have been exposed through their schooling, the media and elsewhere (Woon 2000, 146–47). Ching Kwan Lee, writing about the migration of young rural women to Guangdong in the 1990s, provides an example of the rebellious daughter model. She claims that in leaving home, these women were motivated primarily by a desire to evade familial obligations and parental decisions:

> Young rural women sought to increase their personal autonomy vis a vis parental domination and to redefine their familial gender role in the realms of production and marriage. Having a wage income or economic independence was a precondition for realizing these goals. (Lee 1998, 84)[3]

Figure 5.1 **Migration Decision Makers**

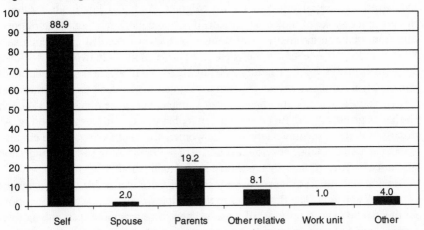

In the next section I compare findings from research undertaken with unmarried *dagongmei* members of the Migrant Women's Club in Beijing with the filial daughter and rebellious daughter models developed by Lydia Kung, Ching Kwan Lee, and others. I argue that, superficially, members of the Migrant Women's Club appear to conform much more closely with Ching Kwan Lee's depiction of rebellious daughters in contemporary Guangdong than with Lydia Kung's discussion of filial daughters in 1970s Taiwan: They are much less under the thumb of their parents than the latter and their out-migration is motivated more by individualist concerns and less by filial obligation. Perhaps this is unsurprising: In Taiwan in the 1970s patriarchal family relations went relatively unchallenged by a neo-Confucian state. In contrast, by the 1990s, rural women and their families in the PRC had been exposed to more than four decades of antipatriarchal discourse. For all this, many of the members of the Migrant Women's Club also come across as very filial to their parents, and there are some striking resonances between their narratives and those of the Taiwanese women that Lydia Kung interviewed.[4]

Deciding to Leave Home

As indicated in Figure 5.1, in response to the question "Who decided you would leave home to work?" the great majority (88.9 percent) of Migrant Women's Club members surveyed in 2000 indicated that they themselves had played a role in the decision. Parents rank second in importance as migration decision makers, but all the same, only about 19 percent said that their parents had been involved in their decision to migrate and even fewer said that others had been involved in the decision.[5] These figures suggest that members of the Migrant Women's Club perceived their decision to migrate to the city as being primarily their own, taken much more independently of parents and others than is implied in the filial daughter model of migration.

This finding is confirmed in the evaluative and explanatory systems apparent in the narratives of my interlocutors in the Migrant Women's Club. In all instances, these women spoke of motivations, decisions, and actions relating to their departure from home in the first person singular. All said "I decided. . . ." None said "they decided . . ." or even "we decided. . . ." Furthermore, only two young women spoke of concerns for their family as being their sole motivation for going out to work—Chen Ailing said she left home to "lighten the burden" on her father, and Liu Yu said she would rather have stayed at home, but as the oldest child she felt she had to go out to work to provide money for her younger siblings' schooling. As discussed in the preceding chapter, other women also spoke of straitened circumstances at home, but they nevertheless talked of their motivations for out-migration primarily in terms of their own personal self-actualization.

Having said this, a more sensitive reading of these women's narratives makes two things apparent. The first relates to the complexity of agency and motivation. As one would expect, for most of these women there was more than one motivation for leaving home. In most of their narratives the balance of motivations seems to lean toward the individual, but in some the mix is so complicated that it is hard to say whether, as a whole, the young woman was motivated more by individual interests and a desire to rebel (or at least be independent) than by family interests and a sense of filial obligation, or vice versa. Indeed, in some cases it seems that individual interests may well have coincided with family interests, rendering the very distinction between the two problematic.

The second point relates to representation. In some instances a set of decisions represented by a young woman as taken by herself and motivated by her own, individual interests could equally well have been represented in terms of a household strategy aimed at maximizing family interests. Curiously, at the other end of the spectrum the women who seem to fit the rebellious daughter model most closely were also the most bent on representing their relations with their parents as filial. We need to bear in mind that both agency and independence, and filial piety are highly desirable qualities in contemporary Chinese society. This is the case in both urban and rural contexts, but most people tend to view independence as a modern, urban quality, while filial piety is associated with a traditional, rural identity. For most *dagongmei* in Beijing it is important to try to be, and to represent oneself as being, both independent *and* filial. Independence and autonomy from the family are desired in their own right and also as symbols of a modern, adult identity. But filial piety is also important for maintaining positive relations with family members and for preserving one's reputation as a respectable and caring woman.

Let us see, then, how all of this unfolds in *dagongmei* narratives. Among my unmarried interlocutors in the Migrant Women's Club, a minority came from areas where the out-migration of young women had been common for many years and was, in fact, the norm when they were teenagers in the mid-1990s. Consequently, these women's own departure from home was almost automatic, involving relatively little conscious decision making on the part of either themselves or their parents. Zhang Ning came from just such an area in Anhui. She began her interview with me by saying:

> I came to Beijing in July 1993. I don't know why I came [laugh]. I was seventeen, with just primary school education. My thinking was very simple: other people had gone to Beijing, so I wanted to go too. Everyone older than me in my village had gone out to work. All my former school-mates had gone and there was just me left. (August 2001)

Here, as throughout her narrative, Zhang Ning portrays herself as having made her own decisions and shaped her own fate. She is by no means a submissive filial daughter, sent out to earn money for the family. Yet her migration hardly seems to have been an act of rebellion either. In fact, staying at home is likely to have drawn more comment from her parents and other villagers than leaving.

Other interlocutors came from areas where out-migration had not yet become *the* norm for young people, but was increasingly common. In these villages, going out to work was generally not considered an act of rebellion, but it was something that involved a weighing up of different options and a certain amount of explanation and justification, both at the time and in retrospect. Most commonly, these women connected their out-migration with a termination of their schooling. They said that they had stopped going to school after having graduated from either primary or junior secondary school because their families could no longer afford it, and their departure from home closely followed this. Migrating to the city to work was the next best thing to continuing an education, offering a chance to escape the boredom of home life and to earn some money, but, in hindsight at least, these women would have preferred to continue their schooling. Ending school and going out to work was not something they said they were pressured into by their parents, though. On the contrary, when questioned, they all insisted that this was their own rather than their parents' decision. The following conversation with Yan Jun, who left her home in Shandong at the age of sixteen, is typical:

Tamara Jacka: Why did you come out to work?

Yan Jun: Because at that time things were hard for my family financially, and it was boring at home. I felt really bad because I thought that if I couldn't go to university I wouldn't have a future. But I didn't try to get into senior high school. I wanted to and my grades were very good, but we didn't have the money.

Tamara Jacka: Was it your parents' decision that you stop school and go out to work, or your own?

Yan Jun: My own. At that age you know when things are tough financially at home and there's a lot of pressure; so I didn't go on [with my schooling], even though I would have liked to.

Tamara Jacka: What did your parents think about that?

Yan Jun: They would probably have liked me to continue, but they didn't put much weight on girls' education. (September 2001)

Should we think of Yan Jun as a "rebellious" or at least independent daughter, or is the "filial daughter" model more appropriate? On the one hand, she represents herself as an independent agent, making her own decisions rather than passively accepting her family's choices. Furthermore, although it is clear that her leaving home is in part a response to her family's straightened financial circumstances, she speaks of this primarily in terms of the problems this presents for the achievement of her own personal interests. The implication is that migration to the city offers an alternative, albeit less desirable, route to self-actualization.

On the other hand, Yan Jun's decision to finish school and go out to work was not opposed by her parents. It could, in fact, be said that for all her professed agency Yan Jun well illustrates the "filial daughter" model in the sense that, as a relatively junior, female member of the family, she did not have the power to fight her parents' low prioritization of girls' education and had no choice but to subsume her own personal desire for an education to the economic interests of her family. Consider the following conversation I had in Haidian, with Han Haiying and her husband:

Han Haiying: Our daughter is fourteen now, she'll be sixteen and graduating from junior high in two years. My hope is for her to finish her schooling—that's my hope, but we can only do so much. If we have only one child going to school, the burden will be lightened. We're planning to send our daughter to Guangdong or Shenzhen to work. It's tough [*xinku*], but we have no choice [*mei banfa*]. In the countryside that's the way it is, there's no choice.

Tamara Jacka: What's your daughter's opinion on this?

Husband: She has no particular opinion.

Han Haiying: She knows [the situation]. In her heart she'd like to study, but she understands that her dad's health is no good. (August 2001)

If I had talked to Yan Jun's parents, they might have told a story similar to Han Haiying and her husband, presenting their daughter's migration as something that they had determined as part of a household strategy for dealing with difficult economic circumstances.

While the termination of schooling after primary or junior high school, followed soon after by migration in search of work, had already become an accepted pattern for young women in Zhang Ning's and Yan Jun's villages, this was not the case for the majority of my interlocutors. Ruan Shilin, for example, said that nowadays (that is, in the early 2000s) all the young women from her natal village in Shandong go out to work soon after leaving school. "If they don't, people ask 'how come you're still at home, why haven't you gone out?'" (November 2001). But when she came to Beijing in 1996, she was one of the first young women to leave home. Other *dagongmei* who migrated in the mid- to late 1990s similarly indicated that they were among the first young women in their area to do so, and their decisions to go were taken in the face of apprehension and in some cases active resistance from their parents. Zhu Jin ran away from home to escape marriage, without the approval of her parents. Others struggled long and hard to persuade their parents to let them go. In general, their migration seemed much more obviously fueled by a determination to escape the constricting bonds of family and village patriarchy than was the case for either Zhang Ning or Yan Jun.

Many parents sought to dissuade their daughters from leaving home for safety reasons and because they felt they were too immature to be able to manage the complexities and risks involved in making the journey to the city and finding work there. Qiao Xue was among the first young women to leave her village in Shaanxi. She did so in 1997, when she was sixteen. When I asked her what her parents thought of her going out to work, she replied:

My mum was happy for me to come out, for me to broaden my horizons and see what the outside world was like. My dad was different. He said it's very dangerous outside and nowadays society is very complex, and you're still not grown up so you're not adapted for this society. (August 2001)

Like many parents, Qiao Xue's father was concerned by reports he had heard that the city was *luan*—chaotic and unsafe, and that both on the train or bus traveling there, and in the city itself, young women were vulnerable to having their belongings stolen, being raped, deceived into prostitution, or else kidnapped and sold in marriage.

Parents' safety concerns were more pronounced for daughters than for sons, and also sometimes greater for junior members of the family than for firstborns. As the firstborn child in her family, Ruan Shilin's decision to go out to work at the age of twenty-three did not meet with opposition from her parents. Like other firstborns, she had taken on chores and responsibilities at a relatively young age and her parents were confident that she had learned to look after herself and could manage in the city. Her classmate, though, had to struggle hard to persuade her parents to let her go, because they worried that as the youngest child in the family she had led a sheltered life and might not be able to look after herself away from home. Others, on the other hand, indicated that their parents were relatively unconcerned about their departure from home, because their older siblings had already migrated to the city, demonstrating that it could be achieved safely.

A second reason why parents sometimes opposed their daughters' migration was that they doubted they would succeed in the city and felt they would do better to accept their lot in the countryside. This is illustrated in the remarks of Zhou Ling, who left her village in Jiangsu in 1982 when out-migration was still very rare:

> Of course my parents would not agree to me leaving home. One reason was they thought people would look down on us even more. The other reason was they thought it would later be even harder for me to find a good husband. Another reason was, once I left, how would it be? What prospects would I have? I'd work as a maid and then quite soon just have to come back. So [our neighbor] didn't want to help me leave home. She said if things didn't turn out, my parents would blame her. But every day I went to her place to help her with her work and gradually I persuaded her. She said she'd write a letter to her cousin [working as a maid in Beijing], and if she agreed I could go, otherwise she could do nothing. Her cousin wrote back very quickly, agreeing. She said that the wages weren't high—only 18 yuan a month, but if I wanted to I could come. So I did. I was probably more determined to go out than other girls because my family situation was unusual. So I was more determined. (August 2001)

Finally, parents worried that other villagers would perceive their daughters as immoral if they went out to work, and consequently the families would lose face and the young women would have great difficulty finding husbands. As Zhou Ling explained,

> At that time it wasn't as open as now, with so many people going out, and if you went out to become a maid, you would have no status, because that was the same as becoming a servant. People would look down on you and later no one would marry you. And also, people seeing a girl leaving home would think "Who knows what she's doing. Could she be doing other things, going off with men?" Chastity is extremely important to Chinese people. Other girls growing up in the village could be observed by everyone. But if you ran so far away, no one could see what you were doing, so later you wouldn't be able to find a husband. Better families, those with promise, wouldn't let you marry their son. (August 2001)

Since the 1990s out-migration has become more generally accepted than it was when Zhou Ling left home, especially for men (single and married) and couples. However, the out-migration of unmarried women, and of married women without their husbands, is still relatively uncommon, and it remains the case that their sexual morality is viewed with suspicion.[6] It was for this reason, for example, that Gao Xinran's desire to go out to work and to experience a little freedom before marriage was met with resistance from her parents and from the family of the man to whom she was engaged.

Women who leave home in the face of village prejudices, and despite parental resistance, come closest to the "rebellious daughter" model. Certainly, they themselves often emphasize their unusual determination and rebelliousness. Zhou Ling, for example, stressed repeatedly that she was "more determined" than other girls to leave home, talked in detail of the effort and persistence she put into finding a means by which to get away, and said that

> at first they [her parents] did not agree [to her leaving home], but then they saw how determined I was. My dad said, "You've already written the letter and you really want to go, so we won't stop you." He also thought about it and said, "There's no way to find a life at home. Go and try it [that is, work in the city], and maybe you can carve out a path [*chuang chulai*] for yourself. Otherwise you'll just come home and farm." (August 2001)

In conversation with me, Chunzi joked about how she responded to her mother's anxious plea that she get married and settle down rather than go off to the city, by threatening to shave off all her hair and become a Buddhist nun if she was not allowed to leave home. This so frightened her mother, she laughed, that she acquiesced (October 2001). On another occasion, though, she wrote an article for the magazine *Zhongguo Funü* (Chinese Women) in which her tone was much more serious. There she emphasized her mother's and her own desperate efforts to make enough money to enable her to continue her education. She wrote of the tears she cried when the work she was doing to pay her school fees finally sent her to the hospital with exhaustion and anemia, making her realize that she could no longer fight the prevailing view that it was pointless for a girl to get educated. And she emphasized the determination with which she left her family and the small mountain village in which she had grown up, making the frightening and arduous trip to Beijing rather than giving in to her mother's request that she stay at home and accept one of the young men introduced to her (Chunzi 1998, 26).

Of all my interlocutors, Chunzi and Zhou Ling represented themselves as the most doggedly independent and rebellious. And yet, they also talked with a great deal of sympathy about their parents and emphasized their love and sense of filial obligation to them. In both cases their narratives suggest that the course their life has taken and their sense of self are deeply intertwined with their relations with their parents; relations that cannot adequately be captured by either the rebellious or the filial daughter models. Thus, while Chunzi talked of how hard she struggled against her mother's insistence that she settle down in the village, she also said, "There are many things for which I love my mother very much. I love her so much that it hurts," and she talked with deep gratitude and respect about the enormous sacrifices her mother made to pay for her children's education:

> I've always wanted to earn enough money to show filial piety [*xiaojing*] to my parents, so that my family would be better off. My great dream . . . I remember back then, other people had TVs. When I was twenty I really hoped that I could earn enough money to buy my mum a TV, or else buy a present for her birthday or something—that was my dream. Later when I came to Beijing—I remember the funds were borrowed actually—my aim in coming to Beijing was to get to know life away from home and find a job. (October 2001)

Later Chunzi added:

> Nowadays our family's conditions are pretty good. Locally, we count as well off. So the price my mum paid in the past was not for nothing. Now my older brothers and younger brothers all show filial piety [*xiaoshun*] to her, and so do I. (October 2001)

The impact of Zhou Ling's relations with her family upon her life course was even more complex. Zhou Ling's paternal grandparents and her parents had at one stage all worked in the city. Her grandmother, who looked after her when she was young, told her stories of when she worked in a Japanese-owned factory in Shanghai before the war. Zhou Ling recalled that the stories were always very exciting—her grandmother never said anything about hardship or suffering. Her mother, too, told her exciting stories about when she worked in an urban steel mill in the late 1950s. But in 1963, in an attempt to ameliorate urban unemployment, the authorities sent most rural workers, including her mother, back to the countryside. With the onset of the Cultural Revolution, and because of her paternal grandfather's bad class status, the rest of the family was also sent to the countryside. Zhou Ling continued:

Their life had been okay, but after going to the countryside things changed. Their status and class background were no good and that meant they were very lonely and depressed. My dad always made us serious. He thought the rest of his life would be like that—he wouldn't be able to turn his life around because there were no opportunities— but he really hoped that later there would be some promise for his three daughters. He felt that if there was some promise, we could bring honor to our ancestors [*guangzong yaozu*] and give our family face [*timian*]. So ever since we were small my grandmother and my parents all tried to educate us. But we couldn't see any hope and my dad really suffered. . . .

The whole time I was growing up, I saw that expression of suffering on my dad's face, so I always tried to be serious, so I would have some promise, so I could let my mum and dad live well [*guo hao rizi*], and so that the people in our village would not look down on us. Later, when Deng Xiaoping came to power, it became possible to sit the exams for university—it was no longer dependent on your class status. So, in the countryside everyone studied really hard. I studied really, really hard, hoping to escape the countryside [*tiaochu nongmen*] and come to the city and later bring my parents to the city, so that they wouldn't have to eat bitterness in the countryside anymore. . . . When I didn't get into university my dad got very angry and yelled abuse at me. I couldn't understand him. I felt that I had tried very hard, but I simply didn't have enough to eat and always got dizzy, so how could I possibly have got into university. I blamed my dad. My dad blamed me. I felt that when I was at home, I always made him angry. I felt my dad didn't understand me and I felt very bad. Originally, the idea of going to university had given me some hope, but when I went back to the countryside that hope disappeared—I had no prospects [*bentou*]. I had to go out to the fields every day from when the sun rose till when it set. There was no hope. When I looked at the fields, I felt desolate. Was this to be my whole life? I had no prospects.

I was only seventeen years old then and my family was poor. So someone came to help me find a husband. We had three daughters and were very poor, so they were kind-hearted and looked for a man who would marry into our family and help with the work. They found one in our village. That family was at the bottom of the barrel. They couldn't get anyone to marry their sons because they were so poor. They had four sons and they didn't have any room, so they thought one son could marry me and live with our family. I was very upset—I couldn't possibly have been interested. Anyway, I was only seventeen and I didn't understand anything. The matchmaker was very persuasive, but my parents and grandmother were very upset. They looked down on those people because they couldn't find a wife for their son. [My family] lost hope even more, seeing that people believed that their daughter could only be married to that kind of man. My grandma got really mad and sent [the matchmaker] packing. I also lost hope. Was that my life? Was that the kind of person I was going to marry? Even though the match was unsuccessful, it made me unhappy. I didn't want to live that kind of life, so I decided to get out. It didn't matter where I went—I just had to leave that place. The wish was very strong. It was partly because I felt my parents didn't understand me and partly because it was so remote and desolate in the countryside. People just worked in the fields—there was no form of pleasure or anything else. Then there was that matchmaker. . . . So I decided to go. (August 2001)

Like other young rural women who left home to join the floating population in the early 1980s, Zhou Ling was a pioneer. At that time rural out-migration was rare, there were few avenues through which it could be accomplished, and it was undertaken in the face of high levels of suspicion and disapproval from parents and other villagers. To leave home and migrate to the city one *had* to be rebellious—to go against dominant patriarchal understandings of the position of young women, and to pursue individual self-interests with great determination and persistence. Such a determination to rebel comes through very clearly in Zhou Ling's narrative. Her decision to leave home was motivated most immediately by her sense that her parents did not understand her, by the desire to get out of the countryside and away from the joyless, constricted life that her parents had led, and by a rejection of what other villagers understood was to be her future as a woman of a poor, low-status rural family.

Ironically, though, it is clear that at a deeper level much of Zhou Ling's determination and motivation for rebellion comes not so much from her independence or separateness from her family, but from the complex imbrication of her own identity and aspirations with those of her family elders. Thus, as Zhou Ling herself recognizes, at least in hindsight, her escape from home and her quest for self-realization cannot be fully comprehended without appreciating the history of her family and the influences—both positive and negative—that history has had on her. From both her mother's and her father's side, Zhou Ling inherited a sense that she was different from the average village girl. Thus, her desire to escape the village was fueled both by her own direct experiences of poverty and discrimination from other villagers and by an internalization of her father's deep sense of frustration and unhappiness at his inability to achieve (or regain) for his family the honor and prospects he felt they should have had as people with education and urban experience. Her father's suffering drove her away from home, but it also left her with an abiding sympathy for her parents and a desire to make things up to them. It is also clear that her parents and her grandmother were important role models for Zhou Ling. They inspired her to pursue an education well beyond the expectations of most villagers, and that higher education undoubtedly contributed to the confidence she needed to pursue an unconventional direction in life. And while an urban life would have been beyond the bounds of imagination for most young women in the village, for Zhou Ling the seeds of desire for such a life were planted by her mother's and grandmother's stories.

In her village Zhou Ling stood out because of her family background. Among rural migrants she is less unusual. In general, migrants tend to be better educated than the rural average and in the case of women it is partly that education that inspires them to break away from dominant patriarchal norms as well as providing them with the information and confidence they need to leave home (Yang and Guo 1999, 933, 937).[7] In the context of the still very strong assumption among Chinese villagers that educating girls beyond a minimum is a waste of resources, a rural woman's higher education is likely to have been made possible by an unusual level of support from her parents.

As rural out-migration has become more common among young women, and as the development of migrant networks has made each person's departure easier to achieve, the significance of inspiration and support from parents may have declined. However, as I have indicated, growth in rural to urban migration has varied considerably across the countryside. In many areas it remains the case that few young women go out to work, and I would surmise that in these areas family background is highly significant for those who do migrate.

Ongoing Relations with Parents

In her study of factory women in 1970s Taiwan, Lydia Kung writes that even once their daughters left home, rural parents exercised a high degree of control over their lives, not only pressuring them to send money home but also telling them which occupations they should enter and even which particular factories they should choose (Kung 1983 [1978], 54, 66). Among my interlocutors, such direct control over daughters was generally not possible simply because parents were mostly ignorant about circumstances in Beijing, and in any case most *dagongmei* were too far away from their parents back in the village and communication between them was difficult. All the same, some women had older siblings and other relatives in Beijing who exercised considerable familial control over them. Deng Yiyan was one example. In the previous chapter I mentioned that Deng Yiyan's family had refused to allow her to return home and take up her portion of the family's land, saying that both she and the family would lose face if she were to go back to farming. But they also intervened in her activities in Beijing. Thus, when she set up a clothing stall in Beijing, her older brother, who felt that such an activity was also demeaning to the family, went to the Bureau of Industry and Commerce and had her business license revoked.

Still, most *dagongmei* felt comparatively independent and free from their families while they were in Beijing, and this was one of the prime attractions of life in the city. At the same time, it is noteworthy that all my *dagongmei* interlocutors said they maintained contact with their families while they were away from home. Even Zhu Jin, who had escaped an arranged marriage and left home without her parents' approval, said that she had now mended relations with her parents. She phoned them once a week and usually went home for New Year every one or two years (December 2002). And Deng Yiyan, who—thirteen years after leaving home—continued to be bitter about the attitudes of her mother and her older brothers and to chafe at the restrictions they placed on her life, nevertheless returned to stay with her mother in the village at irregular intervals and sometimes sent her money.

Most *dagongmei* with whom I talked tried to maintain regular communication with their parents. The minority whose families had telephones phoned them every week. Others wrote letters home instead. There was also a general understanding that migrants return to their hometown every year or two, usually during the New Year holiday period. Several did not return that often, but this was something that they seemed to think required explanation, the usual one being that they could not afford it.[8] In addition, most of my unmarried interlocutors remitted a portion of their earnings home, to help their parents.[9] Some did so on a monthly basis. Others did so every few months or took money back when they visited home. However, some women sent very little or no money home—mostly those who had lived away from home for a relatively long period. Again, though, they seemed to feel that this required justification. Some explained that they could not afford to remit money to their families. Others said that their families were much better off now and that they needed the money for their own self-development, including education, more than their parents.

It needs to be stressed that in maintaining contact with their parents and sending them money, migrant women do not simply obey orders from their parents. Nor are they passive dupes of a discourse on filial piety, though clearly they are influenced by it. Rather, they actively decide to be filial (or not), and they must expend resources and do work to achieve that end. That they have the resources and are able to decide how to use them is evidence of individual empowerment. In this sense, and contrary to what is usually implied in the filial daughter model, filial piety is as much a form of agency as is the struggle for independence from the family.

Dagongmei decide to be filial for a range of reasons. For some, filial piety is a means to an end. This may have been the case for Deng Yiyan, though she did not say so explicitly. In the past, her mother and her older brothers had shown themselves more than capable of interfering in her life and making her miserable. It is likely, therefore, that Deng felt the need to maintain filial relations with her mother, so that she and the rest of the family would not make Deng's life difficult.

For a great many other *dagongmei,* observing filial piety and being *seen* to observe it—for example, by remitting earnings and visiting home regularly—is a strategy for maintaining the approval of elders and others at home in the village. As mentioned in the previous chapter, most *dagongmei* believe that they will one day have to return home to get married. By conforming to the expectation that they maintain filial relations with their parents, they hope to ensure that their reputations and marriage prospects are not damaged by any suggestion among villagers that their sojourn in the city has turned them into "bad" women—women who have been corrupted by urban commercialism and selfish greed and no longer care for their relatives or, even worse, whose sexual immorality makes them too ashamed to keep in touch with their families.

While filial piety is for some purely a means to an end—a strategy aimed at furthering personal interests—this is not always the case. Chunzi and Zhou Ling, for example, no longer needed to maintain good reputations in their natal villages in the same way as other *dagongmei,* because they had already married and established their own families in Beijing. For them, filial piety was an expression of love and gratitude. Furthermore, to be able to fulfill their filial obligations—to repay their parents for the sacrifices they made in bringing them up—was a major personal triumph for these women. As they explained, throughout their childhood they had observed their parents' suffering and had wanted to do something to make their lives better. As a young woman, Chunzi dreamed of buying a television for her mother. Several years later, she succeeded in finding a job in Beijing that enabled her to send several thousands of yuan to her parents annually over a few years. And Zhou Ling, whose dream as a young woman had been to bring her parents to the city with her so they "wouldn't have to eat bitterness in the countryside anymore," succeeded in doing so—a remarkable achievement for a rural woman.

Aside from this, ongoing relations with their parents contributed in important ways to the emotional lives of many *dagongmei,* even though they were conducted at a distance. Many said they had been very close to their parents when they were young, and they missed them terribly after leaving home. In fact, as discussed in the previous chapter, homesickness was a central element in *dagongmei* experiences of the city. Maintaining links with their parents through telephone calls and letters was an important means by which these young women sought to overcome their homesickness and loneliness. It was also a means through which to develop for themselves, and convey to others, pride and a sense of self-worth in the face of multiple challenges and threats to their status and identity. Ruan Shilin, for example, said that she derived a great deal of pleasure from chatting with her parents on the phone, telling them all about her achievements and adventures in the city (November 2001).

Generally though, my interlocutors only talked to their parents about positive things; they did not confide in them or discuss their problems.[10] This resulted in a sense of loss for many. One twenty-seven-year-old from Gansu said that at home she and her father were good friends and she had often discussed her problems with him. Now that she was in Beijing she wrote home regularly, but only to ask after her parents and to give them positive news: "If I wrote about problems, there'd be nothing they could do to help and they'd just worry for nothing, and, anyway, by the time they got the letter I'd be over my difficulties" (November 2001).

"Associational Migrants"? Relations Between Married Migrant Women and Their Husbands

In the literature relating to the migration of married women, relatively little attention has been paid to intrahousehold relations, most scholars having considered such women to be "merely" "associational" migrants. In other words, it is assumed that married women simply passively accompany or follow their husbands, whose opinions on how best to maximize the household's economic returns are what counts in migration decisions (Thadani and Todaro 1984, 37–38).[11] In this section I draw on interviews with married migrant women in Beijing in order to question this model. Do married women migrate simply as part of a "household strategy" and are they merely associational migrants whose migration is an expression of their subjugation to their husbands? Or are these women independent agents, motivated by interests and concerns different from, and perhaps in conflict with, those of their husbands? Finally, how do migration and life in the city affect relationships between rural women and their husbands?

Deciding to Leave Home

In Haidian the majority of the women I interviewed were married and came to Beijing with their husbands, those with children usually leaving them with grandparents at first, bringing them out once they had settled in the city. These women talked of the decision to leave the village as having been a joint one, taken by themselves and their husbands—they did not represent themselves as individual agents in the same way as my unmarried interlocutors. Furthermore, they spoke of their motivations for migration primarily in terms of issues facing themselves and their husbands as a household, rather than in terms of their own, individual interests. On the other hand, the authority with which they explained the factors contributing to the decision to migrate, combined with the fact that they said "we decided" rather than "he decided," suggests that they were actively involved in the migration decision making process—they did not just passively go along with decisions taken by their husbands (or other family members) in the way that is implied in the term "associational" migrant.

Other married women, including those who had gone out to work without their husbands or before them, and those who left after their husbands and in order to join them, presented the decision to migrate much more as their own, and some alluded to conflict with their husbands. Three women in Haidian said that their husbands had gone out to work first and they had followed them some time after. Here, I briefly outline each of these cases in turn, before commenting on the extent to which they conform to the household strategy and associational models of married women's migration.

Case 1. Zhang Xiaohua, aged thirty-six,
primary school education, from Henan

Zhang Xiaohua's husband came to Beijing in 1999 and she and their son, who was eleven at the time, joined him a year later. At home, Xiaohua and her husband grew wheat and rice and he also had a small business selling seeds. However, they had very little land and the seed business did not bring in much money. Added to this, Xiaohua had suffered serious illness for some years and they had spent several thousand yuan on medical bills. She could not work much and the family depended financially entirely on her husband. Because he could not make a decent living at home, he came to Beijing to work in a small private demolition company run by fellow villagers.

Asked why she too came out, Zhang Xiaohua responded that at home she "had nothing to do" [*mei shi gan*]. In the village her son did a lot of the domestic chores—heating water, cooking, washing clothes, cleaning, and so on. In Beijing he went to school and she "just did a bit of housework." At the time that I met Xiaohua, her husband's business was doing poorly, and she was very anxious about their financial situation. Xiaohua wanted a job, but at her age and with little education it was very hard to find work. Another migrant from Henan had found her a job as a maid, but she declined it because it would have meant living in the employer's home, making it impossible for her to look after her son.

When I asked Xiaohua whether she thought things were harder for migrant women or for men, she answered "definitely men, because they have to earn money outside to support the family. Women stay at home and look after the children, wash clothes and cook." (August 2001)

Case 2. Song Shulan, aged thirty-seven, two years
junior secondary school education, from Henan

Song Shulan has two children—an eleven-year-old girl, and a son of seven. Her husband first came to Beijing in 1986, before their daughter was born. He started a business selling cutlery and made a lot of money. In 1996 he returned to the village to build a large new house with his savings. For a few months, Shulan and her two children and her husband's mother and younger brother lived in the house together, but then they all came to Beijing to join her husband. At first, the younger brother worked with Shulan's husband, but when he got married he started up his own business. Shulan works at home, spending a couple of hours each day making gas lighters.

When I asked Shulan why she had come to Beijing, she said it was so the family could be together and because it was too hard for her at home, doing all the farming and looking after two children. At home they have too much land for her to manage on her own. Since she left they have rented out their land and their newly built house stands empty. (September 2001)

Case 3. Yao Min, aged thirty-two, junior secondary school education, from Hebei

Yao Min's story is similar to Song Shulan's. She has a thirteen-year-old daughter and a three-year-old son. Her husband came to Beijing in 1986, before they were married. Over the years—on his visits home—they married and had a daughter, whom Min raised in her husband's village. When Min was due to have her son, however, she and her daughter came to Beijing because there were no longer any relatives in her husband's village who could help her look after the baby, she did not want to have to do the farmwork on her own, and she wanted the family to be together. Back in the village a relative farms their large plot of land and a migrant farm laborer minds their house—a multistoried building that they bought in 1998, on the same day that their son was born.

At the time that I met Min her husband was putting pressure on her to return to the village with the children. His reasoning was that the family's living costs would thereby be reduced and his wife could also earn some money by farming (she was unemployed in the city). Min, however, was resisting, citing the same reasons she gave for following him to Beijing in the first place. In particular, she feared that she would be lonely and overworked in the village and dreaded going back to farming.

It may be that there was more to this than Min was letting on. In their investigation of out-migration in Anhui and Sichuan, Lou Binbin and her colleagues found that married women sometimes followed their husbands out of the village in order to keep an eye on them and ensure that they did not spend all their earnings on cigarettes and the like or have affairs with other women (Lou et al. 2004, 218–19). There are signs that this was also true in Min's case, for she said she often got angry and argued with her husband because he did not always come home at night. (September 2001)

Taken together, these case studies of married rural women following their husbands to the city suggest, unsurprisingly, that marital relations and the decision making processes involved in married men's and women's migration vary from one family to the next and that, in at least some cases, they are rather more complicated than the household strategy and associational models of migration suggest. In all three of these families, the initial decision for the man to work in the city while his wife remained at home was most likely guided by the understanding that he was the main breadwinner in the family and that the opportunity cost of migrating was higher for his wife, because he was less able to take care of child care and domestic work than she. This decision conforms to a simple household strategy model in the sense that it was the most rational way for the family to maximize economic benefits. As feminist critiques of this type of household strategy model point out, however, what is deemed to be "rational" depends on understandings of gender divisions of labor.

In Zhang Xiaohua's case, her illness and lack of education contributed to the assumption that her husband was the main breadwinner in the family and that he should undertake the "more demanding" task of working outside the village. However, even in her case, and certainly in the case of the two other women, had dominant gender divisions of labor and cultural understandings of different types of work been different, the most "rational" household strategy might have been for the women in these families to migrate first. Zhang Xiaohua, for example, could have migrated to the city and earned an income for the family working as a maid, while her husband took charge of what, in another culture, might be considered the heavier task of doing the domestic chores, looking after their son, and tilling the plot of land, even though it was small. And if understandings of gender divisions of labor in Song Shulan's and Yao Min's families had been different, they might have made just as much money with the women earning a wage in the city and the men putting their greater physical strength to work generating an income from their large plot of land. Alternatively, had these women been in a greater position of authority in their families, they might have persuaded their husbands that they should leave home first or without them, regardless of dominant cultural understandings of gender and "rationality." In fact, that is precisely what happened in the case of two of my interlocutors whose stories will be outlined below (see also Lou et al. 2004, 230; Murphy 2004, 265).

When it comes to these women's decisions to follow their husbands to Beijing, the household strategy model seems even less appropriate or useful, especially in the case of Yao Min and Song Shulan. In Zhang Xiaohua's case it is hard to tell the extent to which her decision to follow her husband was motivated by economic considerations. It is possible that she expected initially that, like her husband, she could earn more money for the family in the city than remaining on the land, even though that turned out to be an unrealistic expectation. Judging from her narrative, however, it seems more likely that she was motivated by a belief, first of all, that domestic chores would be easier for herself and her son in the city than in the village, and they might enjoy a better standard of living. Second, life in the city with her husband might be less boring and lonely than staying in the village. And finally, her son might receive a better education in Beijing. As it turned out, the situation of migrants in Haidian took a downturn in the late 1990s and these expectations were unrealized. However, Xiaohua was not to know that at the time she left home.

Song Shulan's and Yao Min's decisions to follow their husbands were even more obviously motivated by personal need rather than by a household strategy for maximizing income. In both cases, these women balanced the income they could generate working at home on the farm against a reduced workload for themselves and the emotional benefits of having the family together in the city, and decided in favor of the latter.

Studies of migration based on the household strategy or the associational models assume that key decisions over family members' activities and the use of resources are made by the male head of the family, with women either not involved in, or simply going along with, those decisions. None of the women discussed here presented their relations with their husbands in that light; each one portrayed herself as an independent agent, with her own opinions, and making her own decisions. In the case of Zhang Xiaohua and Song Shulan, those decisions probably accorded with their husbands' wishes. However, in Yao Min's family there were clearly disagreements, and she refused to go along with her husband's wish that she return to the village.

As I indicated in the first section of this chapter, it is relatively rare, and in some places considered deviant or immoral, for a married woman to go out to work without her husband. In a joint conversation, three of my interlocutors—two from Hebei and one from Gansu—said that this was the case in their home villages. They noted that it was common for single men and women and married men to migrate, but no married woman would be allowed by her mother-in-law to go out to work, "because she would lose face—other people would think the daughter-in-law had been forced to go out to earn money for the family doing something shameful." As they explained further, "other villagers would think she was immoral—they wouldn't know what she was up to in the city and would think that she might work as a prostitute, so her husband's family would lose face if they let her go" (December 2002).

Married women who do try to go out to work on their own often come into conflict with their husbands and others, and require considerable willpower and fortitude to achieve their goals. Some leave home out of sheer desperation. In a story published in *Rural Women*, Pang Hui wrote that her husband's drinking and violence drove her to leave him and her three daughters to work in the city. Pang Hui worked as a cook on a construction site, but when winter came and work stopped at the site, she decided to return home.

> I thought that after half a year of absence my husband would have changed, but I was wrong. When I got home, carrying my cherished money that I'd earned with blood and sweat, the first thing my husband said was: "You shameless thing, how dare you come back? No old bags who go out to work ever come home intact. I'd rather be a bachelor than a cuckold. Even if we were dying of poverty, I wouldn't take the dirty money you earned. Get out!" I said to him, "My money is clean," but he wouldn't listen and pushed me out the door. I shook all over, and it wasn't the wind from the mountains that made me shiver. I secretly gave the money to my oldest daughter, who chased after me in tears, and once more took the road away from home. (Pang 2004, 295)

Among my interlocutors, two women—Ma Hua and Jin Rong—went out to work without their husbands. Unlike Pang Hui, though, they did so from a position of strength rather than desperation. Ma Hua, a twenty-eight-year-old member of the Migrant Women's Club from Guizhou, migrated to Beijing in 1998, leaving her husband and their one-year-old child at home in the village. Ma Hua, like Zhang Xiaohua, said she came to Beijing because she "had nothing to do" at home. However, she denied that her family's poverty was an issue. In fact, she remitted her earnings to her natal family rather than to her husband, because he and his parents did not need the money. When I asked her how it was that she had come on her own, leaving her husband and child at home, she replied, "Everyone asks me about that," acknowledging that it was an unusual thing to do. Her explanation was that since their marriage two years ago she and her husband had lived in the same house as his parents and she found that somewhat difficult:

> I get on okay with them, but the relationship is not that close and we don't understand each other as well as my husband and them. It's easier for my husband to look after them than it is for me, because he understands their habits and needs and moods. Also, he's better at doing the heavy farmwork than I am, and his parents can look after the child. (October 2001)

Ma Hua said that she consulted with her husband about going out to work, but it was her idea. He accepted her decision, but he was not happy about it, and after she left he missed her a great deal and kept urging her to return home.

Jin Rong, a thirty-eight-year-old from Hebei, lives in Haidian with her husband and their two school-age children. Jin Rong explained that in their home village there was a man who had gone out to work and become very successful. She said to her husband, "He earns enough money on his own to raise a family of four! If he can make money outside, why can't we?" Her husband, however, did not want to go. They were quite well off raising a herd of sheep and a cow, and he did not want to risk the uncertainties involved in doing business away from home. So Jin Rong set out without him. Like Zhou Ling, she may have been inspired to go out to work by the example of her parents. Both her mother and father had worked for a time during the 1950s in factories in the city of Shijiazhuang, before being laid off and sent back to the countryside. Jin Rong was also relatively well-educated—she had graduated from senior high school, whereas her husband had only primary school education. She joked that at the time they met she didn't think to ask what school he had graduated from. "Afterward I said to him that if I'd known he only had primary school education, I wouldn't have married him" (August 2001). Her higher level of education may well have given Jin Rong more confidence and a greater desire to seek work away from home.

When Jin Rong first left home, it was to accompany a young nephew to Shijiazhuang, where they met up with her older sister. There, Jin Rong observed that with a three-wheeled cart one could earn more than 100 yuan in a day, transporting goods for other people. So she contacted her husband:

I said, "why can't we earn a bit more money?" So after the harvest he came out. But once we started we found it wasn't so easy. There were people who'd been doing it for a while and they all knew each other. Someone calls you over and asks you to take something somewhere and you can earn several tens of yuan. But we didn't know anyone and no one wanted us to take anything so it was no good and we stopped doing it. . . . Later he came to Beijing and thought it was okay here, so he urged me to come here too. Because living costs here were too high the two children stayed at home with my mum for a year. Then, because she was too old and couldn't look after them, I went and brought the children out. (August 2001)

The stories of Pang Hui, Ma Hua, and Jin Rong defy the simplifications of the household strategy and associational models of migration. All three women left home without or ahead of their husbands, rather than following them, and all three represented themselves as active agents, taking decisions independently of their husbands. Only one did so with the primary aim of making money for the family. And none of these women described relations in their families solely in terms of harmony and accord. On the contrary, one woman's migration was a desperate flight from her husband's abuse and violence, another's was partially motivated by tension between herself and her in-laws, and the third initially left home without her husband because he refused to go with her.

Migrant Marital Relations in the City

In the literature on rural to urban migration in China to date, scant attention has been paid to the impact of migration and urban life on relations between married migrants.[12] In studies of married migrants living in cities elsewhere in the world, two key themes emerge. The first is that, in some contexts following migration, women's social status and their power in family decision making improve as a result of their increased participation in paid employment and other activities in the "public" sphere (Willis and Yeoh 2000, xv). The second is that migration puts enormous stress on family relationships, and this can result in greater domestic discord, violence against women, and other threats to their health and well-being (Murphy 2004, 266; Buijs 1993, 6–8). In the following paragraphs I discuss relationships among married migrants in Beijing in terms of these two themes.

In very few instances were there any signs that my married interlocutors' power or bargaining position in their family had improved since migrating to the city, whether as a result of paid employment or anything else. In her study of returned rural migrants in Jiangxi, Rachel Murphy claims that women returning from work in the city have an improved bargaining position in the family as a result of the knowledge they have accrued of the outside world, and because their demonstrated wage-earning abilities give them a "fall back position" and, hence, a greater degree of leverage in family conflicts (Murphy 2004, 265). It is possible that Ma Hua may have improved her bargaining position relative to her parents-in-law and her husband in this way, even if she remitted her savings to her natal family rather than to her husband and in-laws. However, it is also likely that Ma Hua's standing in her family and in the broader community would have taken a blow as a result of the disgrace entailed in her having left home unaccompanied by her husband. As Pang Hui's story illustrates, economic independence does not necessarily improve a woman's standing in her family's eyes—it can even make it worse. In Ma Hua's case, it is unlikely that experience in waged work in the city would be viewed with quite such contempt. Nevertheless, how increased status resulting from wage-earning abilities would have balanced out against the social stigma of a woman working away from home and unaccompanied by her husband is not at all clear.

While it is possible that their status might improve if or when they return to the countryside, the bulk of evidence suggests that married women living with their husbands in Beijing enjoy little, if any, improvement in status while in the city and may in fact experience a decline in their power and bargaining position. As discussed in chapter 3, migrants enter a labor market in the city that is highly segmented according to both *hukou* (household registration) and gender. This means that, in general, while rural women may find urban employment that earns them a cash income, thereby increasing their status relative to the position they occupied as domestic workers and agricultural laborers in the village, their income is likely to be less than that earned by their husbands. Furthermore, the chances of a married woman having *any* employment are much less than for single women and for men. This is partly age-related, for, as I mentioned earlier, employers of migrant women commonly prefer younger women and discriminate against women over the age of thirty. Married women's difficulties finding paid work are also related to their responsibility for domestic work and childrearing. In the countryside, most women receive help with domestic work and childcare from relatives, especially parents and parents-in-law. In the city, most migrant women have no such support, but neither can they afford maids or urban childcare facilities. Furthermore, while some private schools provide affordable education for migrant children aged six and above, there are very few institutions catering for the needs of migrant children under the age of six.

Most of my married interlocutors, including three out of five married members of the Migrant Women's Club and the majority of those I interviewed in Haidian, had no form of paid work in 2001. This was a source of considerable anxiety, because it meant that their families were stretched financially. Some also talked explicitly of their discomfort at being financially dependent upon their husbands. Furthermore, as elsewhere in the world, domestic work and childcare contribute little to a woman's social status or her authority and bargaining position in the family, because such work is considered trivial compared to paid work, in the sense of being both lighter and easier, and less important. Such a view is apparent in Zhang Xiaohua's narrative above.[13]

In 2001 only two of my married interlocutors, Ma Hua and Zeng Jiping, had independent waged employment in the public sphere. Ma Hua worked as a cleaner, earning an income that may or may not have improved her standing with her husband and his family back in the village. Zeng Jiping worked as a shop assistant in Beijing and her husband had a junior managerial position in a state-run factory in the city. Jiping's wage was less than her husband's, but nonetheless extremely important in enabling her to be independent of her husband. Her independence, however, worked against her. Some months before I got to know her, Jiping and her nine-year-old daughter went back to the countryside for a while to visit her parents. While they were away Jiping's husband had an affair. Later, when Jiping found out, she told him she wanted a divorce. He refused because he was concerned that the stigma of divorce would cost him his job. Jiping kept insisting and moved out of their apartment. In response, her husband started visiting her at the shop where she worked, hurling abuse at her, and on one occasion beating her up. When she visited me, her face swollen and bruised, Jiping explained that her husband was trying to cause trouble in the shop so that she would lose her job. His reasoning was that without a job she would be financially dependent on him and would not dare keep pressing for a divorce (September 2001).

A few other women worked alongside their husbands selling vegetables, or else earned an income by working at home. Chunzi, for example, made a little money by sewing children's clothes and handicrafts at home and selling them, mainly through a network of friends. Song Shulan worked at home assembling and gluing together gas lighters, and Liang Chun sewed quilt covers and took in tailoring and mending work. The significance of this work to the family economy varied. Chunzi's handicraft production was quite time-consuming, but it brought in only a little money on a sporadic basis. Song Shulan said that she worked a couple of hours each day. Though considerably less than her husband's income, her earnings were an important supplement to the family's budget. Liang Chun's sewing was the most significant: Her outline of her daily schedule indicated that she spent at least six hours a day sewing, and her income, of about 600 yuan a month, although on average less than her husband earned doing light construction and interior decorating work, was more regular than his (August 2001). All the same, Liang Chun, like Chunzi and Song Shulan, downplayed the significance of her work, talking of it as merely something she did when she had some "spare time" rather than as a real job. As feminist studies of women's work worldwide have noted, this is not unusual. Work that is conducted by women within the home, because it is done by women and because of its location in the domestic sphere, is frequently devalued both by society generally and by the women who do it. Indeed, it is frequently not considered "work" at all and, like domestic chores, it generally results in little improvement in women's status or power in the family (Mies 1982; Henderson et al. 2000; Jacka 1997, 143–54).

Other studies show that when women work alongside their husbands in a family business, this also contributes relatively little to improved status. In part this is because their income is not distinguishable from their husbands', and therefore cannot serve to demonstrate their individual worth or to improve their economic independence. In addition, like sewing and other work done at home, women's work in family businesses is frequently undervalued because the tasks that women perform cannot always be distinguished from "domestic" work and are considered of lesser value and status than those done by men (Jacka 1997, 156–57; Zhang, Li 2001, 118–23). Among my interlocutors who worked with their husbands selling vegetables, most worked at least as many hours as their husbands: cooking, cleaning, and looking after the children, as well as working at the market stall. The men, however, generally did more of the supposedly more "demanding" work of transporting vegetables between the wholesale market and the stall where they sold them, and took the lead in decision making relating to the business. While these women were probably in a better position, and felt less anxiety, than those without any income at all, their social status and bargaining position in the family were nevertheless still lower than that of their husbands'.

With regard to the second theme I outlined above—the potential for migration to contribute to an increase in domestic discord—three of my married interlocutors talked of conflict and violence between themselves and their husbands. As mentioned above, Zeng Jiping's husband took a lover but refused to divorce his wife, and when she insisted he responded with abuse and violence. Yao Min and her husband argued and he sometimes hit her. As I discussed above, the discord between them seemed to stem primarily from a conflict between the husband's belief that the family would be economically better off if Yao Min were to return to the countryside and Yao Min's dread of returning to her husband's village. There were also indications that extramarital sexual activity on the part of Yao Min's husband exacerbated discord in this family. Yao Min said that on the days when her husband made a lot of money things weren't so bad, but on other days he put enormous pressure on her to return home (to his village). She refused to do so, but, she said laughing, when she got angry she felt like going back to her *own* home, to stay with her parents, and last year she had done so for a time. When I asked if she often got angry, Yao Min said she did, because her husband sometimes did not come home. And, she said, his temper was bad (*piqi bu hao*) and he sometimes hit her. Yao Min made this remark in an offhand way, and when I asked if it was common for men to hit their wives, she nodded. She pointed across the courtyard and said that the woman living there was beaten up the night before last. Her husband's temper was also bad, Yao Min explained (September 2001).

Jin Rong also mentioned discord between herself and her husband. When I asked what effect her husband's low level of education had, she responded:

He speaks crudely. But, then, a lot of men are like that. He doesn't have much education, so he likes to talk like that. When there's trouble between us I generally don't argue with him. What's the use of arguing? We're together so we just have to get by—after all, it's for life, for the children. (August 2001)

I asked Jin Rong if she and her husband often argued and she said:

When we have no money we argue. If we've got work and we're busy, even if we're not earning much he's not inclined to argue. The more he's at home with nothing to do, the more he likes to argue about nothing. (August 2001)

None of these women submitted passively to their husbands' abuse. However, both Jin Rong and Yao Min explained the abuse as relatively common and ordinary. Their narratives point to two understandings of abusive behavior on the part of migrant men. First, they portray men's abusive behavior as stemming from "bad temper" and "crudity," which are common and normal attributes of men (but not women). Second, however, both these women point explicitly to economic stress and, specifically, to their husbands' lack of work as exacerbating their husbands' abusiveness. Both these understandings are very much a part of dominant discourse on gender and sexuality in both rural and urban China. On the one hand, as Harriet Evans notes, post–1949 Chinese writings on sex and sexuality have been dominated by the notion that differences in sexual behavior stem from the fact that men are biologically more inclined to be active and aggressive and women passive (Evans 1997, 33). On the other hand, "the idea that gender and sexual oppression are at root an economic issue is shared by many people in China, including theorists of the Women's Federation" (ibid., 31).

The cases of Zeng Jiping and Yao Min point to men's extramarital sexual activities as a further cause of domestic discord. That this may be relatively common among migrant couples living in the city is suggested by Zhang Li's study of Zhejiangcun, the largest migrant settlement in Beijing. Zhang found that in Zhejiangcun it was common for relatively well-off male entrepreneurs to visit prostitutes and to have affairs with other women. For the men, such sexual practices, alongside the frequenting of karaoke bars, expensive restaurants and the like, were a way of demonstrating economic power and manhood among other male migrants (Zhang, Li 2001, 123). Their wives complained that such behavior would not have occurred in the village and that it was a result of the corrosive effects of the city and of consumption-oriented economic reforms (ibid., 123). Financially, these women had prospered as a result of migration and their husbands' earnings from business. However, rather than having a sense of improved well-being, they felt their status and stability in the family had been undermined in the new context.

Aside from resulting in insecurity for the wives, it is possible that extramarital affairs are also a cause of greater insecurity for migrant men themselves and that they contribute directly to higher levels of domestic violence on their part. As the anthropologist Henrietta Moore has noted, in many cultures male violence against women often occurs when the man feels a threat to his status as a breadwinner and/or his sexual status. Perhaps ironically, the latter threat often emerges when the man engages in extramarital affairs. Moore cites ethnographies undertaken in the Andes as making it clear that

> in the context of these specific extra-marital relations attributes of desirable masculinity, far from being confirmed are challenged, perhaps even denied. The men cannot control their lovers as they would wish, they cannot control other men's access to these women and therefore they cannot control the definition of their own masculinity because they cannot control the definition of or the social practices surrounding the femininity of their lovers. The only women they can control are their wives; and it is they who confirm their husbands' masculinity by their proper adoption of the opposite feminine subject position, and so their husbands hit them. (Moore, Henrietta 1994, 69)

The discussion here supports the argument that migration puts enormous stress on family relationships. The stress arises from challenges to the gender order, in particular a threat to men's economic and sexual power and men's responses to that threat, which can result in domestic discord and damage to married women's health and well-being. However, the case studies outlined here and elsewhere in this book suggest that this is only one aspect of married women's experience of migration, which may or may not be outweighed by other considerations. In her study of the impact of migration on rural women, including those who migrate themselves and those who remain in the village, Rachel Murphy argues that "migration brings more benefits for women when they migrate directly than when they support the migration of other household members by staying on the farm" (Murphy 2004, 251). Murphy further claims that the invisibility of married migrant women's work in the domestic sphere in the city and the consequent lack of status they suffer may well be outweighed by other factors, particularly the satisfaction of sharing life with their husbands rather than being lonely (ibid.). Finally, Murphy finds that married women who return to the village after a sojourn in the city are often bored, lonely and unhappy, and frustrated by both constraining patriarchal norms and the lack of resources preventing them from improving their living standards or escaping farming (Murphy ibid., 264). Despite financial pressures and violence from her husband, Yao Min's case appears to concur with Murphy's general findings, for she claims that she is better off in the city than back in her husband's village where she faces loneliness, boredom, overwork, and the drudgery of farmwork. Not all married women do remain with their husbands in the city of course, but clearly Yao Min is not alone in her sentiments.

Relationships with Fellow Villagers and Urbanites

Kinship, Localistic, and Other Migrant Ties

In addition to emphasizing the effect of household relations and household strategies on decision making relating to migration, studies of labor migration worldwide commonly note the significance of bonds and networks between kin and fellow villagers for shaping migration patterns, the experiences of migrants at destination, and the construction and maintenance of migrant communities. Scholars have argued that in contemporary China, where both labor market mechanisms and government services are poorly developed, informal contacts and networks between migrants, former migrants, and others from the same region are particularly important (see Solinger 1999; Zhang, Li 2001, 54–68, Fan 2004, 189–95; Ma and Xiang 1998; Scharping 1999; Scharping and Sun 1997; Rozelle et al. 1999). Relatives and other fellow villagers, or *laoxiang*,[14] supply information about work opportunities and conditions in particular destinations, and provide contacts in the city that smooth the way for new arrivals. In addition, *laoxiang* often travel together, seek employment in the same factories, or set up their own small businesses together. According to most analysts, they also tend to live together in the same dormitories or migrant settlements, with other migrants from the same province, to socialize with them, and to turn to them first for companionship and support. Laurence J.C. Ma and Xiang Biao write:

> Although a common Chinese term, *laoxiang* as a cultural phenomenon is of particular importance to migration. Migrants who are *laoxiang* normally have a shared sense of common experience, and they are invariably emotionally attached to their common place of origin. Familiar home environment, identical home dialect [*xiangyin*], similar experiences and a sense of common fate can engender an intimate camaraderie that binds them together. This strong feeling is best displayed at the place of destination. Living with the dominant "they" group, *laoxiang* from the same place tend to voluntarily cluster together in a "we" group for mutual support, assistance and friendship. (Ma and Xiang 1998, 560)

Employers and government agencies often use and promote *laoxiang* networks. For example, domestic service companies, many of which are run by Women's Federations, commonly recruit young rural women for work as maids in urban households by signing contracts with county governments to supply young women from that area. And factories commonly encourage migrant employees to recruit new workers from among *laoxiang,* believing that in this way they will obtain a more reliable and easily controlled workforce (Lee 1998, 127). Ching Kwan Lee and others claim that factory managers also promote local identifications and competition among migrant workers with different regional backgrounds as a way of dividing and ruling the workforce (ibid., 116–23; Pun 1999, 7–8).

Localistic ties and networks assist migrants in negotiating the urban labor market, but they also tend to increase regional and gender segmentation in that market. For example, in the mid-1990s in Beijing, more than one-third of construction workers were rural men from Hebei province and one-third of domestic workers were rural women from Anhui (Ma and Xiang 1998, 564). This was not just because urban labor practices and regulations limit migrants to a narrow range of occupations, but because of migrants' reliance on localistic networks, networks that are also gendered: men seek help from their "brothers" from the same village, and women seek help from their "sisters." These networks, then, tend to exacerbate forms of difference, inequality, and exclusion between "locals" and "outsiders" that are created through government structures and the policies and practices of urban officials, employers, and others (see chapter 3). They also increase differences between the work experiences of migrants from different regions and those of men and women while simultaneously homogenizing the work experiences of migrants from the same region and of the same gender (Fan 2004, 193). Having said this, local networks and subsequent labor market segmentation are not absolute, and each migrant trade and occupation in Beijing involves people from around the country (Solinger 1999, 202).

As I discuss in the next few paragraphs, my own research confirms that local networks are crucial for providing rural women with avenues for migration, determining their destinations, places of residence, and occupations in the city, and providing practical help in settling in the city. It suggests, however, that once they have "found their feet" these women rely less and less on such networks over time, and that they may depend upon them for friendship and emotional sustenance less than Ma and Xiang and other scholars have intimated.

Among respondents to the survey of the Migrant Women's Club conducted in 2000, almost half indicated that they obtained their current job through friends or relatives in Beijing. A further 18 percent said that friends or relatives in their home village had been instrumental in their finding employment (N = 94).[15] When asked whether they had friends or relatives already in Beijing when they arrived, two-thirds of the respondents indicated that they did (N = 95).[16] Of them, half said that their friends and relatives had given them information about employment opportunities or had helped them find work. In addition, about 23 percent said that their friends or relatives had provided them with housing and food, and 11 percent had received financial assistance. Only 11 percent said that they received no help from their friends and relatives in Beijing (N = 66). In a further indication of the significance of preexisting contacts, 30 percent of respondents said they already had a job on arrival in Beijing, and 57 percent said that they obtained work within one week of arrival (N = 94).[17]

These responses indicate that relatives and other *laoxiang* are crucial in helping rural women find work and settle in Beijing—a finding that is confirmed in the narratives both of members of the Migrant Women's Club and the women that I interviewed in Haidian. Almost all of these women received help from relatives and others in the village, including information and financial assistance; traveled from home in the company of *laoxiang;* and/or decided upon their destination in large part because they had contacts with relatives or other *laoxiang* already living there. I could detect no clear differences in the significance of networking between women from different regions, between women of different ages and marital status, or between women who had migrated to Beijing at different times—all relied on kin and others from the same village or county as traveling companions, and for information, job openings, and practical assistance. Not surprisingly, however, several members of the Migrant Women's Club indicated that the significance of their ties with relatives and other *laoxiang* had declined over the years that they had been in Beijing, while personal connections (*guanxi*) with other migrants and with Beijingers became correspondingly more important for finding improved accommodation and better jobs. A number of my interlocutors complained that migrant women were at a severe disadvantage in the urban labor market because they lacked *guanxi* with locals.

Aside from providing practical help in getting settled and finding work in the city, *laoxiang* are also important as friends, partners in leisure activities, and sources of emotional support. In my survey of the Migrant Women's Club, most respondents indicated that what little time off they had they spent mostly at home, in activities such as reading, watching television, or resting, involving relatively little interaction with other people. Nineteen out of ninety-eight respondents said that they never went out during their leisure time, from which we can surmise that their interactions while in Beijing were essentially limited to those with co-workers, the great majority of whom were other migrants, and to a lesser extent their managers and employers. Among the respondents who said that they did go out during their leisure time, a mere 2.5 percent said they commonly went out with local Beijing people. Almost half said they commonly went out with *laoxiang*[18] and about 20 percent went out with relatives. Interestingly, though, 40.5 percent also said that they commonly went out with other migrants (see Figure 5.2).[19]

These findings confirm those of other studies showing that migrants have relatively little social interaction with urbanites and that they socialize primarily with *laoxiang*. Nevertheless, they are unusual in two respects. First, they indicate a higher level of socializing between migrants from different regions than other studies; and, second, they suggest even less interaction between migrants and local urbanites than other studies. In comparison, in a Sino-German survey of 600 migrants conducted in the cities of Beijing, Shanghai, and Guangzhou in 1999, 58

Figure 5.2 **Partners on Leisure Outings** (as percentage; N = 79)

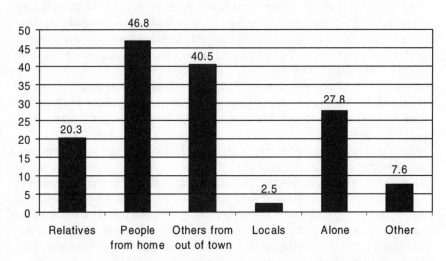

percent of respondents said they often interacted with *laoxiang* and less than 10 percent said they never did. In contrast, only about 20 percent of respondents in this survey said they often interacted with migrants from other provinces and almost 30 percent said they never did. About 43 percent claimed that they often interacted with locals (Cao 2001, 88). This latter high figure may be explained by the inclusion of interactions involved in activities such as shopping, trading, negotiating rent, and dealing with local officialdom.[20]

Several factors might explain my own survey respondents' relatively high levels of interaction with migrants from other provinces. First and most obviously, the Migrant Women's Club itself was an important source of friendships for its members and provided opportunities for social interaction with migrants from all over China that are usually unavailable to migrant workers. Aside from this, differences in work patterns may help explain the differences between the survey findings outlined here, for while the Sino-German survey included migrants engaged in trade and running their own businesses, the Migrant Women's Club survey included only waged workers. Commenting on the Sino-German survey, one researcher explains the low level of interaction between migrants from different regions in terms of intense competition for business between migrant entrepreneurs from different regions (Cao 2001, 87). Such competition may well limit interregional interactions. Perhaps there is less such competition between waged workers, for all that Ching Kwan Lee and others write about workforce segmentation and interregional competition among factory workers.

It is also possible that survey respondents from the Migrant Women's Club were employed in enterprises and types of waged work in which regional segmentation was less marked than in other areas. Certainly, in my interviews with members of the Club who worked in large factories or companies, I was struck by the number who shared dormitory rooms with migrant women from many different provinces. This was surprising in light of other studies that have indicated that migrant women factory workers from the same province most commonly work together in the same workshops and on the same production lines, share the same dormitory rooms, and therefore tend to socialize together more than with other migrant women (Pun 1999; Lee 1998, 117–23). It is possible that this type of segmentation is less pronounced in Beijing than, for example, in cities in southern China, where the majority of studies on migrant women factory workers have been conducted.

One could also speculate that the differences between the survey findings outlined here relate to demographics, for while the majority of respondents in the Sino-German survey were married (62 percent) and male (63 percent), 90 percent of respondents to my own survey were female and 86 percent were unmarried. It could be that young, unmarried women are less enthusiastic about the *laoxiang* tie than others. In Chengdu, Louise Beynon found, in fact, that some unmarried migrant women actively avoided ties with *laoxiang,* instead seeking accommodation with migrants from other provinces. As one woman explained:

> Just because a person is a fellow villager doesn't mean they can be a friend. In fact, I prefer friends who come from outside my village. Otherwise it can get too complicated. They might tell tales about me to the village or gossip too much. I like making friends through my own choice. (quoted in Beynon 2004, 139)

While some migrants may find connections with others from the same province a comfort in the face of new and alienating circumstances, it might be that young, unmarried women, many of whom migrate in order to escape the restrictions of life in the village, are more likely to avoid such connections, especially with migrants from the same village or county (Beynon 2004, 139).

Among married women in Haidian, work and social activities were most commonly conducted with close family members, other relatives, and other *laoxiang.* Once more, though, the *laoxiang* tie seemed less significant in these women's lives than research in other areas has suggested. As I will discuss shortly, there was little sign of community life among *laoxiang* in Haidian. Indeed, some of my interlocutors did not even know who their neighbors were. And none of the women in Haidian were involved in any migrant associations or clubs, whether based on local ties or other forms of identification between migrants.

This is typical of the vast majority of the floating population in contemporary China, for migrant associations such as the Migrant Women's Club are rare and they are mostly not based on local ties. In this, the contemporary period is very different from earlier eras, for between the seventeenth and early twentieth centuries migrant associations based on regional origin were numerous. Termed *huiguan* and *tongxianghui,* these associations played an important role in providing support for rural migrants in China's newly emerging commercial and industrial centers and in furthering the development of those centers. For example, Bryna Goodman writes that in nineteenth-century Shanghai *huiguan* promoted business among immigrants from the same native place built temples and burial grounds; organized religious events; funded hospitals, schools, and benevolent institutions caring for orphans, widows, the ill, and the poor; ran restaurants serving regional cuisine; and sponsored opera troupes from their native place (Goodman 1995, 90–118). In other words, *huiguan* were the focal point for well-developed communities and community-based sociocultural identities among immigrants to the city. They also played a highly significant part in governance and politics. In the late nineteenth century, for example, local officials relied on *huiguan* to settle disputes and when cases entered the courts, they were often referred back to *huiguan* for settlement (ibid., 128).

In the twentieth century, *huiguan* became increasingly politicized. Early revolutionary student groups were organized almost entirely through native-place ties (ibid., 193), and native-place associations played a highly significant role in mobilizing support and providing funding for the republican government and recruiting soldiers for the revolutionary army. Through the Republican period, these activities were accompanied by a reorientation of existing *huiguan* and the creation of new native-place associations, called *tongxianghui.* These reformed and newly created associations absorbed and promoted the aims of the government, performing numerous social, welfare, and quasigovernmental functions and acting as mediators between officials and ordinary people. Later, both the resources and membership of native-place associations were greatly depleted, first by civil war and Japanese occupation and then by the Communist Party's policies of nationalizing property and limiting rural to urban migration. For a while, some survived in attenuated form as social clubs and neighborhood temples, but these were finally destroyed during the Cultural Revolution (ibid., 305).

In contemporary Shanghai, Beijing, and other cities there are no formal native-place associations with a status even approaching that of *huiguan* and *tongxianghui* in the first half of the twentieth century. The governments of individual provinces establish offices in urban centers to facilitate the flow of labor between the province and the city, but by and large these offices provide no services to migrants residing in the city. A few nongovernmental native-place organizations have also been established to promote trade and technological development, but, as Bryna Goodman notes, these differ from pre–1949 native-place associations in being strictly divided along functional and occupational lines. They do not attempt to transcend occupation or class and they do not engage in social activities that serve a broader community (Goodman 1995, 306).[21] Aside from this, there are a few nongovernmental organizations serving the interests of, and promoting a sense of community among, migrants that transcend occupational, class, and regional divisions. These include the Migrant Women's Club in Beijing, the Working Women's

Network in Shenzhen, and a Migrant Workers' Reading Club in Shanghai (Chen Yutao 1995, 12). To my knowledge, however, there are no such associations organized according to native place. This is surprising, given, on the one hand, the burgeoning of nongovernmental and quasigovernmental organizations since the 1990s and, on the other, the size of the floating population and the obvious lack of welfare and community support services that it suffers from.

There are some more informal forms of community organization and leadership among coprovincials, but again they are fairly limited in constituency and function. Some localistic networks in some trades develop into cliques or gangs (*bang*). For example, in 1989 a manager of the March 8th Domestic Service Company in Beijing told me of the existence of an Anhui *bang* among maids. Women in this network exchanged information with each other, passed on the "tricks of the trade," and sometimes engaged in criminal activities. For this reason, the company had stopped recruiting young women from Anhui (interview with Li Ruijin, August 1989). Other reports also suggest that *laoxiang* sometimes band together in criminal gangs, engaging in petty theft and sometimes the kidnap and sale of rural women (Honig 1996, 236). However, none of these *bang* contribute to native-place community or cultural identity in the way that earlier *huiguan* and *tongxianghui* did.

In the contemporary setting, community leadership of large, well-knit migrant settlements like Zhejiangcun in Beijing probably comes closest to the nineteenth- and early-twentieth-century *huiguan* and *tongxianghui* models. In Zhejiangcun in the early to mid-1990s more than half of the population were migrants from two rural areas around Wenzhou in Zhejiang province.[22] In this settlement, some of the wealthier migrant entrepreneurs built large housing compounds, which were then inhabited exclusively by Wenzhou migrants and their employees. Some of these compounds housed several hundred households and employed security guards at the gates. Within and around the compounds, migrant leaders built their own restaurants serving Zhejiang food, post offices, medical clinics, schools, and recreational facilities (Solinger 1999, 254). These facilities contributed to a thriving community in which there was a high degree of social interaction between *laoxiang* households. Zhang Li reports, for example, that the wives of Wenzhou entrepreneurs commonly visited each other, chatted, and played mahjong (Zhang, Li 2001, 124). And some whose husbands had left them, or who had initiated divorce proceedings because they could no longer tolerate their husbands' extramarital affairs, formed mutual support groups among *laoxiang* in similar circumstances (ibid., 134–35).

The majority of migrant settlements, however, have a more mixed population than Zhejiangcun, less organized leadership, and a much less developed community life (Solinger 1999, 256). Certainly this was the case in Haidian. In some lanes and yards (most housing was constructed around large quadrangles) the majority of households were from the same province—usually either Henan or Hubei. In some, in fact, residents were all from the same county. In others, though, there was a mix of local Beijing residents and migrants from all over the country to whom they had rented rooms. Within the settlement there was a primary school for migrant children, some small eateries, grocery shops, and vegetable markets, but few other facilities.

Most of my interlocutors had close connections with one or two other households nearby—most commonly kin and less often other *laoxiang*. These were people they had traveled with or followed to Beijing, and in many cases continued to work with. Beyond this, there was a good deal of variation in the degree to which these women interacted with other migrants around them. Housing was mostly cramped and dark and without running water, so women carried out a lot of their daily activities—preparing food, cooking, and washing clothes—outside in the laneway or courtyard. Some women sat outside on stools, working with their neighbors, exchanging gossip, watching their own and other friends' children running around in the yard, sharing cooking utensils, and the like. This occurred as much in lanes and yards where residents were of mixed regional origin as in those where residents were from a single county or province. To some extent, these migrants were brought together by the difficulties and fears that they shared. In particular, gossip among them was often the only source of information available about changing regulations and impending demolitions. It also provided an outlet for frustration and anger and a source of comfort in the face of shared anxieties and hardships. On the other hand, with buildings being demolished and frequent police raids, this area was not conducive to doing business or living a peaceful life, so the turnover rate among residents was high, with large numbers of migrants leaving and a few new people coming in. This meant that in some yards and lanes women did not know their neighbors and had little to do with them. Sometimes, walking from one interview to another, or on the way to the market, the women or children accompanying me would call out greetings to numerous acquaintances. At other times they recognized very few people in the street.

In the discussion so far I have suggested that socializing between *laoxiang* may be less frequent among rural migrant women in Beijing than previous studies of migrants in China have implied. There are signs also that *laoxiang* ties and, for that matter, relationships with other migrants may be shallower and contribute less to individual migrants' emotional well-being than is implied in other studies, especially studies of migrant communities such as those in Zhejiangcun. Certainly, among my interlocutors both in Haidian and in the Migrant Women's Club, these ties did not appear sufficient to overcome high levels of loneliness and isolation. In Haidian I was forcibly struck by the large proportion of women who looked depressed and unhappy. Sometimes my interlocutors themselves explained this in terms of the enormous pressures they were under as a result of their families' straitened financial circumstances, the lack of employment and business opportunities in the area, and the constant threat of housing demolition and police sweeps that they faced. Other women explained their unhappiness explicitly in terms of loneliness. Undoubtedly, these factors fed into and reinforced each other.

Among members of the Migrant Women's Club there were a number who suffered from loneliness because they were isolated from other migrants. This was particularly the case among those who worked as maids, many of whose employers did not allow them to use the telephone or to invite friends to the apartment, and restricted their time off work. However, even among *dagongmei* who shared dormitories with other *laoxiang* and migrants from other provinces, there were high levels of loneliness. Many of these young women said that they had fun with their workmates and, on the surface, relationships between them were characterized by camaraderie. When I visited women in their dormitories, there was always a lot of joking, laughter, and physical affection between them. Invariably, however, my interlocutor would want to find a quiet space away from her roommates, before she would confide personal concerns to me.

When I visited Liu Yu in 2002, she was working in a factory and sharing a dormitory room with five other women, all of whom were from Liu Yu's home province of Sichuan and one of whom came from the same county as herself. Sitting on their bunk beds during the lunch break, they laughed and chatted happily together, but it quickly transpired that they knew little about each other's personal circumstances—when I inquired after Liu Yu's younger sister and brother, they expressed surprise that she had siblings and that I knew about them. And when Liu Yu led me away so that we could talk in private, her demeanor changed dramatically. Suddenly she was no longer a carefree young girl, but a much older woman, hunched over before me. No one in the factory knew about the rape that Liu Yu had suffered the previous year, and, she said, she had no one to confide in about her nightmares and her anxieties for her future. She liked to play around with her workmates and preferred that they thought of her simply as a happy girl, but it was very hard not having anyone to talk with about personal matters (*xinli hua*) (December 2002).

Research on single factory workers in Taiwan similarly indicates that dormitories "do not function as a substitute for the absence of family ties; nor do they provide a locale for meaningful social relationships; family-type relations were not found to have developed in dormitories and the conclusion was that persons are affiliated for restricted and special purposes only" (Schwartzbaum and Tsai, cited in Kung 1983 [1978], 162). Another scholar writing on Taiwan observes that there is no evidence for the common assumption "that informal patterns of interaction established in the work context result in genuine social groups that share various interests and activities both at the work place and outside it" (Moore 1965, cited in Kung 1983 [1978], 163).

Kung and the other scholars she cites hypothesize that the lack of deep emotional relationships among Taiwanese factory workers stems from traditional Chinese culture and upbringing characterized, in particular, by a distrust of outsiders and an emphasis on the desirability of avoiding both conflict and emotional expressiveness in interpersonal relations. In the case of rural factory workers in the People's Republic of China (PRC), these cultural factors may also apply. However, my inclination is to put more emphasis on the high levels of competition that exist between these workers. To a large extent this is a result of management practices that promote divisiveness and competition, rather than solidarity, among workers. As Ching Kwan Lee, Sally Sargeson, and others have written, managers and middle-level supervisors often manipulate personal relationships in order to "divide and rule," for example by promoting or giving lighter tasks to workers who are from the same province or county as they themselves, or with whom they have some kinship or other personal connections (Lee 1998, 119–20; Sargeson 1999, 128–34). Unsurprisingly, this generates considerable antagonism among workers as well as between workers and their managers. Both Ching Kwan Lee and Sally Sargeson indicate that such antagonism among workers is overcome, in some instances, with workers forming friendships "in order to survive the hostile environment that their class position condemns them to share" (Lee 1998, 122), and uniting to go slow or strike in protest at exploitative management practices (Sargeson 1999, 177–82). All the same, it may be that management-promoted hierarchies and divisions commonly militate against the establishment of deep, personal bonds between migrant workers.

Separate from this, there is also competition among *dagongmei* to conform to the contrasting ideals of chaste and filial rural daughter and "modern" woman. Therefore, as Louise Beynon notes, young women are often reluctant to confide in workmates, particularly *laoxiang,* in case they will gossip about their "immoral" behavior, especially in relation to members of the opposite sex, and damage their reputation back in the village. On the other hand, there is considerable peer group pressure among young women workers to conform to ideals of "modernity" and "urbanity," and this can be very alienating for some. For example, as I will discuss in the next chapter, one young woman writing in *Rural Women* spoke of her discomfort in the face of her migrant co-workers' taunts about her "country bumpkin" hairstyle and unfashionable, conservative dress, and about the fact that, unlike her more "liberated" sisters, she refused to let any of her co-workers see her shower, and was too shy to go dancing with them (Xiao 1993).

Relations with Urbanites

Very few of my interlocutors had made friends with any local Beijing people. Even Zhou Ling, who had lived in Beijing for more than ten years and was married to a local man, had very few Beijing friends. She spent a lot of time on the telephone to other migrant women whom she had befriended through the Migrant Women's Club, but she felt that her husband's friends and co-workers, including those living in neighboring apartments, looked down on her, and she rarely had much to do with any of them.

Other *dagongmei* members of the Migrant Women's Club also had few dealings with urbanites and when they did, their experiences were often negative. As I myself observed, officials, shopkeepers, and bus conductors were commonly very rude to them and served them only with reluctance. At their places of work, *dagongmei* factory workers and others in large enterprises generally lived and worked alongside other migrants, in divisions and areas of work separate from urban employees. They characterized their relationships with these workers and with urban managers and employers most often in terms of distance and inequality. And, as I will discuss in the next chapter, there was little sense of shared interests or identities between migrant workers and their urban employers, or even between migrant and local workers.

Maids' relationships with their employers were more varied. At one extreme, as in the cases of Chen Ailing and Liu Yu, employers treated their maids with abuse and violence. At the other end of the scale, some of my interlocutors spoke with great fondness and gratitude about their employers. Ruan Shilin, for example, said that when she began work as a maid, she was unsure of herself and often made mistakes, but her employers were very understanding and encouraging. The woman comforted her when she missed home and encouraged her to participate in the Migrant Women's Club and the man, who worked for a newspaper publishing house, frequently brought home newspapers for her to read (November 2001). In general, the best employers tended to be older urbanites with relatively high education, who treated their maids like junior members of the family—not as equals, but at least with solicitousness and encouragement.

In Haidian, as in other migrant settlements, migrant women had few interactions of any kind with urbanites. Their husbands often traveled around the city and interacted with urbanites in their business activities, but their own lives were much more circumscribed. Apart from sometimes accompanying their husbands to buy and sell vegetables, these women rarely traveled out of the settlement. They shopped in local stores and markets, most of which were staffed by migrants like themselves. And apart from Liang Chun, who often went to see her sister's family in a nearby district, they rarely visited anyone outside the area. Within the settlement, the only locals they interacted with on a regular basis were their landlords. This relationship was generally one of distance. When asked how they got on with their landlord, Han Haiying and her husband replied: "Okay. We don't have much contact. We say hello when we meet. . . . We don't have contact with any other locals" (August 2001). Zhang Xiaohua said that her landlord looked down on his tenants. When they went to pay their rent he did not let them sit down, and when they met on the street he did not greet them. Aside from this, the only other significant contact that Han Haiying, Zhang Xiaohua, and other women in Haidian had with local Beijingers was with Public Security officers, whose frequent but unpredictable visits were understandably regarded with universal fear and hostility.

Conclusion

In this chapter I have demonstrated the significance of rural women's relations with other people for their experiences of migration. Relationships with family members and with *laoxiang* are particularly important. These relationships are shaped by powerful gender discourses and have a major impact on decision making relating to migration, migrants' destinations, the occupations they take up, and their experiences of life in the city.

Large-scale out-migration of women from the Chinese countryside is a relatively recent phenomenon that has posed a major challenge to family relationships and the dominant understandings of gender roles that underpin those relationships. However, patterns of out-migration have varied enormously as have the adjustments in attitudes and values that people have made in coming to terms with it. In some areas migration and work in the city is considered highly dangerous for women (but not men), and the sexual morality of migrant women is questioned. In these areas women who leave home do so in the face of considerable anxiety and disapproval from parents, parents-in-law, and spouses. In other places large numbers of unmarried women now leave home for a stint of work in the city shortly after they leave school, and their morality is no longer questioned. They are, however, most commonly expected to return home after a few years to marry and assume the role of "virtuous wife and good mother." Once married, it is considered inappropriate and even immoral for a woman to leave her husband and children for work in the city. In some areas the reverse holds true—the migration of young, unmarried women is still frowned upon, while the migration of married women is considered relatively acceptable.

Contrary to the household strategy and filial daughter models, young unmarried women who migrate generally do *not* do so at the behest of their parents or in order to contribute to the family economy. Rather, these women make their own decisions and choices, aimed primarily at improving their lives and prospects for self-realization as modern individuals. Further, for many, if not most, *dagongmei* out-migration is one element in a rejection of dominant rural patriarchal discourses, closely linked with the frustration of a desire for education and a wish to avoid, or at the least postpone, marriage and the traditional role of "virtuous wife and good mother." In this sense, even in areas where it has become commonplace for young women to migrate, those who do so are rebellious daughters who leave home in defiance of patriarchy and in order to escape it.

However, even while pursuing independence in the city, migrant daughters generally maintain connections with their parents and send them remittances. For some this is a strategy for maintaining their reputation in the village and ensuring that they will be able to find a marriage partner. For others, connections with their parents are important for overcoming loneliness and affirming a positive sense of self in a new and alienating environment. And some young women, even the most rebellious, wish to repay their parents for bringing them up and giving them the resources, including education and self-confidence, to be independent. Meeting filial obligations thus continues to be important for young rural migrant women as a way of simultaneously negotiating dominant patriarchal discourses; preserving good relations with loved ones; maintaining connections between past, present, and future subject positions; and cultivating an identity that is both independent and modern, and moral and caring.

When married women migrate, they most commonly accompany or follow their husbands. In view of this, much of the literature on migration has adopted an associational model of women's migration, assuming that men are the main agents in migration decision making and paying little heed to their wives' interests or roles. In this chapter I have challenged this approach on the grounds that it masks dynamics in marital relations that are crucial for understanding how decisions relating to migration are made. In some families men migrate ahead of their wives because they see this as the most rational or economically beneficial division of labor. However, notions of what is rational are shaped by dominant discourses relating to gender and the power relations they embody. Furthermore, they are highly contested. Some women's behavior accords with dominant gender discourses—they remain in the village while their husbands migrate, or follow them once they have settled in the city. Other women defy prevailing norms, leaving home ahead of their husbands or without them. All of these women make active choices and decisions based on considerations of the needs of both their family as a whole and themselves as individuals—they are not, as the associational model suggests, merely passive dependants.

A further limitation of studies based on the associational model of migration is that they neglect the fact that married women migrants' experiences in the city are different from their husbands' and that life in the city can have a profound effect on migrants' marital relations. Some feminists have claimed that migration and work in the city enable women to renegotiate gender relations in the family—in particular, that paid work gives them a degree of power and authority relative to their husbands that they did not have in the village. I find little evidence of this among married migrant women in Beijing. Married migrant women, especially those with children and those over the age of about thirty, are severely disadvantaged in the labor force. Most are unemployed. Furthermore, the minority who have paid work derive relatively little in the way of increased status from it, either because they work alongside their husbands and do not earn an independent income, because their income is much lower than that of their husbands, or because the location of their work in the domestic sphere renders it invisible.

My research does bear out the findings of other studies, according to which migration and life in the city puts strain on marital relations, which may result in threats to married women's health and well-being. In particular, there are signs pointing to relatively high levels of domestic discord and violence among married migrants in Beijing. Migrant women themselves attribute this to economic pressures and to a tendency among rural men to engage in extramarital affairs in the city.

Aside from relations with parents and husbands, localistic bonds and networks play a crucial role in rural peoples' decisions to migrate, in their destinations, and in their occupations and places of residence in the city. These networks are highly gendered—men guide their "brothers" and women guide their "sisters" to the destinations and occupations in which they themselves have worked and have contacts. Consequently, localistic networks tend to contribute to a gendered segmentation of the labor force.

Once settled in the city, migrant women tend to live, work, and socialize primarily with other women from the same region. My research suggests, however, that this *laoxiang* relationship may not always be as deep or as significant to migrant women's emotional well-being as previous studies have intimated. Furthermore, among members of the Migrant Women's Club, ties among migrants from different regions were almost as common as those between migrants with the same regional background. And in the Haidian migrant settlement, residents were of more mixed regional origin than in some other settlements, and there was less community life among migrants than studies of other settlements have indicated.

In common with previous studies, however, I find that rural migrants have few interactions with local Beijingers. This is particularly the case among the numerous unemployed married women living in migrant settlements like that in Haidian. Male entrepreneurs and unmarried women who work as maids or in other forms of paid labor have more contact with locals. However, whether male or female, married or unmarried, migrants rarely count local Beijingers as friends.

6

Identifications

In this chapter my focus is on how migrant women talk about their identities in relation to other people. I have two main aims: the first is to understand how these women experience and respond to the range of conflicting subject positions and values opened up by migration. Do they easily negotiate the transition from rural to urban subject positions or do the disjunctures between rural and urban subject positions and values with respect to identity and interpersonal behavior result in confusion or conflict for them? My second aim is to explore the relationship between the subject positions that migrant women adopt and those expressed through dominant discourses. Do migrant women's identifications of themselves accord with official and urban representations of migrants? Or do they draw upon other discourses and take up other subject positions not found in dominant official or popular urban discourses?

The chapter is further informed by questions about gender, class, and ethnicity. In her 1992 study of divisions among women workers in Shanghai between 1850 and 1980, Emily Honig argues that regional origin was so important a basis for identity, prejudice, and social conflict in the city as to constitute a form of ethnicity. In particular, there was very strong prejudice against Subei people, that is, those whose families originated from the northern part of Jiangsu province. Being a Subei person in Shanghai meant being poor; working in the least lucrative and least desirable jobs; living in slums on the edge of the city; being laughed at for the clothes one wore, the food one ate, and the dialect one spoke; being perceived as dirty, ignorant, and unsophisticated; and having trouble finding a marriage partner (Honig 1992, 1–2). Subei people were not physically different from the rest of the Shanghai population, and yet, Honig says, they were treated as if they were a different race, and their experiences were similar to those of racial minorities in other cities across the world (ibid., 3). Northern Jiangsu natives themselves were not passive actors in the process of ethnic formation. In fact, they rarely identified with the category "Subei people," adhering to more narrowly defined forms of regional identification and in the process resisting the negative characterizations of Subei-ness (ibid., 132–33). However, writes Honig,

In the immigrant city of Shanghai, Jiangnan natives constituted the elite and as such had more power to establish the terms of discourse, both about social categories constructed according to native place identities as well as who qualified as a truly native Shanghainese. Subei people sometimes challenged the categories, but they were not equally positioned in the contest. . . . In Shanghai, Jiangnan natives were the dominant group; it was they who had the power to formulate self and other. Subei people, in contrast, could not "opt out" of the labeling process. (ibid.)

In a later paper Honig reflects upon the potential transferability of her understanding of Subei ethnicity in Shanghai in the nineteenth and early to mid-twentieth centuries, posing the question: "Does the association of migrants with specific jobs and neighborhoods and the prejudice against them evidence the construction of a kind of native-place ethnic identity [in contemporary China]?" (Honig 1996, 237). And if so, is the primary ethnic division between local urbanites and "outsider" rural migrants or is it between people from different provinces or regions? In order to answer these questions, Honig suggests, we need to understand the processes through which social categories are constructed and the meanings they take on. Furthermore, she argues, in addition to knowing the categories constructed by urbanites, we need to understand how migrants identify themselves (ibid., 238). "The point," Honig explains, "is not simply to determine whether or not [a sense of difference] represents ethnicity, but rather to identify the social categories created that inform and fuel structures of inequality" (ibid., 242).

Following Honig's lead, this chapter considers the significance of native-place and rural/urban "ethnicity," as well as gender and class, for an understanding of identities and identifications among migrant women in contemporary Chinese cities.[1] To what extent, it asks, do migrant women identify with and against others on the basis of gender or class? And do regional identifications between migrant women point to something like ethnic divisions between them, or is it rather the rural/urban distinction that functions like ethnicity? What values and understandings about identity are associated with each of these forms of identification and division, and how do they relate to each other? The first section of the chapter looks at where migrant women draw the line between "us"—that is, those with whom they identify—and "them"—those they identify against—in different contexts, and the second section discusses the characteristics that they attribute to these groupings.

Us and Them

Migrants as Nonlocals

In line with the segregation that exists in the employment and residence of migrants and locals, and the lack of interaction between the two groups, rural migrant women in Beijing almost never speak of themselves as "locals" (*bendi ren*),

"Beijing people" (*Beijjng ren*), or "urbanites" (*chengli ren*). In Haidian, migrants identified themselves as "peasants" (*nongmin*) or, when talking about their status and treatment in the city, as "outsiders" (*waidiren*). The locals from whom these migrants rented housing were mostly also "peasants" or "former peasants" (because they had rural, agricultural *hukou*), but migrants generally did not consider this to be grounds for identification with them. Quite the contrary: many smarted at the fact that, though "no better than them," locals treated them with contempt and, by renting out their housing, earned a handsome living sitting around doing nothing, while migrants worked themselves to the bone. Migrants often, therefore, characterized these locals as lazy, crude country bumpkins even lower down the social hierarchy than themselves.

In my survey of the Migrant Women's Club I asked respondents: "Ultimately, deep down, what sort of person do you feel you are?—a rural person (*nongcun ren*), an urbanite (*chengli ren*), neither a rural person nor an urbanite (*bu shi nongcun ren, ye bu shi chengli ren*), or you don't know?" As is illustrated in Figure 6.1, only four out of ninety-five people, or 4.2 percent, responded that they were urbanites, a figure that corresponds with the number of respondents who said that their original agricultural *hukou* had been converted to local nonagricultural *hukou*.

When asked "Do you think of yourself as an urbanite?" and "Do you think of yourself as a Beijing person?" interlocutors from the Migrant Women's Club, including those who had lived in the city for several years, almost invariably responded with a firm "no." Even the responses of those very few women who showed some ambivalence about the question reveal a sense of division between themselves and other rural residents and migrants on the one hand and local Beijing people on the other. For example, I asked Yan Jun, a twenty-two-year-old factory worker who had come to Beijing from Shandong six years previously, if deep down she felt herself to be a rural person or an urban person. After a long pause she responded:

> I think I should be considered an urban person, because I've lived here for so long and I've learned a lot about living here and I don't want to go back because the thinking is too feudal in the countryside. (September 2001)

Just before this, Yan Jun had been telling me that she had a sense of inferiority because she had little education and she came from the countryside, but in continuing her response to my question she said, "I do have some belief in myself. I don't think I'm just a peasant."

Similarly, when I asked Ruan Shilin if, after five years in the city, she felt she was still a rural person or whether she now counted as a Beijing person, she said, "No, I don't count [as a Beijing person]" (November 2001). She then explained at

Figure 6.1 **Self-Identifications** (as percentage; N = 95)

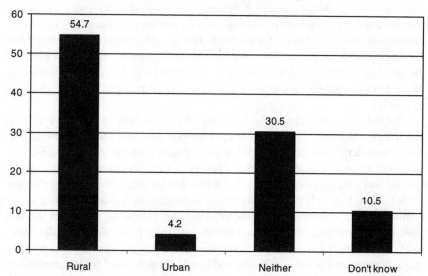

length that she did not put much weight on the distinction between Beijing people and outsiders, and that she felt for everyone who suffered injustice, regardless of whether they were locals or outsiders. However, when I pursued the issue of her own identity further, by asking if she could imagine a context in which she would say "us Beijingers," she insisted she could not:

> I don't think of myself as a Beijing person. I love Beijing and I have a sense of responsibility for things here, but I could never say "us Beijingers." Others ask me, "How is Beijing? What are Beijing people like?" They don't see me as a Beijing person, and I wouldn't say "us Beijingers" either. (November 2001)

When I pressed them to explain how it was that they did not consider themselves to be Beijing people, despite having lived in the city for many years, both the women in Haidian and the members of the Migrant Women's Club unhesitatingly answered that their identification card (*shenfen zheng*) or, more commonly, their *hukou* booklet indicated otherwise. I did not get the sense from my interlocutors that these were merely bureaucratic labels to them. Rather, they determined their fundamental identity; regardless of how long one had lived in Beijing, if one's identity card and *hukou* booklet identified one as belonging elsewhere, one could not think oneself a Beijing person.

However, there is real doubt as to whether a migrant woman would feel herself to be a Beijing person, even if she had lived in the city for many years *and* managed to have her *hukou* converted. Nonmigrant acquaintances have told me that you have to have been born in Beijing to count as a local. Others have said that it sometimes takes generations for people to feel accepted as true Beijingers. When I asked Ruan Shilin whether she would call herself a Beijing person if she obtained Beijing *hukou,* she replied hesitatingly: "I'd say my home [*laojia*] is in Shandong. But I don't know, you have to ask someone who *has* managed to get it" (November 2001).

The only migrant I knew who had managed to have her *hukou* converted was Zhou Ling. She was clear that before the conversion both she and her daughter were "outsiders"—despite the fact that Zhou Ling's husband was born in Beijing, had local urban *hukou,* and, though his parents were from elsewhere, felt no doubt that he was a Beijing person. With her *hukou* (and therefore her daughter's) converted, Zhou Ling felt that her daughter would grow up knowing nothing of the terrible angst that she herself had suffered over her *hukou* and would not feel that she was different from others around her, the way most migrant children did. However, Zhou Ling's conversion to a Beijing *hukou* did not appear to have much impact on her own sense of self. She had fought long and hard for the conversion, but when it came she seemed curiously unmoved. This may have been because she felt that her Beijing *hukou* was neither a redress of the injustices faced by migrants as a collective nor something that she had achieved independently—it had been possible only because of her husband's relatively privileged position as an urbanite in a state-owned work unit. Nor did having local *hukou* have any significant effect on the ways in which Zhou Ling was regarded by the urbanites around her, including her in-laws and her neighbors (August 2001).

Even after the change in her *hukou,* Zhou Ling's conversations with me were characterized by a strong identification, not as a Beijing person, nor as a Jiangsu person (Jiangsu being where she was born and grew up), nor as a rural resident, but as a migrant "outsider"—a *waidiren.* And despite being married to an urban Beijing man, Zhou Ling's identification of *waidiren* as "us" was equally matched by an identification of urbanites as "them," her conversations punctuated by frequent sharp criticisms of urbanites, including urbanites in general, intellectuals, officials, her neighbors, her in-laws, and even her husband.

Identifying with migrant outsiders was emotionally stressful and draining for Zhou Ling. In fact, she told me that while working in the office of the Migrant Women's Club she became so upset at the plight of *dagongmei* and frustrated at her own powerlessness and inability to do anything to improve their situation that she started having problems with her heart. Having her *hukou* converted and then leaving the Migrant Women's Club in 2001 did not change this, at least not immediately. In fact, her bitterness at the treatment migrants received from urbanites was heightened by her unemployment and the fact that her dependence upon her husband had grown even greater than previously. In 2002, though, this all changed. She found a good job in a state-owned work unit and succeeded in her ambition to bring her parents to live with her in Beijing. Outwardly she appeared a good deal more relaxed than she had before. When she was involved with the Migrant Women's Club, she said, she had not paid enough attention to her child and family. Now she was working full-time and concentrating on her family more. She rarely participated in the Migrant Women's Club and was out of touch with its members. Her identification with the *waidiren* subject position had, it seemed, been supplanted by more socially accepted, less stressful identifications as an employee of a Beijing work unit and as a wife and mother (December 2002).

Peasants, Outsiders, and In-Betweeners

Aside from Yan Jun and Zhou Ling, all the migrant women I talked with shared a certainty that they were *not* Beijing people, *not* locals, and *not* urbanites. In terms of more positive identifications, as I mentioned above, my interlocutors in Haidian generally identified themselves as outsiders when discussing their treatment by urbanites and at other times as rural people. Among these women, several years of living and working in an urban environment had not disturbed a fundamental understanding of themselves as rural people.

Among the members of the Migrant Women's Club, however, there was less certainty on this issue. This is reflected in Figure 6.1 above, which shows that while more than half of all respondents to the Migrant Women's Club survey identified themselves as rural people and only a few said that they were urbanites, 30.5 percent said they were neither rural people nor urbanites, and a further 10.5 percent said they did not know what sort of person they were.

In her book about migration in the Philippines, Lillian Trager argues that young women migrating from the countryside to the city and back moved between the two locations and two sets of subject positions with ease. They did not act as, or see themselves as, "peasants" in the city, nor did they see themselves as urban girls no longer able to participate in rural activities when they returned home on visits to their family (Trager 1988, 193). She quotes Philip Bartle as saying: "An individual need not suffer ambivalence from rural-urban contrasting obligations any more than a person has to suffer ambivalence from the daily contrasts in roles at work and roles at home" (Bartle 1981, cited in Trager 1988, 193). Trager then continues:

> It is, in other words, possible to suggest that those involved in migration carry dual or multiple identities involving combinations of ideas and values from rural and urban settings and leading to behavior appropriate to those settings. This suggests, further, that the issue of adaptation to urban settings is less problematic than has often been suggested. (Trager 1988, 193)

Trager is right to emphasize that migrants—like everyone else—carry multiple identities involving combinations of ideas and values. In addition, to reiterate points made in the introduction to this book, it may be that under modernity and postmodernity the range of identities or subject positions that are available to, or forced upon, individuals is multiplied.

Marshall Berman, Craig Calhoun, and other social theorists suggest that this may present major challenges for individuals—in Berman's words, "It pours us all into a maelstrom of perpetual disintegration and renewal, of struggle and contradiction, of ambiguity and anguish" (Berman 1982, quoted in Mills 1998, 301). Bartle and Trager suggest that the struggle and anguish may not be half as bad as Berman indicates—that a continual balancing and shifting between numerous different subject positions may be an easy and normal aspect of ordinary daily life. Lydia Kung, writing about the entry of rural women into urban industry in Taiwan, puts forward a similar argument when she suggests that "allowance must also be made for the possibility that individuals can compartmentalize different facets of their lives and that they are able to balance a variety of traditional and modern attitudes and experiences" (Kung 1983 [1978], 184).

I would argue that the degree of ease with which individuals compartmentalize different aspects of their lives, or combine, balance, or shift between different subject positions, is subject to various contingencies, including cultural expectations, social context, and the gap between subject positions that must be negotiated. It must be approached as an empirical question, on a case-by-case basis, rather than determined *a priori*. In the lowland Philippines, where rural-urban travel and communication are frequent and most rural adults have, therefore, been exposed to urban culture and lifestyles (Trager 1988, 193), it may be that individual migrant women can move untroubled between rural and urban subject positions. However, for *dagongmei* in large Chinese cities it is much harder. For most of the young Chinese women who travel to the city to work, this is the first time they have traveled any further than their local county town and the first time they have had a waged job. Many are initially bewildered by the size and confusion of the city and they struggle to learn how to do their jobs and to become accustomed to high levels of disciplinary control over their time and their bodies, and to long hours of exhausting, menial labor (Lee 1998, 114–15).

In addition, urbanites' coldness toward migrants and their frequent, sometimes violent, efforts to demean them often come as a nasty shock. Pun Ngai writes that on the assembly line in an electronics factory in Shenzhen managers constantly derided new workers as stupid, uncivilized country girls (*xiangxiamei*) with "rough hands and feet" (*cushou cujiao*), who understand nothing and cannot be taught (Pun Ngai 1999, 4). And when a group of these women went out for a drink in a café and the waiter wrongly gave them a drink before passing it to a man at a neighboring table, the man yelled to the waiter: "Their hands have touched the drink. Bring me another one. You don't know how dirty their hands are, those *waishengmei* [girls from another province]!" That evening, one of the young women involved wrote in a letter to her boyfriend:

Shen, why do the local people never treat us as human beings?—Now that I'm out in the world, I find myself a hundred times more worthless than in the village. (ibid., 12)

Once in the city, *dagongmei* become conscious very quickly of the things that mark them out as outsiders, especially their clothes, hairstyles, language, and manners, and they try hard to erase those marks, quickly learning to speak standard Mandarin, cutting their hair, and spending much of their first wages on fashionable new clothes. However, many remain skeptical of their ability to achieve an urban subject position, even on this superficial level. For example, many of my interlocutors were anxious that the police would stop and detain them on the street. When I asked how the police could distinguish them from locals, given that they dressed in the same style of clothes, some women just shrugged their shoulders. Others said the police could tell from their accents that they were from out of town and some replied "We look different, we walk different." (In fact, even I could often identify young migrant women, because they did not walk with the same air of confidence as others and they tended to huddle together in tight groups).

Among *dagongmei* who have been in the city for a while, there is a heartfelt and painful confusion about rural versus urban identity. On the one hand, while the allure of a modern, urban identity is very much promoted by the state, popular discrimination against rural migrants and the structural obstacles put in the way of their integration into urban society are such that few *dagongmei* believe that they are, or will ever be, "true" urbanites. On the other hand, after anything more than about a year in the city, most *dagongmei* feel that they are no longer rural people— they would be unable to readjust to life in the village were they to move back, and villagers would treat them as outsiders, just as urbanites do. As Louise Beynon argues, this sense of "in-betweenness"—of belonging neither to one place nor another—may be harder for migrant women than men, for "unlike men, who have a certain and fixed home to return to, these women have an accentuated sense of insecurity about their future because their natal home can only be temporary" (Beynon 2004, 141–42). As time goes by, migrant women's periodic visits home only serve to heighten the perception of distance between themselves and other villagers. One woman writing for *Rural Women* put it succinctly:

Rural people take me for a city person, but city people take me for a rural person. To both my distant home village and to this city I am forever an outsider. (Mei 1994)

Laoxiang and Dagongmei

While a sense of being neither urban nor rural is a powerful one among *dagongmei*, they do make other, more positive, identifications. The most important of these are based on distinctions between people from different provinces, between workers and bosses (*laoban*), and between those in different occupations. Each of these identifications serves as a basis for the expression of collective identities and shared interests, but each is limited to particular contexts.

A number of studies have alluded to regional origin as a basis for both inclusive and exclusive forms of identification among migrant workers in contemporary China, similar to those noted by Honig in her study of workers in Shanghai in the nineteenth and early to mid-twentieth centuries, discussed above. For example, Ching Kwan Lee reports that in the factory in Shenzhen where she based her research, workers identified each other more by regional origin and by the patron who brought them in than by name. Furthermore, competition and antagonism between workers of different regional origin was accompanied by a stereotyping of identities. Northerners—that is those from north of the Yangtze River—described southerners as greedy, uncouth, profligate, and ostentatious. Southerners, on the other hand, described those from the north as "fierce" and as having no sense of beauty or fashion (Lee 1998, 118–19).

Migrant women have also occasionally commented to me on supposed traits shared by people from particular regions. Northerners, and specifically Beijingers, are described as "cold" (*lengmo*) and "arrogant" (*jiao'ao*). And Anhui people are particularly able to "eat bitterness" (*chi ku*)—they tolerate long hours of grueling labor with less complaint than others. In addition, at the start of activities at the Migrant Women's Club when participants introduced themselves, they automatically said their name and the county and province from which they had come. Commonly, they did not mention their age or their occupation, or had to be prompted to do so. Beyond this, though, identifications based on regional background were rarely brought into play either in formal Club activities or in casual interactions between Club members. At a New Year soiree that members put on, for example, two people performed songs from minority nationalities, but this was for their exotic sound, not because the singers belonged to those nationalities (they did not). In fact, as far as I can recall, the only time individuals' own regional backgrounds became a focus of attention was in relation to food. Occasionally, for example, someone returning from a visit home would bring in some local produce from their home county for other Club members to sample. And dumpling (*jiaozi*)-making sessions involved jokes about the different shaped dumplings that friends from different provinces each fashioned, and the amount of vinegar and chili that those from some provinces ate with their dumplings as compared to others who ate theirs plain. Such jokes, however, served to increase the camaraderie between women from different provinces, rather than heighten the divisions between them.[2] Aside from this, regional origin has rarely been a significant element, either in urbanites' conversations with me about migrants or in migrant women's representations to me of their identities and their experiences. In these contexts, the significance of regional forms of identification has been far outweighed by outsider/local and rural/urban distinctions and cannot be said to constitute a form of ethnicity.

More significant to migrant women's representations of themselves is an identification as a migrant worker or *dagongmei* and a distinction drawn between migrant workers and others. For members of the Migrant Women's Club, the term *dagongmei* provided an important new subject position and basis for identification with other migrant workers. This identification was most commonly defined in negative terms or in terms of lack—"we *dagongmei*," my interlocutors often said, "have no power or rights [*mei you quanli*] and we have a sense of inferiority [*juede hen zibei/ you zibei gan*]." This form of identification was reinforced by Xie Lihua and Li Tao, staff at the *Rural Women* collective, who explained that the reason they had established the Migrant Women's Club was that being both female and rural, *dagongmei* were a "vulnerable group" (*ruoshi qunti*). Negative as it was, this understanding formed an important basis for solidarity among *dagongmei*, although for all Xie Lihua and Li Tao's emphasis on the particular vulnerability of migrant *women*, the solidarity was not gender specific—membership of the Club included some men, and members' discussions of their experiences rarely focused on gender to any significant extent. This lack of gender identification will be further explored shortly.

Outside of the Migrant Women's Club young migrant women refer to themselves as *dagongmei* relatively infrequently. Originally from Hong Kong, the term had become widespread in the cities and special economic zones of south China by the early 2000s, but elsewhere it was still regarded as a new and awkward term. Furthermore, some women felt uncomfortable at what they felt to be the derogatory or condescending connotations of the appellation "*mei*"—younger sister or young girl. Nevertheless, in both Beijing and Hangzhou my interlocutors strongly identified with other migrant waged workers.

This is not to say that there are no antagonisms between *dagongmei*. On the contrary, as indicated in the previous chapter, in the workplace managers and middle-level supervisors often manipulate particularistic ties (*guanxi*), favoring those with whom they have personal connections over those with whom they do not, and this results in resentment and tension, not just between workers of different regional origin but between migrant workers generally. *Outside* the workplace, however, *dagongmei* identifications with other migrant workers commonly override the divisions between them. In some instances these identifications are based on occupation. Women working in the service sector, for example, often talk about their experiences in terms of the discrimination faced by those in the service sector in particular, rather than those faced by migrants in general. As Zhou Hongxia, a woman from Anhui working in a restaurant in Hangzhou, put it:

> For me, working in a restaurant is nothing bad, but Hangzhou people look down on waitresses in restaurants and nightclubs. They say they are troubled places, too many people coming and going, they're not proper. . . . I've worked in several restaurants and they've all been quite proper. It's the same as any other work. But when you say you work in a restaurant, it's as if Hangzhou people view you with contempt. They look down on you. (Jacka 1998, 55)

Similar identifications with others in the same occupation are also commonly made by maids, who represent their experiences as differing from those of other migrants both because their occupation has a particularly low social status and because they have more contact with urbanites than other migrants (see, for example, Mian 2004). Conversely, many migrant women try hard to distinguish themselves from other *dagongmei* who work as escorts (*sanpeinü*) and prostitutes, to avoid being tarred with the same brush. This is a major concern, because both urbanites and villagers tend to lump all migrants together as similarly morally suspect. Therefore, to achieve both a positive, modern, and urbane image in the city and a respectable, filial image back at home in the countryside, most migrant women feel they must do all they can to avoid any association between their own work and that of sex workers. The remarks by Zhou Hongxia, above, evidence this concern.

Apart from their efforts to cast prostitutes as the inferior, negative "other," the occupational identifications made by *dagongmei* do not generally militate against a solidarity with migrant women workers as a collective and across occupational boundaries. In some instances, the identification with *dagongmei* is essentially the same as that with outsiders. In other words, the generalizations made about "us" migrant women workers are the same as those made about migrants more broadly and are contrasted with those about "them" urban locals. In other cases, the distinction drawn is more specifically between migrant workers and bosses, the latter term being used to refer to factory owners and managers, small-scale entrepreneurs and traders, and individual employers of maids—anyone who uses or makes a profit on the labor of others rather than selling their labor to another (cf. Xu, Feng 2000, 86–89).

This identification cuts across the migrant/urbanite divide in the sense that bosses are viewed similarly, regardless of whether they are urbanites or migrants themselves. There is, thus, a major divide between migrant laborers on the one hand and migrant employers and entrepreneurs (and their families) on the other. *Dagongmei* generally do not identify with migrant women like my interlocutors in Haidian who are traders or businesspeople or whose husbands run businesses. The worker/boss distinction also cuts across the migrant/urbanite divide in the sense that the representation of bosses and of local urbanites is very often blurred in *dagongmei* narratives, even though many of the owners of large factories employing *dagongmei* are from overseas, and the proprietors of restaurants and sweatshops are often migrants from other provinces. All bosses tend to be characterized similarly, as exploiting their workers and treating them with contempt. Zhou Hongxia sums up:

> The bosses don't trust us outsiders. If you do everything perfectly it's okay, but if you do one little thing wrong, then [pause]. Bosses are all like that. They like pretty girls, someone presentable. Otherwise they scowl at you and make you feel bad. I've had several different jobs in Hangzhou and the bosses are

all the same. They're only interested in whether the girls are pretty or not, not in their ability. . . . If you do anything wrong they abuse you. These wealthy bosses, Hangzhou bosses, they're all capitalists. They think they can do anything they like. (quoted in Jacka 1998, 54)

Do remarks such as these point to a (nascent) class consciousness? Do they suggest that class is more significant than place to migrants' understanding of who they are?[3] Migrant workers often draw upon Marxist terminology, referring (accurately) to the ways in which capitalist bosses exploit (*boxue*) them. This sets them against contemporary official discourse, in which such language, the hallmark of Maoism, has been supplanted by the notion that "to get rich is glorious." Yet migrant workers do not talk about class (*jieji*), or about belonging to the working class (*gongren jieji*) or proletariat (*wuchan jieji*) (Sargeson 1999, 4–8). As Sally Sargeson in her study of identifications among factory workers in Hangzhou in the 1990s argues, this is not just a case of workers being taken in by official discourse and failing to comprehend their true, objective circumstances and interests. Rather, migrant workers perceive that ownership of property and control over the means of production are not the sole, nor even the key, factors determining relations of subordination. Therefore, while they complain about exploitative capitalist bosses, they also complain about the exploitation and discrimination they receive from state officials and other urbanites, and they represent their own and their exploiters' identities, not in terms of class, but in terms of place, power, privilege, and particularism (ibid., 17) and the intimate connections between all three. The epitome of the exploiter is the powerful, contemptuous (usually male), urban official or employer, who manipulates *guanxi* to further his own interests. Yet, others also get caught up in this image. As I have mentioned, for example, bosses tend to be portrayed in this way regardless of whether they are urban or local.

On the other hand, urban workers are also represented in a similar way. I recall an occasion on which Gao Xinran, some of her *dagongmei* workmates, and I sat talking in the canteen run by the large company in which they worked as cleaners. This was a very up-market canteen, rarely frequented by the cleaners. Gao Xinran and the others had taken me there as a special guest and in order to impress me, but they were very uncomfortable. Gao Xinran watched the urban company staff sitting at other tables with a brooding, resentful look on her face, and she said, nodding her head in their direction, "They're the ones we serve." When I objected that it need not be viewed in that way, since they were all employees working alongside each other in the same company, Gao Xinran retorted, "Yeah, but that's how it is in fact" (December 2002).

For Gao, as for the majority of other *dagongmei,* hierarchical divisions between migrant and local workers, and consequent differences in power, privilege, material circumstances, and income, militate against identifications across the rural/urban and outsider/local divide. But this is also the case in those instances in which migrant workers' situations differ little from those of urbanites. Such instances were rare in the early 1990s, but have become increasingly common, accompanied by growing antagonism between local and migrant workers. This is largely because of growing insecurity of employment among urban workers, and increasing competition between themselves and migrants. During the 1990s the numbers of incoming migrants greatly increased, and some of these rural "outsiders" quickly climbed the ladder to success. Meanwhile, the "iron rice bowl" of the urban working class had been broken. Increasing numbers of urban workers in the state sector lost their entitlement to a life-long job with welfare and other benefits attached and were employed on temporary contracts not much better than those of migrant workers. Others were laid off from state-sector enterprises as a result of employers' efforts to improve productivity or in the wake of bankruptcy, and they were forced to turn to lower status unskilled work that previously was the exclusive domain of migrants. Consequently, according to Zhou Ling, urbanites' attitudes toward *dagongmei* were worse in the early 2000s than they had been when she first arrived in Beijing in the early 1980s:

> They discriminate against us even more. When I first came out, I was always embarrassed about it, so when I talked with urbanites I was always very self-effacing and felt inferior. They thought that was great because it made them feel superior. It gave them a feeling of superiority, so they sympathized with you. They thought you were very pitiful, so they sympathized. Now it's different. Now they discriminate against you. They feel different because there's more people coming out now and there's more [urban] unemployment. Also, when we first came out, we all became maids. Nowadays, not all of us become maids. Some become shop assistants, the same as them. Some work in hotels, some become bosses. So they don't feel the same anymore. . . . Their equilibrium has been disturbed, they're losing their feeling of superiority, so they no longer sympathize with you, they discriminate against you. (August 2001; see also Mei Luxian, quoted in Jacka 1998, 53)

It is conceivable that in the future, growing congruence in their circumstances will lead increasing numbers of workers to construct class-based identities, or at least alliances, which cross the local/outsider and urban/rural divide.[4] To date, however, there has been very little solidarity between migrant and urban workers, and while strikes among both groups are common, they rarely come together. In sum, both urban and rural migrant workers do evince an awareness of class exploitation, but they are also highly conscious of the fact that class in China is riven through and through by hierarchies of particularism and place.

Gender and Individualism

In terms of explicit representations of identity and experience, gender appears much less significant to migrant women than the other forms of identification discussed so far. Neither my interlocutors in Haidian nor those in the Migrant Women's Club identified experiences that they shared with women in general, as distinct from men, and across the rural/urban or local/outsider divide.

In Haidian my interlocutors referred to themselves and other migrant women as peasants and outsiders, but never specifically as peasant or outsider *women*. Furthermore, they very rarely volunteered information about difficulties shared by peasant or migrant women, but not men, nor did they identify patriarchy or sexism as a problem. For instance, a few mentioned that, as children, their educations were limited because their families included several girls—the problem, as they saw it, was the poverty that resulted from having too many mouths to feed. They did not identify discrimination against girls as a factor, even though their brothers commonly received more schooling than they did.

In addition, in talking about their current circumstances, it was relatively rare for these women to indicate that they had interests different from their husbands or from their families as a whole. Some did mention disputes or discord between themselves and their husbands, but most talked in terms of experiences and difficulties shared by themselves and their husbands as a couple. And when I asked what activities they were engaged in, they either talked of the business that they and their husbands had set up together, or about their husbands' income-earning ventures. They either did not mention their own work, whether it was domestic work or income-generating work, or, if they did, they greatly downplayed its significance to the household. When I asked them what hopes they had for the future, they said they had none or responded in terms of hopes for their children's education. None of the Haidian women responded to this question in terms of hopes or desires for themselves as individuals.

Members of the Migrant Women's Club seemed more individualist than the women in Haidian—they emphasized their own individual agency more, and they spoke a good deal more about a desire to "develop themselves" and less in terms of aspirations for, or obligations toward, their families. This difference appears to map easily onto a stereotypical difference between traditional and modern orientations, it being commonly understood that traditional agrarian societies emphasize kinship and community, while individualism and self-interest are necessary for modern, consumer-oriented capitalism (Sahlins 1992, 13). However, several factors complicate this seemingly straightforward distinction between traditional, (slightly) older married migrant women, and their more modern *dagongmei* counterparts. Already in the previous chapter I showed that while *dagongmei* do, indeed, act primarily as modern independent agents, pursing their own self-interests, rather than as cogs in their families' economic strategies, their relationships with their parents are also very important and they are often very filial in the most traditional way. In addition, to the extent that *dagongmei* are relatively individualist, this is partially a reflection of a very long-standing, if not traditional, expectation that young and unmarried people are relatively free to pursue individual interests—to try to "change their fate" and "find a life" for themselves—whereas beyond a certain age both men and women, but especially women, must "settle down," marry, and subsume individual concerns to the needs of children and the family as a whole. On the other hand, recent discourses on modernity, consumption, and (self-) development have contributed to these differences, for these discourses are simultaneously highly individualist and directed primarily at young adults. For example, advertisements urging people to buy products that will contribute to a modern lifestyle are targeted mainly at young people. In addition, women's organizations (in both rural and urban areas) aim to further modernization and development by encouraging women to undertake training courses to improve their individual *suzhi* (quality) and by promoting the "four selfs"—self-respect, self-confidence, self-reliance, and self-strength (*zizun, zixin, zili, ziqiang*). All of their projects target young women and usually exclude those over the age of forty.

The narratives of members of the Migrant Women's Club suggest that they were relatively individualist *before* moving to the city and that a desire to find a life for themselves as individuals was a primary motivation for that migration. This orientation relates partly to their age and partly to the effects of the discourses of modernity outlined above, for these discourses are not limited to the more modern, urban centers—through the media, migration, and the training of officials they have also pervaded the countryside. However, it is clear that, once in the city, these women's individualist aspirations were both reinforced and given a particular shape and language by the general influence of urban consumerism and urban media discourse on development, and by the particular impact of the Migrant Women's Club. Most obviously, self-development (*ziwo fazhan*) is not a term that rural women would normally use, but is something *dagongmei* have picked up from official rhetoric.

In addition to being more individualist, the members of the Migrant Women's Club were more conscious of gender and more critical of patriarchal discourse than my interlocutors in Haidian. But the difference was much slighter than I had expected, given the former group's involvement with an organization dedicated specifically to protecting and promoting the rights of migrant *women*.

When they talked about their lives in the village prior to migration, some members of the Club referred to experiences specific to girls and there was some criticism of patriarchal discourse. In particular, as I discussed in chapter 4, they complained of limitations to rural girls' education. Like the women in Haidian, they identified their families' straitened financial circumstances as the primary cause of this, but some also attributed it to the fact that their home village and/or their family were "feudal" and that they "care more about men than women" (*zhong nan qing nü*). Many also chafed at the limitations that were placed on young women's movements outside the home village, and, almost universally, the unmarried members of the Club dreaded marriage in the village as an end to their autonomy and a subordination to the authority of their husbands and in-laws.

These women's narratives indicate, once more, that they did not just become critical of rural patriarchal discourse after and as a result of their experiences in the city—they were already critical of, and felt limited by, such discourses in the village before they migrated, and that was a primary reason for them leaving home. As discussed in chapter 4, though, it is also clear that their experiences of more liberal urban attitudes toward sexuality, combined with their own experiences of individual autonomy, strengthened their criticism of rural patriarchy and their desire to avoid or at least postpone their return to it.

In talking about their current circumstances as migrants in the city, members of the Migrant Women's Club were unlike the women in Haidian in that they did sometimes refer to themselves in gender-specific terms, as *dagongmei* and *wailaimei*. Surprisingly, however, they were no more likely than the women in Haidian to identify gender or patriarchal discourse as a factor affecting their own and other migrants' lives in the city. Thus, like my interlocutors in Haidian, they never identified with other nonmigrant women in the city, and when they talked of the difficulties they faced, it was as rural migrants and outsiders rather than as women. This stance is reflected in responses to my survey of the Club, in which I asked respondents to identify the three main reasons why *dagongmei* sometimes faced difficulties and could not realize their aspirations while in the city.[5] As can be seen in Figure 6.2, a large proportion of respondents pointed to discrimination against outsiders, discrimination against rural people, and household registration as the primary obstacles. Lack of skills and knowledge, a sense of inferiority (*zibei gan*), and a lack of connections (*guanxi*) were also listed by a relatively large number of respondents. However, it is striking that only 6.8 percent of respondents pointed to discrimination against women as being a factor contributing to the difficulties faced by *dagongmei* in the city.

As I discussed in chapter 3, the urban labor force is highly segmented by gender as well as by *hukou* status. As a result, female migrants generally earn less than male migrants and there are significant differences in the experiences of the two groups. However, while *dagongmei* are quick to point out that migrant wages are lower than urbanites' and that they perform all the dirty, tiring, low-status work that urbanites shun, they very rarely discuss differences in the pay or working conditions of migrant men and women, or identify gender as a factor in their experiences. Even Liu Yu, who had worked as a maid, understood the rape that she had suffered at the hands of her employer in terms of urbanites' contempt for rural people, and not in terms of gender inequalities and patriarchal discourse.

In sum, migrant women identify themselves primarily as outsiders to the city, as rural people, as in-between the city and the countryside, and as *dagongmei*. In

Figure 6.2 Obstacles to the Achievement of Migrant Women's Aspirations in the City (as percentage; N = 88)

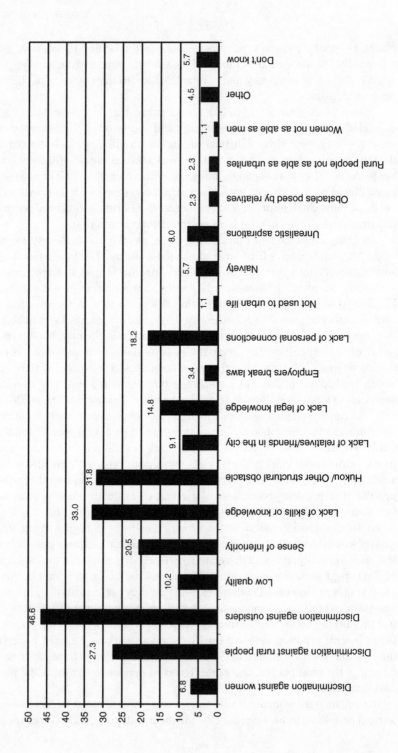

addition, in some contexts they identify with *laoxiang,* as distinct from people of other regional backgrounds, and in others they identify as and with workers in opposition to the bosses. However, explicit identifications based on gender play a very minor role in migrant women's representation of their identities and experiences. This can be read as testimony to the strength of discourses on rural/urban difference and the grossness of inequalities between migrants and urbanites, especially between migrant workers and urban employers and officials, relative to those between male and female migrants—certainly this is how most migrants themselves would read it. But it is also attributable to the orientations of the state, the Women's Federation, and women's groups such as the *Rural Women* collective. As I discussed in chapter 2, the Chinese women's movement has largely accepted the terms of official, dominant discourse, responding to gender oppression primarily in terms of economic (under)development, "feudal remnants" in people's attitudes and customs, and low levels of *suzhi,* or human quality, especially in the rural population. As a result, migrant women, like others, have learned the language of development, underdevelopment, and rural/urban difference. They are also able to challenge some aspects of rural patriarchy. On the whole, however, they do not have the language with which to challenge the profound gender inequalities underlying violence against women and women's disadvantaged position in the labor force.

Traits of Difference

Chapter 1 sketched out the main features of urban representations of rural inhabitants and migrants as inferior to urbanites, not just in relation to opportunities and quality of life but in terms of essential qualities of person. In the next several paragraphs I address the following questions: To what extent do migrant women's own representations of themselves and others, and the evaluative systems underlying these representations, accord with dominant characterizations? To what extent do they repudiate them, and to what extent do they present different understandings of identity?

When I asked my interlocutors whether they thought there were differences between rural and urban people, they almost invariably said "yes" and proceeded to elaborate those differences. This was the case both in Haidian and among members of the Migrant Women's Club and other *dagongmei.* However, there were significant differences in the way these two groups of women characterized and explained rural/urban differences.

Occupation, Wealth, and Education

The women in Haidian most commonly talked in terms of differences in occupation and economic circumstance. For example, when I asked her about differences between rural and urban people, Zhang Xiaohua explained that country people have to work in the fields even when it's hot. City people, when it's hot, go to their offices, where they have electric fans and air conditioners. In the countryside women, children, and the elderly must work outside from morning till night. When the wheat has ripened you have to go and harvest it or you'll lose it. Things are very tough for rural people, and you just live from one day to the next. (August 2001)

In response to the same question Jin Rong said:

When it comes down to it, there are differences, otherwise why would rural people run to the city, even though they can't earn much there? [In the past], city people had a stable wage of several hundreds of yuan each month, but rural people worked a full year and still they owed the production team workpoints [i,e., the team assigned work and sometimes people couldn't finish the tasks they were assigned, so they owed money or labor]. The more people [in the family] the more you owed. So city people had advantages over rural people. Now with reform and opening up the differences are even greater. (August 2001)

In addition, when I said to Jin Rong that I had heard that city people look down on outsiders, she responded: "Who comes out to work if they have money? If you have money you stay at home, you only come out to work if you don't have money." Her understanding, which was similar to that of many other women in Haidian, was that the primary basis for difference and inequality between people is wealth. She did not challenge the validity of a discrimination based on economic circumstances; she challenged instead the justice of rural people's poverty. In other words, it was natural to her that urbanites would look down on rural people because of their poverty. It was wrong, though, that peasants should be so poor.

Aside from economic explanations, the other gloss on rural/urban difference offered by the women in Haidian related to education and what we might understand as manners or civility in interpersonal relations. This was epitomized in the following exchange with Han Haiying:

Tamara Jacka: Some people say that city people look down on outsiders, is that right?

Han Haiying: Some do, but not many. In general, there are more good people [than bad]. Sometimes city people are more civilized [*wenming*] in the way they talk. Rural people speak crudely. They don't have education and culture [*wenhua*], so of course there's going to be a difference. And of course people in the capital are going to be civilized. (August 2001)

In Haidian, my questions about differences between rural and urban people seemed to connect only marginally with my interlocutors' primary concerns. In contrast, among members of the Migrant Women's Club and other *dagongmei* such differences were a much more central concern. Furthermore, the range of distinguishing characteristics that they identified was different. They did not mention rural and urban people's different economic position, but they did talk about differences in education, culture, and civilization. They were also concerned with rural/urban differences relating to language, dress, comportment, sexuality, morality, and personality, and were able to identify and elaborate a vast panoply of such differences. As my *dagongmei* interlocutors described them, these rural/urban differences are marked but not insurmountable. In other words, while the status of a "true" urbanite is practically unattainable, it is possible for a *dagongmei* to become less rural and more urban than previously, and for many this is a highly sought-after goal. In fact, *dagongmei* views on rural/urban difference emerged as commonly in comparisons of the relative urbanity of different *dagongmei* as they did in direct comparisons between rural people and urbanites, and it was very common for *dagongmei* to laugh at the rurality of their former selves and to deride others for being less advanced in their progress toward urbanity.

Why my interlocutors in Haidian and those in the Migrant Women's Club should have such different views on rural/urban differences is, in itself, an interesting question. I would argue that the differences reflect a shift in orientation that has occurred in society more generally. Haidian women's characterization of rural/urban difference in terms of occupation and education is more or less in line with both Confucian and Maoist orientations. It echoes the traditional Confucian distinction between rulers, who use their minds and hearts (*laoxin*), and the ruled, who use their muscles (*laoli*), and the notion that those with education are more civilized and morally superior to those without. Of course, the Communist Party under Mao Zedong reversed the Confucian order by according those who work with their muscles (the peasants and the working class) higher status and by devaluing elite education, culture, and notions of civility. Even so, it did not challenge the significance of education and occupation, instead using them alongside the ownership of property as fundamental markers of class identity and status. In contemporary discourses these remain important, despite the near disappearance of class as a category of analysis. However, as I discussed in chapter 1, in its pursuit of market development, the post-Mao Communist Party has also elevated competition in consumption and *suzhi*. This, in turn, has resulted in a much greater emphasis on objects of consumption, like clothes, food, and leisure, and personal *suzhi,* including everything from physical comportment, language, and know-how, through to morality, psychology, and aspects of personality as not just the consequences of social position and status, but as their determinants.

In general, although competition in consumption and *suzhi* has become a part of life in even the poorest, most isolated villages, it is more intense in the cities because there people are generally more exposed to Party and market rhetoric and because urbanites can afford to compete more vigorously in these arenas than poor villagers. Furthermore, the scale and range of competition is different—villagers mostly compete with others in the village, while urbanites compete on a national, even international, scale.

On the whole, *dagongmei,* especially those working as maids and in the service and retail sectors, have rather more contact with urbanites than migrant women, like those in Haidian, who are not employed in wage labor. They also tend to be more sensitive toward urban constructions of identity and status than the women in Haidian. As I discussed earlier, the women in Haidian had few interactions with urbanites and their fundamental sense of themselves remained as rural people, derived primarily from their relationship with family members and other villagers. Migration to the city was seen as an opportunity for furthering both individual and family goals, but for most it resulted in relatively little change or challenge to identities or relationships with others. In contrast, members of the Migrant Women's Club and other *dagongmei* with whom I spoke were much less certain about who they were. Having come to the city not just to make money but to "find a (new) life" and an identity as an independent adult, separate from their family, these women were fascinated by the modern urban norms and subject positions they absorbed from the media and from their interactions with urban employers and others. Many aspired to be as modern and urban as possible, and it mattered a great deal to them how well they measured up to urban ideals and how they were seen by urbanites.

One might have expected increasing contact between *dagongmei* and urbanites to engender a more nuanced mutual understanding and a repudiation of rural/urban dichotomies and stereotypes. In reality, however, through the 1990s and 2000s, *dagongmei* and other migrant contact with urbanites has on the whole not lessened the prejudices of either group. On the contrary, as I discussed above, urban views of migrants have become increasingly dichotomized and negative, and *dagongmei* have responded in kind. Occasionally, *dagogmei* defend themselves and other rural migrants against urban objectifications by referring to structural inequalities and resulting material disadvantage. Zhou Ling, for example, railed against Beijingers' complaints about migrants being dirty. As we stood on the balcony outside her family's apartment, looking out onto the makeshift huts of migrants working on the construction site below, she said:

Look at how they live! There are no washing facilities down there. And those workers never get paid regularly. Sometimes they just get paid when a job is done and then they're sent away, sometimes they only get paid at the end of a year. They can't afford to go to the public baths, so sometimes they don't wash for months at a time. And then locals complain that they're dirty?! (August 2001)

However, such *dagongmei* challenges to urban stereotyping are rare. More commonly, despite their understanding of structural inequalities, young migrant women are unable to overcome urbanites' essentialized, dichotomized characterizations of the differences between rural people, including migrants, and urban dwellers. Instead, they reproduce them with their own different—sometimes radically different—inflections.

Dress and Sexuality

In China, as elsewhere, dress is an important signal to others about social status, identity and sexuality, indicating not just wealth or one's eye for fashion but also the sort of people with whom one identifies and the kind of person one is "on the inside." *Dagongmei* are highly sensitive to this signifying power of dress. I recall a visit to Zhu Jin, who worked as a salesperson in a dress shop and lived in a small, rented room in Fengtai. During my visit (December 2002) we sat on her bed leafing through her photograph album. She was keen for me to see the most recent photographs of herself and her friends at tourist sites around Beijing, but when we looked together at the earlier pictures, taken when she was still at home or soon after she got to Beijing, she exclaimed several times, "[I look] so rustic, so ugly! [*Tai tu le, zhen bu hao kan!*]." To my own eyes, she did not look at all bad, but there was a marked difference between her presentation in the earlier photographs and the appearance she cultivated a few years later. The day I visited her, Zhu Jin had painted her eyebrows and was wearing mascara and eyeshadow. She wore a close-fitting black sweater and jumpsuit, with a necklace from which hung a large cross, embellished with colorful, artificial jewels. Her hair was cropped short, smart and fashionable. In her early "rustic" photographs her hair was slightly longer and not as smart, and her clothes were less revealing, more asexual (or masculine) and more unkempt. In one picture, for example, she wore a baggy denim jacket and loose trousers with several pockets.

Zhu Jin's contemporary image accords well with the image of feminine modernity that is promoted in the media, including *Rural Women* and *Working Sister.* In its first eighteen months of publication, all but one of the eight covers of *Working Sister* featured a photograph of a model *dagongmei,* whose successes were written up as lead stories (see, for example, Figure 2.1). These cover girls have long hair, some pinned back, some loose, wear make up and fashionable clothing, and smile out at the reader. Some look feminine and sexy, others strike one more simply for their confidence. On two of the covers the *dagongmei* stands alone in color, on five she is highlighted against a faded, obviously poor and rural background, with a smaller, elderly figure standing to one side. In these latter pictures, the vibrant *dagongmei* is graphically removed from, and juxtaposed against, much less appealing images of rurality.

Zhu Jin shares with the editors of *Working Sister* an ideal of the successful, urbanized *dagongmei* as confident and modern—smarter, more fashionably dressed, and more sexy than her rural counterpart. This is an image that many *dagongmei* long for, spending their meager savings and what little leisure time they have shopping for fashionable clothes, lipstick, and skin-whitening creams that they hope will give them a new urban look, if not identity (Pun 2003, 486–87). However, not all *dagongmei* are as positive about, and strive as hard for, this image as Zhu Jin. Some are reluctant to spend any more of their hard-earned wages on changing their appearance than is necessary to blend into the urban setting. Some express disgust at the ways in which their fellow migrants' efforts to adorn themselves make them look like prostitutes.

In 1993 *Rural Women* published a story that vividly conveyed the significance of appearance and its close relationship to norms of behavior and sexuality, the enormous pressure on *dagongmei* to conform to ideals of modern urban appearance and behavior so as to avoid the objectification of peasantness, and the ambivalence that some *dagongmei* nevertheless feel about those norms. The author, a *dagongmei* named Xiao Chun, says:

> I still like to braid the type of plaits that only rural girls wear. When they see this, my friends shake their heads and say "They're so rustic (*tu*)! You're a silly girl, cut them off and be done with them!" I still like to wear the country clothes that I brought from home with me—things with high collars and long sleeves. My friends see them and say: "Such a hot day, look at what you're wearing! Are you still not willing to wear the clothes we helped you buy? . . ."
>
> What makes everyone even more convinced that I'm a lovable bumpkin is that I never allow any of my roommates to shower with me. Because of these things they're always imitating me, laughing till they're sore in the stomach. One day three sisters decided to "reform" me, pushing and pulling me over to the dance hall. But when they got me to the entrance, I held onto the doorframe for dear life. By this time they were panting and out of breath, but one of them had to ask, "Tell us, why don't you want to go?"
>
> "That place isn't right for me. . . . I don't have to tell you that."
>
> Then they attacked me en masse: "You're too feudal, too ignorant, we simply must 'reform' you!" And all I could say was, "I'm not feudal and I really don't want to seem ignorant. To tell the truth, I enjoy watching other people's graceful dancing. I even envy them and wish I could be like that, but I can't."

But they still wouldn't lay off, so in the end I said: "I'm going to wait until I've got a boyfriend and then I'll go dancing."

They laughed themselves silly, but they could not persuade me. Actually, when I think about it, I feel a little ridiculous myself. Why am I like that? I feel I'd be embarrassed to hold my hand out to a man I don't know. And I feel that if I was to behave that way, I'd be turning bad, I'd be betraying the sincere, honest, upright village folk who brought me up. But I can't explain how I feel, even to myself.

It's true, some say I'm "rustic," and I know I am, it's just that sometimes I feel very assured about being "rustic." But at other times it feels stupid, and a burden. You see, I've gradually come to understand: these days the model rural girl doesn't have to be like me. (Xiao Chun 1993)

Aside from language, appearance, comportment, and sexuality, *dagongmei* elaborate a host of rural/urban differences relating to manners, personality, and interpersonal behavior. As can be seen from the following conversation, for example, Zhang Ning shared a belief with Han Haiying and Jin Rong in the superior civility of urbanites:

Tamara Jacka: Do you generally have much contact with Beijing people?

Zhang Ning: Well, before when I was working [as a maid] my jobs were all with Beijing people.

Tamara Jacka: What were your relations with them like?

Zhang Ning: Very good. They had education and culture [*wenhua*] and were good to me.

Tamara Jacka: Do you think there are differences between rural and urban people? Or else, are there differences between Beijing people and Anhui people?

Zhang Ning: [Hesitation] In the countryside, the people you have contact with don't have much education. But in Beijing you meet people with education and culture and they're relatively civilized [*wenming*]. Rural people are crude [*cu de*].

Tamara Jacka: I don't understand. Can you give an example?

Zhang Ning: When they speak, when they do things. [pause] In the countryside, if there's a conflict people just abuse each other. Men hit each other. In the city you get that too sometimes, but not in the families I worked in. Usually they used peaceful means to solve problems. Beijing people very rarely swear, or they swear mildly—not like the awful things rural people say. Rural people swear at you for anything and everything. [pause] In the countryside, if there's a conflict they swear at you, pick out your shortcomings. (August 2001)

Similarly, Ma Hua believed that urbanites were more civilized than rural people, who fought and argued over the pettiest of issues. When she went home for a visit after being in Beijing for two years, the fighting was what struck her most. It made her feel that the village was unsafe and backward. Rural people, Ma Hua explained, can "eat bitterness" (*chi ku*) to a greater extent than urban folk—that is, they are more capable of tiring, physical work. But they are no good at things to do with emotions and relations with others, because they are uneducated and they have little contact with other people (October 2001).

Deng Yiyan's understanding of rural/urban differences was somewhat different. She said:

> I hate having to deal with others here, because in the city relations between people are terribly complicated. You have to cultivate good interpersonal relations [*gao hao renji guanxi*] and ingratiate yourself with the leadership [*taohao lingdao*]. . . . In the countryside people are always very frank [*zhishuai*] with each other, they help each other and are very warm [*reqing*]. There's no conflict of interest between people, because everyone just has their own plot of earth to plant, and if you're not hardworking and you don't farm well, you can only blame yourself. But it's not like that in Beijing. Here there are opportunities to go up in the world—in the countryside there aren't. There it's just a matter of how much you earn. Here, if the leaders appreciate and admire you, you'll have the opportunity to get ahead or you'll be able to get more money. If the leaders don't like you, you won't be able to get a bonus and you won't be able to get ahead. So you must ingratiate yourself with the leadership. I hate that. If the leaders want to talk to me I'll talk to them, but otherwise I don't pay them any attention. (August 2001)

When I asked Gao Xinran and two of her workmates if there is a difference between city people and country people, Xinran responded firmly: "Yes, urbanites are cold [*lengmo*], while rural people are warm [*reqing*], and urbanites look down on us" (December 2002). We talked for a while about discrimination against rural migrants, myself commenting that inequalities and discrimination exist in every society. One of Xinran's workmates then asked me "what about domestic violence—does that happen everywhere too?" I said that yes, I thought it did, but Xinran said "[in China] it only happens in rich, urban households, it doesn't happen in the countryside." Xinran's workmate countered with a story of a rural relative whose husband beat her, but Xinran herself remained of the opinion that such behavior was far more characteristic of wealthy urbanites than of rural people (December 2002).

Dagongmei characterizations of essential rural/urban differences such as these appear to be drawn from the same dominant discourses on modernity as are contemporary urban representations of these differences. Indeed, in broad terms at least, they seem to match understandings about traditional rural versus modern urban traits that are common to discourses on modernity across the world—urbanites, so it is said, are more civilized in their relations with others as well as being more open-minded. But they are also cold, cruel, manipulative, and self-interested. Rural people, in contrast, are uneducated, uncivilized, crude, and rude while also being straightforward and honest, warm and friendly, and hardworking.

On the other hand, the devil is in the detail, and while drawing on similar sets of ideas and values, the specifics of *dagongmei* representations of rural/urban difference are often quite different from those identified in other discourses. Furthermore, among *dagongmei* themselves, identifications of rural and urban characteristics vary, are invested with a variety of different values and judgments, and are highly contested. These identifications are perhaps most usefully understood as performative acts, which reflect an understanding of the context in which individuals are situated at any given moment and serve different functions according to whom they are speaking, the points they are making, and the effects they are trying to achieve. In some contexts, for example, *dagongmei* draw upon highly negative characterizations of urbanites in order to carve out a positive subject position for themselves as rural migrants or to highlight their loneliness, alienation, and/or maltreatment in the city. In others, they paint a more positive picture of urbanites in order to convey an identification with, or an aspiration toward, an urban identity. In yet other contexts, the judgments and characterizations that *dagongmei* make are highly ambivalent, reflecting desires to identify simultaneously with different, conflicting subject positions.

In order to further explain and illustrate these points, I want to discuss two of the most common sets of characterizations and identifications that *dagongmei* make about themselves, rural people, and urbanites. Both of these sets of characterizations revolve around an understanding that, compared with urbanites, rural people are lacking in education and culture (*wenhua*) and lead narrow, closed-in lives, interacting very little with the outside world. This understanding is more or less universal among *dagongmei* as in the rest of the population, but it is elaborated in different ways. Some *dagongmei* contend that lack of education and participation in society results in a lack of civility and civilization (*wenming*) and human quality (*suzhi*) in the rural population, while others contest this link. Yet other *dagongmei* make a connection between education, culture, wide-ranging participation in society, and an ability to engage in "clever talk." According to them, rural women and *dagongmei,* because they lack education and have little experience of the world beyond the village, "do not know how to talk" (*bu neng jianghua*) and have a "sense of inferiority" (*zibei gan*), but are also more honest and straightforward (*laoshi*) than urbanites.

Civilization and Quality

Migrant women frequently represent urbanites as more civilized than rural people, because they are better educated. Civilization, or *wenming,* they explain, is essentially the same as good manners and politeness toward others (*limao*). They commonly assume that the more educated people are, the more civilized their behavior. Thus, when domestic workers explain the particularly good treatment they receive from their urban employers, they usually do so in terms of the employers' high level of education. Conversely, when presented with evidence that abuse and violence against maids is perpetrated not just by the lowliest of urbanites but by the most highly educated, migrants often express great shock and disbelief.

As is illustrated in the quotations above, migrant women often also claim that low levels of education, combined with minimal contact with people outside the family and village, mean that rural people are uncivil and uncivilized and lacking in quality. They are ruder and cruder than urbanites and they fight more. Among migrants, as in official and popular urban discourse, these are ubiquitous and potent characterizations of rurality. They may have some validity—as I mentioned earlier, recent reports indicate that violence, both between villagers and officials and among ordinary villagers, is alarmingly widespread in contemporary rural China. However, it is generally not acknowledged that a great deal of rural violence can be attributed to mounting corruption, social inequalities, economic stress, and a breakdown in governance. Similarly, *dagongmei* do not argue that rural lack of civility may be blamed on the state's failure to provide affordable education to villagers, though Han Haiying and other women in Haidian came close to making this claim. Among *dagongmei,* as among urbanites, lack of education and civility has come to be understood as an essential attribute of rural persons. For urbanites, the figure of the uneducated, uncouth rural peasant (and rural migrant) functions as an inferior other against which notions of urban superiority are constructed. And it performs a similar function for *dagongmei* like Zhang Ning, whose narrative identifies her with a positive new urban subject position by highlighting the negatives in the subject positions she has left behind.

Migrant women's concern with education and civility is far from novel or unusual—traditionally, culture, civilization, and civility were centrally valued and closely intertwined attributes of social status (cf. Brownell 1995, 173). It should also be noted that, even in purely linguistic terms, it is quite difficult to avoid reproducing a discourse that marks out rural inhabitants and rural migrants as being less civilized and of lower quality than urbanites because they are, on average, less educated. The term *wenhua* is generally translated into English as civilization, culture, and education. The phrase *mei you wenhua* means uneducated or illiterate but it also indicates a lack of refinement and culture. *Wenming* is usually translated as civilization, culture, or civility. Both *wenhua* and *wenming* contain the character *wen* which means script, written language, literary, culture, and refined in manner. In Confucianism, the ideal man (and I use the masculine form advisedly) is highly *wen* (Louie 2002).

Superficially, the understandings about *wenhua, wenming,* and *suzhi* found in the narratives of migrant women like Zhang Ning and Jin Rong appear to accord closely with dominant urban discourses on these topics. However, the following more detailed examination of the range of meanings attributed to these terms shows that the apparent unanimity between dominant urban and migrant discourses is illusory, though so, too, is the apparent internal homogeneity of both dominant urban discourse and migrant discourse.

As indicated in chapter 1, *suzhi* has recently become important in a vast range of dominant discourses—not just official, state discourses but also popular, urban discourses. It stands in for a range of attributes, abilities, and qualities, including not just education and civility but also everything from genetic quality and physical fitness to political correctness, entrepreneurial know-how, self-confidence, endurance, and adaptability. My interlocutors in the Migrant Women's Club were quite familiar with the term *suzhi* and highly sensitive to the urban stereotype of migrants as "low *suzhi*" peasants. They were as much caught up in the competition for *suzhi* as anyone else. And yet, they used the term *suzhi* itself only infrequently. Furthermore, on the rare occasions that they did use it, or when responding to explicit questions about the term, my interlocutors usually explained *suzhi* solely in terms of education and civility. In Chunzi's words:

Rural people and migrants don't use the word *suzhi.* Instead, if they think someone has low *suzhi* they say that she is uncivil [*bu wenming*] or impolite [*bu limao*], or else that she does not care about face [*bu ai mianzi,* i.e., she is unconcerned that her behavior might damage her moral reputation]. (October 2001)

The picture with regard to *wenhua* (culture) and *wenming* (civility/civilization) is also complicated. Traditionally, as I mentioned, culture and civility were highly valued attributes of the educated elite. They comprised an expert understanding of, and adherence to, traditional rituals and the patriarchal notions of propriety that they embodied, as well as a high degree of literacy and familiarity with the classics. Peasants were uneducated and, therefore, also considered unrefined and morally inferior. So, too, were merchants. In fact, anyone connected with the world of money and commerce was considered to be even further removed from the elite ideal of propriety and morality than were the peasants.

The words *wenhua* and *wenming* themselves, however, are quite recent—neologisms adopted from the Japanese by nationalist, modernizing intellectuals and officials in the late nineteenth and early twentieth centuries. Though linguistically connected to Confucian concepts of culture and refinement (*wen*), the adoption of the terms *wenhua* and *wenming* was in fact antitradition, anti-Confucian, and modernizing in intent. The ideal "civilization" that the new elite promoted was forward- rather than backward-looking, emphasizing not rituals (now labeled "superstitions"), but rather scientific knowledge, technological progress, and democracy, as well as a smart, clean modern image, discipline and public etiquette. As I mentioned in chapter 1, improving people's manners—teaching them to keep clean, dress neatly, and stop spitting in the street—were key concerns under both Sun Yatsen and Chiang Kaishek's New Life Movement. Both these leaders and their governments also sought to abolish popular religion and customs.

Under Mao Zedong, and in particular during the Cultural Revolution, the Communist Party attacked the privileged status of elite culture and the highly educated. At the same time, the Party reinforced existing understandings of commerce and profit making as immoral. After Mao's death, however, the Party leadership once more promoted the status of education and of the highly educated. In addition, through its campaign to construct a socialist "spiritual civilization" (*jingshen wenming*), which was initiated in the mid-1980s and gained pace through the 1990s, it attempted yet another reconstruction of notions of culture and civilization. Like the modernizers of the first half of the twentieth century, officials implementing the spiritual civilization campaign have promoted science and technology, modern appearance, hygiene, discipline, manners, and the abolition of "backward" customs and religious practices. Indeed, as Sara Friedman notes, the contemporary state's spiritual civilization campaign bears an uncanny resemblance to the New Life Movement of the 1930s and 1940s (Friedman 2002, 187).

However, the post-Mao state has also insisted upon adherence to the "four basic principles" (Communist Party leadership, socialism, dictatorship of the proletariat, and Marxist-Leninist-Maoist thought) and fought "spiritual pollution" from overseas, including pornography and freedom of the press. Aside from this, *wenming* has been understood increasingly in terms of advancing China's market economy and its status as a world economic power. In other words, culture and civilization are no longer set apart from the "uncivilized" world of money and commerce. Instead, authorities try to promote a modern image and to entice foreign investment by adorning the streets of Beijing and other cities with large signs featuring smart new high-rises, surreally blue skies, green lawns, clean, empty streets, and messages urging the citizenry to contribute to the construction of a well-ordered, polite, clean, and environmentally friendly urban community. Kam Louie also notes that images of the ideal Confucian *wen* man have undergone a radical change, so that "although *wen* has never before been rendered as business acumen and managerial skills, that unlikely interpretation seems to have been achieved in recent times" (Louie 2002, 57).

In rural areas, the campaign to construct a socialist spiritual civilization has involved both attacks on backward, feudal rituals, such as those associated with marriage and funerals, and efforts to involve peasants in entrepreneurial activities, freeing them from the "fetters of egalitarianism and traditional small-scale production." Andrew Kipnis reports that in Fengjia village in Shandong in the late 1980s and early 1990s some people actively resisted the spiritual civilization campaign, flaunting their rituals with pride:

> [They] claimed to be past oriented and evaluated this orientation positively. Instead of constructing the future as something new that necessitated the rejection of the past, they constructed the future as something to be purposefully filled with the recreations of past practices. In the village, those who rejected peasant subculture tried to be advanced [*jinbu*] and saw peasant characteristics as backward [*luohou*]; those who valued peasantness saw their subculture as a tradition [*chuantong*] that should be passed on to the future [*chuanxialai*] in order to respect [*xiaojing*] its ancestors. (Kipnis 1995, 124)

I have never met a migrant woman who promoted tradition in quite the same way as some Fengjia villagers did. Rather, *dagongmei* attack rural society for being backward (*luohou*) and feudal (*fengjian*). Their usage of these latter terms, however, almost always refers to poverty and patriarchy and does not touch on other aspects of rural culture or economy. In addition, rural migrant women do not talk of these forms of backwardness as a deficiency of *wenming*. For these women, as indeed for most of the population, the term *wenming* refers to something in between Confucian notions of culture and propriety and the contemporary state's understandings of civilization. It reflects a concern with education, politeness, decency and basic respect in interpersonal relations, and also with cleanliness, order, and appearance. Migrant women do not acknowledge the other meanings that the state has attributed to *wenming* in recent years.

Besides this, not all *dagongmei* agree that urbanites are more civilized than rural people. Despite the power of the linguistic and cultural link between *wenhua* and *wenming*, some women repudiate the notion that urbanites' higher education necessarily makes them more civilized and higher in quality. As Zhu Jin put it, "*suzhi* is much the same as *wenming*. But not everyone who has *wenhua* has *suzhi* and not everyone who has *suzhi* has *wenhua*" (December 2002). Some of my *dagongmei* interlocutors who said that rural people were less educated and less *wenming* in the sense that they tended to abuse each other and fight more than urbanites, also understood the contempt that urbanites, including those with the highest levels of education, displayed toward rural migrants as a form of low *suzhi* and lack of *wenming*. Qiao Xue, for example, said: "Not all rural people are lacking in *suzhi*. Beijing people sometimes say they are, but I think that's not right—their *suzhi* is lacking. Sometimes they really discriminate against outsiders" (August 2001).

Some went even further in challenging the link between *wenhua* and *wenming*, claiming essentially that power and money corrupt even the educated. In the process, these women implicitly challenged the link that the state has tried to forge between *wenming* and a market economy, drawing upon a more traditional (and Maoist) understanding of a contrast between education, culture, and civility on the one hand and uncivil commerce and profit making on the other. For example, when I asked Liu Yu what she thought about the claim that rural people have low *suzhi,* she strongly disagreed:

> Urbanites might have education but that doesn't mean their *suzhi* is high, and just because they have money doesn't mean they have *"suzhi"* either. So many urbanites look down on other people and treat them badly. Rural people are straightforward—they say what they want to say. Urbanites, though, are deceitful and they insult you. All this stuff about *wenming* in the city—people think you can buy it, but you can't. (September 2001)

Characterizations revolving around notions of civility and quality were the most common kind of response that I received when I asked members of the Migrant Women's Club the question "What differences are there between rural and urban people?" I cast this question in gender-neutral terms and the responses about differences in civility that I got were also ostensibly gender-neutral. As readers may have noticed, however, the characterization of rurality that my question evoked for Zhang Ning was first and foremost of fighting between rural *men.* Uncouthness and abusive, violent behavior are not exclusive to the rural male—rural women are also viewed as uncivilized relative to urban men and women. All the same, for most *dagongmei* as for the urban population, the epitome of lack of civilization is the rural male (and the epitome of civilization is the urban male). For the majority, the most potent symbol of rurality and also of the phenomenon of the "floating population" is the uncivilized peasant male, lacking in education and *suzhi.*

When the focus shifts from rural/urban differences in general to the characteristics of specifically female rural people and female migrants, the terms of discussion change. As I discussed in chapters 1 and 2, the Women's Federation, *Rural Women,* and the Migrant Women's Club all stress the need to raise rural and migrant women's *suzhi.* The problem as they see it, though, is not that these women are "uncivilized" or uncouth in the way that rural men are. Rather, they are concerned that rural women are ignorant, naive, timid, and lacking in self-confidence. In order both to improve their social status and to contribute to the market economy, rural women and *dagongmei* must undergo technical training and, most important, they must learn to be independent and confident in themselves. *Dagongmei* themselves do not generally talk about *suzhi* in this way. However, their characterizations of rural women and of themselves and other *dagongmei* are otherwise similar to those of the Women's Federation, being couched in terms of "not knowing how to talk" (*bu neng jianghua*), being "too honest and simple" (*tai laoshi*), and having a "sense of inferiority" (*zibei gan*).

"Knowing How to Talk"

As I discussed in the introduction, "knowing how to talk" (*neng jianghua*) refers to the ability to speak in public with articulateness and persuasiveness. It is a marker of high status, understood to result from formal education and public interactions. *Dagongmei,* like most other people, believe that in general rural inhabitants "do not know how to talk" because they lack formal education and because their lives are confined to the farm and village. Even more than men and older women, unmarried rural girls are understood to be particularly unable to talk because traditionally they are supposed to be confined to the domestic sphere and to "listen to others' talk" (*tinghua*), meaning to be obedient, rather than speak up for themselves. Consequently, it is common for *dagongmei* to represent themselves as unable to talk relative to urbanites and to other migrants who have been in the city longer than they. Frequently, this is linked with being "too honest and simple" (*tai laoshi*) and with having a "sense of inferiority" (*you zibei gan*). As an example, I recount a conversation that I had in Hangzhou with a nineteen-year-old waitress, Cheng Xihua, who had been in the city for only one month. When I asked "Which do you think is better—the country or the city?" Cheng said:

> Of course, the city is better than the countryside, but it's not possible for country people to stay in the city long term. There are some migrant workers who stay in the city. But I'm sure I wouldn't be able to—I'm not as capable as others [*bu ru bieren qiang*]. (Jacka 1998, 58)

When I asked her to explain why she thought that, she replied:

> I don't know. I think I look down on myself [*qiaobuqi ziji*]. I have a sense of inferiority. I'm too honest and simple, I'll never amount to anything [*mei huatou*]. Other migrant workers look down on me because I'm not as able as them—I can't talk the way they can. That's why I have a sense of inferiority. (ibid., 58)

At first sight, Cheng Xihua seems simply to have internalized others' negative characterizations of her as being unable to talk, and therefore as being inferior and having no future. What does it mean, though, to say that one "looks down on oneself" and "has a sense of inferiority"? I suggest that, at the very least, it indicates an awareness of objectification, a split between the "I" that speaks and the "I" that is looked down upon by others. To say "I think I look down on myself" and "I have a sense of inferiority" is not the same as "I am inferior." It conveys an understanding of others' negative objectifications, but simultaneously a degree of ambivalence about those objectifications, perhaps even a challenge to them.

I mentioned above that knowing how to talk is a marker of high status. It has long been so, for it is associated with education and mental abilities. And in post-

Mao China the ability to talk, in the sense of being able to negotiate, bargain, and hold one's own in public, has been accorded even greater value because of its perceived importance in business, trade, and competition. Among both urbanites and villagers, *laoshi*—the opposite of knowing how to talk—is nowadays commonly viewed as a liability. Thus, whereas in the 1960s and 1970s rural parents tried to find a *laoshi* husband for their daughter who would be decent, hardworking, and who would listen to his elders and leaders, nowadays ambitious rural women more commonly avoid such prospective grooms, fearing that they will be too easily taken advantage of and cheated (Yan, Yunxiang 2003, 76–79).[6]

Ostensibly, Cheng acknowledges that, being "unable to talk" and too "honest and simple," she is too dumb (in both senses of the word) to survive in a market-oriented city. And yet, for all the importance attached to the ability to talk, there is another long-standing and powerful strand of thought according to which it is associated with inauthenticity, deviousness, and the cold-blooded pursuit of self-interest. Peasants, in this line of thinking, uncorrupted by education, foreignness, modernity, money, or power, are more caring of others around them, more honest and more moral than the educated urban elite who know how to talk. Deng Yiyan and Gao Xinran (mentioned earlier) both draw upon this set of understandings when they characterize urbanites as cold and violent, and interpersonal relations in the city as complicated. Peasants, in contrast, are warm and frank. *Laoshi*, while indicating simplicity, also evokes, more powerfully than any other term, a positive stereotype of the peasant as being warm, decent, frank, and honest. Cheng's use of the terms *bu neng jianghua* and *laoshi* may thus not be as thoroughly self-denigrating as they first appear. For if she is too *laoshi* for the city, what does that say about the morality and worth of urban relations?

Among members of the Migrant Women's Club in Beijing, Chen Ailing was often described, both by herself and others, in the same terms as Cheng Xihua. Chen Ailing, it may be remembered, was severely abused and beaten in her first job in Beijing, working as a maid. She was later successful in suing her employers in court, but was awarded minimal compensation. In 2002 Chen Ailing took a job as an apprentice to a tailor named Zhao Feng, who was like Chen Ailing in being from outside of Beijing, but unlike her in having urban *hukou* and being relatively highly educated. On one occasion, Zhao Feng invited me, along with a friend of hers, to a meal at the apartment that she shared with Chen Ailing (December 2002). At one stage during the meal our conversation turned to the topic of boyfriends and marriage. Zhao Feng laughed and said that Chen Ailing was very coy about such things. She recounted how, catching a glance of a love scene on the television as she walked past, Chen Ailing became very embarrassed and quickly left the room. I joined in the teasing, telling Chen Ailing that I thought there was a young man at the Migrant Women's Club who liked her, and she blushed furiously, turning away and hiding her face in her hands. In the ensuing conversation she repeated a number of times that she "did not know how to talk." Zhao Feng laughingly countered that she also did not know how to sing—even when there was just the two of them together in the apartment, Chen Ailing refused to sing. Zhao Feng's friend told Chen Ailing that she should loosen up a little—that everyone should feel they could sing if they felt like it.

After this teasing the conversation took a more serious turn, Chen Ailing telling Zhao Feng's friend a little about her court case. When she stood up in court, Chen Ailing said, she was extremely nervous because she did not know how to talk. Even now, she continued,

> I have a real sense of inferiority. My former employers made me feel terrible, but I wasn't able to say anything. My mother died when I was eight, and I had no women around me. When I got my first period, I thought I had cancer like my mum. When I was at school, everyone made fun of me because I didn't have a mother.

"Young rural women often say they don't know how to talk," I commented. "They're too scared to speak," Zhao Feng responded, and her friend said, "People don't listen to them when they speak, so they don't talk and then they don't know how to." Zhao Feng's friend tried to encourage Chen Ailing, telling her she must not feel inferior, and recounting a story about a young woman whose father died when she was very young. She consequently had a very strong feeling of inferiority, but she overcame it, going on to become a famous singer.

Zhao Feng then told us that Chen Ailing was generally too afraid to ask questions. Rather than encouraging Chen Ailing, as her friend had done, however condescendingly, Zhao Feng proceeded to detail a long list of all the simple mistakes that Chen Ailing made when sewing. Chen Ailing, who was sitting next to her boss, hung her head, silent but with a very sullen and angry expression on her face. Feeling very uncomfortable and unable to respond in any other way, I got up and excused myself at the earliest opportunity, and Chen Ailing accompanied me out to the bus stop. On the way, I told her I was sorry about the turn the conversation had taken. Chen Ailing burst out that of course she was not an expert tailor; she had only just started as an apprentice. And it was wrong, she insisted, that her boss should be so critical of her, given that she forced Ailing to work from morning till night but paid her next to nothing. Anyway, it was wrong to say bad things about people, "because you can hurt people with words more than if you hit them." She would not tolerate such treatment much longer, she said—after the New Year holiday she would look for another job (December 2002).

On a later occasion, three members of the Migrant Women's Club talked with me about Chen Ailing's difficult personal circumstances and history. Two were acquainted with her from interactions at the Club, but knew little about her past. The third woman filled in the details for them, whereupon they expressed sincere shock and dismay. Chen Ailing, they sighed, with a mixture of admiration and sadness, was very *laoshi,* by which they meant that she was a very honest and moral person. But then, they said, "That's what happens to people like that" (December 2002). Zhu Jin was less charitable about Chen Ailing, describing her as *wonang,* a derogatory colloquial term that my dictionary glosses as "hopelessly stupid and chicken-hearted." Chen Ailing, according to Zhu Jin, would never get anywhere with anything. When I asked if that was because she had only primary school education, Zhu Jin said no, that even if she herself had so little education, she would still fare better than Chen Ailing because she would stand up for herself and would find a way to make money. Chen Ailing just wasn't extrovert and enterprising enough (December 2002).

In outlining these various conversations with Cheng Lihua, and with and about Chen Ailing, I have sought to fill out the range of meanings and associations that are encoded in a juxtaposition of the terms *laoshi* and *bu neng jianghua.* Beyond indicating a simplicity that is supposedly common to all peasants, male and female, these terms are particularly evocative of an obedient, chaste, innocent, good young village girl who has grown up in the shelter of her family, having little contact with the outside world. This is the same ideal girl described in the account above by Xiao Chun, who wears demure clothes with high collars and her hair in braids, who does not dance and refuses to bathe in public. Traditionally, this has been a very powerful symbol of Confucian morality and order. Under Mao Zedong, though, the Communist Party cultivated a new image of femininity and morality— that of the young rural woman with collar-length hair and plain, loose-fitting jacket and trousers, with hoe (or gun) in hand, working in the fields, and participating in local politics. Between the 1940s and 1970s, this was one of the Party's most frequently promoted images, not just of women's liberation but of the liberatory potential of the revolution as a whole. But since the 1980s the Maoist symbol has no longer been seen as liberated or liberating, either by the state or by rural women themselves. Instead, the young Maoist woman peasant and the demure, chaste maiden have merged, *both* becoming the symbol of tradition and rusticity. Today, this is contrasted with a powerful new symbol of modernity—the extrovert, enterprising, urbane, consumerist, sexy, and sexually liberated young woman who adorns advertising billboards and magazines across the city (Zhang, Zhen 2001).

Young rural migrant women themselves react to these contrasting amalgams of ideas about tradition, modernity, the market, and sexuality in different ways. Some, like Zhu Jin, strive for the subject position of the liberated, modern young urban woman who has money, sex, power, fun, and freedom, not so much as an alternative to the traditional village girl per se, but as an alternative to the future that looms for that girl if she stays in the countryside—that of a married woman subject to the monotony and claustrophobia of farmwork and under the thumb of a patriarchal rural husband and in-laws. As I discussed in chapter 4, most *dagongmei* are relatively positive about their childhoods in the countryside, but they look upon a future as a married woman in the village with dread. Zhu Jin, in escaping an arranged marriage, migrating to the city, and finding work in a dress shop, is relatively confident in her new, more urban, and urbane image. She is able to affirm a positive sense of herself both by celebrating the distance she has come from her own, formerly rustic image and by portraying her transition to urbanity in terms of her personal "get up and go," contrasted with the "chicken-heartedness" of others, like Chen Ailing, who have not managed the transition as successfully.

A great many other *dagongmei*, while still desiring urban modernity, are less confident about their ability to achieve it. Some explain their failure in this regard in terms of being unable to talk, having a sense of inferiority and other associated weaknesses. In part, as can be seen in the example of Chen Ailing, this points to an internalization of others' denigration and a reflection of a lack, or a loss, of self-esteem. And yet, when I met her, Chen Ailing was far from coming across as a passive victim. If she was nervous in court, she was nevertheless impressively articulate, and she prosecuted her case successfully. And on the occasion that I recounted above, although she hung her head in silence in front of Zhao Feng, she later defended herself vigorously against the latter woman's criticisms of her ineptitude. Both Chen Ailing and Cheng Xihua did not merely accept others' denigration. Instead, like other *dagongmei* who refused to acknowledge that urbanites are more civilized than rural people, they challenged the validity of the contempt they faced in the city by questioning urban morality.

Conclusion

The identities and experiences of rural migrant women in urban China are shaped through a complex imbrication of gender, class, local/outsider, urban/rural, and regional forms of identification and division. Of all of these, however, it is the division between locals and outsiders, and that between urbanites and rural people, that dominate both urban and rural migrants' representations of what it means to be a rural migrant woman in the city.

In response to questions posed by Emily Honig, I argue that this local urban versus outsider rural divide constitutes a form of ethnicity and is as significant as the divide between the local population of developed nations such as the United States and Australia, and their ethnic immigrant populations (Honig 1996, 239). On the one hand, as I demonstrated in chapter 3, it forms the basis for institutionalized discrimination, exploitation, and disadvantage very similar to that experienced by overseas immigrants. On the other hand, Chinese rural migrants as a collective are perceived, both by themselves and by others, as more homogenous than overseas immigrants of different ethnic backgrounds, for while gender, class, and regional origin are seen to identify and divide them in some contexts, overall, the rural outsider label is more powerful.

Thus, as I showed in chapter 1, urbanites tend to lump together all members of the floating population and to label them as essentially and fundamentally different and inferior to themselves. And their characterizations of rural migrants as having low *suzhi* are very similar to the descriptions of disadvantaged ethnic groups found in other societies. For their part, migrant women also identify themselves primarily as rural people, outsiders, in-betweeners, and/or migrant workers rather than in terms of native-place ethnicity. Unlike before 1949, and despite continuing segmentation of the labor force along regional lines, there is now almost nothing in the way of native-place culture or community in contemporary urban China, and few migrant women represent their province or county of origin as being more significant to their identity than their rural and outsider status.

Some migrant women's understandings of their identity as rural people are relatively undisturbed by their experiences in the city. For others, especially young, unmarried *dagongmei,* migration to the city presents both profound threats to personal integrity and understandings of self, and exciting opportunities for new subject positions. In responding to these threats and opportunities, *dagongmei* most commonly reproduce the terms of dominant, urban discourse, identifying a host of essentialized markers of rurality and urbanity. However, they inflect this discourse in a variety of ways, accepting some meanings and identifications and not others. Those most keen to take on a modern, urbane image, and confident that they can do so, tend to align themselves with urban constructions of peasants as uneducated and uncivilized, and of young rural (migrant) women as simple, unable to talk, sexually repressed, and lacking in fashion sense. Those hurt more in their encounters in the city, and those less confident of their ability to become modern and urbane, generally lack the power to challenge or disagree with these characterizations in their entirety. Sometimes, however, they seek to construct a more positive identity for themselves by challenging the link between education and civilization and by questioning the superiority and morality of urbanites' clothes, their sexual liberation, their ability to talk, and their treatment of others less fortunate than themselves.

Part IV

Time

7

Narrative, Time, and Agency

In previous chapters I have sought to cast light on rural migrant women's experiences, identities, and values by focusing attention on specific aspects of their narratives. In this last chapter, in contrast, I examine whole plots and the themes, assumptions, explanations, and evaluations that are threaded through them. My concern, above all, is to identify which narrative forms are most common among rural migrant women and, through an examination of these, to understand migrant women's conceptualizations of time, temporal relationships, temporal change, and agency— or, more specifically, how things change and who or what does the changing.

The narrative forms characteristic of rural migrant women's stories, written and spoken, can be categorized broadly in two groups. The first group of narratives portrays and explains migration and life in the city in terms of its role in the speaker's personal life course. These include narratives of migration as an economic strategy, as a reprieve or escape from the countryside, as a chance to see the world and have fun, and as a process of self-development. Most women's life stories and conversations draw upon more than one of these narrative forms, but they commonly give greater priority to one than to others. Each of these forms is discussed in the first part of this chapter.

The second group of narratives is structured around complaints about migrants' circumstances in the city, their status, and the treatment they receive from others. In a previous paper drawing on research conducted with migrant women in Hangzhou in 1995, I referred to narratives of complaint as "speaking bitterness." Since 1995, however, a change has occurred in the language in which migrant women complain. In earlier narratives migrant women spoke bitterness about capitalist exploitation, inequalities, injustices, and indignities. More recently, a new language of human rights has been added. At the same time, recent narratives more commonly include conceptualizations of collective migrant resistance than previously. These changes are the subject of the second part of this chapter.

Migration Narratives and the Life Course

When I asked my interlocutors in the Migrant Women's Club and in Haidian to tell me about their lives, and specifically about their experiences of migration, most began by telling me their age, their province and county of origin, and the length of time that they had been in Beijing. They then talked about their experiences in roughly chronological order, starting with a description of their own and their families' circumstances in the countryside, and the events and motivations leading up to their departure from home. They continued with an account of the sequence of places they went to if Beijing was not their only destination, the jobs they took, and the conditions they encountered, concluding with their current circumstances and, in some cases, reflections on the future. This rough order was interspersed, interrupted, and in some cases thoroughly subverted by generalized statements, most of them negative, about their personal circumstances and the circumstances of rural people and rural migrants as a collective. These latter statements are the subject of the second part of this chapter. Here, I want to concentrate on the more overarching order with which migrant women structured their stories. In some instances this order was imposed primarily by myself, as a result of the prompts that I gave when women said that they did not know how to begin or they did not know what to say next. However, many of my interlocutors presented lengthy and detailed accounts of their lives with very little prompting, and in these cases the ordering of the plot was essentially the same as in other, more structured interviews. The same plot order prevails in the vast majority of autobiographical stories published in *Rural Women* and *Working Sister.*

All of these stories, spoken and written, structure the representation of life as a migrant in the same way that migration as an event is perceived—as a journey across space and time. More specifically, they tend to reflect an understanding of migration as a singular, finite journey between just two points in time and space— an approach with a number of corollaries. The first is that usually only two places— the home village and the city in which the migrant is currently based—are discussed in any detail and, if experiences of work as a migrant in other places come into the story, it is usually only to explain the series of events that led up to the individual's present circumstances and location. In addition, although it is clear that migrants commonly move frequently between village and city during the course of their life, most migrant narratives are structured around an account of life before migration started, followed by a rendition of life as a migrant in the city, and intervening periods back in the village are mentioned only briefly, if at all.

Second, migrant narratives tend to prioritize change in personal circumstances rather than continuity, and show contrasts between the past and the present, between the countryside and the city, and between rural and urban values, living and working conditions, and lifestyles. Some accounts emphasize positive change and contrasts, such as higher incomes, greater autonomy, and a more interesting life. Others focus on negative changes and contrasts, including experiences of discrimination, exploitation, and loneliness. Yet others display an expectation that migration should have led to a positive change, but a disappointment, and in some cases profound bitterness, at the fact that they are now no better off, financially or otherwise, than they were before in the countryside.

A final corollary of the structuring of the life story as a journey between two separate points in time and space is that ongoing connections between those points tend to get downplayed or, alternatively, discussion of such connections—for example, the interactions between young migrant women and their parents back in the village—are underwritten by a consciousness of a large gap between them, and emphasize the effort entailed in traversing that gap.

Beyond this, it is possible to distinguish between five key narrative forms, each of which locate migration and life in the city in different ways with respect to the speaker's life course, and display a different understanding of the relationship between the speaker's past, present, and future. In the remainder of this chapter I discuss each of these narrative forms in turn, bearing in mind, however, that migrant women's stories usually include elements of more than one of these narrative forms, and that there is some overlap between them.

Migration as Rural Economic Strategy

As I mentioned in chapter 4, scholars most commonly view migration as motivated by economic needs. Given this, one would expect that migration narratives would be structured around the possibility or otherwise of making money in different contexts—that life in the countryside prior to migration would be described primarily in terms of economic hardship, that migration would be explained as a strategy for improving income, and that life in the city would be evaluated primarily in terms of the degree to which it led to an improvement in financial circumstances.

In fact, I found such a narrative form to be relatively rare in *dagongmei* stories, whether recounted to me in person or written and published in *Rural Women* or *Working Sister.* It is not that these women did not mention financial difficulties or a desire to make money—often they did.[1] However, their narratives were not consistently and thoroughly dominated by this economic theme. Thus, while they often mentioned poverty at home and talked of it as one motivation for migration, it was not usually described as the *main* motivation. In addition, making money was not a central part of these women's evaluation system. In other words, events and circumstances were not selected or evaluated on this criterion. In relation to their experiences in the city, the chief problem these women identified was rarely low pay per se, but more commonly injustice or indignity. And the positives were not pay but education, self-development, excitement, autonomy, respect, the ability to endure, and employment that enabled the expression and fulfillment of personal abilities.

In contrast, among my interlocutors in Haidian, narratives were much more commonly structured around the theme of earning money. These women alluded to other motivations for migration, including overwork, loneliness and boredom in the village, and a desire for the family to be together. In general, however, these issues took second place to economic concerns. Thus, in descriptions of the past

and the countryside, poverty and economic hardship came first and were emphasized more than other issues, and the move to the city was justified first and foremost in terms of that economic hardship. This included women from
poverty-stricken households, and villages that had been devastated by floods and
other natural disasters (see also Jacka 1998, 44), but also others who were obviously much better off, for whom money was required, not for sheer survival, but
for children's education and for building new housing. Similarly, although other
issues were mentioned, decisions about migration—its timing, whether the woman
migrated alone or with other family members, and the migration destination—
were explained primarily, although not exclusively, in terms of the maximization
of income-earning potential.

When describing their experiences and circumstances in the city, women in
Haidian focused mainly upon the question of whether they and their partners were
able to further their family's long-term prosperity. Most were pessimistic in this
regard, since the downturn in migrant business opportunities in Beijing from the
late 1990s meant they were only marginally more able to earn money in the city
than in the countryside, most of what they earned went toward covering the high
cost of living in the city, and therefore they could save or remit very little. Frustration and disillusionment at this lack of improvement over their previous circumstances in the village were the dominant emotions conveyed in these narratives.

The only other issues that were frequent points of focus in these women's narratives were the injustices of rural/urban inequalities and the corrupt and brutal treatment with which they were threatened by Public Security officers. Anger over these
issues featured prominently in my interlocutors' narratives, but usually not as something separate from their complaints about their inability to further their family's
economic interests. Rather, the one source of frustration and sense of injustice ag-
gravated the other, in some cases snowballing to the extent that the narrative explaining migration as a strategy for earning money was quite overtaken by "speaking
bitterness," a subject discussed in the second section of this chapter.

The dominance of economic concerns in the narratives of the women in Haidian
does not necessarily equate with an overwhelming concern with earning money
and furthering the family's economic prospects. The lack of discussion of personal as opposed to family concerns, or of conflicts within the family, for example, may well have been shaped by the cultural expectation of an emphasis on
the family's interests and needs and on family harmony, and the cultural prohibi-
tion against "airing dirty linen in public." However, I do believe that these women,
because they were married and had children, were more concerned than my single,
childless interlocutors with making money for their families and less concerned
with personal self-fulfillment. Furthermore, the recent downturn in their families' economic fortunes, combined with local government closure of some businesses and pressure on migrants in the area to move out, made worries about
their families' economic future more pressing in 2001 than they might have been
in previous years.

Among the stories of the women in Haidian, there is a fair degree of uniformity with respect to orientation to the past and the future and to the rural and the urban. In chapter 4, I noted that most of these women were reluctant to return to the countryside in the near future, but most felt they would be compelled to do so. On the other hand, there was little sign that the wish to stay in the city long-term entailed a break with the rural family or community, and rural values, or any desire for such a break. Nor, as I discussed in chapters 5 and 6, was there any significant evidence of integration into urban society or the adoption of urban identities. These women were rural in their orientation, and their goal in migrating was to further their interests and needs as rural mothers, wives, and daughters-in-law, and to enhance the welfare and status of their families in the village.

Of course, values are not static, and in this period rural values and expectations were changing rapidly, in part as a result of the impact of migration to the city. As discussed in chapter 4, for example, expectations relating to housing escalated through the 1990s, influenced in part by the absorption of urban tastes by returning migrants and realized with the money those migrants earned in the city. Migrant women in Haidian responded to these changing expectations, but from their perspective this response was not a shift from rural to urban values, but a furthering of rural values.

Taken as a whole, *dagongmei* stories are strikingly different from those of the women in Haidian in their orientation to the rural and the urban, the past and the future. Although *dagongmei* often assert connections with the family back in the countryside, their stories point strongly to an assumption that migration to the city involves, or should involve, not a furtherance and improvement of their old lives and identities, but a break or major change in them. However, the narrative forms of these stories are less homogeneous than those of the women in Haidian and they involve a range of different kinds of break and change. Some conceive migration to the city as a chance to see the bright lights, have a good time, and earn a bit of cash. Almost always this is portrayed as an interlude—a brief diversion from rural life. In others, migration is a flight from rural life. Some narrative forms are built on the conception of life in the city as offering a migrant a new and better set of external circumstances and opportunities; others are dominated by the notion that through migration and life in the city a migrant will transform her *self.* In the following paragraphs I examine each of these different narrative forms in turn.

Migration as Interlude: Seeing the World and Having a Good Time

It's curious, but before, it would never have occurred to me to want to come out and be someone's maid. A country girl [*xiangxia meizi*] is just a country girl, but I had hands and feet and I'd been to school for seven or eight years, so what would I want to go and wait on someone else for? As for my parents, it wasn't as if they wanted me to go and earn money. Their only goal for me as the youngest was to find a good son-in-law. But I had other ideas. It wasn't that I didn't want to get married, I just felt it was too soon. I was only twenty. If they wanted me to go into the confines of the family that early and become like others, already pulling along a snotty-nosed kid at an early age, I wouldn't do it! I still wanted to have a good time for a couple of years, spend a couple of years of complete freedom and happiness. Wanting a good time led me to the city. I'd spent twenty years in the countryside, so I thought it best to change my environment and get some variety. I hadn't suffered any great pain or grief, it was just that I wanted a bit of "novelty." Becoming a maid I just thought I could have a bit of a "novel" city life. (Anon. 1993)

I mentioned in chapter 4 that in Beijing in 1989 and in Hangzhou in 1995, some *dagongmei* explained that they came to the city to experience the "big lights" of the city, see the world, and have a taste of freedom; and/or that they had "nothing to do" at home and wanted to "come out and have a good time" (*chulai wanr*). Like the woman quoted above, most of those who explained their migration in this way gave the (not necessarily truthful) impression that they only wanted to stay in the city for a short time, and that having satisfied their curiosity about the city and having had a taste of freedom they would return to the village to marry and settle down. Another common characteristic of these women's narratives was the sense conveyed that migration was motivated by curiosity and a (frivolous) desire for pleasure or stimulation, rather than by need or desperation. In conversation, when young women said that they came to see the "big lights" or to have a good time, they often did so with a shrug of the shoulders, a smile or a laugh. One twenty-two-year-old from Jiangxi whom I interviewed in Beijing in 1989 laughingly said that other villagers had said the capital was a dangerous and "chaotic" (*luan*) place, and she just wanted to come and see for herself (Jacka 1998, 67).

As mentioned in chapter 5, by the 1990s in some villages a sojourn in the city had become an expected rite of passage for young women in the interstice between leaving school and getting married. Some of the women who laughed that they were motivated simply by a desire to see the world and have a good time came from this type of village. Their laughs can be read either as a trivialization of the question of their motivation or as a sign of embarrassment that they did not have a more "serious" reason for leaving home. However, in other cases the expressed trivialness and frivolity of the wish to go to the city to see the big lights is belied by women's accounts of the resistance with which parents and other villagers met that wish and the lengths they had to go to fulfill it. Either these women were trivializing, or were embarrassed about, what was in fact a very serious and urgently felt need to get away, however briefly, or they were using the "going out to have a good time" explanation to mask different motivations that were harder to talk about.

From one perspective, going out to have a good time (for a short while) was an easy, safe explanation of out-migration for young rural women because it posed no real threat to gender divisions of labor and expectations about women's role in the rural family. As I discussed in chapter 4, female school leavers were often not required to contribute to the family economy, and had nothing to do at home. As long as they returned in their early twenties to fulfill the expectation of marriage, childbirth, and domestic work in their new household, they could be allowed to leave home, spread their wings a little, and perhaps bring home a bit of cash. In addition, the notion that migration was but a brief interlude posed less of a challenge to the state's policy of keeping rural people in the village as much as possible, and keeping strict limits on rural settlement in the larger cities. Finally, speaking to an unfamiliar foreign researcher or writing in a magazine about going out to have a good time was probably a good deal easier than discussing other more complex, weightier, or personal motivations for migration.

On the other hand, in the rural context in particular, going out to have a good time had definitely immoral connotations. As discussed in chapter 5, the sexual morality of a young woman who had moved beyond the controlling gaze of her family was likely to be questioned by other villagers, and this could become a serious obstacle to her marriage prospects. This problem was compounded in the case of women traveling to large cities by the suspicion that such places, corrupted by foreign influences and modernity, were particularly dangerous hotbeds of decadence and immorality. Even in the city, and despite the state's efforts at boosting the market economy by promoting leisure and consumption, for women having a good time had strong connotations of prostitution, and was therefore frowned upon both by ordinary urbanites and by officials (including, and in fact especially, the Women's Federation). For a young rural woman, therefore, giving too much weight to the desire to go out and have a good time could prove more than a little embarrassing or awkward.

These contrasting perspectives may explain why it was that while some of the *dagongmei* with whom I talked laughed that all they wanted in coming to the city was to have a good time for a little while, others hotly denied that this was their motivation. For example, in Hangzhou, Zhou Hongxia said

> I don't have any big ideas. I haven't come to find a rich boyfriend or anything. I just want to have a reasonable job and earn some money. Us migrant workers have only one aim—no one comes to have a good time or see the big city. We all come to earn a bit of money to take back home and do something we want to do. Afterward, when I've earned some money I'll open a shop or something, be a boss—that's a bit better than being a migrant worker, isn't it? (Jacka 1998, 66)

Stories published in *Rural Women* in the 1990s also quite often referred to young women being drawn to the city for its excitement and pleasures, only to then deride that attraction as trivial, foolish, or wrong-headed. This was commonly not achieved through a direct negation of the idea of the city as being exciting. In fact, that conceptualization was generally preserved. Usually, however, it was juxtaposed with another element that diverted attention from the city's excitement and suggested that there were other, more important, things in life. The quotation above, for example, came at the beginning of a brief story recounting the narrator's visit to a dance hall, whose enticing, flashing lights she had seen from her employer's apartment. However, the main point of the story was not the pleasure of the dance hall, but the realization that she, a mere rural girl working as a maid, nevertheless had as much right to be there as anyone else—that the new market economy did not discriminate against people according to class or rural/urban background, and all you needed to go dancing was the money to buy a ticket. In the last paragraph of the story, the narrator notes that a man at the dance hall asked her to later give him a telephone call. She concludes:

> I, of course, was certainly not prepared to make any call, and I wasn't looking for romance either. I came here only to prove to myself that a maid could also use the money she'd earned to enter a high-class dance hall, and what's more, having to pay was no problem. (Anon. 1993)

In other stories, the excitement of the city was juxtaposed with, and subsequently overwhelmed and negated by, homesickness. Often the juxtaposition was repeated more than once, building up a picture of "the brightly colored city as nothing more than a beautiful big hoax" (Bai Mu 1994, 27) and concluding with an overwhelming sense of the importance of maintaining connections with the countryside and/or returning to it. In a typical example, a ten-paragraph story called "My thoughts have left the city," a juxtaposition between the excitement of the city and the pull of home back in the village is repeated no less than eight times. The story begins:

> Shouldering my pack of homesick thoughts, I cross the noisy, argumentative city streets. Even though there are glittering neon lights, highrises that touch the sky, sweet, melodious karaoke, and elegant, sumptuous fashions, they cannot sever my longing for my motherland [*guxiang muqin*].

And it ends:

> In my hands I hold what is flourishing, but my heart belongs to my home. Ah! I'm a stranger from a faraway place. It's mid-autumn, and in my heart there is only the moonlight of my home village; the moon has come to me from the village. (Wang Yingchun 1994).

No doubt the intended message of this story was that migrants should not be lured by the city's pleasures into forgetting or severing their ties with the village.

But why did the author feel it necessary to repeat the message so many times? The underlying assumption of resistance to the message that this implies suggests two things: First, many young migrant women *are,* in fact, drawn to the city primarily because of its pleasures and excitements—the neon lights, towering high-rises, melodious karaoke, and fashions. Second, those enticements *do* lead many women to forget or to sever their connections with the village. (For another example, see the story by Chen Aizhen, discussed in chapter 4.)

In 2001 and 2002 members of the Migrant Women's Club frequently claimed that they came to the city to broaden their horizons or to experience freedom. Furthermore, this was often continued as an important theme through their narratives, with references to the freedom, stimulations, and possibilities of the city, and statements to the effect that they did not want to return to the countryside because it was boring or there was nothing to do (see chapter 4). However, broadening horizons was not linked with having a good time, but rather presented as a component of self-development, something to which I will return shortly. It is noteworthy that none of my interlocutors in the Club said that their original motivation in coming to Beijing was to have a good time. Similarly, in response to the survey of the Club that I ran in 2000, 48.9 percent of participants indicated that one of their prime motivations for leaving home was "to develop themselves," 38 percent said "broaden their horizons," and 32.6 percent said "to exercise independence," but only 9.8 percent said they left home in order "to have a good time" (see Figure 4.1).

It is not clear whether this difference between my earlier interlocutors and the members of the Migrant Women's Club is a result of a change over time or the influence of the Club on its members, or is perhaps due to the fact that a larger proportion of the latter group had been in the city for more than a few months. Whatever the reason, it does confirm that over time young migrant women have not only learned that the chances of having a good time in the city are slim but also that it is inappropriate for them to do so.

Escape

I mentioned above that the "seeing the world and having a good time" migration narrative might sometimes mask a more serious need to get away. Occasionally, migration *is* represented explicitly as a desperate, forced flight, usually from either an impending marriage or from patriarchal oppression and violence. Pang Hui's story, sent in for the story competition, "My life as a migrant worker," and published in *Rural Women* in 1999, is a vivid example of this. The story begins with a description of the speaker's husband as a gambler and a drunkard, who beat her and her three daughters on a daily basis, the introduction concluding: "One of those awful beatings three years ago made me determined to leave him, and that's how I started my life as a migrant worker." Subsequently, there is little sense of improvement, for the narrator, who goes to work as a cook on an urban construction site, is continually subjected to sexual harassment from the male workers and cannot sleep at night because of the fear of rape and because she worries constantly about the daughters that she has left behind. Later, things seem to look up, for

> after four months of life as a migrant worker, I gradually got used to the environment and came to understand those men. Even though they were crude people, they were not bad. . . . Eventually I won their respect through my own efforts.

That brief sense of improvement is, however, abruptly quashed when winter forces work at the construction site to a stop, and the narrator decides to go home.

> I thought that after half a year of absence my husband would have changed, but I was wrong. When I got home, carrying my cherished money that I'd earned with blood and sweat, the first thing my husband said was: "You shameless thing, how dare you come back? No old bags who go out to work ever come home intact. I'd rather be a bachelor than a cuckold. Even if we were dying of poverty, I wouldn't take the dirty money you earned. Get out!" I said to him, "My money is clean," but he wouldn't listen and pushed me out the door.

Once more, the story returns to the theme of forced flight:

> I shook all over, and it wasn't the wind from the mountains that made me shiver. I secretly gave the money to my oldest daughter, who chased after me in tears, and once more took the road away from home.

There is a brief assertion of agency and positive change, but then the story ends in a way that cancels out that agency and reinforces the impression of forced flight by refusing any more positive sense either of achievement or of direction into the future:

> It was different from the last time. Having experienced life as a migrant worker, I was no longer ignorant about the outside world, my steps were no longer as hesitant, and I believed at heart: no matter what happened, I would go on living, living without complaint, regret or shame.

I am a cloud, destined to float around in this life. I do not know where the wind will blow me next (Pang 2004).

As a published narrative, this story is highly unusual. It is, first of all, an example of *Rural Women*'s coverage of issues relating to gender oppression that are rarely addressed in the mainstream press (both because social critique can be politically risky and because critique of gender, in particular, does not sell well). Even in *Rural Women,* Pang Hui's story stands out, not so much for its social critique or its negativity, but because it offers little sense of personal or social progress or optimism for the future. Stories in *Rural Women* frequently discuss rural women's desires to escape problems such as poverty, discrimination against women in education, forced marriage, and the control and violence of husbands and/or in-laws, but almost always temper this with a positive message about the future. As I have noted elsewhere, this narrative form, in which the past is criticized but the future is depicted with optimism, has long dominated Chinese Communist political discourse, literature, and film. And it is generally the refusal of such a narrative form, rather than negativity per se, that is read as politically unacceptable. This might explain why Pang Hui's story—the only published competition entry that does not provide the reader with a way to see out of, or beyond, the tragedies and uncertainties of the narrator's life—received only a commendation rather than first, second, or third prize (Jacka 2004, 284).

Among spoken narratives, Pang Hui's denial of progress and a clear direction into the future is much more common. In Haidian, in particular, my interlocutors conveyed, time and time again, a sense that they were trapped, unable to move either forward or back. As Jin Rong put it,

I don't have any hope anymore. If you want to go back home you can't—you don't have any money. If you go back you have to set up house again and how are you going to do that without money? So you just have to stay here and make do. . . . We endure bit by bit [*manman ao*]. It'd be no good going home now, and it's no good here either. (August 2001)

Among *dagongmei* there was more sense of movement and progress. There was also a greater sense of personal agency and the power of individual migrant women to change their own destiny and less resignation to being blown about by the winds of fate. Nevertheless, among those who had been in the city for some time, the sense of being caught "in between," of "living from one day to the next," and of not having a positive, achievable future was also very potent. As I discussed in chapters 4 and 6, these women felt that there was little chance of improving their economic status in either the city or back home in the village. Socially, also, they felt it unlikely that their marginalization and insecurity in the city would be ameliorated in the future and were concerned that if they returned to the village they would find it hard to readapt and would be treated as outsiders by those who had remained in the countryside.

Changing One's Fate

Migration is rarely represented in terms quite as desperate and as bleak as Pang Hui's. All the same, it was common for migrant women in the 1980s and 1990s to represent out-migration as a search for a (new) life. To most of my interlocutors in Haidian this meant improving upon their existing life in the countryside. To members of the Migrant Women's Club and other *dagongmei,* on the other hand, the search was more commonly for a *new* life—for a way in which to change their fate (*gaibian ziji de mingyun*).

Migrant narratives suggest, however, that this conception of migration met with opposition from both rural and urban quarters—that while it was not done to speak of migration as merely having a good time, it was also not right to have too many grandiose illusions and ideas above one's station. In the quotation above, for example, while Zhou Hongxia emphasized that she had migrated to the city for something other than to have a good time, she also stressed that she did not have any big ideas. "I haven't come to find a rich boyfriend or anything," she said, alluding to the fact that one of the few sources of upward social mobility for a rural woman is marriage to a wealthier man, preferably one with urban *hukou* (household registration).

Both Chunzi and Zhou Ling portrayed their migration to the city in the 1980s explicitly and primarily in terms of looking for a new life and changing their fate. At the same time, both alluded to other peoples' doubts about, and resistance to, this aim. According to Chunzi, her parents advised her to settle down and start a family, rather than tormenting herself trying to achieve an alternative. They understood her desire to change her fate, but they doubted she would be able to. However, Chunzi defied their pessimism: "I knew I wasn't—you know—anything much, but I didn't believe them. I thought if there was something I wanted to do, I'd be able to do it" (October 2001).

Zhou Ling's life story gives the impression that her parents', or at least her father's, entire life had been dominated by the desire to change their family's fate and by the thwarting of that desire. However, when Zhou Ling announced that she wanted to leave home, rather than seizing on the opportunity her parents resisted the idea in the same way that Chunzi's did. They feared that, rather than providing an opportunity to better her life, working as a maid in the city would be a dead end and Zhou Ling would have to return to the village. In the meantime, though, she would have ruined her reputation and her marriage prospects.

Zhou Ling also points to the fact that the rural/urban divide and barriers to rural to urban migration were so strong that through the 1980s not only did urbanites resist the notion that rural people could change their fate through coming to the city, but rural people themselves internalized the belief that they belonged on the farm and nowhere else:

> When I first came out, I felt that I shouldn't be leaving home. I thought there was something wrong with me that I was afraid of farming. So when people asked my why I had left home, I just said that I had come to be a maid because my health was poor and I wasn't up to farming. I didn't dare say that I wasn't willing to farm—that I wasn't willing to stay in the countryside because life is too bitter there and that was why I wanted to come to the city. If you said that, other people would say that your way of thinking was no good. Since then there have been big changes. With opening up, people's ways of thinking have been changing. I think that the *dagongmei* coming out in the future won't have the same way of thinking as we did. They will probably be a bit better than us. At that time, we really did think that rural people should just stay at home and farm. (August 2001)

Despite opposition, both Chunzi and Zhou Ling stuck to their original determination to find a new life. In fact, the conception of migration as (potentially) enabling a change in fate formed the main underpinning of their life stories. Not only did they explain their original departure from home in this way but the event structure and evaluative and explanatory systems of their narratives were all based on this conception. Chunzi portrayed her life in the city as a series of struggles, in which she achieved initial successes in her effort to change her fate, only to suffer setbacks, after which she had to start all over again. Aside from the resistance she faced in the village to obtaining an education (see chapter 4) and then to migrating, and the difficulties she later had with household registration (chapter 3), during her time in Beijing, Chunzi was badly injured in a traffic accident, had troubles with her eyesight, and on one occasion had all her belongings and savings stolen. She also started a restaurant with a friend, only to be cheated, lose a huge some of money, and be forced to close down (Han Chun 1999), and during the birth of her child she suffered complications that left her partially paralyzed and very weak, and that therefore limited her ability to work and earn an income (chapter 3). Each time she suffered a setback, however, she picked herself up and started again. She explained:

> You have to work hard for a life—strive for it, pay for it, and after you've got over the ridge, you'll see hope. If you fall down, get up and you'll have hope. If you don't get up after you've fallen down, it's probably

your fate to fall down. That's how I see it. Each time I've fallen down I've learned a lot. (October 2001)

In presenting her life story Chunzi mentioned that her mother sold blood to help finance her trip to Beijing, and other relatives and friends also lent her a substantial sum of money. She also mentioned receiving help from other people in Beijing in finding employment, in starting up her restaurant, and in introducing her to her husband. However, apart from expressing her enormous gratitude to her mother, Chunzi devoted only very brief attention to this support from other people. And she said nothing about support from her husband. Her narrative thus marginalized the interpersonal connections, discussed in chapter 5, that are vital to any migrant's efforts to improve their circumstances and emphasized, instead, her own individual agency and her persistence in overcoming hardships. One gets the sense, in fact, that Chunzi narrates her series of personal struggles *in order* to highlight her individual agency, the moral importance of acting as an individual agent, and her own moral character.

In Western scholarship, this highly individualist narrative form has been viewed as typically masculine. According to Isabelle Bertaux-Wiame, for example, among rural to urban migrants in France:

Men present their life stories as a series of self-conscious acts, a rational pursuit of well-defined goals. . . . Their whole story revolves around the sequence of *occupations* they have had, as if they insisted on jobs because work is the area where they are more active. They present themselves as the subjects of their own lives—as the actors. Women do not insist on this. Self-conscious acts are not their main interest. Instead, they will talk at length about their *relationship* to such or such a person. They bring into view the people around them, and their relations with these people. In contrast with men's accounts, women will not insist on "what they have done" but rather on "what relationships existed" between themselves and persons close to them. . . . These differences are echoed in the very expressions and speech forms that men and women use. Men will use the "I" much more often than women. The masculine "I" definitely points to the subject of an action. The feminine "I" often takes a different meaning. It does not designate the narrator as subject, but as one pole of a relationship; it is the "I" in relation to another person. And very often, women preferred to use "we" or "one" ("on" in French), thus denoting the particular relationship which underlied this part of their life: "we" as "my parents and us," or as "my husband and me" or still as "me and my children." (Bertaux-Wiame 1981, 256–57; emphasis in original)

This understanding of men and their narratives as rational, individualist, and oriented toward the public sphere, and of women and their narratives as more concerned with relationships, especially in the family, has become a powerful cliché in Western culture, but Margery Wolf and others claim that it does not work well in the Chinese context. In fact, these scholars argue that patrilineal, patrilocal marriage patterns make Chinese women more individualist that men. Growing up with the understanding that upon marriage they must sever ties with their natal family and community and move to an unfamiliar household and village, Chinese women learn that no relationship is permanent and that, although they may be able to construct supportive relations with their children, they must rely on no one but themselves. Chinese men, in contrast, derive security and identity from their knowledge of a permanent place in a family and through the role they take on as the head of a household, building relationships and networks with the male heads of other households (Wolf 1972; Kipnis 2002, 86).

Like Margery Wolf, I believe that patrilineal, patrilocal marriage patterns may play an important role in shaping certain broad differences in the orientations of Chinese men and women—in chapter 4 I discussed this in relation to rural migrant understandings and aspirations relating to place. We should be wary, however, of taking such generalizations too far. Wolf's discussion of the effects of patrilocal Chinese marriage patterns might help to explain why it is that the narratives of Chinese migrant women like Chunzi seem much more individualist than those of the French migrant women in Bertaux-Wiame's study. However, it cannot account for patterns among men and women within the Chinese context, for, as it happens, Chunzi's focus on her individual struggles as a migrant and her neglect of her interconnections with others is characteristic of the narratives of single Chinese migrants, both female and male.

Among the married migrants that I interviewed in Haidian, Bertaux-Wiame's model of "female" relationship-oriented narrative fit a little better, for both husbands and wives, but especially wives, talked commonly in terms of "we," rather than "I"—"we (as a couple) decided to leave home . . . ," "we came to Beijing . . ." and so on. However, we cannot assume from this that married migrant narratives are always more relationship-oriented than those of single migrants. After all, Chunzi was married, but her narrative was highly individualist. Perhaps she would have adopted a different narrative form if her husband had been present, or if the focus of our conversation had been on her present experiences as a wife and mother rather than on her past struggles as an unmarried migrant. Conversely, if I had spoken to my Haidian interlocutors outside the home context, they may have talked more in terms of "I" than of "we." What I am suggesting here, in other words, is that the narrative form an individual uses at any one time relates to the specific subject position that she adopts in that particular context, rather than to any fundamental category of identity to which she belongs.[2]

In Zhou Ling's narrative the central notion that migration is, or should be, a way of changing one's fate operated rather differently from in Chunzi's narrative, or for that matter most other migrant's. Compared with other *dagongmei,* Zhou Ling had been extraordinarily successful in "changing her fate": she had married an urban man with a secure, high-income, high-status job; her *hukou* and that of her daughter had been transferred to Beijing; and she and her family lived in a comfortable, well-furnished apartment. However, in telling her life story she greatly downplayed the struggle to achieve all this, and the value of the achievements themselves. Furthermore, she explicitly denied that her achievements had been the result of her own, individual efforts:

So, how come I can stay in the city? It's just because I have a husband. If I didn't have a husband here, I don't know how I'd manage either. Really, that's how it is. Everything here is my husband's. There isn't anything that's my own. Now that I've left the Migrant Women's Club I'm unemployed. I can't find a good job. So sometimes I'm scared. If I hadn't married, I'd also be destitute. . . . What would I do? All along I've worked really hard and I've studied, but I too can't find a good job. You just can't find a job based on your own abilities. So you see, of all the people who came out early, I'm the only one who's stayed and that's just because I got married here. It's not because I found a good job for myself—it's not because I became independent. (August 2001)

In the past, Zhou Ling told me, she had been written up by journalists as a model *dagongmei*. She herself, she confided, had written articles about how she had become successful through perseverance and hard work.

But now I think that in reality I was deceiving myself. I wasn't telling the truth. I thought I was doing really well, I thought I was better than the others—we all came out together, but the others all went back and only I stayed. But . . . it isn't like that. It's only because of my husband that I've been able to stay. But I do really think I've tried very hard. I've tried really hard all along, but I can't find a good job. You can't get into the better work units because you don't have local *hukou*. Even now that I've got local *hukou* I can't get in. When you're older, how can you get a good job? If you're more than thirty it's very hard to get into a good work unit. Every work unit is saturated. If you don't have *guanxi* [connections], how can you get in? In Beijing you still need *guanxi*—you need power, so these things are really hard. (August 2001)

These remarks confirm that a perception of migration as a chance to change one's fate through one's own, individual perseverance and hard work dominates both the media and the understandings of migrants themselves. Zhou Ling does not directly negate the importance of individual agency that this conception promotes. In fact, it is a source of considerable disquiet to her, first, that her personal achievements in changing her fate are not her own, and that they were not won through merit and hard work; and second, that for the vast majority of rural migrants circumstances are much as they were for her father—no matter how hard they try to change their fate, they cannot. As she puts it, *"dagongmei* come out thinking it's a beautiful dream, but they're mistaken" (August 2001).

Rather than her own personal struggles and achievements, Zhou Ling's story was dominated, first of all, by her explanation and justification of her own, and other young rural peoples', dream to change their fate by leaving the farm and working in the city. Second, much of the narrative was a trenchant criticism of the barriers put in the way of the realization of that dream by state institutions and urban elitism. Migrants, she felt, were caught—staying as long as they could in the city because there was nothing for them in the countryside, but unable to achieve anything better in the city than mere survival in miserable conditions (see her quotation in the last section of chapter 4). But, she said,

The state [*guojia*] is very happy about this state of affairs. They have cheap labor and they can see it's very hard for you—for migrant workers—to cause trouble [*naoshi*]. There's an economist at Peking University—he's very famous. Once on TV he said—it made me so angry—"it's great all these peasants coming into the city, they're like water. When the city needs them we turn on the tap and let them in, and when we don't need them we turn the tap off and send them back home." I was so angry—we're people, not water. You see, we have no way out. He didn't have any thought for our needs as human beings. We need to marry and have children, we need to have a stable family, and we need opportunities to develop ourselves. Young people want to change their fate, to go forward, to realize their worth. That is what they yearn for. (August 2001)

In both Chunzi's and Zhou Ling's narratives, the search for a new life and a new fate that migration entails is primarily a search for a new, improved *environment* and new *opportunities* for self-fulfillment. This understanding was common in *dagongmei* stories of the 1980s and 1990s. Through the 1990s and the 2000s, however, it was increasingly overtaken in prominence by a set of narratives in which both the aim of migration and the difficulties in achieving that aim were conceived differently: Now migration was presented as potentially enabling the achievement not so much of a new set of opportunities as of a new *self*. Furthermore, overcoming the obstacles they faced was not always portrayed as an undesirable necessity that migrants had to achieve *in order* to make progress; it became, instead, a valuable component of progress itself. This set of narratives is discussed next.

"Eating Bitterness Is a Blessing": Migration as Initiation and Self-development

We have seen in chapters 1 and 2 that in the 1990s and early 2000s the press sometimes published didactic accounts of model migrant women (and men) success stories. These generally follow a common "rags to riches" narrative pattern: They trace the migrant's life from her beginnings as an ordinary, poor rural girl and her departure from home in search of something more than the village can offer, through several years of hardship, self-sacrifice and persistent struggle as a migrant worker in the city, to her ultimate success, most commonly as a private entrepreneur.

In these accounts, the migrant's life is portrayed as a self-willed, highly purposeful and unidirectional journey culminating in a single set of achievements. Usually, however, the main focus and raison d'être of the story is not the final success, but rather the journey itself. In fact, in some stories, the final success has not yet been achieved but is projected into the future. An example is the story of Zhang Yangqin, discussed in chapter 2. Zhang, described as an "innocent" (*tianzhen*) and "pure" (*danchun*) young girl with "large eyes and fair skin," goes to Beijing at the age of sixteen. There she works during the day as a salesperson and takes classes at night. The story emphasizes her persistence, hard work, and frugality, and almost one-third is devoted to an account of the money she is able to save each month and send back to her family. Zhang herself, it further emphasizes, sleeps on an old, worn mattress and in the three years she has been in Beijing has bought nothing more for herself than one pair of shoes, a pair of jeans, and two pairs of stockings. I repeat the message with which this story concludes:

> This is without doubt a clever, wise and strong girl—a *dagongmei* with a clear goal, who has come to Beijing in search of an opportunity to study, and with a plan for development. The city has provided girls like her with the possibility to get diplomas and certificates through part-time work and part-time study and training. It is evident that five years from now, ten years from now, Yangqin will no longer be the sixteen-year-old Yangqin who first arrived in Beijing, and nor will she be the Yangqin of today. Hence, we can say that coming into the city and, in particular, striding once more through the school gates, has changed the life trajectory of this rural girl—it has changed her fate. And this change, this opportunity and possibility, provided and created by mobility, has been grasped firmly by Zhang Yangqin herself. (Ma 1998, 27–28)

Like Chunzi's story, narratives such as these highlight both the obstacles that the migrant faces on her journey and the physical resilience and dogged willpower with which she overcomes them. Much more than Chunzi's story, however, they emphasize that the migrant is pursuing more than new opportunities and a new environment—rather, self-development and the improvement of *suzhi* (human quality) is both the means and the end of the migrant's journey. However, what exactly self-development entails, and what sort of new self it achieves, is commonly left vague. Thus, the narrator of Yangqin's story indicates that over the next five to ten years Yangqin will become a different person, but is vague about the nature of the transformation and how it will occur. The sense is that Yangqin will mature and learn new skills, primarily as a result of further education, but, in fact, no information is given about the skills or other benefits that Yangqin will derive from her night classes. Aside from this, the story puts more weight on Yangqin's hard work, filiality, and frugality than on the nature of the classes she takes, conveying the impression that these contribute as much to her maturation as does her formal education.

The vagueness in this narrative reflects the more general lack of clarity in dominant discourse about *suzhi* and self-development discussed in chapter 1. These terms mean different things to different people. The one point of real consensus is that they must be a good thing. In didactic pieces, such as the story of Zhang Yangqin, a vagueness about self-development plays an important part in conveying the message that (temporary) migration and work in the city is a good thing, for if migration results in the development of the migrant, however development is understood, it must be positive.

This message is reinforced by three long-standing cultural assumptions. The first is that altruism, hard work, and self-sacrifice are the highest virtues, and high levels of personal consumption are a sign of immorality. This assumption has come in for a beating with the rise of a consumption-oriented market economy, yet it is still very powerful, especially in rural society. The second assumption is that education is one of the very few avenues of social advancement for rural people, and also highly valuable in and of itself. Some of my interlocutors, after struggling hard and depriving themselves for many years in order to further themselves through night classes, voiced the opinion that, in fact, education did nothing to improve one's chances as a rural migrant. As Deng Yiyan pointed out, migrants are wanted for manual labor, not for skilled work. And as Zhou Ling explained, it is social connections that win better employment in the city, not education. Such critiques of the usefulness of education are quite rare, however. For most *dagongmei*, furthering oneself by taking night classes is a powerful, albeit usually unrealizable, dream.

The third powerful assumption underlying the story of Zhang Yangqin, and many others like it, is that the process of growing up is one of development and maturation. This assumption is combined with the association of migration with the transition from youth to adulthood, achieved in part simply by the coincidence in timing between the two and in part through descriptions of the young woman as initially innocent and pure. Logically, this coincidence between migration and growing up need not imply any connection between the two journeys in life. At an unconscious level, however, the effect of this coincidence on the reader is to suggest both that the experience of migration contributes to the process of personal development and that the two journeys are analogous. And following from this, since most people understand growing up to be a desirable process of maturation, so too must be migration.

Aside from this, a vagueness about the process through which self-development is achieved further contributes to the positive spin on migration that the story of Zhang Yangqin and others like it seek to achieve. Thus, the promise of self-development through further education is held out as the primary incentive for women to migrate to the city to work, while the heroism of hard work and frugality is also emphasized as a means by which to persuade migrant women to do their utmost for national development. However, in this juxtaposition of the promise of self-development through education with the heroism of hard work, the dark side of migrant work—long hours of back-breaking menial labor, meager pay, poor living conditions, loneliness, humiliation at the hands of employers and others, and a struggle to maintain dignity, let alone achieve self-development—is hidden.

In Haidian, the stories of my interlocutors bore little relation to the "migration as self-development" narrative that frames stories like that of Zhang Yangqin. Not only did these women commonly disavow the notion of progress that is integral to these narratives, they also showed no interest or belief in the notion that their sojourn in the city might contribute to their personal maturation and the improvement of their self, as well as to their family's well-being. In contrast, *dagongmei* accounts of the late 1990s and early 2000s, both oral and written, commonly featured significant elements of the migration as self-development narrative form. These included an association of rural people and the countryside with children and childhood, and of migration with the process of growing up; an expressed desire to develop oneself and a belief that there is greater potential for that self-development in the city; an emphasis on the importance of broadening horizons and furthering education; and a portrayal of hardship and struggle as a beneficial component of self-development.

Of course, real life is very messy, and it takes some effort to pare it down to a single, teleological narrative in the way that the author of the story about Zhang Yangqin has done for the purposes of conveying a didactic message. When telling their own stories, whether orally or in writing, most *dagongmei* put less effort into shaping their experiences into such a singular quest for self-development. There are some exceptions, though. One striking example is Ye Ye, a migrant factory worker in Hangzhou, whose entire oral account of her life was structured around a single episode in her youth, during which her senior secondary school teacher swore at her, saying that while at home she was treated like a princess, outside of her family she was worthless. According to Ye Ye, this encounter led her to feel that "she must really be wanting in some way" and to her decision to leave home. In her subsequent explanation of this decision, Ye Ye refers to a desire to "change herself" four times, a repetition that highlights the centrality of migration as self-development in her narrative's explanatory system:

I decided I had to change myself and I couldn't let my parents coddle me anymore. I had to stand on my own two feet and change myself. I decided to find work away from home. I thought I could change if I was away from my own family. I decided to go to Shenzhen. The work was very hard there, and you were closed in. You never saw the sun—you worked from morning till night . . . I thought I could change myself working there. (Jacka 1998, 67)

In Ye Ye's narrative the notion of self-development is taken one step further than in the story of Zhang Yongqin. No longer is self-development achieved through further education and selfless hard work. It is a much harsher affair: a rejection of coddling and a remaking of one's identity through a brutal initiation and tempering process—a trial by fire.

Another example of a trial by fire migrant narrative is the story of Zhao Weiwei, entitled "Eating bitterness is a blessing" (*chi ku shi fu*)—to "eat bitterness" (*chi ku*) meaning to endure hardship and suffering. Zhao Weiwei's first job in the city was as a door-to-door salesperson. In this job she was routinely treated with contempt, abused, and on one occasion sexually assaulted—experiences for which she claims to be thankful because they have taught her how to face difficulties. Her story is particularly disturbing because it is so recent. It was published in December 2002, well after migrants, human rights activists, and even the central government itself had begun to call for more reasonable treatment of migrants in urban areas; after legal activists had begun to seek redress for the many migrant workers whose rights had been violated in the workplace; and after the Cultural Development Center for Rural Women established the Migrant Hotline and the Migrant Rights Group. Still, Zhao Weiwei writes:

Gritting my teeth and shaking all over, I ran back to the company, believing that when I described the encounter today [i.e., the sexual assault] to my bosses, I would receive their understanding. Who would have thought, but they simply laughed disapprovingly: "You're just a working sister from outside [*waidi de dagongmei*]—so what if you suffer a bit. The main thing is to get the business. After all you haven't lost anything." I was so angry that I trembled all over. Are outsider sisters [*wailiamei*] really not humans? Do outsider sisters have no dignity? Why is it so hard for an outsider sister to make a bit of honest money with her own two hands? But for all my anger, I still had to face things as before. The next day, before the sky grew light, I shouldered my heavy pack, loaded with products and samples, and went out peddling. . . . In the blink of an eye, four years have passed. In those four years I changed jobs several times. But the most unforgettable experience remains that one when I first came out into the world, because on that occasion I truly learned life's difficulties. It is really the case that a person only grows up and matures by being put through the mill [*jingguo molian*]. I should be thankful for that experience, because it has meant that, since then, whenever I have run into difficulties I have been able to face them calmly and with composure. (Zhao Weiwei 2002)

In the 1990s and 2000s, Ye Ye and Zhao Weiwei were by no means unusual in representing the hardships and humiliations of migrant work as not just a necessary evil, but as a positive contribution to their own self-development as well as to the development of the nation. This is testimony to the power of the discourse on self-development—a discourse that, as I argued in chapter 1, has been crucial to the Chinese state's promotion of capitalist development in this period. At the same time, however, the darker realities of migrant work that Ye Ye and Zhao Weiwei identify have become the focus for increasing levels of discontent and protest among rural people working in Chinese cities. It is to this discontent that I now wish to turn.

Speaking Bitterness and Fighting for Our Rights: Migrant Narratives of Protest

Speaking Bitterness

In telling her story, Zhao Weiwei works hard to contain, and to make sense of, her past experience of sexual assault and other indignities by explaining them as a tempering process—a trial by fire. All the same, halfway through her account, the rhetorical questions "Are outsider sisters really not humans? Do outsider sisters have no dignity?" seem to break out of the text, making public a cry of protest that the narrator perhaps felt at the time, but could not give voice to. This is quite common in both oral and written migrant accounts. Most migrant women's stories are framed by an attempt to locate work in the city in relation to the rest of the individual's life course. However, regardless of the form the narrative takes— whether it is one of migration as a strategy for earning money, as interlude, escape, or self-development—it is often disrupted by complaints and cries of protest that take the form of statements or rhetorical questions directed, as in the narrative above, straight at the reader or listener. These protests are almost invariably focused not on the material aspects of migrants' lives—the low pay or the difficult conditions—but on the contempt with which they are treated by urbanites. Usually, they are linked to a specific, humiliating incident or set of circumstances narrated in the life story, but the protest is often made in the name of a migrant collective "we" that suffers general injustice, humiliation, and indignity, as in Zhao Weiwei's plaintive questioning. Simultaneously, these protests hail the listener as a member of a collective "you" who are not migrants and whose experiences are different from theirs, but who can be compelled to respond to the migrants' distress because they share with them some basic appreciation of social justice and the value of human dignity.

In its emphasis on dignity, this narrative form is similar to the protests and complaints of poor peasants and workers across the world. Scholars have found that across a variety of historical contexts subordinate people commonly demand not just the minimum resources required for subsistence but also to be treated with the same dignity and respect as other members of their community (Moore, Barrington Jr. 1978; Scott, James 1985, 240; Kerkvliet 1990, 266). On the other hand, how that demand is voiced—the bases on which people rest their claims and complaints, and the discourses and narratives they draw on in making them— varies considerably from one context to another.

I have argued elsewhere that in China migrant women's narratives of protest share similarities with, and are historically connected to, a Maoist practice called "speaking bitterness" (*su ku*) (Jacka 1998, 59–64). This term referred originally to a type of public performance practiced during the land reform campaigns of the 1930s and 1940s. During "speak bitterness" sessions, individual villagers, encouraged and guided by Communist Party officials, would step out into a public forum and give an account of the suffering they had endured at the hands of their land- lords.[3] Through listening to, and themselves enacting, these highly emotional per- formances, villagers learned to publicly voice their suffering, not in terms of unlucky fate or personal shortcomings, but in terms of an unjust and oppressive feudal system. This was a kind of consciousness raising[4] and a means of interpolation— a way of educating people to think in terms of Marxist categories of class and exploitation, and of making them active and enthusiastic agents of revolution. Later, this performance of protest was institutionalized further in the rituals of the struggle session, which reached its greatest prominence during the Cultural Revolution. (Jacka 1998, 60; see also Anagnost 1997, 17–44; Rofel 1999, 137–49).

Just as villagers in the 1940s learned to speak of the hardships and exploitation that they suffered in terms of a class system, personified in their landlords, so too have rural migrant women in contemporary China learned to speak in terms of exploitation by capitalist bosses and of contempt from those on the privileged side of a rural/urban divide—a divide that was condemned in Maoist rhetoric, though actually reinforced and cemented in place under Mao, through the household reg- istration system. The language they use in rejecting urbanites' perceptions and treatment of them and, indeed, their consciousness of exploitation and injustice has been learned, I argue, from Maoist discourse (Jacka 1998, 60–61). Indeed, some migrants refer explicitly to a Maoist model of social relations. For instance, a migrant woman in Haidian named Shen Mei had this to say of her experiences of arbitrary police sweeps in Beijing:

> This Communist Party is worse than the Guomindang [the Nationalist Party]. . . . Under Mao Zedong it was much better. Even though people were poor, everyone was equal. No official would dare to treat ordinary people the way they do today. (August 2001)

Other migrant women make less direct comparisons between the present and the Maoist past, but use similar terms and concepts to frame their complaints as were used under Mao. This is perhaps best illustrated by what they do *not* focus on, rather than what they do: migrant women do not commonly speak the liberal language of (lack) of access to resources and opportunities, and nor are they primarily concerned with gender inequalities. Furthermore, although this is changing in the 2000s, in the 1990s migrants did not generally talk in terms of "human rights." Rather, they focused on (capitalist) exploitation, inequality, corruption, and elitism. In Hangzhou, Zhou Hongxia, for example, was highly critical of the attitude of restaurant owners and managers: "They're only interested in whether the girls are pretty or not, not in their ability," she said. "If you do anything wrong they abuse you. These wealthy bosses, Hangzhou bosses, they're all capitalists. They think they can do anything they like" (Jacka 1998, 54). And in Beijing, a member of the Migrant Women's Club complained that in one of her first jobs as a maid her employer, a private entrepreneur, treated her like a servant from pre-Revolution days. She told him that she had been through ten years of schooling and "knew that under socialism everyone was equal," to which he responded "Who's equal nowadays? To hell with human dignity. You haven't got any money, so you have to do as I say. You lot come to Beijing to be nannies, and then you expect people to look after you for nothing!" (Wang Haiying 1993, cited in Jacka 1998, 56–57).

Aside from sharing similar language and concepts, contemporary migrant women's narrations may serve an emotional function similar to that of the speak bitterness sessions of the 1940s. Both performances give some sense of empowerment by providing a rare chance for the participants to vent their complaints to someone who might be interested and take them seriously.[5] And in both cases the performance of speaking bitterness also enables the participants to assert their own worthiness as human beings, established as the converse of the immorality of those they are denouncing. Finally, in both cases, in the process of speaking bitterness against an oppressive "them," the participants also construct an "us"—that is, they identify themselves not as lonely individuals, but as belonging to a community, albeit an exploited, subaltern one.

For all the similarities between the speak bitterness sessions of the 1940s and the migrant women's accounts, the latter differ from the former in terms of temporality and in how they situate the women in relation to the state. The earlier discourse was promoted by the state and entailed negating the past as a way of affirming present directions and projecting toward a more positive future. As others have noted, this negation of the past and projection toward the future was a crucial component of Maoist revolutionary ideology (Croll 1994, 3–14; Ci 1994). When Deng Xiaoping's regime came to power in the late 1970s, it too sponsored a repudiation of the immediate past, the Cultural Revolution, as a way of reaffirming its own legitimacy and engendering optimism about the future. And Chinese citizens at that time commonly framed their accounts to foreign investigators in terms of bitterness in the past that had been overcome (Jacka 1998, 62).

As indicated above, published migrant stories of the 1990s and 2000s also often end on an optimistic note, but this is less common in oral accounts, which more frequently convey a lack of progress, a sense that the narrator lives "one day at a time," "enduring bit by bit." In any case, even narratives that end on a positive note commonly include within them speaking bitterness, which in contrast to earlier forms of speaking bitterness strongly conveys the understanding that the present is a retreat from the past, and which affirms past Maoist ethics and social values in order to denounce the present sociopolitical order. In speaking bitterness about the present in this way, migrants both draw upon and contribute to a broader nostalgia for the golden age of Maoism that has been particularly powerful in rural areas, where villagers feel that they have lost the moral and political status they gained under Mao as members of the revolutionary poor peasant class (Dorfman 1996, 269).

In Haidian in 2001 my interlocutors spoke a great deal of bitterness about their circumstances and, in particular, about the treatment they received from the Public Security Bureau. There was little sign, though, that speaking bitterness might serve as a platform from which these migrants could move from complaint to collective resistance against the state or the status quo. Rather, there was a sense that power was so overwhelmingly stacked against them that there was nothing they could do to improve their situation. Thus, when I asked Shen Mei and her husband if anything could be done about the demolition of migrant housing and the arbitrary and unjust detention of migrants, they said, "No, who could we complain to, since officials are all so corrupt? If we tried to complain we'd get into worse trouble than before." When I suggested that if migrants united they might be able to do something to redress the situation, Shen Mei simply said, "Yeah, maybe. But last year some migrants in Fengtai got together and they killed two officials. But then they themselves were arrested and executed" (August 2001), a statement that encapsulates both the degree of bitterness shared by migrants about their circumstances, and the lack of a conceptualization of how that bitterness might be converted into effective collective resistance.

In *Rural Women* and the Migrant Women's Club through the 1990s, speaking bitterness narratives were met with scorn by the chief editor, Xie Lihua, and other staff. In late 1994 a nineteen-year-old woman from rural Shandong came to the office of *Rural Women* seeking help in finding work in Beijing. According to Xie Lihua, the young woman said that in coming to Beijing she was not fleeing poverty in the village, but, rather, she came in search of something to satisfy a "spiritual hunger" (*jingshen de ji'e*). Failing the entrance examination for senior secondary school was "a fatal blow," and back in the village she felt out of place in the company of her peers. "She felt it was better to choose to kill herself than be forced to tread the same path as her parents' generation" (Xie 1995, 5). On her arrival in Beijing, Xie Lihua helped her to find work as a maid. Two weeks later, Xie Lihua received a letter from the young woman, which said:

I feel a terrible grief that I cannot overcome. Paying an enormous spiritual price, I came to Beijing stubbornly searching for something—searching, searching—and what did I find? . . . The first time I saw the woman of the household I felt as though she looked at me not as a person, but at best as if she was buying a high-class commodity. I felt so humiliated, and it was as if I could foresee everything. Perhaps I am too bookish, and human dignity [*renge*] doesn't matter in this type of work. But I only want to sell my sweat—I don't want to sell my dignity and my soul. Enough, I've really had enough, I can't take it anymore. What kind of a part am I performing?! I can't bear this grief. (Ibid., 6)

During the Cultural Revolution Xie Lihua might have read this as a model tale of a heroic young woman fighting the evils of capitalism. But, as cadres under a regime promoting a market economy, she and her colleagues had to denounce it. According to Xie, when she showed it to others in the editorial office, they all thought the young woman exceedingly naive:

Didn't she understand what coming to the city was all about? If you come looking for "spiritual food"—if you're looking for equality, justice, and human dignity—no city is going to extend its arms to you. She's come to Beijing and met several kindhearted people—let her go to New York and see what it's like . . . Today's world is like a mobile village, with urbanites going overseas and villagers going to the city. This is already an unstoppable tide. But if you want to join this "mobile army," you must be psychologically prepared. Nowhere is there a ready-made cake just waiting for you to cut. Cakes have to be bought with money you've exchanged for blood and sweat, and without material food it's impossible to produce spiritual food! (Xie 1995, 6)

In the Migrant Women's Club, organizers and invited speakers similarly worked hard to dismiss speaking bitterness narratives. As I noted in chapter 2, for example, a visiting psychological counselor told Club members that they should adapt to their environment rather than complain about it. And when participants in another Club discussion said they felt that much of their life had been thwarted and wasted in exploitative, dead-end jobs, Wang Laoshi countered that, no matter what their situation, everyone had the responsibility to make the most of things.

This profoundly unsympathetic attitude toward speaking bitterness prevailed among the staff of *Rural Women* and the Migrant Women's Club through the late 1990s and into the 2000s. And this meant that while members spoke bitterness among themselves and to others outside the Club like myself, this was largely behind the backs of Xie Lihua and Migrant Women's Club staff. Speaking bitterness about the destruction of human dignity through capitalist exploitation was a rumbling on the sidelines, but by and large it was not admissible in the small public sphere created by groups like the Migrant Women's Club, with "one foot in and one foot out" of the state, tolerated but still vulnerable to criticism and closure.

Human Rights

Meanwhile, however, legal and human rights discourse was emerging as an alternative, more politically acceptable framework for the expression of migrant discontent. In the 1980s the Chinese state responded to criticism by the United States and other nations of its human rights record primarily by denying the validity of Western human rights discourse in the Chinese context. However, with the publication of the first so-called white paper on human rights in November 1991, the state recognized the applicability of human rights terminology (Keith 1997, 29–31), and since then discourse on "(lawful) rights and interests" (*hefa quanyi*) and "human rights" (*renquan*) has become increasingly prominent.

In the late 1990s and early 2000s migrant workers and their supporters across China put this new human rights discourse to use in three different ways. First, in the special economic zones of southern China in particular, migrant workers of an increasing number of enterprises rioted in protest against their employers' violations of the law and of their human rights. Second, it became increasingly feasible for ordinary citizens to sue individuals, corporations, and even local governments for violations of their rights, and with the help of nonprofit legal groups and other activists, migrant workers joined the wave of litigation that ensued.[6] Finally, activists and intellectuals increasingly used the language of human rights in journalism and scholarship to lobby the state to improve the situation of migrants.

In chapter 2 we saw that through the 1990s the *Rural Women* collective, like the Women's Federation, tried to teach women to use the law to protect their rights and interests. By placing the onus on individual women to learn how to protect their rights, the discourse deployed by the *Rural Women* collective tended to deflect criticism away from the endemic, institutionalized rights violations that migrant women faced and the state's failure to stem those violations. However, in the late 1990s and early 2000s the *Rural Women* collective started to become more critical of the violations of migrant women's rights, resulting from both the practices of individual companies and from state policy and regulations, especially on household registration. For example, as I mentioned in chapter 2, in 1999 the collective organized a national forum on the protection of the rights and interests of migrant women workers. Most speakers at this forum emphasized that the greatest problem facing migrant women was their own lack of *suzhi,* but criticism was also directed at companies and local governments for their failure to uphold the Labor Law in their employment of migrant labor; at local governments for failing to provide affordable schooling for migrant children; and at the inequities of the household registration system. This was furthered in a second forum organized by the collective in 2001, which put yet more pressure on the state to reform the household registration system and associated regulations.

The *Rural Women* collective also tried to help individual migrant women seek justice through the legal system. As mentioned in chapter 2, Chen Ailing and Liu Yu were two women whom the collective helped in this way. In 2001 some of my interlocutors in the Migrant Women's Club viewed the legal and human rights discourse with optimism, as an avenue through which they could seek redress for the humiliations and indignities they had suffered, and as a basis from which to resist further bitterness. To Chen Ailing and Liu Yu, for example, the possibility of taking their employers to court was extremely important, not just in order to win financial compensation, but to win back the "face" that they had lost as a result of their employers' violent assaults on their bodies and their dignity. However, the enormous trouble and cost required to get to court, and the ultimate failure of their efforts, were a profoundly dispiriting lesson, not just to Chen Ailing and Liu Yu themselves but to all the other members of the Club, on the limitations of the legal system.

In mid-2001, after she had left the office of the Migrant Women's Club, but before Chen Ailing's court case was finalized and Liu Yu's was rejected, Zhou Ling, too, looked to the legal system and the discourse on human rights as a means to improve the circumstances of migrant women. The previous year, after being nominated by Xie Lihua, Zhou Ling received a grant from an international agency enabling her to join a month-long study tour to the United States to learn about nongovernmental organizations there. She got the grant ahead of more than thirty other applicants from Beijing and was the only one of the four mainland Chinese participants on the tour who was not a university academic or a Women's Federation official. In the United States, she told me, she learned that around the world poor women and laborers are exploited. And now capitalists were coming to China to exploit young migrant women. After returning to Beijing she took up legal studies to put herself in a better position to defend the rights of migrant women, and she started talking about the possibilities of migrant women working together to further the efforts of the Migrant Women's Club:

> I'll study law and my friend will study psychological counseling and another will study management, and then we can all work together, work for ourselves. Later on, the Migrant Women's Club will have to be run by us ourselves. It's no good just relying on a city person, it's no good relying on Xie Lihua. . . . We have to organize to fight for our rights ourselves. (August 2001)

Zhou Ling also recognized, though, the enormity of the obstacles she faced in trying to further this goal without the kind of authority, connections, and other resources that Xie Lihua could draw on:

> The state doesn't allow people to organize. If they see an organization has emerged they won't allow it. So it's very risky to try to organize people. If I tried to organize *dagongmei* it's possible I'd be arrested, so

who's willing to do that? . . . Sometimes I think to myself, should I really be doing these things? The state won't give any support. It won't allow you to set up a social organization [*shehui tuanti*]. Very probably you'll work very hard and remain poor; you'll probably be poor your whole life. You certainly won't make much money. If you do this work—helping people with legal cases—they don't have any money to give you. As well as that, I must go and study. I have to pay 10,000 yuan [tuition fees for a two-year course] and I have to live too and I'm not working. Do I really want to do that? As well, I have a family to look after. I have a child who must go to school. And doing this is being unfair to my husband isn't it? I must live off him— I can't earn any money. Moreover, once I've studied for two years and go and do this work I won't be able to earn money. So is it worth it? You'll be poor your whole life. But then I think, there has to be someone to do it, otherwise it will always be like this. (August 2001)

In the end, Zhou Ling withdrew from her legal studies. Worried about neglecting her family and about her dependency upon her husband, and disillusioned by Chen Ailing's and Liu Yu's failures and other events at the Migrant Women's Club, she largely withdrew from Club activities and concentrated on finding a job.

Back at the Migrant Women's Club, other members did not talk about organizing separately, but they were becoming more assertive and public in their criticism of the circumstances of migrants, drawing increasingly upon the language of human rights. In fact, whereas in 2001 Club members spoke bitterness—at least in private conversation—about capitalist exploitation and the destruction of migrant dignity and referred only occasionally to human rights, twelve months later it was more common for members to draw upon a narrative of protest against the violation of migrants' rights. In addition, Club meetings were full of talk about the need for migrants to unite and fight for their human rights.

As part of a New Year soiree put on by Club members at the end of 2002, one man performed a *kuaibanr*, a traditional form of Chinese popular culture involving rhyming song accompanied by the beat of bamboo clappers. The lyrics, which he had composed himself, concluded with the lines:

I hope we migrant workers can unite and stand up, fight for our holidays, for contracts and for [social] insurance. I really hope the media pays attention and the leaders show concern. We're all Chinese, and we shouldn't be treated like this. (December 2002)

At the end of another performance—a skit about the abuse of a young migrant woman working as a maid—the young woman turned to the audience and asked "what can I do?" and they yelled back: "Go to the Migrant Rights Group!" She finished up by punching the air with her fist, shouting "[We must] defend our rights! [*weihu women de quanyi*])."

Conclusion

Paul Ricoeur once noted that "time becomes human to the extent that it is articulated through a narrative mode" (Ricoeur 1984–88, 3). In this chapter I have explored the ways in which the different narrative forms framing migrant women's stories turn time into something human or, in other words, into a central aspect of human experience and subjectivity, a result of individual agency and creativity, which is simultaneously built upon shared social values and assumptions.

In the first part of the chapter I examined narrative forms that shape an understanding of the time of migration and life in the city in relation to the rest of the migrant's life course. Most migrant stories are framed by an assumption that migration involves temporal change, but, as I demonstrated in this chapter, understandings of what that change constitutes vary enormously. One narrative form, the "migration as rural economic strategy" narrative, situates the change effected by migration solely within a rural framework, seeing migration to the city as a strategy belonging to, and enhancing, the rural identity and fundamentally rural life course of the migrant and her family. This narrative form was particularly common among married interlocutors in Haidian, but rare among *dagongmei*.

Other narrative forms see migration as a break from the rural life course. In the "migration as interlude" narrative the break is temporary, and migration is represented as a brief interlude or escapade—a chance for a bit of freedom and fun before returning to the life of marriage, domestic chores, and work in the fields that is the inevitable fate of rural women in their twenties. This narrative of migration as interlude was common among young, single *dagongmei* in Beijing and Hangzhou in the early and mid-1990s, but rare among interlocutors in Beijing in the early 2000s. Another narrative, migration as escape, was found occasionally among both single and married women. Migration, here, is seen as a desperate flight from the countryside, and the structure of the narrative conveys the impression that the speaker is still looking over her shoulder at what she has left. Other narrative forms, though, are more forward-looking. The "migration as changing one's fate" narrative represents migration as an avenue through which the migrant might completely alter her life course and achieve a more comfortable existence and more favorable set of opportunities than was available previously. Some version of this narrative form is often found in the stories of both *dagongmei* and other migrant women. A similar form, the "migration as self-development" narrative views migration and work in the city as involving a process, either of education and gradual maturation or of harsh tempering, whereby the migrant will be transformed into a new and better person. This narrative form is very common in the stories, especially written stories, of *dagongmei*, but it was not used by my interlocutors in Haidian.

The second part of the chapter discussed narrative forms that locate experiences of migration not in terms of the life course, but in relation to urbanites and urban discourse. The first is what I call speaking bitterness, a narrative of complaint and protest at the injustices and indignities suffered by migrants, which appears in the stories of migrant women in a range of circumstances. This narrative commonly disrupts the flow of other life-course narratives, shifting attention from the life of the individual migrant narrator to the plight of migrants more generally and locating the experience of migration within a contemporary social order that is contrasted unfavorably with the past. The final narrative form that I examined in this chapter was that of human rights. This is similarly a narrative of complaint and protest, but it differs from speaking bitterness in being less obviously backward-looking and in using the language of human rights to protest the harshness of migrant experience in the city. Rare in the 1990s, this narrative form is now becoming more pervasive among *dagongmei*.

Each of these narrative forms relates in a specific way to dominant discourses and constructs a particular kind of link between personal temporality and social temporality and change. None should be seen as representing merely a passive acceptance or reproduction of dominant or official discourses, but neither are any of them totally separate from and opposed to dominant discourses. Rather, each narrative form shapes a different kind of negotiation with the various discourses circulating in contemporary Chinese society, drawing upon elements of some and rejecting others.

The "migration as rural economic strategy" narrative conforms closely with dominant discourses on the rural/urban divide in affirming the notion that rural people belong essentially in the countryside, and poses no real threat to urban identities. It also affirms the validity both of the state's policy of allowing rural to urban migration and of its strategic emphasis on improving the incomes and livelihoods of citizens, even if it often involves discontent at the fact that this has not been achieved satisfactorily. On the other hand, this narrative form does not take on board the contemporary state's understanding of national development as requiring efforts on the part of citizens to improve their *suzhi* and develop themselves.

Similarly, the "migration as interlude" narrative preserves the status quo in the sense that it poses little threat either to urbanites' wish that rural people not settle in the city or to the dominant patriarchal, rural expectation that women should settle down and marry in the countryside when they are in their twenties. However, this narrative does not sit well with the dominant morality, either of villagers or of the state, both of which look upon young women's enjoyment of pleasure and autonomy with considerable misgivings. Nor, again, does this narrative form engage with the state's obsession with (self-) development.

In contrast to the previous two narrative forms, the "migration as escape" narrative challenges the rural/urban divide and the notion that rural citizens belong in the countryside. It is radical in its rejection not only of rural society, but also of the optimistic teleology of the state, but these rejections are forced and unhappy, and the narrative does not present a positive alternative to either. The narratives of "changing one's fate" and "self-development" also challenge the notion that rural citizens belong in the countryside. On the other hand, these narratives are very much in tune with dominant urban and national discourses rather than in opposition to them, in the sense that they affirm the moral value of the individual, and of the striving for material gain, social status and self-development that has become central to contemporary urban culture and to the market-oriented rhetoric of the state. Furthermore, the narrative of self-development, in particular, interpolates the speaker and reader very effectively into a state-promoted teleology because of the causal links and analogies that it draws between migration, personal maturation, self-development, and national development. In addition, this latter narrative reproduces the status quo by accepting the exploitation of migrants as not just a necessary evil, but also a positive contribution to both national development and to migrants' own self-development.

The "speaking bitterness" narrative resists dominant discourse both in the sense that it is an explicit complaint about the status quo, and because it refuses the state's optimistic version of history. Thus, rather than affirming present directions by denouncing past evils, as in the speaking bitterness of the Maoist past, contemporary migrants' bitterness contrasts present trends unfavorably with the past and uses the language of a previous, discredited regime to criticize the present social order. In the process, while opposing the state, it draws on and contributes to a discourse of nostalgia for Maoism that is very much a part of contemporary popular culture.

The human rights narrative is only now emerging in the stories of migrants, but as a basis for collective resistance against practices that exploit and demean migrants it is more promising and practical than speaking bitterness. Perhaps ironically, this is because the state views it as less threatening, for, in theory at least, discontent about human rights abuse can be channeled and contained within the legal system, and some basic human rights can be allowed without undermining either the rule of the Communist Party or capitalist development. This is particularly true if adherence to minimum human rights standards—standards that do not overcome inequalities or exploitation, but merely ameliorate the most glaring forms of abuse and indignity—can be combined with the lure of greater consumerism and prosperity and an ethics of self-development and development.

In practice, though, the discourse of human rights has increased contestation, rather than contained it, both because to date human rights have been so poorly attended to and because, once entered into, the discourse of human rights itself raises popular awareness and expectations as to the standard of rights that is acceptable. Already, protests over human rights abuses made by migrants and their supporters have made a difference in that, as noted in chapter 3, the central government, anxious to head off social instability by pacifying the flood of migrants pouring into the cities, has pushed for more humane, less discriminatory treatment of migrant labor. To what degree global and local capitalist employers and local governments will take notice of the central government in this remains to be seen. At a broader level, the extent to which human rights for everyone can be achieved within a global capitalist socioeconomic order that relies on the maintenance of hierarchies and inequalities for the extraction of profit remains an open question.

Appendix 1

List of Interlocutors Named in the Text

The following table (pp. 280–282) includes only those people interviewed by the author and referred to by name in the text. In order to protect identities, most names and a few personal details have been changed. Unless otherwise stated, all interlocutors are rural migrant women, and information about them pertains to 2001. Education refers to the level of education attained before migration and does not include night classes taken while in the city.

	Age	Province of origin	Occupation	Marital status and number of children	Education	Time of first urban migration
Women interviewed in Haidian, Beijing						
Han Haiying	35	Hubei	unemployed	married, 2	primary	1995
Jin Rong	38	Hebei	unemployed	married, 2	sen. sec.	1997
Liang Chun	34	Anhui	home sewing	married, 2	jun. sec.	1994
Shen Mei	36	Hubei	unemployed	married, 2	jun. sec.	1998
Song Shulan	37	Henan	home production (gas lighters)	married, 2	jun. sec. (incomplete)	1996
Yao Min	32	Hebei	unemployed	married, 2	jun. sec.	1998
Yong Binbin	34	Hubei	unemployed	married, 2	jun. sec.	1995
Zhang Xiaohua	36	Henan	unemployed	married, 1	primary	2000
Members of Migrant Women's Club, Beijing						
Chen Ailing	17	Shanxi	apprentice tailor	unmarried, 0	primary	1999
Chunzi	35	Anhui	home handicrafts	married, 1	jun. sec.	1992
Deng Yiyan	29	Shandong	sales (real estate)	unmarried, 0	jun. sec.	1988
Gao Xinran	21	Hebei	cleaner	engaged, 0	jun. sec.	2001
Liu Yu	17	Sichuan	factory worker	unmarried, 0	primary (incomplete)	2000
Ma Hua	28	Guizhou	cleaner	married, 1	jun. sec.	1998
Qiao Xue	20	Shaanxi	domestic maid	unmarried, 0	jun. sec. (incomplete)	1997

	Age	Province of origin	Occupation	Marital status and number of children	Education	Time of first urban migration
Ruan Shilin	23	Shandong	domestic maid	unmarried, 0	jun. sec.	1996
Wang Lan	22	Shaanxi	domestic maid	unmarried, 0	jun. sec.	1995
Yan Jun	22	Jiangsu	factory worker	unmarried, 0	sen. sec.	1994
Zeng Jiping	30	Shandong	sales assistant	married, 1	jun. sec.	1998
Zhang Ning	25	Anhui	unemployed	married, 0	primary	1993
Zhou Ling (rural migrant woman, *hukou* converted to local, urban)	36	Jiangsu	unemployed	married, 1	sen. sec.	1982
Zhu Jin	30	Jiangsu	sales (dress shop)	unmarried, 0	sen. sec.	1997
Migrant women interviewed in Hangzhou, 1995						
Cheng Xihua	19	Anhui	waitress	unmarried, 0	jun. sec.	1995
Ye Ye	24	Anhui	factory worker	unmarried, 0	senior sec.	1992
Zhou Hongxia	22	Anhui	waitress	unmarried, 0	primary	1994

(continued)

Other	Occupation
Li Tao (rural migrant man)	Head, Cultural Development Center for Rural Women
Li Zhen	Editor, *Working Sister*
Ning Dong (urban migrant woman)	Migrant school principal, Haidian
Wang Laoshi (local urban Beijing woman)	Office staff, Migrant Women's Club
Xie Lihua (local urban Beijing woman)	Chief editor, *Rural Women*
Xu Min (local urban Beijing woman)	Office staff, Migrant Women's Club
Zhang Hong	Office staff, Migrant Women's Club
Zhao Feng (urban migrant woman)	Tailor, employer of Chen Ailing (see above)

Appendix 2
Maps

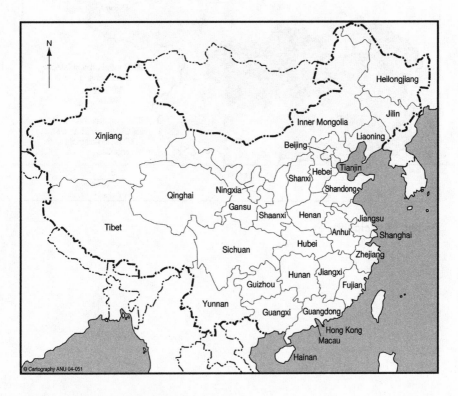

The People's Republic of China

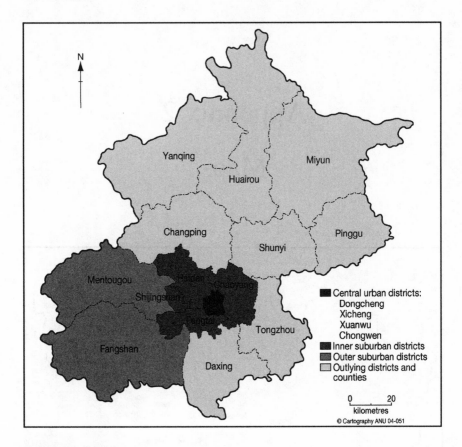

Beijing Municipality

Notes

Notes to Introduction

1. The Ministry of Agriculture estimates that in 2000 roughly 19 out of every 100 rural laborers worked away from home, and the total floating population (including those who had migrated to both rural and urban areas) numbered 94 million ("Rural-to-Town Labour Force on the Rise" 2003). For other recent estimates of the size of the floating population, see Solinger (1999, 18), Rozelle et al. (1999, 374), West (2000, 3–4), Mallee (2000, 35).

2. Definitions vary as to the length of sojourn away from the place of registration that is counted. For a discussion of this, and of other difficulties in defining and quantifying the floating population, see Solinger (1999, 15–23), Scharping (1997), and Chan, Kam Wing (1999). Henceforth in this volume I use the term "migrant" to refer to members of the floating population, and not to those who have had their household registration transferred and are therefore known as "official," "permanent," or "de-jure" migrants (*qianyi renkou*).

3. In the censuses discussed here, the floating population was defined to include anyone without local *hukou* residing in the city for more than a day.

4. A Beijing municipal government spokesperson estimated in 1995 that about half a million construction workers—40 percent of the city's construction labor force—came from outside of Beijing. A further quarter of a million migrants worked in "dirty, tiring and heavy" jobs in textile, sanitation, mining, and coal industries in the city. Finally, more than 70 percent of employees in the capital's burgeoning private sector were migrants (Lei 2001, 490).

5. Nationally, women comprise about 30 percent of the floating population. However, in the Special Economic Zones of Southern China they comprise the majority of the migrant population.

6. One survey of six provinces found, for example, that the probability of women's migration doubled relative to men between 1995 and 2000 (de Brauw et al. 2002, cited in Roberts 2003, 8). Most female (and male) migrants are single, but some studies point to increases in recent years in the migration of married women (Lou et al. 2004). In other countries, increases in the proportion of women, especially married women, in migration streams have been closely related to another highly significant trend—an increase in urban settlement among rural families—for, as analysts of migration have often noted, married women tend to migrate in conjunction with spouses, children, and other family members more commonly than do men, and their desire to remain permanently in the city tends to be greater than that of men (Pedraza 1991, 309–10; Roberts 2003, 7).

7. This book focuses on the experiences of rural women living in the city. It does not discuss the lives of migrant women who have returned to the countryside. For pioneering studies of this important and to date underresearched topic, see Murphy (2002, 2004), Fan (2004), and Lou et al. (2004).

8. Another very significant nongovernmental organization for migrants (also, as it happens, for women) is the Chinese Working Women Network in Shenzhen. It too was founded in 1996 by a group of Hong Kong professionals, headed by the anthropologist Pun Ngai. Its aim is to promote concern for migrant women workers in Guangdong province, enhance their knowledge of workers' rights, improve their health, enrich their social and cultural life and nurture self-empowerment and collaboration among them (*Chinese Working Women's Network* n.d.).

9. We received more than 300 stories from migrant women all over China. Twenty-two were published in Chinese in *Rural Women*. For translations of seven of these, see Jacka (2000b).

10. The questionnaire was prepared by myself, with help from the women working in the Migrant Women's Club office, and was administered by the women in the office and by my research assistant, Arianne Gaetano. The questionnaire was anonymous and confidential and respondents were self-selected. Ninety out of 100 respondents were women. Their ages varied between seventeen and thirty-five, but most were in their twenties; 13 percent were married while another 7 percent were engaged (N = 99). Only 9 percent of respondents had urban *hukou* before coming to Beijing, but at the time of the questionnaire that had increased to 12 percent. Respondents came from a range of different provinces, but the largest numbers were from Shandong (34), Henan (18) and Shaanxi (7). The average time that respondents had spent in Beijing was 3.2 years. One respondent had not finished primary school and 16 percent had primary school education. Of the remainder, most had either junior or senior secondary education (46 percent and 30 percent respectively); 7 percent had been educated to the tertiary technical level (N = 97). In the month prior to the survey, 60 percent of respondents were in waged employment (N = 82). The largest proportions were employed in the service sector (55 percent) and as factory workers (16 percent) (N = 64). These figures correspond roughly to the demographics of the Club membership as a whole. According to a survey of the Club's 399 members conducted in April 1999, members' ages ranged from sixteen to thirty-six, the average being 21.5 years old. Most (81 percent) came from the four provinces of Shandong, Sichuan, Hebei and Henan, but had been in Beijing for three years or more. Some 17 percent had primary school education, and 64 percent junior secondary; 9 percent had graduated from senior secondary school and another 9 percent from secondary or tertiary technical college. A full 72 percent worked as either office cleaners or maids, with smaller numbers employed in other low-status manual jobs (Li Tao 1999a, 75).

11. Another term, *dagongsao,* refers specifically to married migrant women workers, but is rarely used in Beijing.

12. The latter research is discussed in more detail in Jacka (1998).

13. In this book I do not discuss the migration of people of minority nationality or the impact of Han/non-Han ethnicity on migrant experiences. To date, these issues have received very little scholarly attention. They are, however, discussed in Iredale et al. (2001). The authors of this book claim that "to a certain extent the movement of minorities into Beijing is not fundamentally different from the movement of Han from other provinces" but that migrants from ethnic minorities are commonly worse off than their Han counterparts in terms of economic well-being (Iredale et al. 2001, 234).

14. For a range of definitions and discussions of the term "experience" see Scott (1992), Bruner (1986), and Pickering (1997).

15. See, for example, Gluck and Patai (1991) and Thompson (1978).

16. Similarly, Anthony Giddens writes that "In the settings of what I call 'high' or 'late' modernity—our present-day world—the self, like the broader institutional context in which it exists, has to be reflexively made. Yet this task has to be accomplished amid a puzzling diversity of options and possibilities" (Giddens 1991, 3).

NOTES TO PAGES 20–41 287

17. Lou et al. (2004) note, however, that almost all married women were full and active participants in the focus group discussions, regardless of whether they had ever migrated or not.

Notes to Chapter 1

1. I wish to make clear that there is no sharp distinction between state and popular discourses relating to rural to urban migration and migrants. Rather, the history of the construction of rural migrant subject positions has been characterized by a close intertwining and mutual imbrication of popular attitudes, intellectual theorizing and state institutions and policies. See also Lei (2003).

2. I follow Louisa Schein in using the term "internal orientalism" to refer to practices of "othering" that mimic those Western representations of the East referred to by Edward Said as orientalism, but that are, however, engaged in by Asian elites in their representation of groups in their own nation. See Schein (1997, 72–73).

3. Some scholars, for example, have commented on the separation of the gentry from rural life during the late Tang dynasty and others have noted the ways in which urban dwellers during the seventeenth century romanticized the countryside (Kipnis 1995, 113).

4. For a discussion of the profound impact of Smith's writing on Lu Xun, see Liu (1995, 45–76).

5. The May Fourth Movement was named after a demonstration held on 4 May 1919 to protest the Treaty of Versailles transfer of Shandong province from Germany to Japan. It was a nationalist movement involving mostly students and intellectuals, aimed at strengthening China through radical cultural reform.

6. This is not to say that the *shi/min* divide was transformed *solely* into the intellectual/peasant binarism. In fact, it could be argued that throughout the twentieth and twenty-first centuries this divide has persisted or returned in several different guises in a range of discourses in the service of hierarchical power relations.

7. Yet another factor in the way in which modernity has been imagined in China is ethnicity (see Harrell 1995). The construction of Han Chinese images of "minority nationalities" as "ancient," "childlike," and "feminine" that Harrell describes is quite similar to urban Chinese representations of "peasants."

8. The conflation of woman and peasant as "other" is particularly obvious in literature that is structured explicitly around an encounter between intellectual and peasant, for in these works the narrator or main protagonist is invariably the urban intellectual male, and it is frequently an uneducated woman who functions as the key symbol of rural "otherness." The most widely discussed example of this is Lu Xun's story *Zhufu* (New Year Sacrifice), which centers around the tragic fate of a poor, superstitious peasant woman, whose desperate anxieties no one will listen to, and, more particularly, around the moral dilemma of the male intellectual from the city who is unable to help her (Feuerwerker 1998, 245; Chow 1991, 107–12).

9. See, for example, "The Magic Herb" by Hao Ran (1984).

10. For a highly readable case study which supports this claim see Gao (1999).

11. For this reason, both the Iron Girls and the Dazhai production brigade came in for particular scorn by Deng Xiaoping's regime, which based its legitimacy in part on a rejection of Cultural Revolution politics.

12. This series was televised to audiences of hundreds of millions of people in China in 1988. After the crackdown of the Tiananmen demonstrations in 1989, state officials accused the filmmakers of encouraging dissent. One of the principal authors was arrested and the other fled to the United States (Kipnis 1995, 122).

13. Examples include the film *Huang tudi* (Yellow Earth) directed by Chen Kaige; *Zai*

feixu shang (In the Ruins) written by Zhao Zhenkai in 1978; and *Baigou qiuqian jia* (The White Dog and the Swings), by Mo Yan (1985). The latter two stories are discussed in Feuerwerker (1998, 1–8, 210–14, and 240–47).

14. The term *suzhi* originally referred to the chemical composition or characteristics of a substance. In the 1910s the term was used in Japanese to refer to the character, characteristics, or quality of a person's spirit or body, and that usage was adopted into Chinese. However, in Chinese this usage was rare until the 1970s. Until the second half of the 1970s *suzhi* was most commonly used in reference to the quality of the military body, both individual and collective and, less frequently, to that of the bodies of sportspeople. After 1978 the term began to be used also in relation to the quality of other things, including leaders and enterprises. In the early 1980s there was an increase both in the range and quantity of usages of the term *suzhi*. Most notably, the term began to be used frequently in this period in family planning discourse, in the phrase *renkou suzhi*—the quality of the population. In the early to mid-1980s state leaders also began making a close link between improving "spiritual civilization" (*jingshen wenming*) and raising *suzhi*. As can be seen in successive reports to the Party Congress, this link grew in importance through the late 1980s and 1990s. In the late 1980s there was an unprecendented explosion in the usage of the term *suzhi*. Thus, the number of times the word was used in the *People's Daily* (*Renmin ribao*) jumped from 7 in 1970 to 102 in 1980, and then 813 in 1985, 1,066 in 1990 and 2,486 in 2000.

In the many early twentieth-century treatises on the Chinese national character by Liang Qichao, Lu Xun, and others, the term *suzhi* was *not* used. Nor was it used in the numerous translations of Arthur Smith's book *Chinese Characteristics*—that is, until the late 1990s, when a number of scholars translated the title of the book as *Zhongguoren de suzhi*. The text of the 1988 television series *Heshang* (River Elegy), which, as I mentioned above, is highly critical of the backwardness of Chinese tradition and of the peasantry, uses the term *suzhi* a few times, all in one paragraph on the low quality of the peasantry.

15. For further examples indicating the strength of the *suzhi* discourse in contemporary China, see Anagnost (1997), Bakken (2000), and Kipnis (2001).

16. Nigel Harris has likewise noted with regard to international immigrants worldwide that "immigrants rarely catch buses or trains; they 'flood,' 'flux,' 'flow,' 'surge,' 'pour,' 'drain'; they are . . . not just a 'tide' but a 'rising' one, and one flowing into areas which are 'saturated.' Water imagery appears irresistible" (Harris 1995, 186).

17. Other terms that incorporate the character *liu* include *liuluo* (to wander about destitute), *liumin* (wanderer; refugee) and *liumang* (hooligan).

18. For an analysis of media representations of migrants that does distinguish between "official" and "commercial" media, while nevertheless also noting the blurring of the boundaries between the two, see Sun (2004). Recent changes in ownership, funding, and management of the Chinese mass media are discussed in Zhao, Yuezhi (1998).

19. In fact, many articles put even more stress on the negative impact of the floating population, focusing, in particular, on the alleged criminality of its members and the threat they pose to family planning. See, for example, Wang Sigang (1995), "Zhendui Shangye Shichang Tedian . . ." (1994), Li Debin (1993), and Liu Yanling (1994). Zhao Shukai, a senior researcher at the Development Research Centre of the State Council, argues that reports on the criminality of the floating population are blatantly biased and that victimization of, and crime against, rural migrants, lack of support services available to them in the city, and their poor quality of life are problems at least as grave as migrant criminality (Zhao, Shukai 2000). The relationship between rural to urban migration and crime rates is also discussed in Bakken (2000, 387–90).

20. For example, Cai Fang, deputy director of the Institute of Demography in the Chinese Academy of Social Sciences, argued against the common perception of rural to urban

migration as a disorderly, irrational "blind flow" (*mangliu*), using survey data to show instead that rural people's labor migration, settlement, and selection of jobs were rational and ordered, and that most of the negative aspects of migration were the result of distorted policies (Cai 1998, 83). See also, Mallee (1996, 109–11), Yu (1994), and Zhao, Shukai (2000).

21. Despite concern in the media through the 1990s about the lack of social services or cultural activities available to rural migrants in the city, attention to this issue was mostly only cosmetic, and in the early 2000s very few services were available. While I was staying in Peking University in 2001, staff at the office on campus that processed migrant temporary resident permits took down an old sign over the door saying Local Police Department for Managing the Outsider Population (*paichusuo wailai renkou guanli bu*) and replaced it with one saying Office of Services for the Outsider Population (*wailai renkou fuwuzhan*). In fact, however, no "services," apart from the processing of permits, were provided.

22. In 1987 the Thirteenth Congress of the CCP endorsed as Party policy the view that the chief objective of the present "initial stage of socialism" is the development of the productive forces, under which all other goals must be subsumed. This position has been deployed in a number of discourses. For a discussion of the way in which it has been used to justify discrimination against women in employment see Jacka (1990, 19).

23. See Sun (2004), for a somewhat more critical perspective on this type of urban liberalism.

24. See, for example, articles published in *Beijing Qingnian Bao* (Beijing Youth Daily) 5, 6, 8 August and 2 October 2001.

25. The details of one such story are given in Evans (1997, 171–72). For other examples, see "Dangqian Guaimai Funü . . ." (1991); and "1800 Ming Funü . . ." (1993).

26. This explains the heightened shock delivered by one article that reported an instance of kidnapping, not of a rural woman, but of a Shanghai graduate student on her way to Beijing to do research (Anagnost 1997, 134).

27. This aspect of sensationalist stories of *dagongmei* victimhood is discussed in greater detail in Sun (2004). Trafficking in women in rural China is also a favorite topic for Western journalists writing about Chinese society, and for similar reasons. See, for example, "Return of a Medieval Evil" (1991); and "Demand for Wives Fuels Trade in Teenage Girls" (1999).

Notes to Chapter 2

1. The All China Women's Federation is a "mass organization" affiliated with the Communist Party. Its dual role is to further the interests of Chinese women and to promote Communist Party policy among women. For further details see Jacka (1997, 90–100) and Judd (2002).

2. In comparison, *Reading* (*Dushu*), a highly respected intellectual journal, has a circulation of about 100,000.

3. I stress that my concern here is *not* with a distinction between state and nonstate discourses. As discussed in the previous chapter, the migrant subject positions that dominate the Chinese media and other discursive arenas support a range of powerful interests across the state/nonstate divide. And the question of the significance of the Migrant Women's Club is not so much one of its independence from or opposition to the state, but rather of its ability to formulate alternatives to both state and nonstate discourses that subordinate and marginalize migrant women. This approach differs from much recent literature on social organizations in China, which is more commonly concerned with the extent to which such organizations are carving out a public sphere or "civil society" that is independent from, and in opposition to, the Communist state. See, for example, White, Howell, and Shang

(1996). Hsiung, Jaschok, and Milwertz (2001), however, provide a convincing analysis of the Chinese women's movement as straddling the state/nonstate divide.

4. Li Tao and Li Zhen left the *Rural Women* collective in early 2003. The directions that the Migrant Women's Club and *Working Sister* have taken since their departure are beyond the scope of this volume.

5. In the 1990s and early 2000s Public Security staff were under pressure to meet quotas of criminal cases solved. This sometimes meant that if a case appeared too difficult to solve it was not filed. This was a common problem with rape cases.

6. For a report on the first of these forums, see Jacka (2000a). For more details on the Migrant Women's Club, the Cultural Development Center for Rural Women, and the *Rural Women* journal, see their Website at www.nongjianv.org.

7. For further discussion of the intertwining of Chinese women's organizing across the state/nonstate boundary, see Hsiung, Jaschok, and Milwertz (2001).

8. For an example and discussion of the Women's Federation's use of the *suzhi* discourse, see Jacka (2006).

9. At the Forum on the Protection of the Rights of Migrant Women Workers in 1999, not only Li Tao, but, in fact, most speakers blamed migrant women's problems primarily or in part on their low *suzhi*. In speaking to the forum, my colleague Arianne Gaetano and I were critical of this approach, arguing that the greatest problems migrant women faced were social and structural. To say that they were due to the women's "low *suzhi*" was akin to blaming the women themselves for their situation, which would only add to the pressures on them. Xie Lihua observed that these criticisms were not new—she heard them whenever she went overseas. Our arguments were subsequently taken up and elaborated by a number of the participants, and despite being irritated at our critical stance, in her later report Xie Lihua noted that by the end of the forum a general consensus was reached that the "low *suzhi*" epithet must no longer be applied so indiscriminately to migrant women workers (Xie 1999, 4; Jacka 2000a, 137).

10. See Jacka (2006) for further discussion.

11. From 2000 onward, *Rural Women* published far fewer articles and stories about migrant women in urban areas.

12. This is evident in the titles of the columns in which most of the stories appeared. These were as follows: "I am in between the city and the countryside" (*wo zai chengxiang zhi jian*) (1993–95), "Away from home" (*chumen zai wai*) (1993–96), "What does one do in the city?" (*Jincheng yihou gan shenme*) (1995), "Special reports on 'working sisters'" (*'dagongmei' zhuanti baodao*) (1995), "Special reports" (*zhuanti baodao*) (1996), "A home for working sisters" (*dagongmei zhi jia*) (1996–2000), and "My life as a migrant worker" (*wo de dagong shengya*) (1999, 1–12). The last column included stories sent in for a competition that was initiated and funded by myself. The title of this column—the only one to focus explicitly on migrant women's experiences as workers—was also chosen by me.

13. This issue is discussed further in the next chapter.

14. For example, the third issue of the journal carried the following comment, originally posted on www.NewsHoo.com by a Hubei writer:

> As most people know, when he was young, Mao Zedong worked in Beijing. If today's restrictive regulations had been in place then, you can be sure that this "Hunanese peasant" "drifting blindly" into Beijing would not have been allowed to take up his position in the library at Peking University, or if he had, he would have been kicked out soon after. (cited in "Dagong Yulu" 2002, 2)

15. Jane Parpart notes that in the 1990s, the term "vulnerable group"—used to refer to women and other disadvantaged groups in the South—became a rallying cry for develop-

ment experts wishing to challenge the World Bank's structural adjustment policies. Parpart argues that "while an effective weapon against the Bank, this language has further entrenched the image of the helpless premodern, vulnerable Third World woman (Parpart 1995, 228–29). Li Tao notes that "vulnerable group" became a fashionable term in China in 2002, following its adoption by Premier Zhu Rongji. He acknowledges that the term is very controversial, but does not explain the basis for the controversy (see Li Tao 2002, 7).

16. *Laoshi,* literally teacher, is a polite form of address to an educated superior. This is how members of the Migrant Women's Club addressed Wang.

17. In an interview in 1998 Xie Lihua responded to criticisms such as these as follows:

> We cannot know to what degree we have been successful in changing attitudes, but I do have examples of journalists who have changed the perspective of their articles on the migrant population once they came to know the Club and its activities. Some people say that I am just publicizing my own work. I do not agree. I am publicizing a belief and a way of working that represents a trend of development in society, so I really find that media publicity is very important. We bring forward social problems that deserve reflection. (cited in Milwertz 2002, 112)

Notes to Chapter 3

1. The Chinese regimes probably were, in fact, inspired by overseas regulations on "guest workers." In 1995 the Minister of Labor, Li Boyong, proposed to the National People's Congress that a system be set up for controlling the movement of internal migrants "similar to international passport and visa requirements" (Solinger 1999, 4).

2. For a table listing the major regulations pertaining to the floating population that were introduced nationally and locally in Beijing, Shanghai, and Guangzhou/Guangdong in the period 1985–2000 and in effect in 2000–1, see Liu Ling (2001, 128–29). For a diagram setting out the documentation required for, and administrative structures involved in, registering migrants for residence and work in Beijing, and specifically within Haidian district, see Zhou Hao (2001, 191).

3. For further discussion of gender inequalities in land allocation in the 1980s and 1990s, see Judd (1992, 345–46), Jacka (1997, 70–71), and Bossen (2002, 91–98).

4. For a brief discussion of another case, similar to Chunzi's, see Bossen (2002, 98).

5. There are many variations upon this theme. Some villages withdraw all rights to land and collective assets immediately upon a woman's marriage out. Others withdraw some, but not all, rights over a period of several years. For further discussion, see Wang and Zheng (2003).

6. Beijing government regulations require prospective landlords to undergo complex and expensive procedures to obtain permits from the Public Security Bureau and from local housing and land administration departments. District and county land administration departments are required to restrict the number of permits issued to landlords wishing to rent to migrants so that "the proportion of personnel coming to the capital from outside as compared to permanent residents stays within a set ratio." The ratio for each area is set by the local government (HRIC 2002b, 62).

7. The center in Changping has a population of several hundred male and female inmates (HRIC 1999, 54). Other accounts of detention at the Changping center are given in HRIC (1999, 38–51) and "Yi ge Bei Qiansongzhe de Zishu" (Memoir of a Deportee) (2002). For descriptions of conditions at other centers, see HRIC (1999, 6, 32–53).

8. The remaining 9 percent of migrants included those who were unemployed, those who had come to visit relatives and friends, and those who had come on a business trip or for study purposes, tourism, or medical treatment (Beijingshi Tongjiju 2002, 580).

9. As noted earlier, *dagongmei* are, by definition, wage workers. According to a 1999 report from the Migrant Women's Club, 44 percent of its members worked as cleaners, 28 percent as maids, 4.3 percent as waitresses or kitchen hands, and 3 percent as salespeople (Li Tao 1999a, 75).

10. This was in direct contravention of China's Labor Law, according to which all laborers enjoy equal rights to employment and choice of occupation (*Labour Law of the People's Republic of China* 2002, 7).

11. The term *xiagang* refers to people who have been forced to leave their posts in the state sector. Such people continue to be employees, however, and can usually hang onto housing provided by their work unit, and to enjoy subsidized health care and some form of stipend or pension, at least for a few years. In some cases, they are retrained and found alternative jobs (Chan, Anita 2001, 13).

12. In the 1994 Labor Law, the working week was set at 44 hours, but in 1997 that was reduced to forty hours (Chan, Anita 2001, 11 note 28).

13. Of the numerous instances of industrial conflict between factory managers and migrant workers that occurred in the 1990s, the majority were over unpaid wages. In 1998 the Guangdong Labor Bureau secured 450 million yuan owed to migrant workers, mainly by Asian investors (Chan, Anita 2001, 6).

14. All respondents in this survey were migrants with agricultural household registration who had resided in the city for six months or more. Some 7.5 percent of respondents were "managers" (*guanli renyuan*) or "bosses" (*laoban*). The remainder were wage workers. It is not clear how many respondents were male and how many female (Liu Ling 2001, 110).

15. Zhejiangcun is the largest migrant settlement in Beijing, with a population of about 90,000 people. Located in Fengtai District, it is inhabited mostly by migrant entrepreneurs from rural Wenzhou, in Zhejiang province, and their employees. It was demolished in 1995, but rebuilt shortly afterward.

16. One exception is Dorothy Solinger, who discusses migrant circumstances in six trades: construction, manufacturing, domestic service, marketing and services, cottage-style garment processing, and begging and scrap collecting (Solinger 1999, 206–40).

17. For examples, see Mian (2004), and Li, Jianying (2004).

18. The following figures refer to people without Beijing household registration residing in Beijing municipality for more than one day. They are taken from the 2001 Nonnatives Dynamic Control Data of Beijing (Beijingshi Tongjiju 2002, 577).

19. Of the remainder, 405,000 (10 percent) lived in the central urban area, and 133,000 (4 percent) lived in outlying districts and counties.

20. The state began a comprehensive housing reform program in the late 1980s. During the first half of the 1990s, numerous apartments owned by state enterprises and institutions were sold to sitting tenants. Commercially built housing estates also became an important part of the urban and suburban landscape in this period (Wang, Ya Ping 2000, 846).

21. In 2001, 2 percent of migrants bought their own housing in Beijing (Beijingshi Tongjiju 2002, 581).

22. This last description is drawn from Zhang Li's account of the lives of young migrant women who live and work together with their employers in the sewing workshops of Zhejiangcun (see Zhang, Li 2001, 126–30).

23. This has also been documented in several studies of women in similar circumstances elsewhere in the world (see, for example, Constable 1997; Anderson 2000).

24. These issues are discussed in more detail in chapter 4 and in Gaetano (2004, 52–55); see also Jacka (1997, 171–75).

25. In the case of unemployed married women in Haidian, I have calculated the per capita income as one-quarter of their total household income, since most lived in households of four people: two adults and two children. In most cases this income was earned by the husband and amounted to approximately 1,000 yuan per month.

26. The details are as follows: according to the Municipal Statistical Bureau, urbanites earned an average monthly discretionary income per capita of 765.2 yuan in 1999 and 862.5 yuan in 2000. Among the poorest 20 percent of the urban population, the average monthly discretionary income per capita was 389 yuan in 1999 and 481.2 yuan in 2000 (Wang, Ya Ping 2000, 850; Beijingshi Tongjiju 2001, 478). The minimum monthly wage set by Beijing authorities in 1999 was 400 yuan and in 2000 it was 412 yuan (Beijingshi Tongjiju 2002, 516). The 1999 Sino-German survey of 200 male and female migrants in Beijing found that just over two-thirds of respondents earned 800 yuan or less each month. Roughly 17 percent earned 100–400 yuan per month, while 35 percent earned 401–600 yuan. In comparison, in my Migrant Women's Club survey of 2000 I found that, in the month prior to the survey, 91 percent of respondents earned 800 yuan or less per month, 30 percent of respondents earned 100–400 yuan per month, and 48 percent earned 401–600 yuan (N = 90).

27. One exception to this was the women who worked in karaoke bars and nightclubs as hostesses and sex workers. These women could earn several hundred yuan a night. For a discussion of the lives of rural women working as hostesses and sex workers in the city of Dalian, see Tian (2004). Sex work is heavily dominated by rural migrant women, but I do not discuss the experiences of sex workers in this book.

28. The standard rate for domestic service set by one introduction agency, run by the Beijing Federation of Trade Unions, that I visited in 2001 was 200 yuan per month. A little more was paid to those who took care of babies and the elderly.

29. Most of my interlocutors who rented accommodation paid 200–300 yuan per month per room. Each room usually housed three or four people.

30. The "minimum guaranteed cost of living for urbanites" (*Chengzhen jumin zui di shenghuo baozhang biaozhun*) in Beijing was set at 273 yuan in 1999 and 280 yuan in 2000. Below this level, locally registered urbanites were eligible for government payments, but migrants were not (Beijingshi Tongjiju 2002, 516).

31. Fees at the local migrant primary school in which most of my interlocutors' children were enrolled were 300 yuan per semester, or 60 yuan per month. Most of these families had one or two children in school.

32. For a discussion of premarital sex and cohabitation among migrants, see Li Zhen (2002e).

33. Before the late 1970s depression was largely unheard of among ordinary Chinese people and "depressive neurosis" was rarely diagnosed by Chinese psychiatrists. In contrast, complaints of "neurasthenia" amongst the general population were, and continue to be, much more common. Since 1980, however, among academic psychiatrists in urban China there has been a dramatic change in diagnostic labelling, such that "neurasthenia" has effectively been marginalized and reconstituted as "depression" (Lee 1999).

34. This study, conducted in 1998–99, involved twenty-two focus-group discussions with 146 young female migrant workers (seventy-two married, seventy-four unmarried) in the cities of Beijing, Shanghai, Guangzhou, Guiyang, and Taiyuan (Zheng et al. 2001).

35. This is despite the fact that, as a result of declining birthrates, most urban schools had declining numbers of students. According to official figures, in the early 2000s, Beijing had something like 300,000 surplus school places (HRIC 2002a, 4).

36. For a more detailed analysis of the conditions in migrant schools in Beijing, see Han Jialing (2002).

37. This is a good example of the lack of transparency characterizing the migrant regulatory regime. Six months after the introduction of the new categorization of temporary residence permits, the only thing that migrants in Haidian district knew about it was that they were all in the C category (even though many had lived in the city for several years), which meant that they were more likely to be subject to police checks. They believed that an A permit was unobtainable to all except those with official connections. Neither the mem-

bers nor the organizers of the Migrant Women's Club understood the new system. And it took three visits to the local police station, and a good deal of persistent questioning on my part, to obtain the information that I have presented here.

38. On the contrary, according to a large-scale survey conducted in southeastern China by the Ministry of Labor and Social Security, low salaries and poor working conditions have recently been deterring rural people from seeking employment in the manufacturing centers of the Pearl River Delta, southeastern Fujian, and southeastern Zhejiang, with the result that there is now a severe shortage of migrant workers in these areas ("China Facing Severe Shortage of Migrant Workers and Technical Labor" 2004).

39. When asked directly about what most explained their circumstances, members of the Migrant Women's Club stressed household registration, whereas the women in Haidian usually said "poverty." However, the latter also linked their poverty with the household registration system and the inferior status of rural residents.

Notes to Chapter 4

1. China's accession to the World Trade Organization was formally announced the day before this conversation took place.

2. For further discussion see Jacka (1997, 73–84) and Unger (2002, 183–86).

3. Between the 1950s and 1970s people given a "bad class" label, for example because they or their parents were landlords or capitalists before the revolution, suffered various forms of discrimination.

4. In Zhou Ling's case class, family size, and patriarchal attitudes were all at work. Her family suffered both poverty and humiliation because her paternal grandfather had been a minor official under the Guomindang, and her family was therefore labeled as "bad class." This was compounded by the fact that the family had three daughters and no sons.

5. Nine of my interlocutors were born after the one-child policy was introduced in 1979, but none were single children. Three completed primary school, the rest left school after completing junior secondary school. It is possible that in future cohorts of migrant women fewer will feel that their education was stymied by the combination of sexism and large family size. It should be noted, though, that single daughters are still extremely rare in the countryside. It has always been the case that most villagers have gotten away with having a second child if their first was a girl, and since the beginning of the 1990s this has been allowed in official policy across the country.

6. For a discussion of nostalgia in the writing of Shen Congwen and Mo Yan, and the links between the two, see Wang, David Der-wei (1993).

7. For example, Geremie Barmé writes of the emergence of a variety of nostalgias for Maoism and for the Cultural Revolution (Barmé 1996, 1999), Dai Jinhua discusses the rise of nostalgia for both pre-1949 "tradition" and for revolution in urban popular culture and advertisements (Dai 1997) and Zhang Xudong and Wang Ban discuss nostalgia for Shanghai in the 1990s fiction of the writer Wang Anyi (Zhang Xudong 2000; Wang, Ban 2002).

8. See, for example, the film *Yellow Earth* (*Huang Tudi*), the use of yellow earth as a symbol of China in the television series River Elegy (*Heshang*), and Lu Xun's famous story *Guxiang,* which has variously been translated as My Old Home, Hometown, My Native Land and Homeland. In discussing the significance of Lu Xun's story in Chinese culture and his usage of the term *guxiang,* Tang Xiaobing writes:

> Ever since the high Tang period of the eighth century, when poetic giants excelled in elevating homesickness to an archetypal human longing, *guxiang* as subject matter has been fully developed into a fertile field for cultivating communal sentiment as well as artistic and literary sensibilities. The image and concept of *guxiang* best

indicates a primary structure of feeling and frequently provokes a melancholic nostalgia that reaches metaphysical heights while also suggesting allegorical dimensions. Literally meaning "old country," the phrase pits an existential temporality against an external and emphatically rural, often even pastoral, landscape. Like all such key words in a signifying language, *guxiang* describes as well as prescribes a mode of human relationship and experience. In articulating a vital attachment and sense of belonging that is predicated on a spatio-temporal displacement and the subsequent possibility of nostalgia, the phrase, with its layered associations, encodes and transmits a complex conception of home, communal life, and the private self. (Tang, Xiaobing 2000, 74–75)

Significantly, in Lu Xun's story, when the urban male protagonist returns to his childhood home village, it is completely different from his nostalgic memories of the place. Thus, *Guxiang* and the genre of "native land" literature that it inspired is primarily about loss and displacement. The image of home conjures up longing, but it is a longing that cannot be fulfilled—*guxiang*, almost by definition in modern Chinese literature, lies in the past and cannot be returned to.

9. The reasons available for respondents in this survey to mark were "job-related," "improve conditions," "education," "marriage," "family," and "other." For other examples see Scharping and Sun (1997, 107) and Solinger (1999, 154–71).

10. In this, my interlocutors were similar to rural migrants across the developing world. It is widely noted that villagers' out-migration and the usage of remittances from migration are often directed toward education, house building, marriage, and the purchase of consumer goods, rather than toward more immediately productive investment in agriculture or business (Murphy 2002, 88–123; Brettell 2000, 103).

11. It should be noted here, that unlike elsewhere in the world, in rural China to date houses have been essentially unproductive assets. Villagers do not own the land on which their houses are built, and while houses are owned by individuals, the sale and leasing of housing is common only in the vicinity of cities. Part of the reason for this is that legislation aimed at conserving agricultural land prohibits villagers who sell or rent from immediately applying for more land on which to build (Sargeson 2004, 152–53). In addition, in most villages out-migration is greater than in-migration, so there is little demand for rented housing.

12. Aside from "have a good time" *wan(r)* can be translated as "have fun," "play," or "muck about."

13. Respondents were asked to identify up to three of their most important reasons for out-migration. The percentages in Figure 4.1 therefore add up to more than 100 percent. Most respondents to this survey indicated that they made the decision to leave home on their own. This is further discussed in the next chapter.

14. In 1990 there were about 44 televisions per 100 rural households, by 2001 there were 105 (*Zhonghua Renmin Gongheguo Nianjian 2002* 2002, 1194). In the early 2000s some rural families enjoyed a range of television programs. In some areas, however, reception was poor, only one or two local stations could be received, and they broadcast for only a few hours each evening (Murphy 2002, 213).

15. These findings are in contrast to studies in other countries, which show that daughters usually remit more than sons (Murphy 2002, 107).

16. Escaping marriage is often given as a reason for rural to urban migration in stories published in *Rural Women* and *Working Sister.* In addition to Zhou Rencong's story, see Xu Chengbin (1993), Jingjing (1998), and "Guniang Tiaohun" (2002).

17. Until the 1950s most marriages in rural China were arranged by parents without the involvement of the young people themselves. Thereafter, the incidence of arranged mar-

riages declined sharply, and by the 1990s they were rare, though not unheard of. Nowadays, some young people fall in love and become engaged without the intervention of a third party. However, the majority find a partner through the introduction of a relative, friend, or matchmaker (Yan Yunxiang 2003, 45–47).

18. In Chinese, the question is: *Chulai dagong shi bu shi yi tiao chulu?* The term *chulu* means, literally, "a path out." It does not necessarily connote either escape or physical departure, but a way to get a (new) life. Geremie Barmé notes that in the language of the Maoist era the path was that of collective socialism and was something given by the Party and the People, for example to someone who had confessed their crimes and was absolved. Now that the individual has become the center of socioeconomic activity, one can, oneself, search for (*zhao*) a *chulu* (informal communication, July 2003). Aside from being posed in relation to rural to urban migration, in post-Mao China the question of how they are to find a life is often posed of urban women faced with a heavy double burden and with pressure to withdraw from state sector employment (see Jacka 1990).

19. For a discussion of meanings of "old age" and "retirement" in rural China, see Murphy (2004, 255 and 260). Murphy notes that while their labor commonly goes unrecognized, elderly, "retired" villagers often continue to work very hard, farming and caring for grandchildren.

20. In another survey, when 175 migrants were asked "Do you want to work long term in the city?" over half replied that they did not want to and another 22 percent said they did not know. However, subsequent interviews revealed that those who said they did not want to remain in the city actually meant that they believed they had no option but to return home (Zhao Shukai, cited in Murphy 2002, 231–32 note 67).

21. More than one response was possible, so the percentages do not add up to 100.

22. See chapter 3 for details of this survey.

23. See Lee (1998, 130) for similar aspirations among *dagongmei* in Shenzhen.

24. For a detailed discussion, see Murphy (2002, 124–43).

25. For a *dagongmei* discussion of the relative advantages and disadvantages of marriage to a Beijing man, a man from one's home county, or a fellow migrant from a different province, see "Jia gei chengli ren haishi xiangxia ren" (2003).

26. Aside from Liu Yu and Deng Yiyan, discussed here, three other members of the Migrant Women's Club also talked of returning to the countryside. Ma Hua was homesick and was under pressure from her husband to return home so that she could take care of their child. Gao Xinran was torn between missing home and dreading having to go back to get married. However, having been engaged for several months, she felt that the pressure to marry was something she could not escape for much longer. She decided, therefore, to return to the village in the near future. Finally, Chen Ailing dreamed of returning to her home county to set up a tailoring business. However, not only did she lack the necessary capital and skills, Ailing's legal battle with her former employers, who had beaten her severely over several months when she worked for them as a maid, had left her family with huge debts. Furthermore, although she had won the court case, the former employers had migrated overseas and could not be made to pay the compensation that Ailing had been awarded. To return home with neither retribution nor money to repay her debts would be a serious loss of face for Ailing's family. Both she and her sister, therefore, felt compelled to stay in the city to continue to seek justice and to keep working to earn enough to pay back their debts.

27. For a different perspective on the place of the countryside in both dominant discourses and in the narratives of migrant women, see Yan Hairong (2003a). Yan draws on research with women from Anhui who have gone to Beijing to work as maids to argue that "young migrant women's invocations and pursuit of a modern subjectivity, situated in the culture of modernity produced by post-Mao development, has to be understood in the context of a reconfigured rural/urban relationship in China's restructured political economy"

(ibid., 2). This shift in the relationship between rural and urban, she argues, "has robbed the countryside of its ability to be a locus for rural youth to construct a meaningful identity" and amounts to "an epistemic violence against the countryside that spectralizes the rural in both material and symbolic practices" (ibid.). Yan's argument is highly compelling, and in a number of ways is supported by my own research outlined in this chapter. Yet her usage of Gayatri Spivak's phrase "spectralization of the rural" elides some serious issues. First of all, while the countryside is very often dreaded by young migrant women as a "field of death" in the way that Yan suggests, it nevertheless has an important place, both in dominant discourses on modernity and development and in migrant narratives as the site of the past, of childhood and of old(er) age. Second, while she does give them some attention, I believe that Yan underestimates the significance of discourses relating to gender and marriage for migrant women and men's different experiences and understandings of the rural and the urban. Finally, there is the question of when the "spectralization" of the rural began—Yan identifies it with a radical shift in rural/urban relations in the post-Mao period. My own argument emphasizes greater continuities between post-Mao, Maoist, and, indeed, pre-Maoist discourses on rural/urban relations than this would suggest.

Notes to Chapter 5

1. Not all households, of course, are comprised solely of members of a single family. For the purposes of this discussion, however, the distinction between "family" and "household" is not important.

2. For other examples of the filial daughter model, see Woon (2000, 146), Salaff (1981), and Tilly and Scott (1978).

3. For other examples of the rebellious daughter model, see Wolf, Diane (1992), Woon (2000, 147), and Zhang, Heather Xiaoquan (1999).

4. Lydia Kung's description of filial daughters and Ching Kwan Lee's description of rebellious daughters are at opposite ends of a spectrum of writing on young women's labor migration. For studies arguing that such migration is shaped by *both* rebelliousness *and* filial obligation see Woon (2000) and Mills (2002, 11 and 74–91). My own study shares some similarities with these latter works.

5. Respondents could list more than one decision maker. The percentages indicated in the chart therefore add up to more than 100.

6. Ministry of Agriculture household survey data for Sichuan and Anhui provinces indicate that in 1995 most male out-migrants were married (56.3 percent in Sichuan and 51.1 percent in Anhui), but only 31.7 percent of Sichuan and 37.5 percent of Anhui women migrants were married (Du 2000, 77). Migration patterns vary considerably from one area to the next however. In some areas the out-migration of married women has been accepted for many years, but the migration of unmarried women is still frowned upon. In other areas the reverse is the case. See, for example, Lou et al. (2004) for a discussion of contrasting patterns in four counties in Anhui and Sichuan.

7. Using data from a 1988 migration survey in Hubei province, Yang and Guo found that formal education had no significant impact on rural men's out-migration, but that an above-average level of education greatly increased the likelihood of women participating in migration. The highest probability of migration was found among women with 7.7 years of formal education, that is, incomplete junior secondary school. However, among those with senior secondary school education migration was less likely. Yang and Guo suggest that this may be because, while a few more years of education make little difference to the employment opportunities of rural migrants in the city, better-educated women have a much improved chance of obtaining employment in local township and village industries (Yang and Guo 1999, 937–38).

8. In responding to my questionnaire, 20 percent of members of the Migrant Women's Club said that they had not returned home in the previous twelve months; 61 percent indicated that they had returned once; and 19 percent claimed they had returned twice or more (N = 94).

9. In her study of young unmarried rural migrant women in Tianjin, Heather Zhang found considerable variation in the use to which parents put remittances from their migrant daughters. Some used the money to pay for daily necessities and agricultural inputs, others put the money aside for their daughters to use later (Zhang, Heather Xiaoquan 1999, 37). I did not ask my interlocutors detailed questions about the ways in which their remittances were used. However, they gave the impression that the money they sent home was for their parents' own use. This was in contrast to the remittances of married migrants, which were more commonly used by parents to support the migrants' children, or put aside to build a new house for the migrants.

10. A similar point is made by Tan Lin and Susan Short in relation to rural women marrying into Zhangjiagang, a Special Economic Zone in Jiangsu (Tan and Short 2004, 162–64).

11. For exceptions relating to China, see Murphy (2004), Lou et al. (2004), and Zhang, Li (2001).

12. Important exceptions are Zhang, Li (2001), Tan and Short (2004), Murphy (2004), and Lou et al. (2004).

13. In her study of migrants in Zhejiangcun, Zhang Li noted a different problem. She observed that among the wealthiest households, the wives of migrant entrepreneurs did not have jobs, not because they could not find work or because they could not afford childcare, but because their husbands kept them confined to the domestic sphere in a bid to control them and as a way of demonstrating their wealth and status. As one woman explained, "We cannot do anything outside. We would like to do some business, but our husbands [*laogong*] would not allow that. Many people envy us for our comfortable lives, but they do not know that we are really no different from captives. Staying at home is like staying in prison, because you cannot do anything but housework" (Zhang, Li 2001, 124).

14. *Laoxiang* may or may not be related by blood or kinship ties. The term refers most commonly to people from the same village or county, but in some contexts includes those from the same province. For a discussion of the flexibility and instability of *laoxiang* and related terms, see Lee (1998, 84) and Zhang, Li (2001, 55–56).

15. These findings are similar to those obtained by other researchers. For example, according to a survey of migrants from Sichuan and Anhui conducted by the Ministry of Agriculture in 1995, 53.6 percent of female migrants (N = 28), and 51.5 percent of male migrants (N = 140) found their jobs with the help of family members, other relatives, or fellow villagers. Another 10.7 percent of the women and 3.6 percent of the men were directly recruited by employers or rural labor recruitment agencies. Interestingly, only 17.9 percent of female migrants, as compared to 33.6 percent of the men, found their jobs on their own, suggesting that prior information and contacts were more important to women than to men (Fan 2004, 191–92; see also Rozelle et al. 1999, 373; Woon 2000, 153; Scharping 1999, 88–91; Scharping and Sun 1997, 53).

16. Similarly, a large-scale survey of migrants to Shenzhen and Foshan conducted in 1993 found that roughly half of the migrants to each city had relatives and/or good friends living there before they moved (see Scharping and Sun 1997, 50).

17. Another study found that less than 10 percent of migrants to Chinese cities could not find work within one week of arriving (Solinger 1999, 201).

18. Here, the term *laoxiang* includes all those from the same province, rather than just those from the same village or county.

19. More than one response to this question was possible. The figures therefore add up to more than 100 percent.

20. For another example of a survey reporting higher rates of interaction with urbanites and lower rates of interaction with migrants from other provinces, see Scharping and Sun (1997). These authors report that in a 1993 survey of 1,732 migrants in Shenzhen, only 19.5 percent of respondents claim to have spent their leisure time mainly with migrants who were not from their own home province. This was considerably less than the proportion who said their main leisure-time partners were *laoxiang* (55.4 percent), and less, even, than the proportion who indicated locals as being their main leisure-time partners (25.1 percent) (Scharping and Sun 1997, 69).

21. Goodman mentions a Develop Wenzhou Friendly Association and a Develop Fujian Friendly Association in Shanghai (Goodman 1995, 306), and Zhang Li mentions a Ruian Merchant Chamber in Beijing (Zhang, Li 2001, 94).

22. The settlement included 56,000 Wenzhou migrant residents, 40,000 migrants from other provinces, and 14,000 local Beijing residents (Zhang, Li 2001, 19).

Notes to Chapter 6

1. As indicated in the introduction, this volume discusses the experiences of only Han rural migrant women and does not examine the impact of Han/non-Han ethnicity on migrant experiences. See introduction, note 11.

2. *Jiaozi*, because they are roughly round in shape, are a symbol of (re)union and community. Apart from being standard fare at New Year, therefore, parties involving the shared making, as well as eating, of *jiaozi* are a common form of socializing.

3. For an excellent book-length treatment of these important questions, see Sargeson (1999).

4. Sally Sargeson documents one instance in which this happened in a joint-venture factory in Hangzhou in late 1992 (see Sargeson 2001).

5. The question posed was: "*Dagongmei zai chengli de shihou, youshi bu neng shixian tamen de xiwang huo mianlin hen duo kunnan zui zhuyao de yuanyin hezai?*"

6. Lu Xun noted that in 1930s Shanghai *laoshi* was similarly used as a synonym for uselessness (quoted in Yan, Yunxiang 2003, 78).

Notes to Chapter 7

1. Occasionally, though, women explicitly *denied* that their aim in migrating was to make money (see, for example, Cui Jing 1993, 34).

2. For critiques, similar to this, of generalized, dichotomized understandings of gendered narrative forms in non-Chinese contexts, see Bucholtz, Liang, and Sutton (1999).

3. For descriptions of "speaking bitterness" sessions, see Hinton (1966).

4. In fact, the consciousness-raising efforts of Western feminist and other social movements of the 1960s and 1970s were very much inspired by Chinese "speaking bitterness" (Rofel 1999, 295 n. 9).

5. This issue is further explored in Jacka (1998).

6. For documentation and discussion of both strikes and litigation cases on the part of migrant workers, see Chan (2001).

Glossary

anquan	安全	safe
bang	帮	clique; gang
baozheng fei	保证费	pledge fee
Beijing ren	北京人	Beijing person
bendi ren	本地人	local person
bentou	奔头	prospects
boxue	剥削	to exploit
bu ai mianzi	不爱面子	to not care about face, i.e. unconcerned that one's behavior might damage one's moral reputation
bu limao	不礼貌	impolite
bu manyi	不满意	dissatisfied
bu neng jianghua	不能讲话	does not know how to talk
bu ru bieren qiang	不如别人强	not as capable/strong as others
bu shi nongcun ren, ye bu shi chengli ren	不是农村人，也不是城里人	neither a rural person, nor an urbanite
bu wenming	不文明	uncivilized
chabuduo	差不多	more or less; much the same
chenggong zhe	成功者	successful person; success story
chengli ren	城里人	urbanite
chengshi jumin	城市居民	urban resident
chengzhen jumin zui di shenghuo baozhang biaozhun	城镇居民最低生活保障标准	minimum guaranteed cost of living for urbanites

chi ku	吃苦	to eat bitterness; endure hardship and suffering
chi ku shi fu	吃苦是福	eating bitterness is a blessing
chuang chulai	闯出来	to carve out a path; blaze a trail
chuantong	传统	tradition
chuanxialai	传下来	to pass on to the future
chulai dagong shi bu shi yi tiao chulu?	出来打工是不是一条出路？	Is coming out to work the way to find a (new) life?
chulai wanr	出来玩儿	to come out and have a good time
chulu	出路	a way out; a way to find a (new) life
cu de	粗的	crude
cushou cujiao	粗手粗脚	rough hands and feet
dagong	打工	to work as a waged laborer
Dagongmei zhi Jia	打工妹之家	Migrant Women's Club (literally Home for Working Sisters)
Dagongmei	打工妹	*Working Sister*
dagongmei	打工妹	working sister; (unmarried) migrant woman working as a waged laborer
dagongsao	打工嫂	working wife; married migrant woman working as a waged laborer
dagongzai	打工仔	working son; migrant man working as a waged laborer
danchun	单纯	pure
dang ge xiao laoban	当个小老板	to be a little boss
danwei	单位	work unit
duanlian yixia ziji de duli shenghuo nengli	锻炼一下自己的独立生活能力	to exercise independence
feishui wailiu	废水外流	fertilized water (that will) run into someone else's garden; a daughter

fengjian	封建	feudal
fuwu dagongzhe, tuijin chengshihua	服务打工者，推进城市化	to serve migrant workers, and further urbanization
gaibian ziji de mingyun	改变自己的命运	to change one's fate
gao hao renji guanxi	搞好人际关系	to cultivate good interpersonal relations
gongren jieji	工人阶级	working class
guangzong yaozu	光宗耀祖	to bring honor to the ancestors
guanli renyuan	管理人员	managers
guanxi	关系	personal connections
guo hao rizi	过好日子	to live well
guojia	国家	state, nation
guomin xing	国民性	national character
guxiang	故乡	home village; native land
guxiang muqin	故乡母亲	motherland
hai suan manyi	还算满意	(it still counts as) satisfactory
hefa quanyi	合法权益	lawful rights and interests
hei hukou	黑户口	"black householder," i.e., a person without household registration
hen cha	很差	lacking
hen manyi	很满意	very satisfactory
huang tudi	黄土地	yellow earth
huiguan	会馆	Native-place association
hukou	户口	household registration
hunyu zheng	婚育证	marriage and reproduction permit
jia	家	family; home
jiao'ao	骄傲	arrogant
jiaozi	饺子	dumpling
jiating fuwuyuan zheng	家庭服务员证	domestic service permit
jiaxiang luohou, jiali qiong	家乡落后，家里穷	the home county is backward and the family is poor

jiechu wailai wugong qingnian	杰出外来务工青年	outstanding migrant worker youth
jiedu fei	借读费	temporary schooling fee
jieji	阶级	class
jinbu	进步	advanced
jingguo molian	经过磨练	to be put through the mill; to be tempered
jingshen de ji'e	精神的饥饿	spiritual hunger
jingshen wenming	精神文明	spiritual civilization
juede hen zibei	觉得很自卑	to feel inferior
kechixu fazhan	可持续发展	sustainable development
kong gua	空挂	"empty register"; i.e., a person who is formally registered as residing in a particular place, but who does not enjoy the rights to which her registration legally entitles her
kuaibanr	快板儿	traditional form of rhyming verse, accompanied by sticks beaten rhythmically
laoban	老板	bosses
laodong	劳动	labor
laogong	老公	husband
laojia	老家	home
laoli	老力	those who use their muscles; the ruled
laoshi	老实	honest and simple
laoshi	老师	teacher; a polite form of address to an educated superior
laoxiang	老乡	person from the same native village, county, or, less often, province
laoxin	老心	those who use their minds/hearts; rulers
lengmo	冷漠	cold (hearted)

li tu bu li xiang, jin chang bu jin cheng	离土不离乡，进厂不进城	leave the land but not the village, enter factories but not towns and cities
li tu you li xiang, jin chang you jin cheng	离土又离乡，进厂又进城	leave the land and the village, enter factories and towns and cities
liangchong xing	两重性	dual nature
lienü	列女	female martyr; a woman who would rather die than have her virtue compromised
limao	礼貌	good manners, politeness
liqi	力气	physical strength
liu	流	to flow, float, drift
liudong renkou	流动人口	floating population
liulian	留恋	nostalgia
liuluo	流落	to wander about destitute
liumang	流氓	hooligan
liumin	流民	wanderer; refugee
luan	乱	chaotic; unsafe
luohou	落后	backward
mangliu	盲流	blind drifters; blind flow
manman ao	慢慢熬	to endure bit by bit
mei	妹	younger sister; girl
mei banfa	没办法	no choice; nothing to be done
mei huatou	没花头	to have no prospects; will not amount to anything
mei shi gan	没事干	to have nothing to do
mei you quanli	没有权利	to have no power/rights
mei you wenhua	没有文化	uneducated; illiterate; lacking culture
men dang hu dui	门当户对	the doorways are well matched; matching bride and groom in terms of socioeconomic status
min	民	the people
mingong chao	民工潮	tide of peasant workers
minzu	民族	race

mixin	迷信	superstition
mu	亩	unit of measurement. One *mu* = 0.0667 hectares
nan zhu wai, nü zhu nei	男主外女主内	men rule outside, women rule inside
naoshi	闹事	to cause trouble
neng jianghua	能讲话	to know how to talk
nongcun ren	农村人	rural person
nongfu	农夫	farmer
Nongjianü Baishitong	农家女百事通	*Rural Women Knowing All*
nongmin yishi	农民意识	peasant consciousness
nongmin	农民	peasant
Paichusuo Wailai Renkou Guanli Bu	派出所外来人口管理部	Local Police Department for Managing the Outsider Population
pingfang	平房	single-storied buildings
piqi bu hao	脾气不好	bad-tempered
qianyi renkou	迁移人口	official or permanent migrants
qiaobuqi ziji	瞧不起自己	to look down on oneself
ren fanzi	人贩子	human peddler
renge	人格	human dignity
renkou	人口	population
renkou suzhi	人口素质	the quality of the population
renquan	人权	human rights
renzhong	人种	a people
reqing	热情	warm (hearted)
ruguo keneng ni xiang zai Beijing changqi shenghuo xiaqu ma?	如果可能你想在北京长期生活下去吗？	If it is possible, do you think you will live long term in Beijing?
ruoshi qunti	弱势群体	vulnerable group
san da chabie	三大差别	the three great differences: inequalities between city and countryside, mental and manual labor, and workers and peasants

sanpeinü	三陪女	escort; bar hostess
sanwu renyuan	三无人员	three-without personnel: people without legal documentation, stable employment, and residence
shehui tuanti	社会团体	social organization
shehui xingbie yishi	社会性别意识	gender awareness
shenfen zheng	身份证	identity card
shenghuo tiaojian	生活条件	living conditions
shenghuo yali	生活压力	the pressures of life
shenjing shuairuo	神经衰弱	neurasthenia
shequ fazhan	社区发展	community development
shi	士	scholar-officials
shoudao wenming de xili	受到文明的洗礼	to be baptized in civilization
sixiang guannian	思想观念	ideas and concepts
sixiang suzhi	思想素质	quality of thinking
sizi	四自	the four selfs (self-respect, self-confidence, self-reliance, self-strength)
su ku	诉苦	to speak bitterness
suzhi	素质	(human) quality
tai laoshi	太老实	too honest and simple
tai tu le, zhen bu hao kan	太土了，真不好看！	so rustic, so ugly!
taohao lingdao	讨好领导	to ingratiate oneself with the leadership
tianzhen	天真	innocent
tiaochu nongmen	跳出农门	to escape the countryside
timian	体面	face; dignity; honorable
tinghua	听话	to be obedient
tongxianghui	同乡会	Native-place association
tuqi	土气	rustic air; rusticity
tutou tunao de	土头土脑的	dirt-head, dirt-brain
waichu renyuan liudong jiuye dengji ka	外出人员流动就业登记卡	registration card for personnel leaving the area for work

waidi de dagongmei	外地的打工妹	a migrant woman laborer from outside
waidiren	外地人	outsiders
wailai renkou	外来人口	outsider population
Wailai Renkou Fuwuzhan	外来人口服务站	Office of Services for the Outsider Population
wailai renyuan jiuye zheng	外来人员就业证	work permit for personnel coming from outside
wailaigong	外来工	outsider workers; migrant waged laborer
wailaimei	外来妹	(younger) sisters from outside; migrant woman.
waishengmei	外省妹	girl from another province
wan(r)	玩（儿）	to have a good time; have fun; play
weihu women de quanyi	维护我们的权益	defend our rights
weile ziji de jiaoyu	为了自己的教育	for one's education
wen	文	script; written language; literary; refined
wenhua	文化	education and culture
wenhua shuiping	文化水平	level of culture and education
wenhua suzhi	文化素质	cultural and educational quality
wenming	文明	civilization; civilized; civility
wonang	窝囊	hopelessly stupid and chicken-hearted
wuchan jieji	无产阶级	proletariat
xiagang	下岗	laid off
xiang fazhan ziji	想发展自己	to want to develop oneself
xiang kaikuo yanjie	想开阔眼界	to want to broaden one's horizons
xiangxia mei(zi)	乡下妹（子）	country girl
xiangyin	乡音	home dialect
xiaojie	小姐	miss; (young) lady

xiaojing	孝敬	to show filial piety; to respect one's ancestors (also *xiaoshun*)
xiaokang	小康	comfortable living
xiaokang lou	小康楼	a comfortable, multistoried house
xiaoshun	孝顺	to show filial piety
xinku	辛苦	bitterness; hardship; suffering; tough
xinli hua	心里话	talk about personal matters
xinli suzhi	心理素质	psychological quality
yi ban	一般	so-so; ordinary
yi wu suo you	一无所有	destitute
you zibei gan	有自卑感	to have a sense of inferiority
yu shijie jiegui	与世界接轨	to join tracks with the world order
yuan	元	the Chinese monetary unit (also Renminbi)
zai	仔	son
zanzhu fei	赞助费	donation fee
zanzhu zheng	暂住证	temporary residence permit
zhao	找	to search for
zhishuai	直率	frank; candid
zhiye	职业	occupation
zhong nan qing nü	重男轻女	to accord importance to/care about males and neglect females
Zhongguo Funü	中国妇女	*Chinese Women*
zibei gan	自卑感	sense of inferiority
zili	自立	self-reliance
ziqiang	自强	self-strength
ziwo fazhan	自我发展	self-development
ziwo fuquan	自我赋权	self-empowerment
zixin	自信	self-confidence
zizun	自尊	self-respect
zou yitian, suan yitian	走一天，算一天	to live one day at a time

Bibliography

"1800 ming funü zai chongwenmen 'laowu shichang' bei guaimai" (1800 Women Were Kidnapped and Sold at a "Labour Market" in Chongwenmen). 1993. *Baokan wenzhai* (News Digest) 745 (August): 23.

Abu-Lughod, Lila. 1991. "Writing Against Culture." In *Recapturing Anthropology: Working in the Present*, ed. Richard G. Fox, 137–62. Santa Fe, NM: School of American Research Press.

Anagnost, Ann. 1997. *National Past-Times: Narrative, Representation, and Power in Modern China*. Durham, NC: Duke University Press.

Anderson, Bridget. 2000. *Doing the Dirty Work? The Global Politics of Domestic Labour*. London: ZED Books.

Andors, Phyllis. 1983. *The Unfinished Liberation of Chinese Women, 1949–1980*. Bloomington: Indiana University Press.

Anon. (Anonymous). 1993. "Chu jin wuchang" (Entering the Dance Hall for the First Time). *Nongjianü baishitong* (Rural Women Knowing All) May: 5.

Appadurai, Arjun. 1996. *Modernity at Large: Cultural Dimensions of Globalization*. Minneapolis: University of Minnesota Press.

Bai Mu. 1994. "Wo de gen zai xiangcun" (My Roots Are in the Countryside). *Nongjianü baishitong* (Rural Women Knowing All) February: 26–27.

Bakken, Børge. 2000. *The Exemplary Society: Human Improvement, Social Control, and the Dangers of Modernity in China*. Oxford: Oxford University Press.

Bammer, Angelika. 1994. "Introduction." In *Displacements: Cultural Identities in Question*, ed. Angelika Bammer, xi–xx. Bloomington: Indiana University Press.

Barmé, Geremie. 1996. *Shades of Mao: The Posthumous Cult of the Great Leader*. Armonk, NY: M.E. Sharpe.

———. 1999. *In the Red: On Contemporary Chinese Culture*. New York: Columbia University Press.

"Beijing qunian wailairenkou yu 386wan ren" (Last year, Beijing's Outsider Population Exceeded 3.86 million). 2003. Zhongguo xinwen wang (China News Net). www.cpirc.org.cn. 21 January.

Beijingshi Gong'an Ju (Beijing Public Security Bureau). 1995. "Beijingshi waidi laijing renyuan huji guanli guiding" (Regulations on the Management of Household Registration of Outsiders Entering Beijing). Accessed at the Beijing Public Security Bureau website, www.bjgaj.gov.cn.

Beijingshi Tongjiju (Beijing Municipal Statistical Bureau). 2001. *Beijing tongji nianjian 2001* (Beijing Statistical Yearbook 2001). Beijing: Zhongguo tongji chubanshe.

———. 2002. *Beijing tongji nianjian 2002* (Beijing Statistical Yearbook 2002). Beijing: Zhongguo tongji chubanshe.

Bertaux-Wiame, Isabelle. 1981. "The Life History Approach to the Study of Internal Migration." In *Biography and Society: The Life History Approach in the Social Sciences*, ed. Daniel Bertaux, 249–66. Beverly Hills, CA: Sage Publications.

Beynon, Louise. 2004. "Dilemmas of the Heart: Rural Working Women and Their Hopes for the Future." In *On the Move: Women and Rural-to-Urban Migration in Contemporary China*, ed. Arianne Gaetano and Tamara Jacka, 131–50. New York: Columbia University Press.

Bianco, Lucien. 1971. *Origins of the Chinese Revolution, 1915–1949*. Stanford, CA: Stanford University Press.

"Bianzhe de hua" (Editor's note). 1993. *Nongjianü baishitong* (Rural Women Knowing All) April: 5.

Bossen, Laurel. 2002. *Chinese Women and Rural Development: Sixty Years of Change in Lu Village, Yunnan*. Lanham, MD: Rowman and Littlefield.

Brettell, Caroline. 2000. "Theorizing Migration in Anthropology: The Social Construction of Networks, Identities, Communities, and Globalscapes." In *Migration Theory: Talking Across Disciplines*, ed. Caroline B. Brettell and James F. Hollifield, 97–135. New York: Routledge.

Brownell, Susan. 1995. *Training the Body for China: Sports in the Moral Order of the People's Republic*. Chicago: University of Chicago Press.

Bruner, Edward. 1986. "Experience and Its Expressions." In *The Anthropology of Experience*, ed. Victor Turner and Edward M. Bruner, 3–32. Urbana: University of Illinois Press.

Bucholtz, Mary; Liang, A.C.; and Sutton, Laurel A. 1999. *Reinventing Identities: The Gendered Self in Discourse*. New York: Oxford University Press.

Buijs, Gina. 1993. "Introduction." In *Migrant Women: Crossing Boundaries and Changing Identities*, ed. Gina Buijs, 1–20. Oxford: Berg.

Butler, Judith. 1993. *Bodies That Matter: On the Discursive Limits of "Sex."* New York: Routledge.

Cai, Fang. 1998. "Economic Reasons for Migration, the Organization of the Labor Force and the Selection of Jobs." *Social Sciences in China* 19, no. 1 (Spring): 77–84.

Cai Peng. 1994. "Qingchun wu hui" (Being Young Without Regrets). *Nongjianü baishitong* (Rural Women Knowing All) January: 26–27.

Cai, Qian. 2003. "Migrant Remittances and Family Ties: A Case Study in China." *International Journal of Population Geography* 9: 471–83.

Calhoun, Craig. 1994. "Social Theory and the Politics of Identity." In *Social Theory and the Politics of Identity*, ed. Craig Calhoun, 9–36. Oxford: Blackwell.

Cao Ziwei. 2001. "Zhiye huode yu guanxi jiegou—guanyu nongmingong shehui wang de ji ge wenti" (Job Attainment and the Structure of Relationships—Some Questions Concerning Social Networking of Peasant Workers). In *Dushi li de cunmin—Zhongguo da chengshi de liudong renkou* (Villagers in the City—Rural Migrants in Chinese Metropolises), ed. He Lanjun (Bettina Gransow) and Li Hanlin, 71–94. Beijing: Zhongyang bianyi chubanshe.

CDCRW (Cultural Development Center for Rural Women). 2001. Publicity leaflet.

———. 2002. *Dagongmei zhi jia weiquan xiaozu gongzuo jianbao* (Newsletter of the Migrant Rights Group, Migrant Women's Club), 7 September.

Chan, Anita. 2001. *China's Workers Under Assault: The Exploitation of Labor in a Globalizing Economy*. Armonk, NY: M.E. Sharpe.

Chan, Kam Wing. 1999. "Internal Migration in China: A Dualistic Approach." In *Internal and International Migration: Chinese Perspectives*, ed. Frank N. Pieke and Hein Mallee, 49–71. Richmond, Surrey: Curzon Press.

Chant, Sylvia, and Radcliffe, Sarah A. 1992. "Migration and Development: The Importance of Gender." In *Gender and Migration in Developing Countries*, ed. Sylvia Chant, 1–29. London: Belhaven Press.

Chen Aizhen. 1994. "Gebuduan de xiangqing" (Feelings for my Village that Cannot be Severed). *Nongjianü baishitong* (Rural Women Knowing All) May: 17.

Chen Yutao. 1995. "Shanghai youge 'dagongzhe duzhe zhi jia'" (Shanghai has a Migrant Workers' Reading Club). *Nongjianü baishitong* (Rural Women Knowing All) 4:12.

Cheng Jianwei. 2002a. "Nongmin jincheng you duo nan" (Rural People Entering the City Have so Many Difficulties). *Dagongmei* (Working Sister) April–May: 10–13.

———. 2002b. "Shehui baozhang li ni you duo yuan" (How Far Away are You from Social Insurance?). *Dagongmei* (Working Sister) October–November: 6–10.

———. 2002c. "Tuoqian gongzi nianguan da zhuitao" (The Large Scale Pursuit of Unpaid Wages at the End of the Year). *Dagongmei* (Working Sister) December: 10–15.

"China Facing Severe Shortage of Migrant Workers and Technical Labor." 2004. Interfax. http://www.interfax.com/com?item=China&pg=0&id=5755262&req=. Accessed 30 September.

Chinese Working Women's Network. n.d. Publicity leaflet. Hong Kong.

Chow, Rey. 1991. *Woman and Chinese Modernity: The Politics of Reading Between East and West*. Minneapolis: University of Minnesota Press.

———. 1994. "'Love Me, Master, Love Me Son': A Cultural Other Pornographically Constructed in Time." In *Boundaries in China*, ed. John Hay, 243–56. London: Reaktion Books.

Chunzi. 1998. "Ba lei liu gei ziji" (Keeping My Tears to Myself). *Zhongguo Funü* 5: 26–27.

———. 2001. "Hukou, ni daodi neng jiyu wo shenme?" (What do I Get from the Household Registration System?). Unpublished manuscript.

Ci, Jiwei. 1994. *The Dialectic of the Chinese Revolution: From Utopianism to Hedonism.* Stanford, CA: Stanford University Press.

Cohen, Myron L. 1993. "Cultural and Political Inventions in Modern China: The Case of the Chinese 'Peasant.'" *Daedalus* 122, no. 2: 151–70.

Constable, Nicole. 1997. *Maid to Order in Hong Kong: Stories of Filipina Workers.* Ithaca, NY: Cornell University Press.

Croll, Elisabeth. 1994. *From Heaven to Earth: Images and Experiences of Development in China.* London: Routledge.

Cui Jing. 1993. "Jingcheng dagongnü yi pie" (A Quick Look at the Migrant Women of Beijing). *Nongjianü baishitong* (Rural Women Knowing All) January: 34–36.

"Dagong Yulu" (Migrant Workers on Record). 2002. *Dagongmei* (Working Sister) August–September: 2–3.

Dai, Jinhua. 1997. "Imagined Nostalgia." *Boundary 2*, 24, no. 3: 143–62.

"Dangqian guaimai funü ertong xianxiang yanzhong, yi fa yanli chengchu ke bu rong huan" (Currently, the Kidnapping and Sale of Women and Children is a Serious Phenomenon, and it is Urgent that the Law be Used to Punish the Criminals Strictly). 1991. *Fazhi ribao* (Legal Daily) 23 August.

Davin, Delia. 1997. "Migration, Women and Gender Issues in Contemporary China." In *Floating Population and Migration in China: The Impact of Economic Reforms*, ed. Thomas Scharping, 297–314. Hamburg: Institut für Asienkunde.

"Demand for Wives Fuels Trade in Teenage Girls." 1999. *The Weekend Australian* 13–14 November.

Dikötter, Frank. 1995. *Sex, Culture and Modernity in China: Medical Science and the Construction of Sexual Identities in the Early Republican Period.* London: Hurst and Company.

Dong Wei. 2002. "Chengqu nongye renkou jiang zhi sishiwuwan" (The City's Agricultural Population has Declined to 450,000). *Beijing qingnian bao* (China Youth Daily) 27 November: 1.

Dorfman, Diane. 1996. "The Spirits of Reform: The Power of Belief in Northern China." *positions: east asia cultures critique* 4, no. 2: 253–89.

Du, Ying. 2000. "Rural Labor Migration in Contemporary China: An Analysis of its Features and the Macro Context." In *Rural Labor Flows in China*, ed. Loraine A. West and Zhao Yaohui, 67–100. Berkeley: Institute of East Asian Studies, University of California Press.

Dutton, Michael. 1992. *Policing and Punishment in China: From Patriarchy to "The People."* Cambridge: Cambridge University Press.

Emirbayer, Mustafa, and Mische, Ann. 1998. "What is Agency?" *American Journal of Sociology* 103, no. 4 (January): 962–1023.

Escobar, Arturo. 1991. "Anthropology and the Development Encounter: The Making and Marketing of Development Anthropology." *American Ethnologist* 18 (November): 658–82.

Evans, Harriet. 1997. *Women and Sexuality in China: Dominant Discourses of Female Sexuality and Gender Since 1949*. Cambridge: Polity Press.

Fabian, Johannes. 1983. *Time and the Other: How Anthropology Makes its Object*. New York: Columbia University Press.

Fan, Cindy C. 2004. "Out to the City and Back to the Village: The Experiences and Contributions of Rural Women Migrating from Sichuan and Anhui." In *On the Move: Women and Rural-to-Urban Migration in Contemporary China*, ed. Arianne Gaetano and Tamara Jacka, 177–206. New York: Columbia University Press.

Feng, Xiaoshuang. 1997. "The Costs and Benefits of Rural-Urban Migration: A Report on an Inquiry Conducted among Rural Women Employed in the Service, Retail, and Other Trades in Beijing." *Social Sciences in China* 18, no. 4: 52–65.

Feuerwerker, Yi-tsi Mei. 1998. *Ideology, Power, Text: Self-Representation and the Peasant "Other" in Modern Chinese Literature*. Stanford, CA: Stanford University Press.

Fitzgerald, John. 1996. *Awakening China: Politics, Culture, and Class in the Nationalist Revolution*. Stanford, CA: Stanford University Press.

Foucault, Michel. 1977 [1975]. *Discipline and Punish: The Birth of the Prison*, trans. Alan Sheridan. London: Allen Lane.

Fraser, Nancy. 1999 [1992]. "Rethinking the Public Sphere: A Contribution to the Critique of Actually Existing Democracy." In *Habermas and the Public Sphere*, ed. Craig Calhoun, 109–42. Cambridge, MA: The MIT Press.

Friedman, Sara L. 2002. "Civilizing the Masses: The Productive Power of Cultural Reform Efforts in Late Republican-Era Fujian." In *Defining Modernity: Guomindang Rhetorics of a New China, 1920–1970*, ed. Terry Bodenhorn, 151–94. Ann Arbor: Center for Chinese Studies, The University of Michigan.

Gaetano, Arianne. 2004. "Filial Daughters, Modern Women: Migrant Domestic Workers in Post-Mao Beijing." In *On the Move: Women and Rural-to-Urban Migration in Contemporary China*, ed. Arianne Gaetano and Tamara Jacka, 41–79. New York: Columbia University Press.

Gao, Mobo C.F. 1999. *Gao Village: A Portrait of Rural Life in Modern China*. London: Hurst and Company.

Geertz, Clifford. 2000. *Available Light: Anthropological Reflections on Philosophical Topics*. Princeton, NJ: Princeton University Press.

Giddens, Anthony. 1991. *Modernity and Self-Identity: Self and Society in the Late Modern Age*. Cambridge: Polity Press.

Gluck, Sherna Berger, and Patai, Daphne, eds. 1991. *Women's Words: The Feminist Practice of Oral History*. New York: Routledge.

Goldstein, Alice, and Goldstein, Sidney. 1996. "Migration Motivations and Outcomes: Permanent and Temporary Migrants Compared." In *China: The Many Facets of Demographic Change*, ed. Alice Goldstein and Wang Feng, 187–212. Boulder, CO: Westview Press.

Goldstein, Sidney; Zai, Lian; and Goldstein, Alice. 2000. "Migration, Gender, and Labor Force in Hubei Province, 1985–1990." In *Re-Drawing Boundaries: Work, Households,* and Gender in China, ed. Barbara Entwisle and Gail E. Henderson, 214–30. Berkeley: University of California Press.

Goodman, Bryna. 1995. Native Place, City, and Nation: Regional Networks and Identities in Shanghai, 1853–1937. Berkeley: University of California Press.

"Guniang Tiaohun" (A Girl Escapes Marriage). 2002. Dagongmei (Working Sister) April– May: 29.

Guowuyuan Bangongting (General Office of the State Council). 2003. "Guoban: zuohao nongmin jincheng wugong jiuye guanli he fuwu gongzuo" (General Office of the State Council: Improving Management and Services for Rural Labor Migrants Entering Cities). www.people.com.cn 16 January.

Han Chun. 1993. "Dui xiao baomu zai jing bei da" (On the Beating of a Nanny in Beijing). Nongjianü baishitong (Rural Women Knowing All) April: 9.

———. 1999. "Diedao le, ni hai neng paqilai ma? (Can You Pick Yourself Up After a Fall?). Nongjianü baishitong (Rural Women Knowing All) August: 26–27.

Han Jialing. 2002. "Beijingshi liudong ertong yiwu jiaoyu zhuangkuang diaocha baogao" (A Report on an Investigation into the Situation of Compulsory Education among Children in the Floating Population in Beijing). In Huji zhidu yu nüxing liudong: di er jie quanguo dagongmei quanyi wenti yantaohui lunwenji (The Household Registration System and the Movement of Women: A Collection of Papers from the Second National Forum on the Rights and Interests of Migrant Women Workers), ed. Beijing Nongjianü Wenhua Fazhan Zhongxin (Beijing Rural Women's Cultural Development Center), 267– 78. Guiyang: Guizhou renmin chubanshe.

Hao Jiaozhen. 1990. "Zhongguo nongmin 'suzhi cha' ma?" (Are Chinese Peasants "Low in Quality"?). In Heshang bai miu (One Hundred Errors in Heshang), ed. Li Fengxiang, 48–49. Beijing: Zhongguo wenlian chubanshe.

Hao, Ran. 1984. "The Magic Herb." In Paragons of Virtue in Chinese Short Stories During the Cultural Revolution, ed. Par Bergman, 167–77. Goteborg, Sweden: Skrifter Utgivna av Foreningen for Orientaliska Studier.

Harrell, Stevan. 1995. "Civilizing Projects and the Reaction to Them." In Cultural Encounters on China's Ethnic Frontiers, ed. Stevan Harrell, 3–36. Seattle: University of Washington Press.

Harris, Nigel. 1995. The New Untouchables: Immigration and the New World Worker. London: I.B. Tauris.

Harvey, David. 1990. The Condition of Postmodernity. Cambridge, MA: Blackwell.

Henderson, Gail E. et al. 2000. "Re-Drawing the Boundaries of Work: Views on the Meaning of Work (gongzuo)." In Re-Drawing Boundaries: Work, Households and Gender in China, ed. Barbara Entwisle and Gail E. Henderson, 33–50. Berkeley: University of California Press.

Hickling, F.W. 1991. "Double Jeopardy: Psychopathology of Black Mentally Ill Returned Migrants to Jamaica." International Journal of Social Psychiatry 37, no. 2: 80–89.

Hinton, William. 1966. Fanshen: A Documentary of Revolution in a Chinese Village. New York: Vintage Books.

Honig, Emily. 1992. Creating Chinese Ethnicity: Subei People in Shanghai, 1850–1980. New Haven, CT: Yale University Press.

———. 1996. "Regional Identity, Labor, and Ethnicity in Contemporary China." In Putting Class in its Place: Worker Identities in East Asia, ed. Elizabeth Perry, 225–43. Berkeley: China Research Monograph, Center for Chinese Studies, Institute of East Asian Studies, University of California.

HRIC (Human Rights in China). 1999. Not Welcome at the Party: Behind the "Clean-up" of China's Cities—A Report on Administrative Detention Under "Custody and Repatriation." http://iso.hrichina.org/iso/article.adp?article_id=41&category_id=30.

———. 2002a. Shutting out the Poorest: Discrimination against the Most Disadvantaged

Migrant Children in City Schools. http://iso.hrichina.org/iso/article.adp?article_id =2432&category_id=30.

―――. 2002b. Institutionalized Exclusion: The Tenuous Legal Status of Internal Migrants in China's Major Cities. http://iso.hrichina.org/iso/article.adp?article_id= 3441&category_id=30.

Hsiung, Ping-chun; Jaschok, Maria; and Milwertz, Cecilia, eds. 2001. Chinese Women Organizing: Cadres, Feminists, Muslims, Queers. Oxford: Berg.

Hu, Xiuhong, and Kaplan, David H. 2001. "The Emergence of Affluence in Beijing: Residential Social Stratification in China's Capital City." Urban Geography 22, no. 1: 54–77.

Huang Chenxi. 1995. "Mingong Qianliu Dui Nongcun Renkou Suzhi de Yingxiang ji Duice" (The Impact of the Migration of Peasant Workers on the Quality of the Rural Population, and Policy Measures). Shehui 10: 26–27, 48.

Huang, Zhihua. 2004. "The Law Is By My Side." In On the Move: Women and Rural-to-Urban Migration in Contemporary China, ed. Arianne Gaetano and Tamara Jacka, 287–89. New York: Columbia University Press.

Iredale, Robyn et al. 2001. Contemporary Minority Migration, Education and Ethnicity in China. Cheltenham, UK: Edward Elgar.

Jacka, Tamara. 1990. "Back to the Wok: Women and Employment in Chinese Industry in the 1980s." Australian Journal of Chinese Affairs 24 (July): 1–23.

―――. 1997. Women's Work in Rural China: Change and Continuity in an Era of Reform. Cambridge: Cambridge University Press.

―――. 1998. "Working Sisters Answer Back: The Representation and Self-Representation of Women in China's Floating Population." China Information 13, no. 1: 43–75.

―――. 2000a. "Other China/China's Others: A Report on the First National Forum on the Protection of Migrant Women Workers, Beijing." New Formations 40 (Spring): 128–37.

―――. 2000b. "On the Move: The Life Stories of Rural Migrant Women in Contemporary China." Intersections: Gender, History and Culture in the Asian Context, no. 4. http:// wwwsshe.murdoch.edu.au/as/intersections/, accessed September 2000.

―――. 2004. "Migrant Women's Stories." In On the Move: Women and Rural-to-Urban Migration in Contemporary China, ed. Arianne Gaetano and Tamara Jacka, 279–85. New York: Columbia University Press.

―――. 2006. "Approaches to Women and Development in Rural China." Journal of Contemporary China, forthcoming.

Jacka, Tamara, and Gaetano, Arianne. 2004. "Introduction: Focusing on Migrant Women." In On the Move: Women and Rural-to-Urban Migration in Contemporary China, ed. Arianne Gaetano and Tamara Jacka, 1–38. New York: Columbia University Press.

"Jia gei chengli ren haishi xiangxia ren" (Should One Marry an Urbanite or a Rural Person?). 2003. Dagongmei (Working Sister) October: 34–37.

Jiang, Wenran. 2004. "Unimaginable Poverty, Unbelievable Tragedy." South China Morning Post 14 February.

Jingjing. 1998. "Weile zunyan" (For My Dignity). Nongjianü baishitong February: 36–37.

Johnson, Kay Ann. 1983. Women, the Family and Peasant Revolution in China. Chicago: University of Chicago Press.

Judd, Ellen. 1992. "Land Divided, Land United." China Quarterly 130 (June): 338–56.

―――. 2002. The Chinese Women's Movement Between State and Market. Stanford, CA: Stanford University Press.

Kearney, Robert N., and Miller, Barbara Diane. 1987. Internal Migration in Sri Lanka and its Social Consequences. Boulder, CO: Westview.

Keith, Ronald. 1997. "Legislating Women's and Children's 'Rights and Interests' in the PRC." China Quarterly 149: 29–55.

Kelliher, Daniel. 1994. "Chinese Communist Political Theory and the Rediscovery of the Peasantry." Modern China 20, no. 4 (October): 387–415.

Kenyon, Gary M. 1996. "The Meaning/Value of Personal Storytelling." In *Aging and Biography: Explorations in Adult Development*, ed. Gary M. Kenyon and Jan-Erik Ruth, 21–38. New York: Springer.

Kerkvliet, Benedict J. Tria. 1990. *Everyday Politics in the Philippines: Class and Status Relations in a Central Luzon Village*. Berkeley: University of California Press.

Khan, Azizur, and Riskin, Carl. 1998. "Income and Inequality in China: Composition, Distribution and Growth of Household Income, 1988 to 1995." *China Quarterly* 154: 221–53.

———. 2005. "China's Household Income and its Distribution, 1995 and 2002." *China Quarterly* 182: 356–84.

Kipnis, Andrew. 1995. "Within and Against Peasantness: Backwardness and Filiality in Rural China." *Comparative Studies in Society and History* 37: 110–35.

———. 2001. "The Disturbing Educational Discipline of 'Peasants.'" *China Journal* 46: 1–24.

———. 2002. "Zouping Christianity as Gendered Critique? An Ethnography of Political Potentials." *Anthropology and Humanism* 27, no. 1: 80–96.

Knight, John, and Song, Lina. 1999. *The Rural-Urban Divide: Economic Disparities and Interactions in China*. Oxford: Oxford University Press.

"Kua shiji nongcun funü gongzuo de liu da renwu" (The Six Major Tasks for Work with Rural Women in the Transition to the New Century). 1999. *Nongjianü baishitong* (Rural Women Knowing All) July: 1.

Kung, Lydia. 1983 [1978]. *Factory Women in Taiwan*. Ann Arbor: University of Michigan Press.

Kwan, Daniel. 2003. "Powers of Police to Detain Migrants Will Be Scrapped." *South China Morning Post* 19 June.

Labour Law of the People's Republic of China (Chinese-English version). 2002. Beijing: Law Press.

Lague, David. 2003. "The Human Tide Sweeps into Cities." *Far Eastern Economic Review* January 9: 24–26.

Lawson, Victoria A. 2000. "Arguments Within Geographies of Movement: The Theoretical Potential of Migrants' Stories." *Progress in Human Geography* 24, no. 2: 173–89.

Lee, Ching Kwan. 1998. *Gender and the South China Miracle: Two Worlds of Factory Women*. Berkeley: University of California Press.

Lee, Sing. 1999. "Diagnosis Postponed: Shenjing Shuairuo and the Transformation of Psychiatry in Post-Mao China." *Culture, Medicine and Psychiatry* 23: 349–80.

Lee, Sing, and Kleinman, Arthur. 2000. "Suicide as Resistance in Chinese Society." In *Chinese Society: Change, Conflict and Resistance*, ed. Elizabeth Perry and Mark Selden, 221–40. London: Routledge.

Lei, Guang. 2001. "Reconstituting the Rural-Urban Divide: Peasant Migration and the Rise of 'Orderly Migration' in Contemporary China." *Journal of Contemporary China* 10, no. 28: 471–93.

———. 2003. "Rural Taste, Urban Fashions: The Cultural Politics of Rural/Urban Difference in Contemporary China." *positions: east asia cultures critique* 11, no. 3: 613–46.

Li Dazhao. 1984 [1919]. "Qingnian yu nongcun" (Youth and the Countryside). In *Li Dazhao wenji* (The Collected Works of Li Dazhao), 648–52. Beijing: Renmin chubanshe.

Li Debin. 1993. "Liudong renkou yu shehui wending" (The Floating Population and Social Stability). *Shehui* 8: 42–43.

Li, Jianying. 2004. "Working for Myself." In *On the Move: Women and Rural-to-Urban Migration in Contemporary China*, ed. Arianne Gaetano and Tamara Jacka, 304–7. New York: Columbia University Press.

Li Tao. 1999a. "Lun dagongmei zhi jia de renwu ji qiantu" (A Discussion of the Mission and Prospects of the Migrant Women's Club). In *Shoujie quanguo dagongmei quanyi wenti yantaohui, lunwenji* (The Collected Works of the First National Forum on the Rights of Migrant Women Workers), ed. Rural Women Knowing All Collective, 73–78. Beijing.

———. 1999b. "Kuayue yu fenlie: eryuan jiegou zhong de chengxian lianyin—dui bai ming 'wai jia jing' de diaocha fenxi baogao" (Surmounting and Splitting: Marriage of the Town and Country in a Binary Structure—A Report on the Analysis of a Survey of One Hundred Rural Migrant Women who Married Beijingers). In *Huji zhidu yu nüxing liudong: di er jie quanguo dagongmei quanyi wenti yantaohui lunwenji* (The Household Registration System and the Movement of Women: A Collection of Papers from the Second National Forum on the Rights and Interests of Migrant Women Workers), ed. Beijing Nongjianü Wenhua Fazhan Zhongxin (Beijing Rural Women's Cultural Development Center), 119–39. Guiyang: Guizhou renmin chubanshe.

———. 2001. "Ta weishenme ai da?" (Why Did She Endure the Beatings?). *Dagongmei* (Working Sister). Inaugural Issue: 40–42.

———. 2001b. "Dou shi hukou re de huo" (They're All Disasters Caused by Household Registration). *Dagongmei* (Working Sister). Inaugural Issue: 6–11.

———. 2002. "2002 Dagong da pandian" (Taking Stock of Issues Facing Migrant Workers in 2002). *Dagongmei* (Working Sister) December: 4–8.

Li Zhen. 2002a. "Yuan jia—ni zai ta xiang hai hao ma?" (Those Who've Married Far Away—Are You Still Okay in That Other Place?). *Dagongmei* (Working Sister) October–November: 15–25.

———. 2002b. "Huixiang: Jiaxiang de yun shifou yijiu?" (Going Back to the Countryside: Are the Clouds at Home Still the Same as Before?). *Dagongmei* (Working Sister) December: 18–24.

———. 2002c. "Zanzhuzheng: Wu yuan gongben fei de beihou" (The Temporary Residence Permit: Behind the Five Yuan Administration Fee). *Dagongmei* (Working Sister) June–July: 6–9.

———. 2002d. "Liushuixian shang de huayang nianhua" (The Flower of Youth on the Assembly Line). *Dagongmei* (Working Sister) August–September: 16–23.

———. 2002e. "Chuzuwu li de tongju shenghuo" (Cohabitation in a Rented Room). *Dagongmei* (Working Sister) June–July: 18–22.

Linde, Charlotte. 1986. "Private Stories in Public Discourse: Narrative Analysis in the Social Sciences." *Poetics* 15: 183–202.

Liu Ling. 2001. "Chengshi li de cunmin: zhongguo da chengshi nongcun wailai renkou de zhuangkuang he ziwo ganshou" (Villagers in the City—Presentation and Self-Perception of Rural Migrants in Chinese Metropolises). In *Dushi li de cunmin—zhongguo da chengshi de liudong renkou* (Villagers in the City—Rural Migrants in Chinese Metropolises), ed. He Lanjun and Li Hanlin, 95–129. Beijing: Zhongyang bianji chubanshe.

Liu, Lydia. 1995. *Translingual Practice: Literature, National Culture, and Translated Modernity—China, 1900–1937.* Stanford, CA: Stanford University Press.

Liu Xinping. 1997. "Dagong de rensheng ye zhuangli" (Life of the Migrant Worker is Also Glorious). *Zhongguo qingnian* (Chinese Youth) no. 2: 12–16.

Liu Yanling. 1994. "Dangqian wo guo nongye laodongli liudong zhong de shehui wenti ji qi duice" (Social Problems Associated with the Current Movement of Rural Labour, and Countermeasures). *Shehuixue yanjiu* (Sociological Research) no. 2: 76–82.

Lou, Binbin et al. 2004. "The Migration Experiences of Young Women from Four Counties in Sichuan and Anhui." In *On the Move: Women and Rural-to-Urban Migration in Contemporary China*, ed. Arianne Gaetano and Tamara Jacka, 207–42. New York: Columbia University Press.

Louie, Kam. 2002. *Theorising Chinese Masculinity: Society and Gender in China.* Cambridge: Cambridge University Press.

Lyengar, Jayanthi. 2003. "Beijing Unveils Land Reform Policy." *Asia Times Online* www.atimes.com. Accessed 11 March.

Ma, Laurence J.C., and Xiang, Biao, 1998. "Native Place, Migration and the Emergence of Peasant Enclaves in Beijing." *China Quarterly* 155: 546–81.

Ma Xiaoshuang. 1998. "Zhang yangqin qiu xue" (Zhang Yangqin Pursues her Studies). *Nongjianü baishitong* (Rural Women Knowing All) September: 27–28.

McHoul, Alec, and Grace, Wendy. 1993. *A Foucault Primer: Discourse, Power and the Subject*. Melbourne: Melbourne University Press.

McLaren, Peter. 1995. *Critical Pedagogy and Predatory Culture: Oppositional Politics in a Postmodern Era*. London: Routledge.

Mallee, Hein. 1996. "In Defence of Migration: Recent Chinese Studies on Rural Population Mobility." *China Information* 10, nos. 3/4: 108–40.

———. 2000. "Agricultural Labor and Rural Population Mobility: Some Observations." In *Rural Labor Flows in China*, ed. Loraine A. West and Zhao Yaohui, 34–59. Berkeley: Institute of East Asian Studies, University of California Press.

Mei Lin. 1994. "Yongyuan de wairen" (The Eternal Outsider). *Nongjianü baishitong* (Rural Women Knowing All) February: 28.

Mian Xiaohong. 2004. "Burdened Youth." In *On the Move: Women and Rural-to-Urban Migration in Contemporary China*, ed. Arianne Gaetano and Tamara Jacka, 289–93. New York: Columbia University Press.

Mies, Maria. 1982. *The Lace Makers of Narsapur: Indian Housewives Produce for the World Market*. London: Zed Press.

Mills, Mary Beth. 1998. "Gendered Encounters with Modernity: Labor Migrants and Marriage Choices in Contemporary Thailand." *Identities* 5, no. 3: 301–34.

———. 2002. *Thai Women in the Global Labor Force: Consuming Desires, Contested Selves*. New Brunswick, NJ: Rutgers University Press.

Milwertz, Cecilia. 2002. *Beijing Women Organizing for Change: A New Wave of the Chinese Women's Movement*. Copenhagen: NIAS Press.

Moore, Barrington Jr. 1978. *Injustice: The Social Bases of Obedience and Revolt*. White Plains, NY: M.E. Sharpe.

Moore, Henrietta. 1994. *A Passion for Difference: Essays in Anthropology and Gender*. Cambridge: Polity Press.

Murphy, Rachel. 2002. *How Migrant Labor is Changing Rural China*. Cambridge: Cambridge University Press.

———. 2004. "The Impact of Labor Migration on the Well-Being and Agency of Rural Chinese Women: Cultural and Economic Contexts and the Life Course." In *On the Move: Women and Rural-to-Urban Migration in Contemporary China*, ed. Arianne Gaetano and Tamara Jacka, 243–76. New York: Columbia University Press.

Pang, Hui. 2004. "I am a Cloud." In *On the Move: Women and Rural-to-Urban Migration in Contemporary China*, ed. Arianne Gaetano and Tamara Jacka, 294–95. New York: Columbia University Press.

Parpart, Jane L. 1995. "Deconstructing the Development 'Expert': Gender, Development and the 'Vulnerable Groups.'" In *Feminism/Postmodernism/Development*, ed. Marianne H. Marchand and Jane L. Parpart, 221–43. London: Routledge.

Pedraza, Sylvia. 1991. "Women and Migration: The Consequences of Gender." *Annual Review of Sociology* 17: 303–25.

Personal Narratives Group. 1989. "Origins." In *Interpreting Women's Lives: Feminist Theory and Personal Narratives,* ed. Personal Narratives Group, 3–15. Bloomington: Indiana University Press.

Pickering, Michael. 1997. *History, Experience and Cultural Studies*. London: Macmillan.

Poston, Dudley, and Duan, Chengrong Charles. 1999. "The Floating Population in Beijing,

China: New Evidence and Insights from the 1997 Census of Beijing's Floating Population." Austin: Texas Population Research Center Paper.

Pun, Ngai. 1999. "Becoming *Dagongmei* (Working Girls): The Politics of Identity and Difference in Reform China." *The China Journal* 42: 1–20.

———. 2003. "Subsumption or Consumption? The Phantom of Consumer Revolution in 'Globalizing' China." *Cultural Anthropology* 18, no. 4: 469–92.

Ralston, Helen. 1992. "Religion in the Life of South Asian Immigrant Women in Atlantic Canada." *Research in the Social Scientific Study of Religion* 4: 245–60.

"Return of a Medieval Evil." 1991. *Time* 11 November.

Ricoeur, Paul. 1984–1988. *Time and Narrative*, vols. 1–3, trans. Kathleen McLaughlin and David Pellauer. Chicago: University of Chicago Press.

Roberts, Kenneth. 2003. "The Changing Profile of Chinese Labor Migration." Paper presented at the Workshop on Population Changes in China at the Beginning of the 21st Century, Australian National University, Canberra, 10–12 December.

Rofel, Lisa. 1999, *Other Modernities: Gendered Yearnings in China after Socialism*. Berkeley: University of California Press.

Rozelle, Scott et al. 1999. "Leaving China's Farms: Survey Results of New Paths and Remaining Hurdles to Rural Migration." *China Quarterly* 58 (June): 367–93.

"Rural-to-Town Labour Force on the Rise." 2003. *China Daily* 23 January.

Sahlins, Marshall. 1992. "The Economics of Develop-Man in the Pacific." *Res: Anthropology and Aesthetics* 21: 13–25.

Salaff, Janet. 1981. *Working Daughters of Hong Kong*. New York: Cambridge University Press.

Sargeson, Sally. 1999. *Reworking China's Proletariat*. London: Macmillan, and New York: St. Martin's Press.

———. 2001. "Assembling Class in a Chinese Joint Venture Factory." In *Organising Labour in Globalising Asia*, ed. Jane Hutchison and Andrew Brown, 48–70. London: Routledge.

———. 2004. "Building for the Future Family." In *Chinese Women—Living and Working*, ed. Anne E. McLaren, 149–68. London: RoutledgeCurzon.

Scharping, Thomas. 1997. "Studying Migration in Contemporary China: Models and Methods, Issues and Evidence." In *Floating Population and Migration in China: The Impact of Economic Reforms*, ed. Thomas Scharping, 9–55. Hamburg: Institut für Asienkunde.

———. 1999. "Selectivity, Migration Reasons and Backward Linkages of Rural-Urban Migrants: A Sample Survey of Migrants to Foshan and Shenzhen in Comparative Perspective." In *Internal and International Migration: Chinese Perspectives*, ed. Frank N. Pieke and Hein Mallee, 73–102. Richmond, Surrey: Curzon Press.

Scharping, Thomas, and Sun, Huaiyang, eds. 1997. *Migration in China's Guangdong Province: Major Results of a 1993 Sample Survey on Migrants and Floating Population in Shenzhen and Foshan*. Hamburg: Institut für Asienkunde.

Schein, Louisa. 1997. "Gender and Internal Orientalism in China." *Modern China* 23, no. 1: 69-98.

Scott, James C. 1985. *Weapons of the Weak: Everyday Forms of Peasant Resistance*. New Haven, CT: Yale University Press.

Scott, Joan. 1992. "Experience." In *Feminists Theorize the Political*, ed. Judith Butler and Joan Scott, 22–40. New York: Routledge.

Shanshan. 1998. "Beiqi xingzhuang" (Shouldering My Travel Bag). *Nongjianü baishitong* (Rural Women Knowing All) November: 52–53.

Shostak, Marjorie. 1989. "'What the Wind Won't Take Away': The Genesis of *Nisa*–The Life and Words of a !Kung Woman." In *Interpreting Women's Lives: Feminist Theory and Personal Narratives*, ed. Personal Narratives Group, 228–40. Bloomington: Indiana University Press.

Skultans, Vieda. 1998. *The Testimony of Lives: Narrative and Memory in Post-Soviet Latvia*. London: Routledge.

Smith, Arthur. H. 1894. *Chinese Characteristics*. New York: Fleming H. Revell.

Solinger, Dorothy. 1999. *Contesting Citizenship in Urban China: Peasant Migrants, the State, and the Logic of the Market*. Berkeley: University of California Press.

Song, Lina. 1999. "The Role of Women in Labour Migration: A Case Study in Northern China." In *Women of China: Economic and Social Transformation*, ed. Jackie West et al., 69–89. London: Macmillan.

State Family Planning Commission. 1998. "Measures on Administration of Family Planning Among the Migrating Population." www.isinolaw.com.

Steinmetz, George. 1992. "Reflections on the Role of Social Narratives in Working-Class Formation: Narrative Theory in the Social Sciences." *Social Science History* 16, no. 3 (Fall): 489–516.

Stockman, Norman. 2000. *Understanding Chinese Society*. Cambridge: Polity Press.

Sun, Wanning. 2004. "Indoctrination, Fetishization, and Compassion: Media Constructions of the Migrant Woman." In *On the Move: Women and Rural-to-Urban Migration in Contemporary China*, ed. Arianne Gaetano and Tamara Jacka, 109–28. New York: Columbia University Press.

Swacker, Robert Bruce. 1983. "The Concept of the Chinese Peasantry in the Writings of Karl Marx and Mao Tse-Tung." Ph.D. Dissertation, New York University.

Tan, Lin, and Short, Susan. 2004. "Living as Double Outsiders: Migrant Women's Experiences of Marriage in a County-Level City." In *On the Move: Women and Rural-to-Urban Migration in Contemporary China*, ed. Arianne Gaetano and Tamara Jacka, 151–74. New York: Columbia University Press.

Tan Shen et al. 2002. "Beijingshi wailai nüxing jiben zhuangkuang baogao" (A Report on the Basic Situation of Women Migrants in Beijing). In *Huji zhidu yu nüxing liudong. di er jie quanguo dagongmei quanyi wenti yantaohui lunwenji* (The Household Registration System and the Movement of Women: A Collection of Papers from the Second National Forum on the Rights and Interests of Migrant Women Workers), ed. Beijing Nongjianü Wenhua Fazhan Zhongxin (Beijing Rural Women's Cultural Development Center), 199–207. Guiyang: Guizhou renmin chubanshe.

Tang, Can. 1998. "Sexual Harassment: The Dual Status of and Discrimination Against Female Migrant Workers in Urban Areas—A Speech Delivered at the Asia University in Japan." *Social Sciences in China* 19, no. 3 (Autumn): 64–71.

Tang, Xiaobing. 2000. *Chinese Modern: The Heroic and the Quotidian*. Durham, NC: Duke University Press.

Thadani, Veena N., and Todaro, Michael P. 1984. "Female Migration: A Conceptual Framework." In *Women in the Cities of Asia: Migration and Urban Adaptation*, ed. James T. Fawcett, Siew-Ean Khoo, and Peter C. Smith, 36–59. Boulder, CO: Westview Press.

Thompson, Paul. 1978. *The Voice of the Past: Oral History*. Oxford: Oxford University Press.

Tian, Zhengzheng. 2004. "From Peasant Women to Bar Hostesses: Gender and Modernity in Post-Mao Dalian." In *On the Move: Women and Rural-to-Urban Migration in Contemporary China*, ed. Arianne Gaetano and Tamara Jacka, 80–108. New York: Columbia University Press.

Tilly, Louise A., and Scott, Joan W. 1978. *Women, Work, and Family*. New York: Holt, Rinehart and Winston.

Trager, Lillian. 1988. *The City Connection: Migration and Family Interdependence in the Philippines*. Ann Arbor: University of Michigan Press.

Unger, Jonathan. 2002. *The Transformation of Rural China*. Armonk, NY: M.E. Sharpe.

Wang, Ban. 2002. "Love at Last Sight: Nostalgia, Commodity and Temporality in Wang Anyi's *Song of Unending Sorrow.*" *positions: east asia cultures critique* 10, no. 3: 669–94.

Wang, David Der-wei. 1993. "Imaginary Nostalgia: Shen Congwen, Song Zelai, Mo Yan, and Li Yongping." In *From May Fourth to June Fourth: Fiction and Film in Twentieth-Century China*, ed. Ellen Widmer and David Der-wei Wang, 107–32. Cambridge, MA: Harvard University Press.

Wang, Fei-ling. 2004. "Reformed Migration Control and New Targeted People: China's *Hukou* System in the 2000s." *China Quarterly* 177 (March): 115–32.

Wang Jinhong, and Zou Jingqin. 2003. "Guanyu nongcun "waijianü" quanyi wenti de sikao yu tantao" (Thoughts and Questions on Issues Relating to the Rights and Interests of Rural Women Marrying Out). www.ccrs.org.cn. Accessed 10 July.

Wang Ju; Shi Chongxin; and Zong Chunsheng. 1993. "Beijingshi liudong renkou de zhuangkuang ji guanli duice" (The Situation with Regards to Beijing's Floating Population, and Policy Countermeasures). *Renkou yu Jingji* (Population and Economics) 79, no. 4: 35–39.

Wang Lingshu. 1993. "Shuoming shenme. Liang ge baomu zai meng jia de bu tong jieguo" (What Does it Tell Us The Different Fates of Two Maids in the Meng Household). *Nongjianü baishitong* (Rural Women Knowing All) April: 4–5, 7.

Wang Shucheng, and Li Renhu. 1996. "Wuwei: Baomu xiaoying" (Wuwei: The Effect of the Nanny). *Ban yue tan* (Half Monthly Forum) 8: 23–25.

Wang Sigang. 1995. "Shanghai mangliu chuxian 'san duo'" ("Three Manys" Emerge Among Shanghai's Blind Drifters). *Shehui* (Society) 7: 44–45.

Wang, Ya Ping. 2000. "Housing Reform and its Impacts on the Urban Poor in China." *Housing Studies* 15, no. 6: 845–64.

Wang Yingchun. 1994. "Chengshi li xu" (My Thoughts Have Left the City). *Nongjianü baishitong* (Rural Women Knowing All) June: 22–23.

Werbner, Pnina. 1996. "Stamping the Earth with the Name of Allah: Zikr and the Sacralizing of Space among British Muslims." In *Making Muslim Space in North America and Europe*, ed. Barbara Daly Metcalf, 167–85. Berkeley: University of California Press.

West, Loraine A. 2000. "Introduction." In *Rural Labor Flows in China*, ed. Loraine A. West and Zhao Yaohui, 1–13. Berkeley: Institute of East Asian Studies, University of California Press.

White, Gordon; Howell, Jude; and Shang, Xiaoyuan. 1996. *In Search of Civil Society: Market Reform and Social Change in Contemporary China*. Oxford: Clarendon Press.

Williams, Raymond. 1973. *The Country and the City*. London: Chatto and Windus.

Willis, Katie, and Yeoh, Brenda. 2000. "Introduction." In *Gender and Migration*, ed. Katie Willis and Brenda Yeoh, xi–xxii. Cheltenham, UK: Edward Elgar.

Wolf, Diane. 1992. *Factory Daughters: Gender, Household Dynamics, and Rural Industrialization in Java*. Berkeley: University of California Press.

Wolf, Margery. 1972. *Women and the Family in Rural Taiwan*. Stanford, CA: Stanford University Press.

———. 1985. *Revolution Postponed: Women in Contemporary China*. London: Methuen.

Woon, Yuen-fong. 2000. "Filial or Rebellious Daughters? *Dagongmei* in the Pearl River Delta Region, South China, in the 1990s." *Asian and Pacific Migration Journal* 9, no. 2: 137–69.

Xiao Chun. 1993. "'Tu' zai wo de shengming li" (The Place of the "Rustic" in My Life). *Nongjianü baishitong* (Rural Women Knowing All) August: 16–17.

Xie Lihua. 1995. "Guniang, ni weishenme jin cheng?" (Young Girl, Why have You Come to the City?). *Nongjianü baishitong* (Rural Women Knowing All) January: 4–6.

———. 1999. "Zhubian de hua: daodi shei de suzhi di?" (Editorial: Ultimately, Whose Quality is Low?). *Nongjianü baishitong* (Rural Women Knowing All) August: 4–5.

Xu Chengbin. 1993. "Wo shi yi wei tiaohunzhe" (I am Escaping Marriage). *Nongjianü baishitong* (Rural Women Knowing All) November: 8–9.

Xu, Feng. 2000. *Women Migrant Workers in China's Economic Reform*. London: Macmillan, and New York: St Martin's Press.

Yan Hairong. 2001. "'Suzhi,' 'Ziwo fazhan' he jieji de youling" ("Quality," "Self-Development" and the Ghost of Class). *Dushu* (Reading) March: 18–26.

———. 2002. "Self-Development of Migrant Women: Production of Suzhi (Quality) as Surplus Value and Displacement of Class in China's Post-Socialist Development." Unpublished paper.

———. 2003a. "Spectralization of the Rural: Reinterpreting the Labor Mobility of Rural Young Women in Post-Mao China." *American Ethnologist* 30, no. 4: 1–19.

———. 2003b. "Neo-Liberal Governmentality and Neo-Humanism: Organizing Suzhi/Value Flow Through Labor Recruitment Networks." *Cultural Anthropology* 18, no. 4: 493–523.

Yan, Yunxiang. 2003. *Private Life Under Socialism: Love, Intimacy, and Family Change in a Chinese Village 1949–1999*. Stanford, CA: Stanford University Press.

Yang, Li and Xi, Yinsheng. 2004. "Women's Rights to Land Under China's Land Contract System." Paper presented at the Symposium on Women's Participation in Policy Implementation and Institutional Change in Rural China, 14–16 April, at the University of Nottingham.

Yang, Mayfair Mei-hui. 1994. *Gifts, Favours and Banquets: The Art of Social Relationships in China*. Ithaca, NY: Cornell University Press.

Yang, Xiushi and Guo, Fei. 1999. "Gender Differences in Determinants of Temporary Labor Migration in China: A Multilevel Analysis." *The International Migration Review* 33, no. 4: 929–54.

"Yi ge bei qiansongzhe de zishu" (Memoir of a Deportee). 2002. *Dagongmei* (Working Sister) April–May: 7.

Yu Dapeng. 1994. "Chengxiang guanxi zhong de 'cheng che xiaoying'" (The 'Riding the Train Effect' in Relations Between the City and the Countryside). *Shehui* 3: 37–39.

Zhang, Heather Xiaoquan. 1999. "Female Migration and Urban Labour Markets in Tianjin." *Development and Change* 30: 21–41.

Zhang, Li. 2001. *Strangers in the City: Reconfigurations of Space, Power, and Social Networks within China's Floating Population*. Stanford, CA: Stanford University Press.

Zhang Shenhong. 1996. "Xiang jia de rizi" (Days when I Think of Home). *Nongjianü baishitong* (Rural Women Knowing All) July: 37.

Zhang Xudong. 2000. "Shanghai Nostalgia: Postrevolutionary Allegories in Wang Anyi's Literary Production in the 1990s." *positions: east asia cultures critique* 8 (Fall): 249–387.

Zhang, Zhen. 2001. "Mediating Time: The 'Rice Bowl of Youth' in Fin de Siècle Urban China." In *Globalization*, ed. Arjun Appadurai, 131–54. Durham, NC: Duke University Press.

Zhao, Shukai. 2000. "Criminality and the Policing of Migrant Workers." trans. Andrew Kipnis. *The China Journal* 43: 101–10.

Zhao Weiwei. 2002. "Chiku shi fu" (Eating Bitterness is a Blessing). *Dagongmei* (Working Sister) December: 39.

Zhao, Yuezhi. 1998. *Media, Market, and Democracy in China: Between the Part Line and the Bottom Line*. Urbana: University of Illinois Press.

"Zhendui shangye shichang tedian zhua hao liudong renkou jisheng gongzuo" (We Must Pay Special Attention to Family Planning Work Among the Floating Population in Accordance with the Characteristics of the Commercial Market). 1994. *Zhongguo renkou bao* (China Population Daily) 10 August: 3.

Zheng, Zhenzhen et al. 2001. "Sexual Behaviour and Contraceptive Use Among Unmarried, Young Women Migrant Workers in Five Cities in China." *Reproductive Health Matters* 9, no. 17: 118–27.

"Zhi dagongmeimen de yi feng gongkai xin" (A Public Letter to Working Sisters). 1996. *Nongjianü baishitong* (Rural Women Knowing All) April: 5.

Zhonghua renmin gongheguo nianjian 2002 (People's Republic of China Yearbook 2002). 2002. Beijing: Zhonghua renmin gongheguo nianjian she.

Zhou Hao. 2001. "Liudong ertong de guishu yu quanli" (The Place and Rights of Migrant Children). In *Dushi li de cunmin—Zhongguo da chengshi de liudong renkou* (Villagers in the City—Rural Migrants in Chinese Metropolises), ed. He Lanjun (Bettina Gransow) and Li Hanlin, 174–91. Beijing: Zhongyang bianyi chubanshe.

Zhou, Rencong. 2004. "Leaving Huaihua Valley: A Sichuan Girl's Own Account of Being a Migrant Worker." In *On the Move: Women and Rural-to-Urban Migration in Contemporary China*, ed. Arianne Gaetano and Tamara Jacka, 297–304. New York: Columbia University Press.

Index

Tamara Jacka is Senior Fellow, Gender Relations Center, Research School of Pacific and Asian Studies, Australian National University. She is the author of *Women's Work in Rural China: Change and Continuity in an Era of Reform,* and coeditor of *On the Move: Women and Rural-to-Urban Migration in Contemporary China.*